EARLY CHILDHOOD EDUCATION

EARLY CHILDHOOD EDUCATION

An International Encyclopedia

Volume 1
A–D

Edited by
Rebecca S. New and Moncrieff Cochran

PRAEGER

Westport, Connecticut
London

Library of Congress Cataloging-in-Publication Data

Early childhood education [four volumes] : an international encyclopedia / edited by Rebecca S. New and Moncrieff Cochran.

    p. cm.

    Includes bibliographical references and index.

    ISBN 0-313-33100-6 (set : alk. paper)—ISBN 0-313-33101-4 (vol 1 : alk. paper)—
    ISBN 0-313-33102-2 (vol 2 : alk. paper)—ISBN 0-313-33103-0 (vol 3 : alk. paper)—
    ISBN 0-313-34143-5 (vol 4 : alk. paper)

    1. Early childhood education—Encyclopedias.   I. New, Rebecca Staples.   II. Cochran, Moncrieff.

  LB1139.23.E272   2007
   372.2103—dc22   2006035011

British Library Cataloguing in Publication Data is available.

Library of Congress Catalog Card Number: 2006035011
ISBN: 0-313-33100-6 (set)
     0-313-33101-4 (vol. 1)
     0-313-33102-2 (vol. 2)
     0-313-33103-0 (vol. 3)
     0-313-34143-5 (vol. 4)

First published in 2007

Praeger Publishers, 88 Post Road West, Westport, CT 06881
An imprint of Greenwood Publishing Group, Inc.
www.praeger.com

Printed in the United States of America

The paper used in this book complies with the
Permanent Paper Standard issued by the National
Information Standards Organization (Z39.48-1984).

10 9 8 7 6 5 4 3 2 1

Contents

Alphabetical List of Entries

VOLUME 1

VOLUME 2

VOLUME 3

Guide to Related Topics

Act for Better Child Care
(ABC)
Advocacy and Leadership
Child-care Subsidies and Tax
Provisions
Children's Defense Fund
(CDF)
Child Development
Group of Mississippi
(CDGM)
Convention on the Rights of
the Child (CRC)
Early Head Start
Even Start
Good Start, Grow Smart
Head Start
National Association for the
Education of Young
Children (NAEYC)

National Black Child
Development Institute
(NBCDI)
National Center for Children
in Poverty (NCCP)
National Education Goals
Panel (NEGP)
National Head Start
Association (NHSA)
No Child Left Behind Act
((NCLBA)
Organisation for Economic
Cooperation and
Development (OECD)
Philanthropy and Young
Children
Poverty, Family and Child
Race and Ethnicity in Early
Childhood Education

Socioeconomic Status (SES)
State Prekindergarten
Programs
Teacher Education
and Compensation Helps
(TEACH)
United Nations Children's
Fund (UNICEF)
United Nations Educational,
Scientific and Cultural
Organisation (UNESCO)
The World Forum on Early
Care and Education
World Health Organization
(WHO)
World Organisation
for Early Childhood
Education (OMEP)
Worthy Wage Campaign

Child Care

Accreditation of Early
Childhood Programs
Act for Better Child Care
(ABC)
Attachment
Black Caucus (NAEYC)

Center for the Child Care
Workforce (CCW)
Child Care
Child Care and
Development Fund
(CCDF)

Child Care Subsidies, Tax
Provisions
Day Nurseries
Early Care and Education
Programs,
Administration of

Families
Infant Care
National Association
  for the Education of
  Young Children
  (NAEYC)
National Association
  for the Education of
  Young Children

(NAEYC)
Academy for Early
  Childhood Program
  Accreditation
National Association
  of Child-care
  Resource and
  Referral Agencies
  (NACRRA)

National Committee on
  Nursery Schools
Program for Infant Toddler
  Caregivers (PITC)
School-Age Care
Worthy Wage
  Campaign
Yale University Child Study
  Center

Child Development Domains, Theories, and Research

Attachment
Behaviorism
Biculturalism
Bilingual Education
Binet, Alfred
Bowlby, John
Bronfenbrenner, Urie
Bruner, Jerome
Bullying
Child Abuse and
  Neglect
Child Study Movement
Constructionism
Constructivism
Culture
Development, Brain
Development, Cognitive
Development, Emotional
Development, Language
Development, Moral
Development, Social
Developmental Delay
Developmental Systems
  Theories
Disabilities, Young Children
  with
Ecology of Human
  Development

Erikson, Erik H.
Freud, Anna
Freud, Sigmund
Gender and Gender
  Stereotyping
Gesell, Arnold
Hall, G(ranville)
  Stanley
Intelligence
Intelligence Quotient (IQ)
Kohlberg, Lawrence
Language Diversity
Luria, A. R.
Maslow, Abraham
Mathematics
Maturationism
Multiple Intelligences,
  Theory of
Narrative
National Black Child
  Development Institute
  (NBCDI)
Parents and Parent
  Involvement
Pavlov, Ivan Petrovich
Peer Culture
Peers and Friends
Piaget, Jean

Play
Play and Gender
Poverty, Family and Child
Psychosocial Theory
Race and Ethnicity in Early
  Childhood Education
Rousseau, Jean-Jacques
Second-Language Acquisition
  in Early Childhood
Self-Esteem and Self-Concept
Sex and Sexuality in Young
  Children
Sexual Abuse
Social Cognitive Theory
Social Competence
Social Constructionism
Social Constructivism
Socio-cultural Theory
Socioeconomic Status (SES)
Spiritual Development
Temperament
Vygotsky, Lev Semenovich
War Play
Watson, John B.
Whiting, Beatrice
Whiting, John W. M.
Yale University Child Study
  Center

Early Childhood Education Curriculum and Pedagogy

Academics
Bank Street
Behavior Management and
  Guidance
Bilingual Education
*The Creative Curriculum for
  Preschool*

Curriculum
Curriculum, Emotional
  Development
Curriculum, Mathematics
Curriculum, Music
Curriculum, Physical
  Development

Curriculum, Science
Curriculum, Social
Curriculum, Social Studies
Curriculum, Technology
Curriculum, Visual Art
Developmental-Interaction
  Approach

Developmentally
   Appropriate Practice(s)
Direct Instruction
   Model
Documentation
Early Childhood Environment
   Rating Scales (ERS)
Family Literacy
High/Scope
Jumpstart
Literacy
Literacy and Disabilities

Mathematics
Montessori Education
Multicultural and Anti-Bias
   Education
Open Education
Parenting Education
Pedagogy
Pedagogy,
   Activity-Based/Experiential
Pedagogy, Child-Centered
Pedagogy, Social
   Justice/Equity

Play
Play and Pedagogy
Play as Storytelling
Program for Infant-Toddler
   Caregivers
Progressive Education
   Project Zero
The Project Approach
Reggio Emilia Approach to
   Early Childhood Education
Symbolic Languages
Waldorf Education

Family and Society

Adoption
Biculturalism
Child Abuse and Neglect
Children's Media
Computer and Video
   Game Play
Convention on the Rights of
   the Child (CRC)
Culture
Domestic Violence
Families
Family Literacy
Fathers
Feminism in Early Childhood
   Education

Gay or Lesbian Parents,
   Children with
Incarcerated Parents,
   Children of
Immigration
Individualized Family Service
   Plan (IFSP)
Mothers
Parental Substance
   Abuse
Parenting Education
Parents and Parent
   Involvement
Peer Culture
Peers and Friends

Philanthropy and Young
   Children
Poverty, Family and Child
Race and Ethnicity in Early
   Childhood Education
Sexual Abuse
Socioeconomic Status (SES)
Spirituality Development
Technology Curriculum
Television
Temporary Assistance to
   Needy Families (TANF)
Violence and Young Children
Women, Infants and Children
   (WIC)

Health and Special Needs

Attention Deficit
   Disorder/Attention Deficit
   Hyperactivity Disorder
   (ADD)/(ADHD)
Augmentative and Alternative
   Communication (AAC)
Autism
Cerebral Palsy (CP)
Child Abuse and Neglect
Child Abuse and Neglect,
   Prevention of
Council for Exceptional
   Children (CEC)
Deaf Children
Development Cognitive
Developmental Delay

Developmental Disorders of
   Infancy and Early
   childhood, A Taxonomy of
Disabilities, Young Children
   with
Division for Early Childhood
   (DEC)
Domestic Violence
Down Syndrome
Early Childhood Environment
   Rating Scales (ERS)
Early Childhood Special
   Education (ECSE)
Early Intervention
Environmental Assessments
   ECRS only of Safty

Fetal Alcohol Syndrome (FAS)
Gifted and Talented Children
   in the United States
Individualized Education Plan
   (IEP)
Individualized Family Service
   Plan (IFSP)
Individuals with Disabilities
   Education Act (IDEA)
*Journal of Early
   Intervention (JEI)*
Jumpstart
Learning Disabilities (LD)
Literacy and Disabilities
Mental Health
Montessori, Maria

Nutrition
Obesity
Parental Substance Abuse

Play Therapy
Sensory Processing Disorder
  (SPD)

Sexual Abuse
Visual Impairment
Young Children

Historic Figures in Child Development/Early Childhood Education

Addams, Jane
Almy, Millie
Ashton-Warner, Sylvia
Bandura, Albert
Binet, Alfred
Blow, Susan Elizabeth
Bowlby, John
Bronfenbrenner, Urie
Bruner, Jerome
Comenius, John Amos
Dewey, John
Eliot, Abigail Adams
Erikson, Erik H.
Frank, Lawrence Kelso
Freud, Anna
Freud, Sigmund
Froebel, Fredrich
Gesell, Arnold
Gordon, Ira J.
Hailmann, Eudora Lucas
Hailmann, William Nicholas

Hall, G(ranville) Stanley
Hawkins, David and
  Hawkins, Frances
  Pockman
Hill, Patty Smith
Hunt, Joseph McVicker
Hymes, James L., Jr.
Isaacs, Susan
Kohlberg, Lawrence
Lowenfeld, Viktor
Luria, A. R.
Malaguzzi, Loris
Maslow, Abraham
McMillan, Margaret
McMillan, Rachel
Mitchell, Lucy Sprague
Montessori, Maria
Naumburg, Margaret
Osborn, D. Keith
Owen, Grace
Owen, Robert

Parker, Francis W.
Parten, Mildred
Pavlov, Ivan Petrovich
Peabody, Elizabeth Palmer
Pestalozzi, Johann
Piaget, Jean
Pratt, Caroline
Read, Katherine
Rogers, Carl
Rousseau, Jean-Jacques
Steiner, Rudolf
Temple, Alice
Thorndike, Edward L.
Vygotsky, Lev Semenovich
Watson, John B.
Wheelock, Lucy
White, Edna Noble
Whiting, Beatrice
Whiting, John
Wiggin, Kate Douglas
Wollstonecraft, Mary

Professional Journals

*Child Care and Early
  Education Research
  Connections*
*Contemporary Issues in
  Early Childhood*
*Early Child Development
  and Care*
*Early Childhood Education
  Journal (ECEJ)*
*Early Childhood Research &
  Practice (ECRP)*
*Early Childhood Research
  Quarterly (ECRQ)*
*Early Years: An
  International*

*Journal of
  Research and
  Development
  Education 3-13*
*European Early Childhood
  Education Research
  Journal (EECERJ)*
Exchange
*International Journal of
  Early Childhood (IJEC)*
*International Journal
  of Early Years
  Education*
*International Journal of
  Special Education*

*Journal of Early Childhood
  Research*
*Journal of Early Childhood
  Teacher Education
  (JECTE)*
*Journal of Early
  Intervention
  (JEI)*
*The Journal of Special
  Education Leadership*
NHSA Dialog
*Topics in Early Childhood
  Special Education
  (TECSE)*
Young Children

Professional Groups, Programs, and Organizations

American Associate Degree Early Childhood Educators (ACCESS)

Association for Childhood Education International (ACEI)

Association for Constructivist Teaching (ACT)

Black Caucus (NAEYC)

Center for the Child Care Workforce (CCW)

Child Development Associate (CDA) National Credentialing Program

Child Development Group of Mississippi (CDGM)

Children's Defense Fund (CDF)

Council for Exceptional Children (CEC)

Division for Early childhood (DEC)

Early Childhood Music Education Commission (ECMC)

International Kindergarten Union (IKU)

International Reading Association (IRA)

McCormick Tribune Center for Early Childhood Leadership

National Association for Regulatory Administration (NARA)

National Association for the Education of Young Children (NAEYC)

National Association for the Education of Young Children (NAEYC) Academy for Early Childhood Program Accreditation

National Association of Childcare Resource and Referral Agencies (NACRRA)

National Assoc of Early Childhood Teacher Educators (NAECTE)

National Black Child Development Institute (NBCDI)

National Center for Children in Poverty (NCCP)

National Committee on Nursery Schools

National Council for Accreditation of Teacher Education (NCATE)

National Education Goals Panel (NEGP)

National Head Start Association (NHSA)

National Institute for Early Childhood Professional Development

North American Reggio Emilia Alliance (NAREA)

Organisation for Economic Co-operation and Development (OECD)

Reggio-Inspired Teacher Education (RITE)

Southern Early Childhood Association (SECA)

United Nations Children's Fund (UNICEF)

United Nations Educational, Scientific and Cultural Organisation (UNESCO)

The World Forum on Early Care and Education

World Health Organization (WHO)

World Organisation for Early Childhood Education (OMEP)

Worthy Wage Campaign

ZERO TO THREE

Research and Early Childhood Education

Action Research

Brain Development

Child Care and Early Education *Research Connections*

Child Study Movement

Documentation

Early Childhood Environment Rating Scales (ERS)

Early Child Development and Care

Early Childhood Research & Practice (ECRP)

Early Childhood Research Quarterly (ECRQ)

Early Years: An International Journal of Research and Development

European Early Childhood Education Research Journal

High/Scope Perry Preschool Study

IEA Preprimary Project

International Journal of Early Childhood (IJEC)

Journal of Early Childhood Research

Laboratory Schools

Organisation for Economic Co-operation and Development (OECD)

Portage Project

Preschool Curriculum
  Evaluation Research
  Program (PCER)

Qualitative Research
Quantitative Analyses/
  Experimental Designs

Teacher Research
Young Children

Schools and Schooling, Educational Settings, and Contemporary Issues

Academics
Accreditation of Early
  Childhood Programs
Assessment in Early
  Childhood
Assessment, Visual
  Art
Bank Street
Behavior Management and
  Guidance
Bilingual Education
Bullying
Child Abuse and Neglect,
  Prevention of
Child Art
Child Care
Children's Media
Children's Museums
Classroom Discourse
Classroom Environments
*Contemporary Issues in
  Early Childhood*
Curriculum
Curriculum, Emotional
  Development
Curriculum,
  Mathematics
Curriculum, Music
Curriculum, Physical
  Development
Curriculum, Science
Curriculum, Science
  Start
Curriculum, Social
Curriculum, Social
  Studies
Developmental-Interaction
  Approach
Developmentally
  Appropriate Practice(s)
Dewey, John
Direct Instruction Model
Division for Early Childhood
  (DEC)
Documentation

Early Childhood Environment
  Rating Scales (ERS)
Early Head Start
Ecology of Human
  Development
Eliot, Abigail Adams
Emergent Curriculum
Environmental Assessment in
  Early Childhood Education
Even Start
Families
Family Literacy
Gifted and Talented Children
  in the United States
Grade Retention
Grouping
Head Start
High/Scope
History of U.S. Early
  Childhood Care and
  Education
Infant Care
Inclusion
Jumpstart
Kindergarten
Laboratory Schools
Literacy
Literacy and Disabilities
Literacy Curriculum
Mathematics
Mixed-Age Grouping in
  Early Childhood
  Education
Montessori Education
Multicultural and Anti-Bias
  Education
Narrative
No Child Left Behind Act
  (NCLBA)
Open Education
Parenting Education
Pedagogy
Pedagogy, Activity-Based/
  Experiential
Pedagogy, Child-Centered

Pedagogy, Social
  Justice/Equity
Peer Culture
Peers and Friends
Play
Play and Gender
Play and Pedagogy
Play as Storytelling
Play and the Teacher's Role
Playgrounds
Preschool/
  Prekindergarten Programs
Professional Development
Professional Ethics
The Project Approach
Race and Ethnicity in Early
  Childhood Education
Read-Alouds and Vocabulary
  Development
Readiness
Reconceptualists
Reggio Emilia Approach to
  Early Childhood Education
Reggio-Inspired Teacher
  Education (RITE)
Ruggles Street Nursery
  School and Training Center
  (Boston, Massachusetts)
School-Age Care
Second-Language Acquisition
  in Early Childhood
Self-Esteem and Self-Concept
Social Curriculum
Standardized Tests and Early
  Childhood Education
State Prekindergarten
  Programs
Symbolic Languages
Teacher
  Certification/Licensure
Teacher Education,
  Early Childhood
Technology Curriculum
Waldorf Education
War Play

Social Policies

Act for Better Child Care
(ABC)
Child Abuse and Neglect,
Prevention of
Child Care and Development
Fund (CCDF)
Developmentally
Appropriate Practice(s)
(DAP)
Early Head Start
Early Intervention
Even Start
Head Start
Individualized Education Plan
(IEP)
Individuals with
Disabilities Education Act
(IDEA)

Interagency Education
Research Initiative (IERI)
Jumpstart
National Association for
Regulatory Administration
(NARA)
National Association for the
Education of Young
Children (NAEYC)
National Association for the
Education of Young
Children (NAEYC)
Academy for Early
Childhood Program
Accreditation
National Association of Child-
care Resource and Referral
Agencies (NACCRRA)

National Center for Children
in Poverty (NCCP)
National Education Goals
Panel (NEGP)
No Child Left Behind Act
(NCLBA)
State Prekindergarten
Programs
Teacher Education and
Compensation Helps
(TEACH)
Temporary Assistance to
Needy Families
(TANF)
Women, Infants and Children
(WIC)
World Health Organisation
(WHO)

Preface

Early Childhood Education: An International Encyclopedia is unique in form and contents, providing in four volumes a compilation of understandings, controversies, theories, policies, and practices in early childhood education as currently found in the United States and 10 other nations around the world. Admittedly biased in the attention we pay to U.S. early childhood education and our reliance on English-language professional literature, the Encyclopedia acknowledges prevailing controversies in the field and presents multiple perspectives on early childhood education as understood and practiced in representative nations of Europe, Asia, Africa, and South America. The Encyclopedia has been prepared with a large and diverse audience in mind, including undergraduate and graduate students of education, child development, social policy, and cross-cultural studies; parents and teachers of young children in the United States and abroad; scholars—national and international; program administrators; policy makers and analysts; and the general public.

The purpose of this four-volume work is to serve as a useful reference source on the period of early childhood and the field of early childhood education. Its principal aim is to provide the curious reader—student, parent, teacher, policy maker, citizen—with information on key historical and contemporary issues, including research, theoretical perspectives, policies and practices, in select nations around the world. Given the rapid rate of change and contemporary pace of knowledge generation, the Encyclopedia shares the same limitations as do other published works—it represents a particular period of time in the history of a field as interpreted by particular groups of people and as written by individuals with their own sense of priorities. The meaning of "contemporary" as reflected in the pages of these four volumes is associated with events and understandings of the first decade of the twenty-first century. The definition of "historical," as the reader will see when reviewing entries on the history of early childhood education in the various nations included in Volume 4, ranges widely from one cultural context to another. The Encyclopedia's usefulness is not limited, however, to its representation of the past and the present. The second aim is to present the *status quo* of early childhood education, as interpreted by the contributors, as a catalyst for continued debate about and engagement in future actions and advocacy on behalf of young children's early learning and development.

Process

This innovative project represents a rich and diverse array of scholarship and opinions about the early care and education of young children. The topics themselves were originally identified by established scholars, teachers, and students of child development and early childhood in the United States. This list was revised several times over the course of production, first in response to international contributors who identified topics essential to their respective national contexts. As the word list circulated, contributors proposed unanticipated or emerging topics of interest and importance. An Editorial Advisory Board consisting of 12 leading scholars in the field was indispensable to the identification of appropriate authors and the editing of entries to insure an accessible reading style for a broad audience. An International Advisory Group insured the selection of qualified authors and relevant topics in each country; each International Advisor also authored the country profile describing contemporary early childhood policies and practices.

Special Features

The scope of this four-volume encyclopedia has both breadth and depth. Volumes 1, 2, and 3 include over 300 entries that reference one hundred years of early childhood education in the United States; Volume 4 includes another hundred-plus entries describing past and present interpretations of early childhood in ten other nations: Australia, Brazil, the Czech Republic, China, France, Italy, Japan, South Africa, Sweden, and the United Kingdom. The total number of national and international contributors to this encyclopedia is over 300.

Topics covered in this four-volume encyclopedia include those associated with the period and study of *child development*—for example, parenting, cognitive development, and friendships and peer relations; *child care*—for example, infant and toddler care, family child care, and after-school care; *early childhood education*—for example, academics, assessment, curriculum, pedagogy, and teacher training; *professional organizations in the field*—for example, the National Association for the Education of Young Children (NAEYC), the National Association of Early Childhood Teacher Educators (NAECTE), and the Southern Early Childhood Association (SECA); and English-language *professional journals*—for example, the U.S.-based *Early Childhood Research Quarterly (ECRQ)*, *International Early Childhood Education* from the United Kingdom, and Australia's *Contemporary Issues in Early Childhood*. Entries on *key historic figures* in the field of U.S. early childhood education—for example, John Dewey and Abigail Eliot—are joined by those whose work has influenced early childhood education around the world—for example, Frederich Froebel and two Italians, Maria Montessori and Loris Malaguzzi.

This encyclopedia does more than serve as a resource to traditional features of the field. In addition to entries on children's social development, early literacy, and various means of assessment, Volumes 1, 2, and 3 include entries on contemporary *concerns and controversies*—for example, the No Child Left Behind Act, corporal punishment, domestic violence, obesity, and poverty. The changing nature of *family structures* is reflected by entries on adoption, children of gay and lesbian parents, and second language acquisition. Multiple perspectives on an early childhood *curriculum and pedagogy* are found in entries on a child-centered pedagogy, pedagogy for social justice, progressive education, and the Reggio Emilia Approach. In addition to entries on contemporary theories of teaching and learning, alternative and post-modern perspectives on the field are represented by entries on the reconceptualist movement, feminist theory, and children's sexuality. The work also includes extensive discussions of the particular needs and potentials of diverse populations of children, including children with disabilities, children of incarcerated parents, and children who are bilingual. The inclusion of multiple entries on complex topics—such as the education of young children with special needs—provides both breadth as well as alternative perspectives on topics of critical importance.

The provision of multiple perspectives goes global in Volume 4 (see the separate introduction to Volume 4). The countries included were selected because their early care and education systems are interesting and dynamic reflections of the cultures they serve. They represent each of the five inhabited continents other than North America, and include societies experiencing rapid political or economic change over the past quarter century (e.g., Brazil, China, the Czech Republic, and South Africa) as well as those characterized by relative continuity over that same period (Australia, France, Italy, Japan, Sweden, and the United Kingdom). Another macro-level variation of interest was in economic systems, ranging from the largely free-market capitalist systems of Australia, Japan, and the United Kingdom (more similar to the United States) to systems in Sweden and France with larger public sectors and greater public investment in social welfare. Volume 4 includes national profiles of current early childhood educational policies and practices in these ten countries. Those seeking to understand how early childhood education serves the goals and needs of nations in Europe, Asia, Africa, South America, and Oceania will find rich descriptions and deep insights from authors in these 10 countries beyond North America.

These profiles also create contexts for invited essays from many authors outside the United States on key topics—for example, *literacy*, *parent education*, *technology*—selected by international consultants as they correspond to contemporary scholarship and concern in their respective cultural contexts. For that reason, the number of entries per topic varies considerably, with *curriculum* as the sole topic selected by each country. Entries on *family involvement* and *teacher preparation* describe current practices in eight of the ten international settings. Other topics, such as *health*, *violence*, and *assessment*, were less frequently selected topics and are addressed by authors in only two or three international settings. Early childhood educators wishing to expand their understanding of curriculum, play, literacy, and creativity will be stimulated by the international perspectives these experts provide. Researchers interested in topics ranging from teacher preparation to early childhood pedagogy and the ecology of childhood can mine these data for useful insights from a variety of cultural contexts. For parents wishing to understand the singular experience their child is having in the local child care center or family child care setting as it corresponds to children's experiences in settings around the world will find much to ponder. Thus, for example, the reader can review international perspectives on early literacy in six nations outside the United States.

Organization

Topics are arranged alphabetically in Volumes 1, 2, and 3; and countries are presented in alphabetical order in Volume 4. In addition to a table of contents in the front pages of each volume, topics are cross-referenced, with boldfaced items in text and "See also" lines at the ends of entry text. All entries conclude with lists of cited works and additional resources, including books, journal articles, and Web sites. A detailed subject index provides further access to the information in the entries, while a Guide to Related Topics allows readers to trace broad themes and concepts across the entries of the first three volumes. Thus, readers interested in a topic such as "literacy" will find references to multiple entries associated with that topic in Volumes 1, 2, and 3; as well as discussions of literacy in six different national contexts in Volume 4. A detailed introduction places the field of early childhood education into current context.

These unique features insure that this encyclopedia will provide useful information based on current understandings of early childhood policies, theories, and practices. They have also been designed to provoke further debate on the role of early childhood education in the lives of young children and their families, and on the priorities and policies of diverse nations around the world with respect to their youngest citizens. As such, this set serves as both a resource and a catalyst for reflection and global conversation on the broad field of early childhood education.

Acknowledgments

The preparation of this encyclopedia was a joint effort. The two of us conceived and organized its contents together. The coordination of entries, communications with authors, and editing for Volumes One, Two, and Three were carried out primarily by Rebecca New. Mon Cochran assumed primary responsibility for Volume Four, including international correspondence, topic coordination, text editing and assistance with translations.

Supporting us in this work has been a strong social support network of old and new friends and colleagues. Indeed, a project the size of this undertaking could not succeed without the assistance, encouragement, and patience of numerous others. Of course, any future usefulness of this encyclopedia is dependent upon the knowledge and writing skills of its more than 300 contributors. Many of these contributors are also our friends and colleagues; some are our students; still others are new acquaintances. We thank them each for their hard work, their patience with the editing process, and their willingness to persist with requested revisions. There were also many others, behind the scenes as well as working closely with the editors and contributors, whose confidence in our vision was instrumental to its attainment. Although the total number of well-wishers is surely too large to itemize, some who made direct contributions must be acknowledged.

Thanks to Marie Ellen Larcada for the original invitation to do a project on early childhood, and for believing in and advocating for its expansion to include international contributions from around the world. Without this initial support, the project would have remained nothing more than an idea. Once begun, Joanna Krablin (now Joanna Krablin Nelson) became indispensable to the day-to-day operations and, especially, to the ongoing communication with each of the contributors. Her meticulous record-keeping and soothing demeanor kept both editors and contributors on an even keel, even through the roughest of weather. John Wagner of Greenwood played his long-distance role with grace and a sense of humor appointed, providing sage advise, practical editorial assistance, and gentle pressure about looming deadlines—each critical to the completion of this project.

As word lists were generated and authors identified, members of the Editorial Advisory Board reminded us of why we had invited them in the first place. Individually and collectively, Board members joined in email-hosted debates on the merits of topics to include and to leave out, about whom to invite to write essential but unclaimed topics, and how best to organize the entries. All Board members wrote one or more entries, and a majority of them helped with the editing, with an eye to accessible language and comprehensive coverage tempered by respect for each author's writing style and position on the subject. Group discussions with several Board members—Carolyn Edwards, Stacie Goffin, and Sharon Ryan—about U.S. interpretations of curriculum and pedagogy not only resolved critical issues in the production and organization of the manuscript; they were also stimulating in their own right and one of the unanticipated highlights of this project.

Another boon for the editors as well as future readers of this encyclopedia is the International Advisory Group, most of whom were known to one or both of us previously, each of whom became a source of support and inspiration to each other. Their willingness to serve as representatives, collectors, and editors of the material from their own countries was matched by their willingness to share their ideas and questions about various topics in an open forum with other Group members so as to generate a framework for the national discussions. The sort of cross-cultural discussion that went on between Group members is just the sort of dialogue that we hope the encyclopedia will generate.

And last but not least, we wish to acknowledge and thank our families and friends for their patience, indulgence, and support for our work on this project. Far too many late dinners—some missed entirely—were explained by "I was working on the encyclopedia." It is with a sense of relief as well as gratitude that we can say, by way of a final "thank you," *it's done*—and we couldn't have done it without you.

Rebecca S. New
Moncrieff Cochran

Introduction

What Is Early Childhood Education?

Early Childhood Education (ECE) has been described as many things: a form of applied child development, purposeful and targeted early intervention, or any of an array of services designed to support the learning and development of children in the first years of life. For most people, as acknowledged in the following passage from a forthcoming publication by one of the editors (Cochran, 2007), early childhood education refers to services provided during the period from birth to the age of compulsory schooling:

> Early care and education policies and programs involve the provision of (a) child care to preschool-aged children, and care before and after school to school-aged children while their parents are employed or receiving further education; (b) other child development focused and early educational experiences to preschool-aged children; and (c) child development, child care, and early education information made available to the parents of preschool-aged children.

This definition provides room for many of the more narrowly focused child care and early education programs and providers found across the country, including child-care centers, family and group family child-care programs and networks, preschools, nursery schools, Head Start programs, and prekindergarten programs. It also includes efforts to inform and educate parents about child development, child-care alternatives, and approaches to teaching preschool children appropriate social, cognitive, and language skills. For some in the field, however, this definition does not capture all of the meanings of early childhood education. The term "preschool children" in the definition refers to children during the period immediately prior to their entry into primary school. In the United States, this age group is typically three- and four-year-old children, and the endpoint of this definition wavers between the ages of four, five, and six. In the absence of national policies, kindergarten (for five-year-olds) remains nonobligatory in many states across the country but is a part of compulsory schooling in others. Further acknowledging the socially constructed nature of this time in the life of the child, the **National Association for the Education of Young Children** (NAEYC) defines early childhood as the period from birth to age eight. As editors, we agreed to avoid a fixed definition of the age range of the field, given these vast disparities in common use. As the reader will soon learn, a majority of the contributors have interpreted the age range of these volumes to encompass the period from birth through age five. The absence of early childhood perspectives in the primary grades has emerged as an area of major concern to many in the field.

Nor did we delimit the language used to describe the field. For many Americans, child care (of infants and toddlers) is distinct from early childhood education (interpreted as a form of early schooling). For others—the editors included—the *field* of early childhood education embraces the multiple *systems* of early *care* and education, as acknowledged in the previous definition. For some, the politics of this discourse is central to the controversy in that adults who are identified as caregivers typically earn less than those identified as teachers. On the other side of this particular coin is a growing concern about increased efforts to "teach" infants and toddlers so as to promote early brain growth and development. Many of our international contributors refer to systems of early *care* and education.

This introduction to the field of ECE is not a digression; rather, it acknowledges the fact that much of what is thought about and done for young children is wed to the particular sociocultural and historical contexts within which children live and learn and grow up. It is for that reason that we have solicited entries on the ecology of early childhood, represented in Volumes 1, 2, and 3 with entries on the changing nature of families, the growing prevalence of media and technology in children's lives, and new concerns about children's physical health (e.g., obesity), and their mental well-being (e.g., violence, drug abuse). We also invited contributors in Volume 4 to describe the "place" of childhood as interpreted and experienced in their various cultural contexts. These entries include discussions on how childhood has changed, both from a legal point of view (as expressed through laws and conventions of children's rights) as well as the position of the child in various extra-family spaces. Throughout the four volumes of this work, contributors from various fields have responded to our invitation to add to the ongoing debate about the nature and meaning of early childhood, drawing upon literatures in anthropological studies, child development, education, psychology, sociology, social policy, and the history of childhood itself. Their entries provide a compelling case for the complexity of the field, its dependence on collaboration, its varied positioning within diverse cultures, and its inevitable controversial nature.

An Abbreviated History of a Field-in-the-Making

Whatever it means to contemporary readers, the contested terrain of early childhood education has a long history in the United States. Described eloquently by Stacie Goffin and Valora Washington, the **history of U.S. early childhood care**

and education (in Volume 2) is replete with examples that illustrate its almost chameleon-like place in American history. At the same time, a careful review of this history reveals the field as constantly struggling against the status quo, illustrated by the legions of progressive reformers—many of them women—who revolted against the harsh **pedagogy** of traditional schools and advocated for a new, child-centered pedagogy. The ensuing debates about programs designed to rescue children from the streets, or from overzealous practitioners who insisted on straight rows and straight letters, are echoed in contemporary debates about effective pedagogy for young children in Head Start and public preschool programs. These debates are linked to another, that associated with two enduring images of the young child—one "at risk" and the other as "normal"—images generated and reified well over one hundred years ago that reveal much about the politics and the science that have accompanied the endeavors of early childhood educators over the course of the twentieth century. That these two different images have continued, throughout the history of the United States, to be associated with different groups of children as a function of their ability, race, ethnicity, language, or religious background should give pause to professionals in the field and readers of these volumes.

That some philosophical debates have remained constant about children's early learning needs and capacities should not be interpreted, however, as suggesting that the field has remained stagnant. Far from it. The field of early childhood education as understood and practiced in the United States has grown and changed by leaps and bounds over the course of the last century. These advances in the field reflect changes in society as well as new understandings and creative innovations in the field itself. Beyond the recognition that early childhood is a distinct period of human development, the following four broad themes capture some of the most compelling ways in which the field has grown and struggled over the past 100 years:

• Early childhood as worthy of and requiring scientific study
• Early childhood as a time to intervene
• Early childhood as a time for teaching and learning
• Early childhood as contested terrain

The following discussion is brief because the entries in these volumes take up these issues person by person, policy by policy, innovation by innovation. These features are summarized here to help the reader gain a better appreciation of the status of the field as informed by its history and interpreted by contemporary scholars.

Early Childhood as a Period of Human Development Worthy of Study

It was within the context of industrialization and the modernist project at the end of the nineteenth century that the pursuit of scientific knowledge and social progress began to influence the study and education of young children (Lubeck, 1995). The twentieth century was proclaimed as the "Century of the Child" and students of child development became partners with social advocates for an early childhood education. William James proposed that child study serve as a scientific basis for pedagogy; and G. Stanley **Hall** urged mothers to observe and record their children's development. Eventually rejected as not sufficiently "scientific," Hall's informal approaches to child study (see **Child Study Movement**) were replaced by more systematic and "scientific" methods, many based on Edward **Thorndike**'s ideas on educational measurement. As the notion of "ability" as a measurable characteristic became more widely accepted, the emerging field of child development embraced notions of normative development and soon asserted its scientific status over the field of early childhood education. Child Study and Child Welfare Institutes, among them the Iowa Child Welfare Research Station, and university **laboratory schools** created new settings in which professionals could work with and study young children. Throughout the second quarter of the century, early childhood institutions continued to develop in response to new understandings of child development. In this new century, amidst growing controversy, much of it fueled by Western European scholars and philosophers, child development theory and research remains the primary knowledge base for early childhood education in the United States. New brain research has added to the conviction that there is much to learn about, and much to promote during, the period of early childhood (see **Brain Development**).

Early Childhood as a Time to Intervene

Early educational initiatives have historically been vulnerable to social causes and, in the United States, many have focused on children deemed underprivileged. Decisions about which children needed an out-of-home educational experience were reflected in the charity movement and the day nursery movement (see **Day Nurseries**); some of these innovations also reflected the changing work habits of American **families.** Concerns about child labor and child welfare drew attention to children's physical and psychological needs—especially those born in **poverty** or to uneducated **parents.** In 1912, the Children's Bureau was established as a symbol of federal interest in young children as well as the beginnings of a concern with the "at risk" child.

Throughout the second half of the twentieth century, early childhood educational services expanded in directions established decades earlier. Wealthy children stayed home or enrolled in **play** groups or private nursery or preschools (see **Preschool/Prekindergarten Programs**). Children of poor families and/or those whose mothers worked enrolled in federally run or privately funded daycare centers, nursery schools, or **kindergartens,** with family daycare in the homes of nonfamilial adults the most common. At a time when notions of universal stages of **cognitive development** were being detailed and the role of constructive play took on a new importance in promoting early intelligence, President Lyndon Johnson launched Head Start as a centerpiece to the War on Poverty. Begun in 1965 as an eight-week summer program, Head Start soon became a large-scale social welfare program that has varied as a function of politics as well as growing understandings of child development. In 1975, another group of children—those with disabilities—was identified as entitled to publicly funded early intervention services. Eventually renamed and amended in 1997 to include younger children, The **Individuals with Disabilities Education Act** (IDEA) effectively changed the landscape and the language of early childhood education, from the classroom to **teacher education** to a new field of **early childhood special education**. To date, U.S. policies have continued to prioritize funding for children needing **early intervention** over the provision of universal early care and educational services.

Early Childhood as a Time to Learn

Understandings of early childhood as a time for learning emerged from child development laboratories such as John **Dewey**'s at the University of Chicago. The mantra of "learning by doing" was soon part of the discourse of the early nursery school movement of the 1920s, and children were not the only ones who were busy. Social activists and others committed to progressive education traveled abroad and returned with new perspectives on early educational practices. As Friedrich **Froebel's** kindergarten came under criticism, the ideas of Maria **Montessori** gained favor. Abigail **Eliot** returned from England with new ideas about the "total child" concept, including a focus on parents. Teacher training schools were launched, and by 1925 a **National Committee on Nursery Schools** was convened— a group of women who eventually served as founding mothers of the **National Association for the Education of Young Children**.

As laboratory schools and research centers spread across the United States— some at major research universities—so too did the influence of child development research on teacher preparation. By the 1930s, many middle-income children attended nursery school and/or kindergarten for purposes of enhancing their development and their teachers sought training in departments of home economics, psychology, or education. By mid-century, the kindergarten was increasingly viewed as the first and best place to establish children's "**readiness**" for formal schooling. Jean **Piaget's** treatises on the child's distinctive ways of reasoning—most disseminated decades after they were first published—provided new windows on children's developmental processes and new rationale for an early childhood education.

Ideas about the period of early childhood—and children's early education— were also reflected in and supported by businesses. For example, by the end of the nineteenth century, major toy companies were marketing toys as educational games. The twentieth century saw a dramatic increase in mass-produced toys, many of them designed for solitary play. Lincoln Logs, Erector sets, and Crayolas enhanced constructive and creative activities and provided new interest, in play that could take place indoors. Subsequent debates on the value and nature of toys, and their roles in educational environments, were sparked by such leading figures as Montessori, Roland Barth, and Erik **Erikson**, among others. Controversy surrounding the contributions of play to children's learning, identity, and development became a part of the early childhood education discourse.

Early Childhood as Contested Terrain

Each of the above features—the notion of scientific research as a basis for decisions about early childhood, the premise of early intervention into the lives of children deemed "at risk," and the presumed benefits of capitalizing on children's early learning potentials—has generated controversy as well as new policy initiatives throughout the twentieth century and into the twenty-first century.

There is little doubt that decisions by governors and state legislatures to invest public revenues in early childhood programs has been influenced by advances in child development knowledge that have occurred during the past quarter century, including new understandings of the infant brain as brimming with neurological potential waiting for stimulation rather than as an empty vessel seeking to be filled.

Such political involvement in ECE has brought long-desired recognition as well as unanticipated challenges, as evidenced by the **No Child Left Behind Act** and new performance standards for Head Start that are more akin to those of elementary schools than what many believe is appropriate for young children. The nature and aims of science are also at stake, as funding agencies increasingly emphasize the importance of empirical evidence to the exclusion of qualitative forms of inquiry in the determination of developmentally appropriate educational practices as essential to maintaining the "scientific" and professional status of the field.

As the stakes increase for research that can demonstrate "what works" in early childhood classrooms, postmodern scholars and contributors to the **reconceptualist** movement question the capacity of research to tell it "how it is," and caution against the certainty based on empirical knowledge, especially when such "truths" include a standardized image of childhood. Within this oppositional context, professionally derived determinations of quality and **developmentally appropriate practices** in the United States continue to be informed by child development research; and comparative studies of early education, in turn, continue to demonstrate alternative interpretations of high quality early care and education. In short, debates about the role of early childhood education and the consequences of various curricula and teaching methods on children's lives echo many of the debates of a century ago. And yet the field has much to acclaim, as the following policy initiatives show.

Recent Policy Developments Influencing American Early Childhood Education

Interest and activity in the field of early childhood education has reached an unprecedented level both within the United States and worldwide during the past twenty-five years. In the United States, this attention has been generated by the confluence of many different but complementary trends and policy initiatives. One influence contributing to decisions to invest public revenues in programs serving young children has been the previously described advances in child development knowledge. The accumulation of long-term longitudinal studies showing benefits from participation in intensive early education programs during the preschool years has also resulted in a number of specific policy initiatives and accompanying new debates.

Concern with School Readiness

The first of these trends has been an increased emphasis on insuring that young children are well prepared for success in primary school, stimulated in part by a

National Education Goal established at the federal level in 1991 specifying that "All children in America will start school ready to learn." "School readiness" became a mantra during the 1990s that has carried over into the new century, and has led to concerted efforts within the fifty states and the District of Columbia to find policies and programs with demonstrated capacity to enhance the competencies and skills needed by young children to be successful in the early grades.

The primary school readiness strategy employed by the states during the past decade has been funding of prekindergarten. At least thirty-eight states and the District of Columbia now fund state prekindergarten programs for four-year-olds (Barnett et al., 2005). As of this writing, four of these states (Georgia, New York, Oklahoma, West Virginia) are implementing universal programs, and two others (Florida, Massachusetts) have laws in place to do so. Currently these state programs serve four-year-olds, although extending this opportunity to three-year-olds is under discussion in several states. Many of these ECE programs serve children in both school and nonschool (child care, family support) settings. Their schedules may be part- or full-day, and typically are limited to the school year.

The Expansion of Comprehensive Early Intervention Systems and Services

Federal laws and policy initiatives have also contributed greatly to the heightened interest in early education and care. By the late 1990s, the federal law required that the states provide for the development of comprehensive early intervention systems for infants and toddlers with developmental delays or disabilities, in addition to the services developed for 3–6-year-olds. The interest in the birth-three age period is also reflected in changing policies and programs in Head Start.

Head Start and Early Head Start

The federal Head Start program, although under way since the mid-1960s, received substantial funding increases during the Clinton administration (1993–2001), both for expansion and for program improvement. In 1993, the U.S. Department of Health and Human Services undertook a review of the Head Start program that led to a number of recommendations, including the development of services for infants and toddlers living in low-income families (U.S. Department of Health and Human Services, 1993). **Early Head Start**, created in 1994, has grown from 68 to more than 650 programs, serving more than 62,000 families and their very young children in the ten years between 1995 and 2004. As importantly, the positive findings from the longitudinal study of the impacts of Early Head Start have stimulated increased interest in services for 0–3-year-olds and their families at the state and local levels (U.S. Department of Health and Human Services, 2002).

Changes in the Welfare System

A major shift in federal policy toward low-income families occurred in the mid-1990s in the area of welfare reform. In 1996, the Aid to Families with Dependent

Children (AFDC) law, which had provided modest monthly financial support to unemployed single mothers with children as an entitlement, was allowed to lapse. It was replaced by a new law, **Temporary Assistance to Needy Families** (TANF), which provides funds to the states to assist families with young children under certain conditions. These conditions include immediate participation in work preparation programs and entrance into the labor market within two years. No family is eligible for support for more than five years. One effect of this new emphasis on employment for parents with young children and little income has been more attention by states and local communities to the provision of subsidized child care for these families, much of which is family based and some of which is provided by kith and kin (family child care and family, friend, and neighbor care).

Efforts to Help Parents and Communities Assess Quality

The generally mediocre quality of U.S. early care and education programs has been identified as an enduring problem, that approaches the level of a national crisis, especially when accompanied by concerns regarding the lack of equity (equal access to comprehensive supports) and inadequate infrastructure (NICHD, 2005). One recent policy response to the quality challenge has been the development of quality rating systems. A quality rating system (QRS) is a way of assessing, improving, and publicizing the level of quality achieved by an early childhood setting. State QRS systems have five elements: standards (based on widely accepted guidelines), accountability (through assessment and monitoring), outreach and support to practitioners (to improve quality), financing incentives (such as bonus payments for quality, tiered reimbursement rates based on quality, etc.), and parent education. Thus these systems have dual purposes: to assist the parent consumer in making an educated choice and to improve the overall quality of the ECE system. In 2004, nine states and the District of Columbia reported having a QRS with several levels of quality available throughout their jurisdiction, and a number of other states were in earlier stages of implementation. This quality improvement and parent education strategy has the added advantage of bringing the state's early care and education into the public eye, in the hope that this visibility will expose shortcomings in the system, spur public discussion, and lead to improvements in access and infrastructure as well as program quality.

Immigrants

Social characteristics that exacerbate these issues include the increased presence and diversity of immigrants in American schools and communities. The United States was founded by immigrant settlers from England who left their homes under duress and then took over the lands and lives of Native Americans. By the nineteenth century, the pattern began to change and immigrants—many from southern and eastern Europe—were often, although not always, wealthy members of Jewish, Catholic, and Eastern Orthodox religions. These groups came together in the "melting pot" of the United States, where the goal of assimilation

far outweighed the goal of maintaining distinguishing cultural and linguistic traditions. A century later, the United States continues to be a nation of old and new
immigrants, but the new immigrants are now helping to constitute a radically
different version of U.S. multiculturalism that includes people, languages, and traditions from Arab nations as well as Cambodia, the Caribbean and Latin America,
China, South Korea, Russia, and Eastern Europe.

The Economic Impacts of Early Childhood Education

Although the long-term pay-offs from early investment in early care and education services have been understood by social scientists and educators for
more than a decade, economists have become fully aware of the implications
of these findings for macro-economic policy only since the turn of the century
(Dickens, Sawhill, and Tebbs, 2006). The realization by economists that the "return of investment" of early childhood programs is very high over the long term
(20 years) and substantial even in the medium term (5–10 years or more) has
led them to urge expansion of such services at the state and federal levels, and
to recommend that ECE programming be included in the community development strategies promoted by a number of major national foundations. Exciting
work is also under way that documents the economic impacts of the early care
and educational sector on local community development, through wages paid
to the very sizable ECE work force, capital investments in early childhood programs, and the employment opportunities afforded parents who would otherwise need to be caring for their children themselves (Warner et al., 2004; OECD,
2006).

Multiple Perspectives on Early Childhood Education

In conceptualizing this four volume encyclopedia, we did not set out to simplify
early childhood education concepts, programs, and policies to appeal to some
"average" reader, nor have we sanitized the entries to make the early childhood
education field seem cleaner and more coherent than it in fact is. Combining as
it does ideas and perspectives from child development, health, education, early
intervention, and family support, our intention has been to represent early childhood education as it is—complex, dependent upon collaborative relationships,
and unwieldy as a field of study. Because public involvement with young children
must by definition encroach upon the private domain of family life, there must
be controversy. The cultural dimension of the ECE field is also a given because
the field concentrates on that stage of the life course when cultural values, beliefs, and norms are first being introduced to the developing child, and reinforced
through daily routines, social practices, program structures, communal activities,
and interpersonal relations and interactions. The recently released report by the
OECD (2006) attests to the global interest and the cultural diversity in approaches
to early childhood. It is at this cultural level that we believe Volume 4 makes its
greatest contribution, by allowing readers to explore early childhood education
within cultural contexts outside their own, and in so doing to see and appreciate

the cultural dimensions of their own policies and practices in new ways. These features—complexity, controversy, cultural differences, and collaboration—have also characterized development of these volumes and their contents, and this was intentional rather than accidental. They have led to productive conversations among contributors and editors, which hopefully will be extended and expanded by publication of the four volumes. We hope that the ideas and perspectives contained herein will stimulate productive and valued conversations both within and across cultures, so that the lives of all our children and their families can continue to be enriched in new and exciting ways by caring and wise teachers and other caregivers who think globally and teach locally.

References and Further Readings

Barnett, S., J. Hustedt, and K. Schulman (2005). *The state of preschool: 2005 state preschool yearbook*. New Brunswick, NJ: The National Institute for Early Education Research, Rutgers University.

Cochran, M. (2007). *Finding our way: American early care and education in global perspective*. Washington, DC: Zero to Three.

Dickens, W., I. Sawhill, and J. Tebbs (2006). *The effects of investing in early education on economic growth*. Washington, DC: The Brookings Institution, Policy Brief #153.

Lubeck, Sally (1995). Policy issues in the development of child care and early education systems: The need for cross-national comparison. In A. Hatch (ed.) *Qualitative research in early childhood settings*. Westport, CT: Praeger.

Moss, P. (2005). Making the narrative of quality stutter. *Early Education and Development, 16*(4), 405–420.

Meisels, S., and J. Shonkoff (2000). Early childhood intervention: A continuing evolution. In J. Shonkoff and S. Meisels, eds., *Handbook of early childhood intervention*, 2nd ed. Cambridge: Cambridge University Press, pp. 3–31.

National Research Council (2003). *Understanding others, educating ourselves: Getting more from international comparative studies in education*. Committee on a Framework and Long-term Research Agenda for International Comparative Education Studies. Washington, DC: The National Academies Press.

New, R. (2005). Legitimizing quality as quest and question. *Early Education and Development, 16*(4), 421–436.

NICHD Early Child Care Research Network (Eds.). *Child care and child development: Results from the NICHD study on early child care and youth development*. New York: The Guilford Press.

Oberhuemer, P. (2005). International perspectives on early childhood curricula. *International Journal of Early Childhood, 37*(1), pp. 135–142.

OECD (2006). *Starting strong II*. Paris: The Organization for Economic Cooperation and Development.

Tobin, J. (2005). Quality in early childhood education: An anthropologist's perspective *Early Education and Development, 16*(4), 421–436.

U.S. Department of Health and Human Services (1993). *Creating a 21st Century Head Start: Final Report of the Advisory Committee on Head Start Quality and Expansion*. Washington, DC: Author.

U.S. Department of Health and Human Services (2002). *Making a Difference in the Lives of Infants and Toddlers and their Families: The Impacts of Early Head Start*.

Washington, DC: The Commissioner's Office of Research and Evaluation and the Head Start Bureau, Administration on Children, Youth and Families.

Warner, M., S. Adriance, N. Baria, J. Hallas, B. Markeson, T. Morrissey, and W. Soref (2004). *Economic development strategies to promote quality child care.* Ithaca, NY: Cornell University, Department of City and Regional Planning. Available at http://www.earlychildhoodfinance.org/publicationspub.htm.

A

AAC. *See* Augmentative and Alternative Communication

ABC. *See* Act for Better Child Care

Abecedarian Program

The Abecedarian Program, also known as the Carolina Abecedarian Project, was established in 1972 at the Frank Porter Graham Child Development Institute at the University of North Carolina at Chapel Hill. The Abecedarian Program was an experimental early childhood program aimed at studying the long-term effects of high-quality early intervention with infants judged to be at high risk as a result of **poverty** and maternal education. Follow-up studies after twenty-one years indicated that the Abecedarian program intervention had positive long-term results.

The Abecedarian Program began in 1972 and served children of low-income, predominantly African American families. A total of 111 infants, divided into two groups, participated in the study. Fifty-seven infants were assigned to the treatment group and 54 were in the control group. The average age of the infants at the beginning of the program was 4.4 months and all were in good health. Infants in the treatment group received child care and early educational services for six to eight hours per day, five days per week, for fifty weeks per year, up to kindergarten entry at age 5. In addition, families received medical, social, and nutritional services. Children and families in the control group received the additional services, but not the focused early childhood education program.

The early childhood education program consisted of planned activities in specific targeted developmental areas, namely, language, cognitive and fine motor, social and self-help, and gross motor. The child to caregiver ratio was 3:1 for infants and 6:1 for toddlers and preschoolers, and each caregiver was trained to place particular emphasis on language development through daily conversational interactions with the children. The program offered individualized activities for infants and a learning center approach for the toddlers and preschoolers. Parents of children in the program attended social functions, served on the advisory board, and received counseling in child health and development.

During the summer prior to **kindergarten** entrance, the Abecedarian treatment group children participated in a six-week transition program that included other community children. The intent of this program was to introduce the Abecedarian children to others they would encounter in school.

Upon school entry, half the children in both the treatment and control groups were randomly assigned to a school-age intervention program for kindergarten through third grade. A Home-School Resource Teacher (HST) was assigned to a group of fourteen children and served as a liaison between the children's teachers and their families. The HST consulted with the school teachers and provided families with activities to support children's learning of **mathematics** and reading. The HST also referred families to social services as needed. The purpose of this follow-up intervention was to assess the relative impact of timing of intervention on outcomes.

All but seven participants in both the treatment and control groups of the Abecedarian program were assessed at ages three, four, five, six and a half, eight, twelve, fifteen, and twenty-one years. Beginning at age 3 and throughout the study, treatment group children had significantly higher scores on I.Q. tests, as well as reading and math tests. By age 15, significantly fewer treatment group children had been retained in grade or had been placed in special education classes. By age 21, significantly more treatment group children were enrolled in or had graduated from a four-year college, and on average were a year older than control group participants at the birth of their first child.

Because of the school intervention feature of the Abecedarian Program, outcomes can be compared in terms of timing and duration of intervention. Some children received early and continuing intervention, others received **early intervention** only, and still others received later intervention only. In terms of IQ, reading, and math measures, the most persistent positive results were obtained by children in the early and continuing intervention group up to age 12. The next best outcome accrued to children in the early intervention group, followed by the later intervention group. By age 15, however, continuing benefits were discernible only for participants in the two groups that had experienced early intervention. *See also* Cognitive Development; Development, Language; Development, Social; Intelligence Quotient; Intelligence Testing.

Further Readings: Burchinal, Margaret R., Frances A. Campbell, Donna M. Bryant, Barbara H. Wasik, and Craig T. Ramey. (1997). Early intervention and mediating processes in cognitive performance children of low-income African American families. *Child Development* 68(5), 935–954; Campbell, Frances A., Elizabeth P. Pungello, Shari Miller-Johnson, Margaret Burchinal, and Craig T. Ramey. (2001). The development of cognitive and academic abilities: Growth curves from an early childhood educational experiment. *Developmental Psychology* 37(2), 231–242; Campbell, Frances A., and Craig T. Ramey. (1995). Cognitive and school outcomes for high risk African American students at middle adolescence: Positive effects of early intervention. *American Educational Research Journal* 32(4), 743–772.

Stephanie F. Leeds

Abuse of Children. *See* Sexual Abuse

Academics

Academics in early childhood education generally refer to the specific focus on academic content areas such as mathematics, reading, writing, and other **curriculum** domains. Although attention to school readiness and to preparing children for success in school has long been part of the early childhood landscape in the United States, controversies over the role and nature of "academics" in early education gained urgency in the 1980s and continue today.

In the context of what was called a back-to-basics movement in education, David Elkind's books about the "hurried child," and the "miseducation" of preschoolers sounded an alarm in the field, as he described the pushing down of formal academic content and teaching into the years before **kindergarten**. At the same time, similar concerns about early academic pressures influenced the **National Association for the Education of Young Children** (NAEYC) to develop its position statement on **developmentally appropriate practice**. In this publication, NAEYC stated that "in recent years, a trend toward increased emphasis on formal instruction in academic skills has emerged in early childhood programs. This trend toward formal academic instruction for younger children is based on misconceptions about early learning" (Bredekamp, 1987, p. 1). The position statement was intended to counter these misconceptions with a different view of early development and learning, and guidelines for a different set of practices.

At the same time, several lines of research sought to explore issues around "academic instruction" in early childhood. Typically, the designs of these studies contrasted "academic instruction," an "academic focus," or an "academic curriculum" on one hand, with a "child-centered curriculum" or a "developmentally appropriate focus" on the other. Academic instruction was viewed as necessarily didactic and adult-directed, with the child in a passive role, and emphasizing rote learning or drill-and-practice. Contrasted with this was a form of education in which children chose their activities, adults served as facilitators rather than providing instruction, and in which explicit teaching of skills in **mathematics** and **literacy** was considered inappropriate. Results of several studies using this child-centered pedagogy appeared to find disadvantages to the "academic" emphasis, including greater child anxiety and lower motivation on the part of children, without a significant improvement in academic skills except for perhaps some short-term gains in specific knowledge. These results have been found both with economically advantaged and poor children. A well-known longitudinal study in this research tradition was the curriculum comparison study conducted by the High/Scope Educational Research Foundation, in which outcomes for children who had been randomly assigned to an academically oriented curriculum were compared to those for children in a more child-focused, constructivist curriculum (Schweinhart, Weikart, and Larner, 1986). The researchers interpreted the results as showing clear long-term advantages, especially in the domain of social competence, for the more active, constructivist curriculum rather than the curriculum that emphasized academic skills.

For a number of reasons, these results have not ended the discussion about the place of "academics" in early childhood education. First, the findings of these studies have sometimes been criticized on methodological grounds, and the interpretation of results has been questioned. Second, deep-seated, differing perspectives on the importance of academic instruction persist not only across cultures but also within cultures. Family and community expectations for what children should learn are frequently in conflict with the beliefs of early childhood professionals. Additionally, several new developments later in the 1990s and into the present make the picture more complex than it may have appeared fifteen years ago.

For example, developmental and educational research, especially in the area of literacy, indicates that one can predict later school success from children's acquisition of specific academic skills such as alphabet knowledge before they enter kindergarten. These kinds of findings have caused even traditional early childhood educators to consider the extent to which they should include some degree of academic instruction in their programs.

Additionally, as every state in the United States has developed or is developing "early learning standards," academic skills are increasingly emphasized to a greater extent in programs for children below first grade. Although they vary in emphasis, state early learning standards typically include "academic" content areas such as literacy, mathematics, and **science**, with efforts to link or align these standards to those previously developed for grades K–12. And at the federal level, policy debates over the Congressional reauthorization of **Head Start** have focused on strengthening its academic components. Similar issues have surfaced in the United Kingdom (see Volume 4) and other countries with changes in education policies.

In an effort to distinguish early learning from that which takes place in later grades in the United States, the term "preacademic" has sometimes been used to describe foundational school **readiness** skills such as knowledge of shapes, visual perception, copying letters, and so on. Internationally, the **IEA Preprimary Project** used this term in its "Preacademic Skills Measure." Some have criticized this terminology as placing emphasis on the value of early learning for its contribution to what is to come later, rather than having value for its own sake.

Part of the difficulty in conceptualizing early "academics" has been definitional. At times, "academics" refers to a certain type of content (e.g., content and skills in literacy, mathematics, science, and so on), and at other times it refers to teaching methods (e.g., decontextualized, adult-directed, and didactic). Additionally, there has been a failure to distinguish between specific academic skills and broader intellectual competencies and dispositions, which some believe are given short shrift or undermined when narrower academic skills are emphasized. Katz argues that by using project work, the early childhood curriculum might focus on "at least a trio of goals: (1) social-emotional development and (2) intellectual development, and (3) the acquisition of meaningful and useful academic skills" (Katz, 1999, p. 4).

Within this context, the issue today may be reframed, moving away from a dichotomous view. Within this reframed perspective, the question is not whether academic skills and content are an appropriate component of early childhood curriculum and teaching, but how these may be integrated and taught in ways that are engaging and effective. To do this, early childhood educators would need to select academic content that is important and appropriate; continue to promote social and emotional competence, teacher–child–family relationships, and positive approaches to learning; prepare teachers to integrate academic content effectively; and embed academic content within appropriate curriculum and teaching strategies including investigation and **play**. *See also* Curriculum, Science; Pedagogy, Child-Centered.

Further Readings: Bowman, Barbara, ed. (2002). *Love to read: Essays in developing and enhancing early literacy skills of African American children*. Washington, DC: National Black Child Development Institute; Bredekamp, S., ed. (1987). *Developmentally appropriate practice in early childhood programs serving children birth through age 8*. Washington, DC: National Association for the Education of Young Children; Elkind, D. (1987). *Miseducation: Preschoolers at risk*. New York: Knopf; Fuller, Bruce, Costanza Eggers-Pierola, Susan Holloway, Xiaoyan Liang, and Marylee F. Rambaud (1996). Rich culture, poor markets: Why do Latino parents forgo preschooling? *Teachers College Record* 97(3), 400–418; Hyson, M. (2003). Putting early academics in their place. *Educational Leadership* 60(7), 20–23; Katz, L. G. (1999). *Curriculum disputes in early childhood education*. ERIC Digest. Champaign, IL: ERIC Clearinghouse on Elementary and Early Childhood Education; Kwon, Y.-I. (2002). Changing curriculum for early childhood education in England. *Early Childhood Research and Practice* 4(2). Available online at http://ecrp.uiuc.edu/v4n2/kwon.html; Marcon, Rebecca. (1992). Differential effects of three preschool models on inner-city 4-year-olds. *Early Childhood Research Quarterly* 7(4), 517–530; New, R. (1999). What should children learn? Making choices and taking chances. *Early Childhood Research and Practice* 1(2), 1–25; Rescorla, L. A., M. Hyson, and K. Hirsh-Pasek, eds. (1991). *Academic instruction in early childhood: Challenge or pressure?* New Directions for Child Development, No. 53. San Francisco: Jossey-Bass; Schweinhart, L. J., D. P. Weikart, and M. B. Larner (1986). Consequences of the three preschool curriculum models through age 15. *Early Childhood Research Quarterly* 1, 15–45; Scott-Little, C., S. L. Kagan, and V. S. Frelow (2005). *Inside the content: The depth and breadth of early learning standards*. University of North Carolina at Greensboro: SERVE Center for Continuous Improvement.

Marilou Hyson

ACCESS. *See* American Associate Degree Early Childhood Educators

Accreditation of Early Childhood Programs

Accreditation systems provide an organized process for self-study and improvement, and for program recognition. Accreditation systems exist for a wide range of professional activity, including health care services, museums, adventure clubs, colleges and universities, public school systems, and many other kinds of programs and services. Program accreditation became a visible resource to the early childhood field when the **National Association for the Education of Young Children** (NAEYC) launched its center-based early childhood program accreditation system in 1985.

Within the United States, participation in early childhood program accreditation systems is voluntary. Early childhood program accreditation systems are different from regulatory systems such as state licensing standards for child care. States establish regulatory systems to monitor the minimum health and safety of early childhood programs. These public governmental regulations establish the requirements by which early childhood programs may operate in a particular state and are monitored by government officials for on-going compliance. In contrast, early childhood program accreditation systems in the United States provide a voluntary mechanism by which a profession sets and monitors the standards for its own professional practice.

Limited research exists on the impact of early childhood program accreditation systems on program quality. As the most mature of the early childhood field's early childhood program accreditation systems, NAEYC's accreditation system has been the focus of most of the research. Often, research on accreditation's impact is embedded within larger studies. Because the criteria presently associated with NAEYC's early childhood program accreditation system are also tied to research, it is assumed that participation in NAEYC's early childhood program accreditation system will be beneficial. This confidence appears to be warranted; available evidence suggests that NAEYC-accredited programs provide higher levels of program quality than nonaccredited programs.

Structure and Intent of Early Childhood Program Accreditation Systems

NAEYC accreditation is the field's largest early childhood program accreditation system. An inclusive program accreditation system, NAEYC's accreditation system serves the full array of center- and school-based early childhood programs: not-for-profit; for-profit; faith-based; public, and private. In 2005, over 10,000 US center-based programs had been accredited. Even so, fewer than 10 percent of center-based early childhood programs are NAEYC-accredited. Considerable opportunity exists, therefore, for increasing the number of early childhood programs engaged in a systematic and comprehensive process of self-examination and quality improvement.

After fifteen very successful years of operation, dramatic growth in demand for its accreditation services led NAEYC to launch the Project to Reinvent NAEYC Accreditation in late 1999. This five-year project has resulted in a reinvented accreditation system with a new mission and design, new performance expectations, and newly developed accreditation assessment instruments; the new accreditation system is scheduled to be fully operational in 2006.

NAEYC's center- and school-based early childhood program accreditation system is not the only one available for early childhood programs. The early childhood field also has specialized early childhood program accreditation systems for family child care, school age care, Montessori programs, and for faith-based and for-profit programs, many of which offer Web sites with helpful information. While varying in their sponsorship, cost, focus, performance expectations, and the age range encompassed by the programs being accredited, these accreditation systems share in common their desire to help early childhood programs improve the quality of programs so young children will have better early learning and development experiences. They also share in common a system design that (1) engages programs in a process of self-study against a set of professional standards; (2) provides review by an externally assigned group of individuals; (3) includes a process for deciding whether a program has achieved accreditation; and (4) provides a process for programs to maintain and renew their accreditation status. Early childhood accreditation systems vary considerably, however, in their program standards and in how they make these four common structural elements operational. They also vary in their emphasis on continuous program improvement versus a set level of program quality as the desired outcome for the accreditation process. Each early childhood program accreditation system includes unique features, processes, and terminology.

By definition, early childhood program accreditation systems are designed to support program improvement and almost all accreditation systems seek to make the process of program improvement an on-going characteristic of the programs they accredit. This desired result is usually achieved through three features of accreditation systems:

(1) A set of consensually derived professional **standards** that programs use to examine and assess their program's performance; these program standards usually address, but are not limited to, expectations regarding the relationship between children and teaching staff; the management of the program; facilities; **curriculum** and teaching; health performance expectations, and relationships with **families**,

(2) A process by which programs systematically engage in assessing their performance against the system's program standards, and

(3) An external review process that provides programs with feedback about the extent to which their self-assessment coincides with what a neutral reviewer would say about the program's performance. Usually this occurs via a site visit, but accreditation systems vary in how they review a program's self-study of its performance against the system's program standards.

Despite these similarities, accreditation systems can vary in their purpose. While all accreditation systems invoke a process of self-study and quality improvement, continuous improvement is the only possible intent of an accreditation process. Three possible functions of program accreditation systems are of particular relevance to early childhood program accreditation: (1) Granting a seal of approval; (2) Providing a report to users; and (3) Conferring assurance. Clarity regarding the purpose of an early childhood program accreditation system is important because it shapes the way in which the accreditation system is designed and managed.

When the accreditation system grants a seal of approval, it validates the claims made by an early childhood program. Programs assess their own performance relative to the profession's performance standards, and outside reviewers confirm the validity of the program's self-assessment. The accreditation system testifies through its validation and accreditation decision-making processes that the program is delivering what it promises. If a program achieves accreditation from a system with this intent, the program is deemed to be doing what it says it does.

When the accreditation system focuses on the users of early childhood programs by providing them with an assessment of a program's performance, it is recognizing families and other purchasers of early childhood programs as consumers—and as the primary customer of accreditation results. Consumers, in this instance, refer to those individuals who choose and/or pay for an accredited program on behalf of an individual child or children. When the intent of the accreditation system is to provide assessment results to users of early childhood programs (in contrast to the providers of the program), the focus is on evaluating the extent to which an early childhood program's practices coincide with established standards, recognizing their success in conforming to the program standards, and making the program's accreditation status known to families and others so they will use this information in selecting an early childhood program for children. While the stakes of user-focused program assessment are higher for early childhood programs, so are the potential benefits, since achieving accreditation status under these circumstances differentiates high-performing programs from others and elevates their visibility with critical stakeholders, including families.

These two functions might sound similar, but they are conceptually and practically different. When an accreditation process focuses on recognizing programs that comply with its professional program standards, the early childhood program is being evaluated, not just validated, against a set of criteria. The focus is on the program's level of performance. The process of continuous improvement, therefore, is the means to a higher level of performance; it is not, however, the source of accreditation status.

The third function of accreditation is "conferring assurance." The concept is borrowed from industry. Accreditation systems that emphasize this function evaluate programs in terms of their potential to cause damage or harm. Accreditation status provides assurance that the program is safe to use. Achievement of accreditation in this instance affirms that the basic health and safety of children in the program will be protected. In the absence in the United States of consistent public and private regulations that ensure that children are in healthy and safe early childhood programs, this can be an important function for an accreditation system to perform.

No one of these functions is necessarily more important than another. Most early childhood program accreditation systems perform some measure of each function. But the leaders of strong accreditation systems prioritize their functions. They know very clearly what they want their accreditation systems to achieve and organize their work in ways that correspond to their priorities.

Changing Demand for Early Childhood Program Accreditation

With the success of advocacy efforts to increase public and private support for high-quality early childhood programs and the movement for increased accountability, increased demand exists for program accreditation. State legislatures, national organizations such as United Way and Easter Seals, and philanthropic groups have begun to look to early childhood program accreditation as a means for improving program quality, for attaching higher levels of program quality with public and private financial support, and for providing an accountability measure for their investment. More than 30 states now have tiered reimbursement systems or quality rating systems that link public funding with levels of program quality, including achievement of program accreditation. In addition, numerous organizations that fund early childhood programs serving low-income children have linked their financial support with a program's achievement and maintenance of accreditation status.

These public and private policies are helping drive demand for early childhood program accreditation, making achievement of accreditation status more high-stakes for early childhood programs, and placing more pressures on early childhood program accreditation systems to function efficiently, effectively, and reliably.

The increased visibility of early childhood program accreditation also offers new opportunities for the early childhood field. It offers early childhood program accreditation systems and their sponsors the opportunity to make the program standards for high-quality early childhood programs more visible to those who can help make quality programs more available to young children, families, and communities. Ultimately, children most benefit from being in caring and engaging early learning environments. Early childhood program accreditation, especially in conjunction with the support services increasingly available to programs seeking accreditation, offers an effective strategy for increasing the daily quality of children's out-of-home early learning experiences and for improving the impact of these experiences on their learning and development.

Information on NAEYC's accreditation reinvention project can be found in NAEYC's journal, *Young Children*, in articles published bimonthly between July 2000 and September 2004. Information is also available on NAEYC's Web site www.naeyc.org. *See also* Teacher Certification/Licensure.

Further Readings: Bredekamp, S. (1999). When new solutions create new problems: Lessons learned from NAEYC Accreditation. *Young Children* 54(1), 58–63; Bredekamp, S., and Barbara A. Willer, eds. (1996). *NAEYC Accreditation: A decade of learning and the years ahead*. Washington, DC: National Association for the Education of Young Children.

Stacie G. Goffin

ACEI. *See* Association for Childhood Education International

ACT. *See* Association for Constructivist Teaching

Act for Better Child Care (ABC)

The Act for Better Child Care (the ABC bill) was introduced to Congress in November 1987 as the result of efforts by the Alliance for Better Child Care, a coalition that eventually included over 130 national groups. The goal of the bill was to improve the availability, affordability, and quality of child care by providing new federal funds to states. This bill was eventually revised and renamed, culminating in the **Child Care and Development Block Grant**. The history of the ABC bill describes a critical period in the history of early childhood education in the United States and the influence of coordinated advocacy efforts.

In 1971, President Richard Nixon had vetoed comprehensive child-care legislation that had passed the House and Senate with broad bipartisan support, thereby putting a chill on the child-care debate at the federal level for almost 15 years. The issue began to regain currency in 1984 when Representative George Miller (Democrat from California) selected child care as the first priority issue for his new Select Committee on Children and Youth. The Committee held a series of hearings and issued a report on **child care**. During the late 1980s, interest in child care skyrocketed. Mothers had gone to work in record numbers but child-care policy lagged behind. By 1986, the huge gap between women's labor force participation and public investments in child care had generated significant and continuous press attention, which helped to finally force the issue to the top of the Congressional agenda. That year, the **Children's Defense Fund** and a host of national organizations representing children, child-care providers, labor unions, religious groups, educators, women, and others joined together to begin a process that resulted in the Act for Better Child Care.

These efforts were fueled by the belief that if a child-care bill was moving in Congress prior to the 1988 presidential election, child care could become a top issue in the presidential campaign debate. The coalition sought to draw enough attention to the issue to ensure that a bill would be enacted during the first year of a new president's term.

In the summer of 1986, a steering committee began a year-long process of working with representatives of national organizations and early childhood advocates across the country to develop a child-care bill. The original bill provided child-care assistance to families earning up to 115 percent of their state's median income. Funds were also targeted to improve the quality and expand the supply of child care. The bill authorized $2.5 billion annually to be sent to states based on a formula that factored in the number of young children, state per capita income and number of children receiving free and reduced-price lunch. States could use the funds to offer parents certificates to purchase child care or for contracts with providers. In addition, a percentage of funds was reserved to help part-day preschool programs provide full-day, full-year services. Providers receiving funds were required to meet federal standards that would be developed by an advisory committee.

On November 19, 1987, a joint House Senate press conference was held to introduce the ABC bill, which had 126 Representatives and 22 Senators as cosponsors. The lead cosponsors of the Senate bill were Senator Christopher Dodd (D-CT) and Senator John Chafee (R-RI). The House version was cosponsored by Representative Dale Kildee (D-MI) and Representative Olympia Snowe (R-ME). Congress debated the bill during 1988 and child care indeed became a prominent issue in the presidential election campaign with both candidates supporting an expanded Federal role in child care. In January 1989, Senator Orrin Hatch (R-UT) asked to replace Senator John Chafee as the Senate bill's chief Republican cosponsor and became a strong advocate for the bill's passage.

As debates over the bill proceeded, President George Bush supported using tax credits as opposed to providing direct **child-care subsidies** to families. The Democrats who controlled both the Senate and House took advantage of the Administration's willingness to extend tax credits for low-income families and added an expansion of the Earned Income Tax Credit (EITC) to the ABC bill before it was brought to the Senate floor for a vote.

The ABC bill passed the Senate in June 1989. It passed the House in October 1989 but because of budget technicalities, had to pass the House again in March 1990. Congress was scheduled to adjourn in October 1990.

That fall, an unusual conference took place. The Senate worked out a compromise bill with the White House. These discussions did not include the House because of jurisdictional conflicts between various House committees. The Senate and White House announced their agreement on a compromise bill during a press conference that included Senate Majority Leader George Mitchell (D-ME) and Senate Minority Leader Bob Dole (R-KS), as well as the key Senate sponsors of the bill, Senators Dodd, Kennedy, and Hatch. The Senate then met with the House to reconcile any remaining differences. On November 5, President Bush signed a Budget Reconciliation bill that included the ABC bill, renamed the Child Care and Development Block Grant, and authorized $750 million in fiscal year 1991, $825 million in fiscal year 1992, $925 million in fiscal year 1993, and such sums as necessary for fiscal years 1994 and 1995 for child-care assistance to low-income working families and to improve the quality and expand the supply of child care. It also included a small additional program, the "At-Risk Child Care Program." This program guaranteed states $1.5 billion over five years to help low-income working families, who were at risk of being on welfare, pay for child care. In addition, the bill provided for $12.4 billion over five years to expand the Earned Income Tax Credit for working families with children under age 19, as well as a very small Supplemental Credit for Infants costing $700 million over five years.

Federal standards were extremely controversial, and were eliminated early in the process. When the bill went to the Senate floor for a vote in June 1989, the standards were replaced by **state standards** because Senate leaders believed that federal standards would have led to a filibuster on the Senate floor and that they would not have the 60 votes necessary for cloture to end the filibuster. The final standards that were the product of negotiation with the Senate and the Bush White House required that programs had to meet applicable state child-care **licensing** or registration requirements. Providers that were not required to be regulated by the state had to meet very minimal health and safety standards, with the exception of certain relatives. The bulk of funds were reserved for child-care assistance. Families earning up to 75 percent of their state's median income were eligible for help. States had to offer parents the choice of a certificate or contract to purchase child care. Twenty-five percent of total funding was reserved for quality improvements and initiatives targeted to early childhood development and before-and **after-school child care**.

While many compromises were made along the way, advocates were heartened by the results as the process led to the first comprehensive federal child-care program and also a major expansion of the Earned Income Tax Credit. This not only helped low-income parents but also countless child-care providers whose incomes were low enough to qualify them for the EITC.

The battle for a federal child-care program was successful in large part because of a strong grassroots campaign that was driven by the child-care community with support from labor, children's organizations, women's groups, religious organizations, state and local elected officials and many others. It happened without the assistance of e-mail and fax machines and involved countless mailings and phone calls. The campaign was kicked off by meetings in almost 40 states that brought together a coalition of groups that were spearheading their state's efforts to win passage of the bill. The next several years were focused on ongoing communications with these state coalitions urging them to contact their members of Congress both through letters and phone calls and visits, write letters to the editors and op-eds, visit their editorial boards, and participate in various events and projects to build support for the bill. Governors, state legislators, mayors, religious, and business leaders also supported the legislation and appeared at a series of events. In addition there were targeted media efforts involving editorial memorandum, briefings for reporters in Washington, radio actualities, radio public service announcements, op-eds, letters to the editor, a significant number of press conferences, and paid media.

Advocates strongly believed that if a child-care bill was not enacted into law by the time the Congress adjourned in the fall of 1990, it would be almost impossible to sustain momentum on this issue through another session of Congress. They planned a series of activities to be staged in September. Findings from a Children's Defense Fund report about shortcomings in state child-care licensing provisions and other gaps in quality were released right after Labor Day. The report generated hundreds of stories. Miles of paper chains were put together by the grassroots network across the country and were sent to Washington. Staff working for members of the alliance stretched the chains from the Capitol steps to the White House in mid-September. Members of Congress then attached the chains to their doors. Mothers whose children died or were injured in child care also held a September press conference in the Capitol and fanned out to visit their members of Congress to urge them to finish work on the ABC bill.

The extraordinary efforts of thousands of child-care advocates, parents, and public officials made child care a must win issue for the Congress and the Bush Administration. The Act for Better Child Care remains as a source of inspiration for child-care advocates and early childhood education professionals.

Further Readings: Cohen, Sally S. (2001). *Championing child care.* New York: Columbia University Press.

Helen Blank

Action Research

Action research is generally understood as a type of applied research in which the researcher is actively involved in the setting that is the focus of inquiry as well as in the research itself. Most often, the aim of action research is to investigate practice (as in the case of teacher action research) and to improve the quality of an organization and its performance. Bogden and Biklin (1982) describe it as "the systematic collection of information that is designed to bring about social change" (p. 215).

Action research is usually organized in a seven-step, iterative cycle that begins with (1) identifying a problem, proceeds through (2) observation, (3) data collection, and (4) reflection on the dimensions of the problem, to (5) designing a change that addresses the problem, (6) implementing the change/taking action, and (7) assessing its effectiveness through observation, data collection, and reflection. At the heart of this process is systematic reflection on action that leads to action. Action vis-à-vis action research, as McCutcheon and Jung note, "implies that the practitioner will be acting as the collector of data, the analyst, and the interpreter of results" (p. 144).

As a method of inquiry, action research is situated in a very rich and quite mature tradition of research that reaches back to Dewey (1933) and his call for "reflective action" that would lead toward inquiry-oriented practice. As a specific form of research, it is most often associated with the work of Lewin and his colleagues in the 1940s and 1950s whose work was centered on social and psychological problems created by prejudice, segregation, and isolationism. Today, action research figures prominently in formal inquiry in a variety of areas from education to government to business—any area in which understanding interrelationships and practice is useful in determining ways to initiate and support change.

The methodological precedents for action research emerge from qualitative research particularly in the areas of anthropology and sociology—fields that seek to describe the human condition in all of its variety. The analytic methods employed in action research are often generated from and synchronous with actual practice. Thus, a teacher doing action research might use everyday formative assessment tools like classroom maps, running records, or samples of student work to address her inquiry; and a social worker might use interviews, anecdotal notes, and log entries to address hers. Because action research is capable of bringing together numerous variables to define understandable portraits of the complex dynamic of human interaction, it can serve both as a contrast and a complement to experimental studies where the variables must be few and precise.

Further Readings: Bogden, R. C., and S. K. Biklen (1982). *Qualitative research for education.* Boston: Allyn & Bacon; Dewey, J. (1933). How we think: A restatement of the relation of reflective thinking to the educative process. In Jo Ann Boydston, ed. *The later works (1925-1953).* Vol. 8. Carbondale, IL: Southern Illinois University Press, 105-352; McCutcheon, G., and B. Jung (1990). Alternative perspectives on action research. *Theory into Practice* 29(3), 144-151.

Frances Rust

ADD/ADHD. *See* Attention Deficit Disorder/Attention Deficit Hyperactivity Disorder

Addams, Jane (1860–1935)

Jane Addams is best known for opening Hull-House in the heart of the industrial district of Chicago on September 8, 1895. Its purpose was to serve the needs of the poor, most of whom were first- and second-generation newcomers to America seeking work during the Industrial Revolution. She modeled Hull-House after Toynbee Hall, a settlement she had visited in London. Settlements were part of a social movement based on a desire by the more privileged to cross social class lines and offer more than traditional relief to the less fortunate. She regarded the educational activities, philanthropic, civic, and social undertakings of the Settlement to be different manifestations of an attempt to socialize democracy— to put theory into practice. During a visit to East London, she witnessed the poorest of the poor bidding on fruit and vegetables so rotten they were not fit for sale. She later wrote that she was never able to escape the memory of the white arms and hands waving in a huddle to bid for the decaying food. She devoted her life to caring for the underprivileged and oppressed and to working for the rights of workers, women, and children.

The first organized undertaking of Hull-House was a kindergarten, conducted by a volunteer teacher in the parlor. Mothers working long hours in factories were forced to leave their children locked inside their tenements, or during hot summer days they were locked out. Ms. Addams reported that these children began to wander into the kindergarten and fill the cool halls of Hull-House, where they were fed and bathed. As the Settlement rooms became filled with children, an apartment was leased. Finally, a special building was designed and constructed on a side street, known as the Children's House. It was sustained by Hull-House as a day nursery for sixteen years before being taken over by a charity. Ms. Addams recognized how important the Children's House was for the health and safety of the tenements' youngest members, and further how vital it was for the connection it provided to the immigrant mothers who could be taught how to make life in America more possible. Hull-House was expanded to include an art gallery, a public library, the first public playground, public baths, Boys' Clubs, gymnasiums, and much more. At its peak, Hull-House was used by at least 2,000 people a day.

In her first autobiography, *Twenty Years at Hull-House* (1961), Ms. Addams acknowledged the ideological challenges passed down by her father, a Quaker pioneer and miller, who began the Republican Party in Illinois. His close friendship with Abraham Lincoln underscored his determination to help build America—the great experiment in democracy. Born on September 6, 1860, in Cedarville, Illinois, Ms. Addams was among the first women to graduate from Rockford College in 1882. She recalls an inner restlessness as an educated woman in a time when women did not vote and were not expected to accomplish much more than their grandmothers. Despite these limitations, she was the first president of the Women's International League for Peace and Freedom, campaigned for social justice and, as a delegate to the first national convention of the Progressive Party in 1912, seconded the nomination of Theodore Roosevelt. In 1931 she was cowinner of the Nobel Peace Prize. Ms. Addams died in Chicago on May 21, 1935.

Further Readings: Addams, Jane (1961). *Twenty years at Hull-House*. New York: Penguin Putnam; Addams, Jane (1972). *Spirit of youth and the city streets*. Champaign: University of Illinois Press; Addams, Jane (2002). *Democracy and social ethics*. Chicago: University of Illinois Press; Addams, Jane (2002). *The long road of woman's memory*. Chicago: University of Illinois Press; Elshtain, Jean B. (2002). *Jane Addams and the dream of American democracy: A life*. New York: Basic Books; Elshtain, Jean B. (2002). *The Jane Addams reader*. New York: Basic Books.

Ann-Marie Clark

Adoption

Adoption, which involves the legal transfer of parental rights and responsibilities from birth parents to adoptive parents, is a worldwide phenomenon with a long history. In recent years, over 120,000 children have been adopted annually in the United States (National Adoption Information Clearinghouse, 2004). The adopted child, adoptive parents, and birth parents constitute the adoption triad: three persons who are profoundly affected by this process. Most adoptive placements are made by public child welfare agencies or licensed private adoption agencies. Attorneys also facilitate independent adoptions when children are placed with adoptive parents directly by birth parents.

Throughout many countries in which adoption is practiced, there are variations in the age when children are adopted, and the type of adoption. In the United States, children can be placed in adoptive homes as infants or not until they reach adolescence. Transracial adoptions involve the placement of children of one race or ethnicity with a family of a different racial or ethnic background; and in international adoptions, children from one country are placed with families in other countries. In some countries (e.g., the United States, Great Britain, and the Netherlands) some children who are placed internationally also are in transracial adoptive families. Adoptions also vary in their degree of openness—the amount of information or contact to be shared between birth and adoptive parents. Confidential adoptions have no contact; mediated adoptions feature the sharing of nonidentifying information through a third party (typically an attorney or adoption agency; and fully disclosed adoptions occur when identifying information is shared and often includes in-person meetings.

In the past forty years, adoption has become more widely known and accepted, due in part to the increasing numbers of children of many ages in need of permanent families who can provide a nurturing, safe, and supportive home. The increase also has been due to the recognition by adoption practitioners that good homes can be found among families of different races/ethnicities, income levels, marital statuses, ages, nationalities, etc. As a result, many more individuals have a connection to adoption. Although 2–4 percent of children in the United States are adopted, 65 percent of the population in the United States is touched by adoption, as a relative, friend, or member of the adoption triad (Evan B. Donaldson Institute, 2002).

Adoption and Children's Development

One important question that gets asked about adoptees is whether they develop more positively than they would have in foster care, institutions or with their birth families. Coping with the loss of the birth parent can be an important theme for adopted children. However, research shows that children who are adopted tend to have a better emotional and behavioral adjustment than do children who remain in foster care, in institutions, or with birth families who continue to have serious problems that impair parenting. For example, adoption in infancy can greatly minimize the many problems in learning, social relationships, and emotional development among children who were prenatally exposed to drugs (Barth, Freundlich, and Brodzinsky, 2000). Thus, adoption can be an appropriate solution for children whose birth families fail to provide sufficient nurturance and safety.

Another question posed about adopted children is how they fare in comparison to nonadopted children in families that more closely resemble their adoptive families. Adopted children tend to receive more mental health services, in part, because adoptive parents are more likely to seek out support services than are nonadoptive parents. Most research indicates that adopted children also tend to have more adjustment problems than nonadopted children. These problems include school adjustment and learning problems, impulsive, hyperactive, or rule-breaking behavior, and drug use. However, for most adopted children, these problems fall within what is considered a normal range of functioning.

Parenting the Preschool Adopted Child

Once the child has been placed in the family, parents ideally begin the process of creating a care-giving environment that promotes a healthy and stable parent-child bond. Security in **attachment** is facilitated when parents are emotionally attuned to the needs of their child and when there is a good match between parental expectations and the child's characteristics and behavior. Research generally has found little difference in the quality of attachment between infant-placed adopted children and their mothers compared with nonadopted mother–infant dyads.

The advent of language and symbolic thought during the toddler and the preschool years paves the way for adoptive parents to begin the process of sharing adoption information with their child. Unfortunately, there is often a great deal of confusion and anxiety among adoptive parents as they begin this process. Whereas previously the primary foci of the couple were on *integrating* the child into the family and fostering a strong and secure parent–child bond, there is now a growing recognition of the importance of initiating a process of *family differentiation*. This is the developmental period in which most parents are advised by adoption professionals in the United States to begin to talk to their children about adoption. Children might be told of their connection to two families—one that is familiar and the source of their emotional security; the other that is unknown but the source of their biological origins. During this phase of family life, parents face numerous uncertainties about what information to share, when to share it, and in what ways the discussion about adoption will have an impact on their child. Some parents consciously decide not to tell their children about the adoption, a decision believed by many adoption and mental health professions to increase the psychological risk for these youngsters should they find out at some later date that their parents chose not to reveal information about the nature of their adoptive family relationships.

Although disclosing adoption information during the preschool years does not appear to undermine children's psychological adjustment or to disrupt parent–child attachment, it also does not lead to much genuine understanding about adoption, which can be confusing to parents who might overestimate their child's adoption knowledge. Once the telling process begins, parents typically report a growing curiosity on the part of children about birth and reproduction. Children usually begin to label themselves as adopted and quickly learn their "adoption story" at least in some rudimentary form. However, for many adoptees, this early adoption knowledge is superficial as it is not until 5–7 years of age that most children begin to clearly differentiate between birth and adoption as alternative ways of entering a family (Brodzinsky, Singer, and Braff, 1984).

Factors that Buffer Adoptive Families

Although the challenges faced by adoptive parents in the early period of family life cycle are greater, on average, compared with those faced by nonadoptive parent, there are also a number of factors that help buffer the adoptive couple from these unique stressors, leading to quite positive outcomes in postplacement child, parent, and family adjustment. Adoptive couples usually are older than nonadoptive couples when they first become parents, and they are more likely to be settled into their careers and to be more financially secure. They also have been married longer before becoming parents than nonadoptive couples, which may be associated with greater marital sensitivity, communication, and stress management. The adoptive couple is likely to feel a powerful sense of fulfillment with the arrival of a child, which in turn may serve as a protective factor.

Moreover, the need to work with adoption agencies in order to become parents has a beneficial impact on adoptive parents in that they often have more formal preparation for the transition to parenthood than nonadoptive couples. Over the past two decades, adoption-related services and counseling have evolved to address the enduring and changing needs that adoptive families have. Innovative models, such as Generations of Hope (Eheart and Hopping, 2001), demonstrate how the planned creation of a community of foster and adoptive families and senior citizens, with support services integrated into the community, can provide critical supports for families adopting from foster care. Some agencies facilitating transracial adoptions now require prospective parents to undertake an experiential examination of race/ethnicity prejudice and its potential impact on transracial adoptive families. Medical clinics featuring coordinated medical care for children adopted from institutions in other countries now operate in several major cities. Additional examples of innovative and promising practices can be found on The National Adoption Clearinghouse Web site (http://naic.acf.hhs.gov).

Early childhood professionals also have a critical role to play in helping children and parents in adoptive families. Because of the diversity among adoptive families in talking about adoption and living as an adoptive family, it is important for early childhood professionals to provide an open and safe atmosphere for parents to share information about the family's adoption-related choices. With knowledge about the choices made by adoptive families of children in their class, teachers can help proactively and reactively. Proactively, teachers can plan activities, discussion and experiences designed to promote children's understanding of the typical variations in families. Reactively, teachers must be prepared to use "teachable moments" as foundations for additional learning, whether these moments arise from peers' naïve questions, teasing, or adults' comments. The ultimate goal would be for teachers to provide experiences in which all children and members of their families feel respected and supported for their choices in becoming a family.

Conclusions

Adoption provides children and families with a viable alternate path to family life, one that features similarities to and differences from biological family life.

The keys to successful parenting of adopted children include good preparation, realistic expectations, effective behavior management skills, good communication, and adequate supports—all of which are common to other families, as well. Parenting adopted children poses unique challenges and complications for family life and children's development; however, most adoptees tend to adjust as normally as do nonadopted children. Early childhood professionals can enhance their support of adoptive children and families first by developing a heightened professional awareness of adoption and its variations, and second, by incorporating this understanding in programming for and interactions with all children. *See also* Development, Emotional; Development, Language; Parenting Education; Race and Ethnicity in Early Childhood Education; Symbolic Languages.

Further Readings: Barth, R. P., M. Freundlich, and D. M. Brodzinsky (2000). *Adoption and prenatal alcohol and drug exposure: Research, policy and practice.* Washington, DC: Child Welfare League of America; Brodzinsky, David M., and Jesus Palacios, eds. (2005). *Psychological issues in adoption: Research and practice.* Westport, CT: Praeger; Brodzinsky, D. M., and E. E. Pinderhughes (2002). Parenting and child development in adoptive families. In M. H. Bornstein, ed. *Handbook of parenting*: Vol.1, 2nd ed. Mahwah, NJ: Erlbaum, pp. 279-311; Brodzinsky, D. M., Singer, L. M., and Braff, A. M. (1984). Children's understanding of adoption. *Child Development* 55, 869-878; Eheart, B. K., and Hopping, D. (2001). Generations of hope. *Children and Youth Services Review* 23 (9/10), 675-682; Evan B. Donaldson Institute (2002). National Adoption Attitudes Survey. Available online at http://adoptioninstitute.org/survey_intro.html; Grotevant, H. D., Y. Perry, and R. G. McRoy (2005). Openness in adoption: Outcomes for adolescents within their adoptive kinship networks. In D. Brodzinsky and J. Palacios, eds. *Psychological issues in adoption*. Westport, CT: Greenwood; Howe, D. (2002). Talking and telling. In A. Douglas and T. Philpot, ed. *Adoption: Changing families, changing times.* London: Routledge; Juffer, F., and M. H. Van IJzendoorn (2005). Behavior problems and mental health referrals of international adoptees: A meta-analysis. *Journal of the American Medical Association* 293, 2501-2515; Lee, R. M. (2003). The transracial adoption paradox: History, research, and counseling implications of cultural socialization. *Counseling Psychologist* 31(6), 711–744; National Adoption Information Clearinghouse (2003). Adoption statistics. Available online at http://naic.acf.hhs.gov/index.cfm.

Ellen E. Pinderhughes and Neda Bebiroglu

Advocacy and Leadership in Early Childhood Education

To *advocate* is to give voice to a particular issue or concern through the processes of persuasion, argument, or direct action intended to draw attention to the cause and propose concrete changes or solutions. In early childhood education, the work of advocacy entails speaking up on behalf of young children and their families in order to create more just, equitable, and effective social policies or community services. In addition, early childhood advocates often teach parents to become self-advocates, capable of speaking directly to teachers, administrators, or policymakers on matters that affect their ability to care for and educate their own children and the children of others.

Early childhood advocates focus on the ethical, social, and practical responsibilities that arise in the context of work with children and families. Advocates identify social and personal barriers that prevent families and communities from fostering children's healthy development. In turn, advocates challenge those barriers and participate in their removal through changes in practice or policy at the local or national level. In doing so, advocates often take conscious and calculated risks aimed at altering the status quo in order to improve the lives of young children. Advocates use a range of tools that incorporate comprehensive data about the status and plight of children and apply specific strategies meant to change the ways in which institutions or communities respond to the needs of children. Such strategies may include collaborative, participatory organizing at the grassroots level as well as less direct means such as support for political candidates or testifying before local, state, or federal legislative bodies in order to enact child-focused social policies. In this light, advocates must be capable of analyzing and critiquing federal and state social policies as they affect the lives of young children. Advocates must be able to effectively communicate in oral and written forms their understandings, views, and positions on issues related to children's well-being, for both lay and professional audiences.

The Arguments Used by Advocates

Early childhood advocacy generally relies on multiple rationales to argue on behalf of children and families. The *custodial* rationale argues that society has a collective or shared responsibility to care for young children while their parents work. A *developmental* rationale asserts that high-quality early experiences both in home and out of home benefit young children and provide them with the skills and dispositions necessary to succeed in school and community. A *human capital* rationale assumes that early financial investment in the lives of children produces long-term returns that will ultimately save society subsequent expenses associated with remediation, compensation, or even incarceration. A *citizenship* rationale, more prevalent in western European nations, views young children as citizens with fundamental civil and human rights, including access to the same level of support and education enjoyed by youth and adults. Finally, an *ethical* rationale suggests that society should provide high-quality, accessible, affordable services to young children and their families because it is the right thing to do. This moral stance is concerned less with saving money, enabling parents to work outside of the home, or improving children's later academic achievement than it is with acknowledging a collective responsibility to and for all citizens, including those in the earliest stages of their lives.

Early childhood advocates are especially concerned with enhancing the lives of children who experience social and/or economic disadvantage because of their race, ability, ethnicity, native language, family income, or place of residence. In this light, the work of advocates has been especially influenced by the strategies and successes of the U.S. Civil Rights Movement beginning in the late 1950s, in which a wide range of methods have been applied effectively including civil disobedience, street protests, petitioning, legislative action, and community organizing.

The focus of civil rights advocacy on universal social justice has become a core principle of child advocacy. In 1973, the **Children's Defense Fund** (CDF) was founded by Marian Wright Edelman to "provide a strong, effective voice for all the children of America who cannot vote, lobby, or speak for themselves. [The Children's Defense Fund] pays particular attention to the needs of poor and minority children and those with disabilities" (from the CDF mission statement). A year later, the *Harvard Educational Review* published a landmark collection of essays on "The Rights of Children," the first comprehensive set of arguments that the social and economic needs of children deserve as much attention as those of other disenfranchised groups in the United States. The social justice emphasis in child advocacy has also been advanced considerably by the writings of Jonathan Kozol over the past two decades in such books as *Savage Inequalities* (Kozol, 1991) and *Amazing Grace* (Kozol, 1995). This focus on social and economic justice has expanded in recent years to include such areas as children's sexual understandings and identity and the particular realities of AIDS as experienced by parents and teachers as well as children (cf., Silin, 1995). Evolving social conceptions of **inclusion** and children's rights have been responsive to such realities, in turn demanding of advocates a broader set of lenses than has been the case in the past.

In the 1980s, child advocates were especially challenged by the Reagan administration, which attempted to significantly reduce federal support for many of the antipoverty and civil rights policies enacted in the previous two decades. The administration attempted to reduce funding or weaken regulations for programs such as **Head Start**, the Education for All Handicapped Children Act (PL 94-142), and federal subsidies for low-income families in need of day care. At the same time, however, the human capital rationale described earlier was gaining credence, partly because of the values that became dominant during the Reagan years. Corporate and political leaders began to see that the inability of the United States to compete economically with **Japan** (see Volume 4) and Western Europe was due in part to insufficient investment in the lives of young children.

This growing concern led directly to the 1989 Education Summit, at which the nation's governors declared a set of National Educational Goals for the first time ever. The first of the eight goals stated, "By the year 2000, all children in America will start school ready to learn." This simple statement in turn led to a national Success by Six movement organized by the United Way in conjunction with hundreds of community-based organizations. Also in 1989, the United Nations promulgated the **Convention on the Rights of the Child,** which proclaimed that, "childhood is entitled to special care and assistance [and therefore] the family, as the fundamental group of society and the natural environment for the growth and well-being of all its members and particularly children, should be afforded the necessary protection and assistance so that it can fully assume its responsibilities within the community." These two statements, one at the national level and one at the international level, have provided significant support for those who advocate on behalf of children and families.

Principles of Advocacy

As noted earlier, early childhood advocates exercise a range of strategies depending on their circumstances and goals. The options can be characterized along the following dimensions:

Internal versus external advocacy. Internal advocacy occurs when teachers, social workers, health care workers, or others use their positions within schools, hospitals, day-care centers, and other child-serving organizations to speak on behalf of children and families. These professionals attempt to improve the way the institutions in which they work meet the needs of their clients, patient, and customers by arguing for more responsive, accessible, and affordable services. External advocates are those who are not employed by the organization of concern or who do not live in the immediate community but who identify systematic injustices or inequities that they believe should be addressed. Often, internal and external advocates form alliances to put pressure on administrators or elected officials in order to stimulate change.

Individual versus organizational advocacy. Advocates may work on behalf of individuals or through formal advocacy organizations. In the former, friends, allies, guardians, or lawyers speak on behalf of a child or family that does not otherwise have the skills, knowledge, or confidence to speak for themselves. This is especially effective when a child or family is confronted with a complex bureaucracy with multiple regulations that require expertise to negotiate or receive the desired service. Formal advocacy organizations are concerned with practices or policies that affect groups of individuals or multiple communities. The Children's Defense Fund cited earlier is perhaps the most widely known of these advocacy organizations. Others include the Child Welfare League of America and the National Association of Child Advocates, which represents state-level organizations such as the Children's Alliance of New Hampshire or the Advocates for the Children of New York. The **National Association for the Education of Young Children**'s (NAEYC) annual Week-of-the-Young-Child, held each April, is another example of advocacy conducted by an organization consisting of some 100,000 early childhood teachers and administrators.

Data-based advocacy. In addition to operating from core values such as a commitment to social justice, advocates rely on empirical data to argue on behalf of children. To muster support for the issue being addressed, advocates turn to state and national data sources provided in the annual Kids Count profiles of child well-being published by the Anne E. Casey Foundation or the State of America's Children reports released each year by the Children's Defense Fund. At the federal level, the U.S. Department of Education's Office for Civil Rights and the National Center for Educational Statistics are important sources of data for child advocates.

Coalition building. Perhaps the most essential strategy for child advocates is to form coalitions with others in order to speak with one voice that will be heard by those who are in a position to effect change. The child advocacy organizations mentioned earlier are one example of such coalitions or alliances. In a democratic society with elected governing bodies, the power of numbers is the key to the change process. Often alliances of groups with similar missions or values are developed by advocacy leaders. Teachers, social workers, and community organizers may come together to advocate for after-school care for elementary-aged children. Judges, lawyers, and police may share work together to strengthen child protection systems in order to reduce child abuse and offer prevention programs. Business leaders and real estate agents might be concerned about the affordability of housing in a community in order to reduce homelessness. The most effective advocacy coalitions bring all these groups together in nonpartisan organizations such as the Voices for Katrina's Children network formed after the 2005 Gulf Coast hurricanes and supported by the Packard Foundation.

The Link between Leadership and Advocacy

Early childhood educators are expected not only to be effective advocates, but they must also take on broader leadership roles in their schools, agencies, communities, and at the state and national level. By nature, good advocates make good leaders, as they articulate the needs of children and families and offer concrete solutions to the barriers that face those who are too young to vote or whose economic or social status puts them on the margins. In this light, early childhood educators must not only be good teachers, but they must also understand the processes of systems change, policy development and implementation, how to use the media effectively, how to supervise and support beginning teachers, and how to connect children and families to networks of social services.

Lambert et al. (1995, p. 47) offer a comprehensive inventory of the skills most needed by those who serve as leaders in social service organizations. These include the following:

- A sense of purpose and ethics, because honesty and trust are fundamental to relationships.
- Facilitation skills, because framing, deepening, and moving the conversations about teaching and learning are fundamental to constructing meaning.
- An understanding of constructivist learning for all humans.
- A deep understanding of change and transitions, because change is not what we thought it was.
- An understanding of context so that communities of memories can be continually drawn and enriched.
- A personal identity that allows for courage and risk, low ego needs, and a sense of possibilities.

These are broad concepts but are applicable to early childhood advocates who work simultaneously with children, parents, colleagues, policymakers, community leaders, and other allies. By definition, the most effective leaders will also be conscientious and articulate advocates. As Rodd (1994, p. 2) states it, "Leadership is about vision and influence. . . . Leadership [is a] process by which one person sets certain standards and expectations and influences the actions of others to behave in what is considered a desirable direction. Leaders are people who can influence the behavior of others for the purpose of achieving a goal." As indicated throughout this entry, these leadership attributes are synonymous with those of effective child advocates. *See also* National Education Goals Panel.

Further Readings: Charnov, D. J., and C. Rutsch (2000). *Making a difference: A parent's guide to advocacy and community action.* Washington, DC: Children's Resources International; Kagan, S. L., and B. T. Bowman (1997). *Leadership in early care and education.* Washington, DC: National Association for the Education of Young Children; Kozol, J. (1991). *Savage inequalities: Children in America's schools.* New York: Crown; Kozol,

J. (1995). *Amazing Grace: The lives of children and the conscience of a nation*. New York: Crown; L. Lambert, D. Walker, D. P. Zimmerman, J. E. Cooper, M. D. Lambert, M. E. Gardner, and P. J. Ford Slack (1995). *The constructivist leader*. New York: Teachers College Press; *The Rights of Children* (1974). Reprint series no. 9, *Harvard Educational Review*; Rodd, J. (1994). *Leadership in early childhood: The pathway to professionalism*. New York: Teachers College Press; Silin, J. G. (1995). *Sex, death, and the education of Children: Our passion for ignorance in the age of AIDS (the politics of identity and education)*. New York: Teachers College Press.

Bruce L. Mallory

Almy, Millie (1915–2001)

A twentieth-century leader in the field of early childhood education and psychology, Millie Almy played a critical role in shaping the science of child development, identifying the contribution of play to children's social, emotional, and cognitive development, and interpreting and popularizing the theories of Jean **Piaget.** Dr. Almy's career in early childhood education began during her undergraduate studies at Vassar College, where she majored in Child Study and worked in the Vassar nursery school. Following college and prior to attending Teachers College at Columbia University, where she earned her master's and doctorate degrees, Dr. Almy taught in a day nursery and directed a regional alliance of federally funded nursery schools near Buffalo, NY, for the Works Progress Administration, as well as federally funded "Lanham Act" child-care centers established during World War II.

Dr. Almy is widely credited with bringing Piagetian theory into the discourse about young children in the United States, and was widely acknowledged as one of the foremost Piagetian interpreters and theorists in the world. She helped to explain how young children came to understand complex subjects such as science, **mathematics**, and literature through direct experience, manipulation, and visualization before they could understand abstract concepts. Her writings and research about **play** and observation of young children remain classics in the field. Her scholarship reflected her extensive "hands-on" experience with young children in early care and education programs. She served on the faculty of Teachers College at Columbia (1944–1948, 1952–1971) and of the Education School at the University of California at Berkeley (1971–1980), and was President of the National Association of Nursery Educators, as well as a delegate to the Mid-Century White House Conference on Children.

Dr. Almy recognized that the United States "needed greatly expanded programs for young children and their families." She also believed that the success of early childhood programs depended on "the availability of a special kind of early childhood educator . . . described as a double specialist, one who could both teach young children and assess their development, work equally well with adults as well as with children, think concretely as one must in dealing with children, but also think abstractly and formally as one must in planning and executing programs and researching them." To this end, she led an Interdisciplinary Program for Leaders in Day Care at the University of California at Berkeley from 1974 to 1978, funded by the Carnegie Corporation of New York, reflecting her belief that teachers need information from diverse disciplines as well as skills from other professions. She favored professional training for those working with young children, and lamented the poor compensation and low status that drove many skilled practitioners from the field.

Beloved by her students, Dr. Almy continued to mentor graduates long after they had completed studying under her tutelage. Following her retirement, she continued to conduct research across the world, including as a Fulbright Fellow in New South Wales. She also served as a Visiting Professor at Mills College in Oakland, and as a docent at the Oakland Museum. *See also* Curriculum, Science.

Further Readings: Almy, M. C. (1966). *Young children's thinking: Studies of some aspects of Piaget's theory.* New York: Teachers College Press; Almy, M. C. (1975). *The early childhood educator at work.* New York: McGraw-Hill; Almy, M. C. (1979). The impact of Piaget on early childhood education. In Frank B. Murray, ed. *The impact of Piagetian theory on education, philosophy, psychiatry, and philosophy.* Baltimore: University Park Press; Almy, M. C. (1979). *Ways of studying children: An observational manual for early childhood teachers.* New York: Teachers College Press; Stewart, D. (1991). *The oral history of Millie Almy, Ph.D.* Unpublished manuscript, University of California at Berkeley; Lannak, Jane (1995). Millie Almy: Nursery school education pioneer. *Journal of Education* CLXXVII(3), 39–55.

Marcy Whitebook

American Associate Degree Early Childhood Educators (ACCESS)

American Associate Degree Early Childhood Educators (ACCESS) is an organization that provides national visibility and voice for associate early childhood degree programs, faculty, and students. ACCESS began in 1989 as a network of faculty who met at the annual conference of the **National Association for the Education of Young Children** (NAEYC). Today, ACCESS is a national, nonprofit 501(c) (3) membership association with members in the majority of states, a handful of state affiliates, a presence at national early childhood and higher education conferences, and membership resources offered primarily through its Web site.

ACCESS members include full-time and adjunct faculty with early childhood assignments at associate degree programs, campus children's center faculty, and other individuals who share an interest in early childhood teacher career development and education. The organization offers professional support through its Web site, presentations at national and state conferences, and member networks and state affiliates.

The organization's purpose is to support and advocate for strong associate degree programs that provide professional development to those who teach and care for young children from birth through age 8 across a variety of settings— public elementary schools, Head Start programs, child-care centers and homes, and other community early childhood programs. Advocacy for associate to baccalaureate articulate agreements and for a national associate degree accreditation system have been at the center of the organization's work since its founding.

ACCESS national board members worked with NAEYC to develop national standards for associate degree programs in 1992 and again in 2002. ACCESS endorsed both sets of standards. ACCESS participated in a feasibility study workgroup and in the Advisory Council, supporting NAEYC's initiative to develop a national early childhood associate degree accreditation system.

National and state ACCESS efforts focus on supporting innovative, high-quality practices in early childhood teacher education; offering expertise regarding the role of associate degree programs in the early childhood teacher education system; and advocating for policies and systems that strengthen professional qualifications while increasing diversity in our nation's early childhood teachers.

Further Readings: American Associate Degree Early Childhood Educators (ACCESS): Available online at www.accessece.org.

Alison Lutton

Antibias/Multicultural Education

The United States is a nation of many peoples: many races, cultures, religions, classes, lifestyles, and histories. It is also a nation where access to the "inalienable right" to "life, liberty and the pursuit of happiness," has not been equal for all. The white, male European immigrants to the New World established institutions and laws that advantaged them while disadvantaging many other groups based on race, gender, and class. Since the founding of the United States, people have worked to make real the goals of a democratic, free republic that originally served only one part of the society. The increasing cultural diversity and accompanying racism, discrimination, and **poverty** create particular challenges for early childhood educators who wish to honor the professional mandate to foster every child's full potential and to prepare all children to function effectively as members of a democratic society.

Antibias and multicultural education has been a significant force for addressing these challenges and has profoundly influenced early childhood **curriculum** and practice. The hybrid term of "antibias/multicultural education" (Ab/Mc) reflects the roots and evolution of the multicultural movement as expressed in the antibias curriculum created for young children.

Multicultural Education

The multicultural education movement grew out of the Civil Rights Movement and the War on Poverty. It first emerged during the 1970s, spearheaded by several African American scholars, notably James Banks, Geneva Gay, and Carl Grant (e.g., Banks, 1996). Its philosophical roots reflect the work of early African American scholars such as W.E.B. Du Bois and Carter Woodsen, which exposed the myths of equality that prevailed in the White version of the history of the United States. It also had roots in the intergroup education movement of the late 1940s and early 1950s, when some of the classic studies of young children's racial awareness and attitudes toward self and others were conducted.

The original objectives of multicultural education included sensitizing all individuals to ethnic and racial differences, increasing individual awareness of cultural traditions and experiences, helping all individuals value their own race and **culture** as worthy of existing on an equal basis with mainstream American values and experiences, and ensuring that all children have access to high quality education. Multicultural education challenged existing education approaches to diversity, which denied the validity of cultures other than the dominant European-American one.

Multicultural education advocated an approach of "cultural pluralism" and supports the right of every group to maintain their unique cultures while also equally participating in and enhancing the whole society. Cultural pluralism offered an alternative to the "melting pot" ideology, which had claimed that all people would be amalgamated into a new breed of American, but, in truth, meant that immigrants were expected to assimilate completely into the dominant European American society created by the "founding fathers." Cultural pluralism also undermined the ideology of "color blindness," which challenged white superiority but, at the same time, denied the cultural orientations of many groups and their experiences of racism. Early multicultural education was often described as the "salad" approach in which children could maintain and develop their own cultural values, traditions, languages, and lifestyles while also learning to be equal participants in the larger society.

During the 1980s, a wide range of multicultural practices emerged. Sleeter and Grant (1988) organized the different approaches and the political messages they embody into a typology of multicultural education. They articulated the following categories: (1) *education of culturally different children*, adapting programs for specific racial and cultural groups to encourage academic achievement and assimilation into the mainstream; (2) *single group studies*, formerly called "ethnic studies," focused on the literature, art, history, culture of specific ethnic groups; (3) *human relations*, enhancing positive intergroup relationships and reducing prejudice; (4) *multicultural education*, emphasizing the positive, adaptive value of cultural pluralism and encouraging children to be competent in more than one cultural system; and (5) *education that is multicultural and reconstructionist*— promoting profound social, economic, political, and educational changes to foster equal relationships among all groups. The antibias curriculum approach (Derman-Sparks and the ABC Task Force, 1989) is an application of the social reconstructionist approach to early childhood education.

In the 1990s, the scope of multicultural education broadened from the original focus on race and culture to more closely align with the early childhood antibias approach. Multicultural theorists began to implicitly or explicitly include a focus on social class and economic discrimination. The feminist movement influenced multicultural theorists to include gender as a dimension of inequity that cut across race, culture, and class. The passage of the Americans with Disabilities Educational Act in 1990 led to increasing numbers of children with disabilities being "included" in regular classrooms, and disability issues were woven into multicultural curricula. More recently, wider recognition of the hate crimes targeting gay men and lesbian women has led to sexual orientation becoming a theme in multicultural education, an addition that has caused controversy both within and outside the field. In addition, the ethnic groups included as part of multicultural work has broadened to reflect the increasing number of such groups as Mexican and Central Americans and Asian/Pacific Americans living in the United States. Moreover, increased hate crimes and discrimination targeting Arab Americans and Muslims after the September 2001 attack on the World Trade Center has called on multicultural educators to include these issues as well. Some writers (e.g., Ramsey, 2005) have further expanded the definition of multiculturalism to incorporate the ecological justice movement because environmental degradation (e.g., the concentration of highly polluting factories and destructive agricultural practices) has a disproportionate effect on poor communities and countries of color. They have also incorporated discussions about how hyper-consumerism (e.g., the media-inspired competition to purchase the latest clothes and cars) exacerbates the disparities between economic groups and undermines interpersonal and intergroup relationships

The Antibias Approach

The 1989 publication of *Antibias Curriculum: Tools for Empowering Young Children* by the **National Association for the Education of Young Children** (NAEYC) introduced the concept of antibias education to the field of early childhood care and education. It stated that antibias education is "an active/activist approach to challenging prejudice, stereotyping, bias and systemic "isms," grounded in the premise that it is necessary for each individual to actively intervene, to challenge and counter the personal and institutional behaviors that perpetuate oppression" (Derman-Sparks and ABC Task Force, 1989, p. 3). As outlined by the authors, the goals of antibias curriculum are to: (1) nurture each child's construction of a knowledgeable, confident self-concept and group identity; (2) promote each child's comfortable, empathic interaction with people from diverse backgrounds; (3) foster each child's critical thinking about bias; and (4) cultivate each child's ability to stand up for her/himself and for others in the face of bias. These goals are reflected in the National Association for the Education of Young Children (NAEYC) **accreditation** standards. However, the specific tasks and strategies for working toward these goals depend on children's backgrounds, ages, and life experiences.

Motivation for developing the antibias approach arose in the 1980s from dissatisfaction with the prevailing practice in early childhood education of "additive" or "tourist" multicultural education. In this simplistic form of the multicultural approach, curriculum "visits" cultural groups other than the mainstream, white, middle-class culture from time to time, while the content and teaching styles of the "regular" curriculum continues to reflect only the dominant culture. Classroom activities focus on special times, such as a holiday celebration, or an occasional "multicultural" event or unit. Materials used during these special multicultural "excursions" from the regular curriculum are frequently inaccurate, set in the past rather than present, focus on countries of origin rather than the current experience of various immigrant groups, and are presented from the perspective of the dominant culture. Consequently, even with good intentions, a "tourist" multicultural approach results in exposing children to inaccurate information, has little relationship to the children's lives, and sends the message that the dominant culture is normative (Derman-Sparks and ABC Task Force, 1989).

Three core concepts underlie the antibias educational approach. First, it is impossible to teach about diversity without paying attention to the societal systemic power dynamics that assign advantage or disadvantage based on race, gender, class, physical ability, and sexual orientation. These dynamics influence children's developing ideas and feelings about themselves and others and affect every educator's sense of practice with children and families. Second, research about young children's identity and attitudes should inform curriculum. Third, antibias education should utilize principles of constructivist theory and an activity-based pedagogy, which treats learners as active participants in their own learning and requires teachers to scaffold learning experiences to mesh with children's ideas and stages of development. Constructivist classrooms engage children in interactive activities that support active learning about their daily life experiences.

In the years since the antibias approach was introduced, teacher experience has deepened, extended and fine-tuned its conceptual and pedagogical frameworks. Several subsequent books reflected this growth. (e.g., Bisson, 1997; Pelo and Davidson, 2000). In addition, educators in several other countries (Australia, Belgium, Canada, Denmark, Greece, Ireland, Japan, South Africa, The Netherlands, The United Kingdom) are also building theory and practice as they explore what antibias education work looks like in the context of their particular history, population demographics, and cultures (see Van Keulen, 2004).

Current Themes of Antibias/Multicultural Work

Antibias/multicultural (Ab/Mc) education work continues to develop its theory and practice. One theme is the inclusion of more aspects of diversity, as previously discussed in the section about the history of multicultural education. A second theme is the explicit incorporation of critical pedagogy, which has profoundly transformed the scope and methodology of Ab/Mc work (Nieto, 2004). Critical pedagogy emphasizes that teaching and learning occur in specific historic, cultural, and social contexts and power dynamics; and promotes children's capacity to engage in critical thinking about their lives and society. It includes the following goals: to (a) affirm students' cultures without trivializing them; (b) challenge hegemonic knowledge (i.e., the knowledge that is constructed by the dominant group that assumes that they know how the world works for all people); (c) complicate pedagogy so that there is not only one right way to teach; (d) challenge the simplistic focus of tolerance forms of multicultural education on self-esteem as the operative factor in breaking bonds of oppression; and (e) encourage "dangerous discourses" that name and challenge inequities.

A third theme in antibias/multicultural education is a push to critically examine the identities and socialization of white people and to more explicitly develop curriculum that addresses these dynamics for children and adults (Derman-Sparks and Ramsey, 2006; Sleeter, 2001; Tatum, 1997).

A fourth theme is the promotion of teacher reflections on how their own cultural and economic backgrounds and the societal structures of power and advantage influence teaching beliefs, styles, and interactions. Accordingly, effective teacher pre- and in-service training uses a critical pedagogy approach that engages adult learners in experiential and peer learning and in a *process* of change (Derman-Sparks and Phillips, 1997). It also promotes teachers' openness to unfamiliar views and experiences, their ability to challenge one's owns assumptions, and a passion for social and economic and political justice (Ramsey, 2005).

A fifth theme, based on the experience of several decades, is reflected in the understanding that effective antibias/multicultural education requires more than individual efforts within centers and classrooms. It involves community-building and local and national organizing for institutional and political changes that are grounded in a vision of a new society that includes all people equitably. It is centered on the complexities and conflicts inherent in all people's experiences, with a primary goal of liberating people from oppression by challenging the societal, economic, and political structures that maintain these inequities.

Antibias/Multicultural Education in Practice

Diversity, oppression, and social justice may seem to be a world away from young children. However, children are constantly absorbing information about power, privilege, and stereotypes in their families, schools, and communities and from the media. The challenge for early childhood educators is to find meaningful and hopeful ways to nurture young children's positive identity, cross-cultural respect and skills, and capacity to recognize and challenge prejudice and discrimination.

Ab/Mc education is not a set curriculum but rather a framework of goals, principles and strategies. How it is practiced depends largely on the setting: the population of the community and school; the backgrounds and experiences of the teachers and parents; and the specific children in a particular classroom. For example, in a community that has suffered long-term discrimination, the emphasis might be on fostering positive identities and self-worth, while encouraging children and families to play more assertive roles in the community and larger world. In contrast, children who are racially and economically privileged may need to see their own lives in a broader and more critical perspective and to challenge their sense of superiority and learn how to listen to others rather than always express their own views. Therefore, teachers need to be able to work closely with families and know how to gather information about children's communities.

Ab/Mc perspectives and themes can be woven into all curricular themes and teaching practices. The following examples are a few of the many possibilities. The specific themes generated in a classroom should reflect the interests of specific children, families, and teachers. For example, the theme of "family" can embrace all aspects of physical, cultural, economic, and gender differences, as well as the diversity of family composition. The themes of "community" and "work" should incorporate blue and pink-collar workers, artists, and community activists as well as professional jobs. Stereotypes of people with disabilities and women and men should be challenged by showing them in a wide range of activities. Activities such as roleplaying (e.g., shopping) can be constructed to draw children's attention to inequities in the outside world.

In such classrooms, art materials include the range of human skin colors in paint, crayons, paper and play dough and are available to children at all times. The aesthetic environment includes art from all the children's home and community cultures. Music and movement activities expand children's ideas about how different people make and move to music and show how music and dance are ways to express resistance to injustice (e.g., protest songs). Dramatic play props reflect all the children's family culture as well as those in the children's larger community. Photos and posters illustrate diversity of people, families and home environments. Teachers pay attention to issues of power and bias that emerge during children's play and use these as teachable moments.

Discussions about classroom rules and conflict solving provide opportunities to reflect on how people see the world differently and how they need to find commonalities and compromises to live together. Children's comments and questions about the many aspects of diversity as well as incidents of discomfort or bias provide valuable "teachable moments" upon which to build learning activities.

In sum, contemporary multicultural/antibias educators have identified the following goals to help children navigate the contradictions and challenge the inequities of contemporary society in the twenty-first and subsequent centuries:

- Develop strong identities—as individuals, as members of communities, of a country and as living beings on this planet.
- Develop a sense of solidarity with all people and the natural world.
- Become critical thinkers.
- Become confident and persistent problem solvers so that they see themselves as activists rather than simply feeling overwhelmed by the challenges of the world.
- Ensure that *all* children gain the academic skills that will give them access to the knowledge of our society, the power to make a difference and hope for their future.

Educators and families must push for excellent schools in all communities, especially those with high rates of poverty, and help all children understand that academic skills are a source of power that can be acquired without giving up their identities and critical awareness of the world. To these ends, many early childhood professional and leaders (e.g., National Association for the Education of Young Children) argue that antibias/multicultural and **bilingual education** are essential to quality education.

Controversies and Challenges

As well as being accepted as a part of the early childhood education canon and having many advocates and practitioners, antibias/multicultural education has also become a source of controversy and target of criticism from both the left and the right. Advocates themselves have disagreed on its parameters and priorities. Some argue that the original focus on race, ethnicity, and culture should remain primary, because adding other aspects of identity and oppression dilutes the work on racism, which they consider the most intransient oppression in our society. Others insist that expanding the focus strengthens the work because it enables people to understand the core dynamics and intersections between the various forms of systemic and interpersonal oppression, and creates the possibility of collaboration among larger numbers of people. Criticism also comes from people who believe that Ab/Mc work is less relevant to children of color than to white children. Some argue that children of color need to focus on their own identity and group's issues, while others think it is essential to make Ab/Mc education relevant to a range of cultural communities. Some critics from a more progressive stance argue that multiculturalism obscures the real underlying causes of inequality, thus undermining rather than advancing social and economic change.

The most vehement political opposition has come from conservative groups who have targeted both the work and some of its leaders. Opposition includes the argument that Ab/Mc education's focus on cultural pluralism is divisive to the nation, and that education should keep its focus on assimilating everyone into one national culture. Another argument claims that Ab/Mc education distracts from, rather than enhances, academic learning. A third insists that the topics of Ab/Mc education belong only within the family. Some critics highlight the inclusion of rights for gays and lesbian people as evidence that Ab/Mc education is anti-Christian or anti-American. Antibias/multicultural educators argue that this backlash is best understood in the context of wider social conservatism directed against people of color, gays, lesbians and transgender people, immigrants of color and people on welfare. It reflects the tension between those who want to press forward toward creating a more open and equitable society and those who insist on maintaining the old lines of racial, cultural, gender, and class power. This conservative backlash is an indication that the dialogue must be expanded to include people who feel threatened by educational reforms.

In addition to resistance from various quarters, several obstacles within the educational system can derail the full implementation of antibias/multicultural education. Teachers often do not have the time to fully study current social, economic, and political issues and to develop related curricula. They may also lack the confidence and skills to tackle potentially contentious or controversial issues. Administrators may pressure teachers to adhere to the standard curriculum to ensure that children pass mandated tests. Community members and parents may resist the implementation of Ab/Mc education as too radical and contrary to traditional values or as a frivolous distraction from academic curriculum. Despite the many existing resources and evidence that it can be woven into all curricula, Ab/Mc education is still all too often relegated to occasional "add-on," "tourist" activities or simply dismissed all together.

Another impediment to the implementation of Ab/Mc education is the lack of substantial research related to it. Very little empirical information exists about the extent to which teachers' curricula and practices actually reflect multicultural perspectives. Moreover, aside from anecdotal data from teacher observations and documentation (e.g., Pelo and Davidson, 2000; Whitney, 1999), little information is available about how children respond to Ab/Mc activities and whether or not these efforts have any lasting effects on children's ideas about the world. There are many challenges specific to carrying out this research, including designing longitudinal research that enables reliable measures of the effects of Ab/Mc work on children's development, including cognitive changes and relationships with family and peers, within the context of diverse family and community settings. This lack of research is not unique to early childhood settings; overall there has been very little research on the implementation and effects of multicultural education at all levels. However, this type of research is needed to continue to develop the field and to demonstrate to skeptics that it is a worthwhile endeavor. *See also* Constructivism; Disabilities, Young Children with; Feminism in Early Childhood Education; Gay or Lesbian Parents, Children with; Pedagogy, Activity-Based/Experiential; Race and Ethnicity in Early Childhood Education.

Further Readings: Banks, J., ed. (1996). *Multicultural education, transformative knowledge* and *action: Historical and contemporary perspectives.* New York: Teachers College Press; Bisson, J. (1997). *Celebrate! An anti-bias guide to enjoying holidays in early childhood programs.* St. Paul, MN: Redleaf Press; Clark, K. (1995). *Prejudice and your child.* Boston: Beacon Press; Derman-Sparks and the ABC Task Force (1989). *Anti-bias curriculum: Tools for empowering young children.* Washington, DC: National Association for the Education of Young Children; Derman-Sparks, L., and Phillips, C. B. (1997). *Teaching/learning anti-racism: A developmental approach.* New York: Teachers College Press; Derman-Sparks, L., and P. Ramsey. (2006). *"What if all the kids are White"? Anti-bias multicultural education with young children and Families.* New York: Teachers College Press; Nieto, S. (2004). *Affirming diversity: The sociopolitical context of multicultural education.* 4th ed. Boston: Allyn & Bacon; Pelo, A., and Davidson, F. (2000). *That's not fair: A teacher's guide to activism with young children.* St. Paul, MN: Redleaf Press; Ramsey, P. (2005). *Teaching and learning in a diverse world.* 3rd ed. New York: Teachers College Press; Sleeter, C. (2001). *Culture, difference and power.* New York: Teachers College Press. CD-ROM; Sleeter, C., and Grant, C. (1988). *Making choices for multicultural education: Five approaches to race, class, and gender.* New York: Macmillan; Tatum, B. D. (1997). *"Why are all the Black kids sitting together in the cafeteria?" and other conversations about race.* New York: Basic Books; Van Keulen, A., ed. (2004). *Young children aren't biased, are they?! How to handle diversity in early childhood education and school.* Amsterdam, The Netherlands: SWP; Whitney, T. (1999). *Kids like us: Using personal dolls in the classroom.* St. Paul, MN: Redleaf Press.

Louise Derman-Sparks and Patricia G. Ramsey

Art. *See* Assessment, Visual Art; Child Art

Ashton-Warner, Sylvia (1908–1984)

New Zealand's Sylvia Ashton-Warner exemplified the reflective teacher, studying the response of the children in her classroom to her work, and modifying it in turn so that their learning would be optimum. Ashton-Warner wrote eleven books (1959–1979). In the most important of them, *Teacher,* she tells of her struggle to teach beginning reading to very young Maori children, who found the books and lessons used with white children incomprehensible and boring.

Her methods strongly influenced many other teachers who found themselves in cross-cultural settings and who wished to avoid "colonizing" the children. She worked during a time when reading primers still depicted only white, middle-class children. Children of color had little to identify with and little incentive to learn from the sterile text or European urban illustrations of the available primers. Ashton-Warner's passionate writing and her ability to portray classrooms in a way that made them come alive on the page earned her a worldwide audience. Her books have been translated into more than 17 languages.

Social critic Paul Goodman wrote about Ashton-Warner:

Consider . . . the method employed by Sylvia Ashton-Warner in teaching little Maoris. She gets them to ask for their own words, the particular gut-word of fear, lust, or despair that is obsessing the child that day; this is written for him on strong cardboard; he learns it instantaneously and never forgets it; and soon he has an exciting, if odd, vocabulary. From the beginning, writing is by demand, practical, magical; and of course it is simply an extension of speech—it is the best and strongest speech, as writing should be. What is read is what somebody is importantly trying to tell. (p. 26)

Ashton-Warner was motivated by the artist's urge to express strong feelings, and saw the same urge in the children. That observation led her to develop her reflective instructional method. She also orchestrated the school day so it would alternate between expressive activities chosen by the children and activities in which the teacher imparted new information. She called this alternation "breathing in and out." Ashton-Warner also wrote about the relationship of early education to world peace, believing that if children have peaceful means of expression they will not be aggressive or violent.

Ashton-Warner was unable to reconcile her artistic life with her family life. Her drawing, painting of watercolors, and playing piano could not directly be reconciled with her life as a wife and a mother. She and her husband, Keith Henderson, worked out an unusual domestic arrangement. She created in her twenties, and re-created in each place she lived afterwards, a separate writing space she called "Selah" (a place of rest). Although it scandalized the neighbors, her husband, Keith, was the main child-care provider for the family.

She was more honored in the United States, and in other countries, than in her own New Zealand. Despite her receipt of the New Zealand Book Award in 1979 for her autobiography, *I Passed This Way*, she had felt neglected by her country for most of her life. Many in New Zealand education still speak of her as if she was not special. In the rest of the world, her influence is felt, although usually not in the mainstream. Her work was implemented in early **Head Start** programs (notably **Child Development Mississippi**) and in many of the alternative schools of the 1960s in the United States. Teachers in scattered classrooms around the world continue to use her methods to introduce young children to reading. Ashton-Warner has influenced the work of Vivian Gussin Paley, Karen Gallas, Cynthia Ballenger, and others, as well as the activities of the centers for young children in **Reggio Emilia**.

Further Readings: Ashton-Warner, Sylvia (1971). *Bell call.* New York: Simon and Schuster. Originally published 1964; Ashton-Warner, Sylvia (1967). *Greenstone.* New York: Simon and Schuster. Originally published 1966; Ashton-Warner, Sylvia (1979). *I passed this way.* New York: Knopf; Ashton-Warner, Sylvia (1960). *Incense to idols.* New York: Simon and Schuster; Ashton-Warner, Sylvia (1969). *Myself.* New York: Simon and Schuster. Originally published 1967; Ashton-Warner, Sylvia (1974). *O children of the world...* Vancouver: The First Person Press; Ashton-Warner, Sylvia (1972). *Spearpoint.* New York: Knopf; Ashton-Warner, Sylvia (1959). *Spinster.* New York: Simon and Schuster. Originally published in 1958; distributed by Heinemann; Ashton-Warner, Sylvia (1986). *Stories from the river.* Auckland, New Zealand: Hodder and Stoughton; Ashton-Warner, Sylvia (1963). *Teacher.* New York: Simon and Schuster; Ashton-Warner, Sylvia (1970). *Three.* New York: Knopf; Clemens, Sydney Gurewitz (1996). *Pay attention to the children: Lessons for teachers and parents from Sylvia Ashton-Warner.* Napa, CA: Rattle OK Press; Goodman, Paul (1964). *Compulsory education.* New York: Vantage; Hood, Lynley (1988). *Sylvia! The biography of Sylvia Ashton-Warner.* Auckland, New Zealand: Viking Penguin.

Sydney Gurewitz Clemens

Assessment in Early Childhood

Assessment in early childhood typically refers to the measurement of a child's developmental status, whether at a given point in time or at multiple points to track change over time. Although an assessment can be narrowly targeted at achievement in specific areas (such as mathematics or reading/literacy), early childhood professionals are urging a wider perspective. For example, assessment has been recently defined as "the process of observing, recording, and otherwise documenting what children do and how they do it as a basis for a variety of educational decisions that affect the child ... [and] involves the multiple steps of collecting data on a child's development and learning, determining its significance in light of the program goals and objectives, incorporating the information into planning for individuals and programs, and communicating the findings to families and other involved people" (NAEYC, 2003). In general, evaluation is a term referring to a broader enterprise of which assessments are a component. Evaluations often include multiple assessments over time, in the context of other sources, such as the quality of program implementation, staff qualifications, and participant demographics.

Purposes of Assessment

Assessments of young children generally have two primary purposes: first, to serve as yardsticks to measure the ways individual children are developing and second, to determine whether early childhood programs are effectively supporting children's development and learning in the aggregate. The **National Association for the Education of Young Children** (NAEYC) considers assessment integral to planning curriculum and instruction for individuals and groups, communicating with families, identifying children who need services or intervention, and improving program practice (NAEYC, 2003). Parents and caregivers want to know whether a child in their care demonstrates particular strengths, is performing within normative ranges, or shows lags that signal a need for intervention. Developmental assessment refers most often to screening processes intended to identify the need for specialized services or intervention. Meisels and Atkins-Burnett (2000) define screening as "a brief assessment procedure designed to identify children who, because they might have a learning problem or disability, should receive more extensive assessment." Screening tools often focus on visual-motor abilities, language-communicative competence, and gross motor abilities. Other types of screening include hearing and vision, health, and physical development, which could also affect a child's educational needs and experiences (Gullo, 2005).

Early childhood programs develop theories of change and set goals with the expectation that particular practices will lead to expected learning outcomes for participants; assessment provides information that can demonstrate progress toward those goals. It is often beneficial to conduct assessments at multiple time points geared to age or program entry or exit to provide information for purposes ranging from planning individualized instructional approaches to rating the quality of instructional practice. Any intervention that attempts to change behavior or improve learning ideally seeks to assess change at many levels: management and supervision, classroom environment, professional development, as well as child knowledge and skills.

Concerns about Inappropriate Assessment in Early Childhood

Accountability and assessment are closely linked concepts that undergird public policy decisions. With the **No Child Left Behind Act** of 2001, the federal government mandated annual testing of reading and math beginning in grade three and sanctions for schools that do not improve student performance. Many states have adopted early learning standards that extend benchmarks for elementary grades downward into preschool. In addition, federal programs such as **Head Start** have implemented testing requirements in the year prior to kindergarten entry on a limited set of early language, literacy, and numeracy indictors. Much debate continues about the constructs, domains, and indicators for young children's learning and development that should be assessed, and the best means of measuring performance on these indicators. Standards, and the tests to measure progress in achieving them, are often externally imposed for accountability purposes, rather than derived from appropriate developmental expectations. The formats of early childhood assessment are crucial because if implemented out of context, using a single source or method, testing instruments can yield unrepresentative or inaccurate results. Early childhood organizations are concerned that excessive emphasis on assessment could result in inappropriate changes to early childhood environments if, for example, teachers were to focus children's learning activities on specific items of a test rather than provide a range of classroom experiences related to the broad developmental constructs being assessed. An additional concern would be a program-wide reallocation of resources devoted to educational materials and facilities, professional development, and support for teachers based on a narrow conception of what is being assessed (NAEYC, 2003).

What Constitutes High-Quality Assessment?

The value of any assessment hinges on the quality of the information collected. Assessments of young children are inherently difficult to do well, and the importance of obtaining good information is directly related to the way that information will be used. The higher the stakes of the assessment (i.e., the more far-reaching the decisions made based on the results of the assessment), the more stringent the quality of the process should be. In response to increased emphasis on assessment in early childhood programs, NAEYC and the National Association of Early Childhood Specialists in State Departments of Education (NAECS/SDE) released a statement supporting assessments that are "developmentally appropriate, culturally and linguistically responsive, tied to children's daily activities, supported by professional development, inclusive of families, and connected to specific, beneficial purposes." In general, high-quality assessments (1) include information from multiple sources on multiple dimensions, (2) are administered by highly qualified assessors, (3) are reliable, and (4) are valid. These standards apply equally to observational, contextual assessments, and to more direct, test-like assessments of young children.

Assessments that include multiple domains, modes, and perspectives are particularly important for young children. Child-specific indicators based on a comprehensive view of what the child knows and can do were developed by the National Education Goals Panel (Kagan, Moore, and Bredekamp, 1995; Love, 2003; Love, Aber, and Brooks-Gunn, 1994) and have been adopted by Head Start and other early childhood programs. Domains include physical and motor development, social and emotional development, language usage, cognition and general knowledge, and approaches toward learning. Assessments should capture the breadth of children's development, including all five domains. Further, assessment through multiple modes is desirable to more accurately represent a child's development and abilities. Modes of assessment include direct assessment (typically what is referred to as "testing"), parent or teacher ratings, observations, and self-report. Multiple perspectives (e.g., teacher and parent ratings) provide information about the child in different settings. The information from these multiple modes and multiple reporters can be combined to form a more complete picture of an individual child's strengths and needs; in the aggregate, they can provide information on program performance in these areas.

Comprehensive alternative assessments are based on collection of information through a wider range of sources, such as portfolios and anecdotal records. One example of a standards-based approach is the Work Sampling System (Gullo, 2005; Meisels et al., 2001), which features developmental guidelines and checklists in seven learning domains (personal and social development, language and literacy, mathematical thinking, scientific thinking, social studies, the arts, and physical development and health). Teachers rate children on the checklists, select the contents of a portfolio to document each child's learning in the context of the curriculum, and complete a summary report on children's progress three times a year using specific criteria.

As a measure of growth or progress, assessment can be criterion- or normatively referenced. Criterion referenced assessments are those in which performance is judged in terms of mastery of items within given content areas (e.g., reading level). Normatively referenced assessments are those in which performance is judged relative to that of others within the same age group on the same instrument. For all assessments, but in particular for assessing young children, the training and competency of the assessor are critical. Assessors must be able to work effectively with young children in order to measure their performance accurately. Assessors should demonstrate extensive experience with young children as well as thorough training in the proper administration of the assessment tool. It is usually advisable to monitor assessors' performance to ensure their fidelity to the administration procedures of each assessment instrument.

When selecting the individual components of an assessment, it is important that each is reliable and valid for the areas to be measured, and for the children to be assessed. Reliability refers to the ability of an assessment instrument or procedure to produce the same results if administered to the same child within a reasonable timeframe (test–retest reliability), and in the case of ratings, if completed by a different person for the same child (interrater reliability). Reliability of assessments of young children may be lower as a result of numerous factors including uneven development, behavioral fluctuation, situational variables, and prior experience with testing/assessment, all of which may affect the results in ways that have little to do with the child's competence in the domain being measured.

Validity refers to the extent to which the assessment captures what it purports to measure. A perfectly reliable but invalid assessment is useless. Similarly when working with different populations, it is important to know whether the assessment has been used with specific groups and found to be valid for all of them. There are many kinds of validity, including face validity (the extent to which the assessment items appear to measure what they purport to measure), concurrent validity (children perform similarly on different measures of the same domain), and predictive validity (children's performance on the assessment predicts later performance, usually in school). The utility of assessment in early childhood often hinges on the expectation that performance on the assessment predicts the children's later performance. Assessment should be followed by specific planning to address areas of need and to maintain areas of strength. It is hoped that assessment is the first step in a process to remedy problems and improve later performance.

Conclusion

All early childhood assessments should take into account the family, care settings, and cultural contexts in which the child is developing. Optimally, assessment should be carried out within such contexts, but key adults must be informed about and involved in any decision making that results from assessments. Given the lack of consensus about goals and methods of assessment in early childhood, experts have concluded that the field should be considered emergent. The National Research Council has called for a broad program of research and development to advance the state of the art in assessment in the areas of (1) classroom-based assessment to support learning, (2) assessment for diagnostic purposes, and (3) assessment of program quality for accountability and public policy (Bowman, Donovan, and Burns, 2000). *See also* Families; Standards.

Further Readings: Bowman, Barbara, M. Suzanne Donovan, and M. Susa Burns, eds. (2000). *Eager to learn: Educating our preschoolers*. Washington, DC: National Academy Press; Gullo, Dominic F. (2005). *Understanding assessment and evaluation in early childhood education (2nd ed.)* New York: Teacher's College Press; Kagan, Sharon L. (1995). *By the bucket: Achieving results for young children*. Washington, DC: National Governors Association; Kagan, Sharon L., Evelyn Moore, and Sue Bredekamp, eds. (1995). *Reconsidering children's early development and learning: Toward common views and vocabulary*. National Education Goals Panel, Goal 1 Technical Planning Group on Readiness for School. Washington, DC: U.S. Government Printing Office. Available at www.negp.gov/reports/child-ea.htm; Love, John M. (2003). Instrumentation for state readiness assessment: Issues in measuring children's early development and learning. In Scott-Little, Catherine, Sharon L. Kagan, and Richard M. Clifford, eds. *Assessing the state of state assessments: Perspectives on assessing young children.* Greensboro, NC: The Regional Laboratory at SERVE; Love, John M., Lawrence Aber, and Jeanne Brooks-Gunn (1994). *Strategies for assessing community progress toward achieving the first national educational goal.* Princeton, NJ: Mathematica Policy Research; Meisels, Samuel J., and Sally Atkins-Burnett (2000). The elements of early childhood assessment. In Jack P. Shonkoff and Samuel J. Meisels, eds. *Handbook of early childhood intervention.* New York: Cambridge University Press;

Meisels, Samuel J., Judy R. Jablon, Margo L. Dichtelmiller, Aviva B. Dorfman, and Dorothea B. Marsden (2001). *The Work Sampling System* (4th ed.). Ann Arbor, MI: Pearson Early Learning Group. Available online: http://www.pearsonearlylearning.com; National Association for the Education of Young Children (NAEYC) (2003). Early childhood curriculum, assessment, and program evaluation—Building an effective accountable system in programs for children birth through age 8. Available online at www.naeyc.org/resources/position_statements/pscape.pdf; *No Child Left Behind Act of 2001*, Public Law 107-110, *U.S. Statutes at Large* 115(2002), 1425.

Cheri A. Vogel, Louisa Banks Tarullo, and John M. Love

Assessment, Visual Art

Teachers of young children assess visual art in a variety of ways, and for a range of purposes. For teachers in public schools, part of art assessment means ensuring that classrooms for young children are in compliance with frameworks and standards prescribed by the state. In addition, most teachers collect samples of children's artwork to include in child portfolios. Finally, the inspiring work of **Reggio Emilia** has encouraged teachers to use diverse **documentation** of children's artwork and the artistic process in order to make learning visible to children, parents, and the larger community.

Standards and Frameworks

A recent push toward increased accountability in schools has led to the development of a complex set of national and state learning standards for many subject domains. Currently, both national and state-specific standards exist for the arts. An example of one state standard for the visual arts drawn from Massachusetts is shown below:

PreK–12 STANDARD 1: Methods, Materials, and Techniques

Students will demonstrate knowledge of the methods, materials, and techniques unique to the visual arts.

GRADE LEVEL	LEARNING STANDARDS
By the end of grade 4	Students will 1.1 Use a variety of materials and media, *for example, crayons, chalk, paint, clay, various kinds of papers, textiles, and yarns,* and understand how to use them to produce different visual effects 1.2 Create artwork in a variety of two-dimensional (2D) and three-dimensional (3D) media, *for example: 2D – drawing, painting, collage, printmaking, weaving; 3D – plastic (malleable) materials such as clay and paper, wood, or found objects for assemblage and construction* 1.3 Learn and use appropriate vocabulary related to methods, materials, and techniques 1.4 Learn to take care of materials and tools and to use them safely

As a result of this increased push for academic accountability and increase standardized testing even of young children, many perceive that the arts are receiving less attention than more "academic" subjects such as literacy and science. A current trend in art curriculum is tied to these realities: educators such as Carol Seefeldt advocate integrating the arts across domains, thereby including artistic learning and development alongside literacy, mathematics, science, and social studies curriculum. Many teachers are embracing this idea, which is also supported by Gardner's theory of **multiple intelligences** and ideas from the schools of Reggio Emilia, Italy. Each of these sources acknowledges that children learn in different ways and possess different "languages" for communicating and understanding the world. Integrating the arts allows all children a chance to make sense of and communicate their understandings about other topics through artistic means.

Portfolios

Classroom teachers often compile portfolios of children's work throughout the year to assess their artistic development. Although children like to take work home to show parents, teachers may retain work that represents a shift in the child's use of materials or thinking, to look at development in terms of what concepts, materials, and forms appear in the child's artwork. In some instances, the children themselves may self-evaluate, choosing what work should be included in the portfolio. The teacher and the child may look at the portfolio together at different points throughout the year. This also helps children become objective and evaluate their own work, and gives them a new perspective on the work they are currently doing in the classroom. By continually taking notes of what children say about their work, and using these comments as points of departure for discussion about work, teachers can assess what is important to each child about the artwork he/she is producing. For the teacher, knowing what engages the children is helpful in planning future lessons, considering what new materials to introduce, and offering meaningful experiences in which to practice skills.

Documentation

In addition to taking anecdotes, teachers will also take photos, sound recordings, and even videotape classroom activity to assess learning. These photos, transcriptions of conversations, and anecdotes are displayed in the classroom or school by the teacher alongside children's artwork. Documentation includes text articulating what the work might have meant to the teacher and the child. This form of assessment serves as another point of reflection and evaluation for the teacher. Teachers may use documentation to start dialogue with the children, parents, or other faculty. Documentation and conversations that emerge from documentation help teachers as they plan future lessons for children.

Conclusions

Assessing children's artistic work serves multiple purposes. By collecting, displaying, and examining pieces of children's art, teachers may better understand artistic and representational strengths of the children they teach. Observing and documenting the process of creating art can inform teachers about children's fine motor abilities, as well as provide insight about the ways in which children make decisions and plan during artistic experiences. *See also* Child Art.

Further Readings: Massachusetts Department of Education (2000). Massachusetts curriculum frameworks (Visual Arts). Available online at http://www.doe.mass.edu/frameworks/current.html; McWhinnie, Harold J. (1992). Art in early childhood education. In Carol Seefeldt, ed. *The early childhood curriculum: A review of current research*, 2nd ed. New York: Teachers College Press, pp. 264–285; Seefeldt, Carol (1999). Art for young children. In Carol Seefeldt, ed. *The early childhood curriculum: Current findings in theory and practice*. 3rd ed. New York: Teachers College Press, pp. 201–217.

Megina Baker and Maggie Beneke

Association for Childhood Education International (ACEI)

The Association for Childhood Education International (ACEI) is a not-for-profit professional organization of educators, parents, and other caregivers interested in promoting the highest quality educational practices. More specifically, its mission, as presented on the ACEI Web site, is "to promote and support in the global community the optimal education and development of children, from birth through early adolescence, and to influence the professional growth of educators and the efforts of others who are committed to the needs of children in a changing society."

ACEI was founded in 1892 by a group of kindergarten teachers who wished to expand the pioneering work with young children begun by Friedrich **Frobel** in Germany during the 1820s and 1830s. Since that time, the organization's goals (as defined in its constitution) have expanded to include the following:

- The promotion of the inherent rights, education, and well-being of all children in the home, school, and community.
- The promotion of desirable conditions, programs, and practices for children from infancy through early adolescence.
- The raising of the standard of preparation for teachers and others who are involved with the care and development of children.
- The encouragement of continuous professional growth of educators.
- The promotion of active cooperation among all individuals and groups concerned with children.
- Informing the public of the needs of children and the ways in which various programs must be adjusted to fit those needs and rights.

To achieve its goals, ACEI has a membership of nearly 10,000 professionals throughout the United States and sixty other countries. The organization hosts an annual conference that features national and international presenters who focus on a broad range of topics of interest to educators worldwide. The organization also plans a world conference outside the United States every three years. Further, the voice of ACEI is shared with the world through its award-winning journals, such as *Childhood Education* and the *Journal of Research in Childhood Education*. In addition to its prestigious journals, ACEI has an extensive publication program that includes: Focus Newsletters, position papers on contemporary problems and issues, "ACEI Speaks" pamphlets that provide concise information on topics of general concern, and a host of books and resources. The association's goals are also supported through its active liaison with various government agencies, such as the United Nations, the National Commission for the Rights of Children, and the Alliance for Curriculum Reform. Finally, to achieve its mission of providing children with high-quality education, ACEI serves as the lead organization responsible for accreditation of teacher education programs through the **National Council for Accreditation of Teacher Education** (NCATE).

The association actively seeks volunteers for its many committees, which provide direction to the organization. Committees include Awards, Conference, Diversity, Heritage, Infancy/Early Childhood, Intermediate/Middle Childhood, International/Intercultural, Membership, Nominating, Professional Standards/Teacher Education, Program Development, Public Affairs, Publications, Research, Retired Members, Student, Technology, and Week of the Classroom Teacher.

For additional information, view the organization's Web site at www.acei.org or contact ACEI directly at the following address:
17904 Georgia Avenue, Suite 215
Olney, MD 20832-2277
(301) 570-2111 or (800) 423-3563
Fax (301) 570-2212

Jim Hoot

Association for Constructivist Teaching (ACT)

The Association for Constructivist Teaching (ACT) is a professional educational organization dedicated to fostering teacher development based on constructivist learning theory.

Constructivism is a theory about knowledge and learning, describing both what knowledge is, and how it evolves. Initially based on the work of Jean **Piaget** and Lev **Vygotsky** in cognitive psychology, it was extended to the fields of philosophy and education by von Glasersfeld, Duckworth, Forman, Kamii, and Fosnot (among many others). It currently draws further support from complexity theories in science, that is, physics and biology (Prigogine, Maturana, Varela, and Kauffman). The theory describes knowledge not as truths to be transmitted or discovered, but as emergent, developmental, nonobjective, viable constructed explanations as humans engage in meaning-making in cultural and social communities of discourse. Learning from this perspective is viewed as a self-regulatory, organizing, evolutionary process by humans in dynamic "far-from-equilibrium" states as they struggle with the conflict between existing personal models of the world and discrepant new insights. As humans act on and attempt to interpret their surround (assimilation), they construct new representations and models of reality (accommodation) with culturally developed tools and symbols, and further negotiate such meaning through cooperative social activity, discourse, and debate in communities of practice. Although constructivism is not a theory of teaching, it suggests taking a radically different approach to instruction from that used historically in most schools. Teachers who base their practice on constructivism reject the notions that meaning can be passed on to learners via symbols and transmission, that learners can incorporate exact copies of teachers' understanding for their own use, that whole concepts can be broken into discrete subskills, and that concepts can be taught out of context. In contrast, a constructivist view of learning suggests a developmentally appropriate, student-centered, active workshop approach to teaching that gives learners the opportunity for concrete, contextually meaningful experience through which they can search for patterns, raise questions, and model, interpret, and defend their strategies and ideas. The classroom in this model is seen almost as a mini society, a community of learners engaged in activity, discourse, interpretation, justification, and reflection. The traditional hierarchy of teacher as the autocratic knower, and learner as the unknowing, controlled subject studying and practicing what the teacher knows, dissipates as teachers assume more of a facilitator's role and learners take on more ownership of the ideas. Autonomy, mutual reciprocity of social relations, and empowerment become the goals.

The ACT was the natural evolution of the Annual New England Piaget Conference, a small annual conference for teachers held every fall at the Park School in Norwalk, Connecticut. The school was established and directed by Rose Park, an educator interested in applications of Piagetian theory to educational practice. In the late 1980s, the Association for Constructivist Teaching incorporated as a nonprofit and Catherine Fosnot was elected as the first president. Some of the early board members were Barry Wadsworth, George Forman, Lloyd Jaeger, and Calvert Schlick. Annual conferences were held around the New England area. Since 1990, the organization has had more of a national presence, and the annual conferences are rotated around the country.

The mission of ACT is to enhance the growth of all educators and students through identification and dissemination of effective constructivist practices in both the professional cultures of teachers and the learning environments of their students. ACT membership is open to anyone interested in the field of education. Current ACT members are practicing classroom teachers, school administrators, supervisors, consultants, college and university personnel, students, parents, and retired educators. Membership continues to flourish with recent members joining from as far away as Japan and Mexico. The meeting format of the annual conference is usually one that includes two keynote speakers and several sessions of concurrent hour-and-a-half workshops over a two- or three-day period. Presentations include research, curriculum ideas, panel discussions, hands-on workshops, all focused on applying constructivist theory about learning to classroom practice at many levels of education.

In addition to the annual conference, the organization publishes a scholarly journal, *The Constructivist* (now available online), distributes CDs of keynote conference speakers, sponsors an online discussion group, compiles a list of constructivist schools and teacher-education programs. Conference and membership information, ACT board contacts, and news are available on the ACT website at http://www.odu.edu/act.

Catherine Twomey Fosnot and Alice Wakefield

Atelier

In French, the word *atelier* is a common term meaning an artist's studio or workshop. Within the field of early childhood education, an "atelier" is understood as a physical space within a school dedicated to children's exploration and use of many materials, tools, symbolic languages, and forms of representation.

Current understanding of the concept of the "atelier" in schools can be traced to the preschools of the municipality in the city of **Reggio Emilia**, Italy. The first ateliers were established in 1963 in the preschools in Reggio Emilia by Loris **Malaguzzi** and his colleagues. Later, in the 1970s, ateliers were also developed in the city's infant and toddler centers. The presence of the atelier is one of the fundamental aspects that distinguishes the preschools and infant toddler centers in Reggio Emilia from other schools for young children. Closely linked to the concept of atelier within the context of early education is the role of the "atelierista," a teacher with a background in the visual arts, who usually works with small groups of children in the atelier. The atelierista forms a close collaborative relationship with the classroom teachers, as well as supports curriculum development, research, and documentation throughout the entire school.

An essential purpose of the atelier is to offer a variety of high-quality materials to all ages of children and to serve as the central place in the school where many collections of materials are located and used. These collections often include traditional art media, such as paint, drawing, or clay, but also may contain nontraditional materials, such as found objects, recycled items, and such natural materials as stones, shells, leaves, dried flowers, and sticks. The many types of rich and interesting materials in the atelier are used to facilitate children's learning.

The concept of the atelier, as well as learning through materials, is integrated into the entire school. This learning occurs in the physical organization of the space as miniateliers are set up in, or adjacent to, each classroom. The term "miniatelier" refers to a space in the classroom where rich materials are organized for children's daily interactions with symbolic languages. Miniateliers may contain materials similar to the ones in the larger atelier, or they may be adjusted to the particular needs of the children and the teachers in each classroom. The relationship between the atelier and the classroom and the atelierista and the classroom teacher is one of collaboration, exchange, and reciprocity. The atelierista works closely with the classroom teachers to make flexible plans that are carried out over days, weeks, and months, to accomplish agreed upon goals and intentions.

An atelier is very different from the traditional interpretation of an "art class" or "art center" found in many North American early childhood educational programs. The presence of an atelier usually means that the adults believe that children make sense and create understanding of experience through a network of relationships and meaningful interactions with adults, other children, the environment, and materials. In Reggio Emilia, this point of view about children's learning has grown from **social constructivism** and **sociocultural theory.**

Today, educators in the United States who are exploring implications of Reggio Emilia's interpretation of early care and education are finding ways to translate characteristics of the atelier into their own school settings. Educators in the United States interested in the concept of the atelier may or may not have a separate space designated for an atelier, or a teacher who is an atelierista. Still, they are able to incorporate many of these ideas into their schools. For example, some teachers may work these ideas into their own classroom by setting up a miniatelier, giving careful attention to the role of materials in children's projects, documenting their findings, and then sharing them with parents and other teachers. Inspired by the spirit of the atelier, some traditional art teachers are looking for ways to expand their role by collaborating with the classroom teachers on shared goals and projects.

The atelier also plays an active role in developing and supporting research, documentation, and communication within the school community. Adults use the atelier to support pedagogical research through an ongoing cycle of observation, documentation, and interpretation of children's learning. Because of this, the atelier is the primary location within the school where important tools for documentation, such as written notes, photographs, audiocassette recording, or video, are frequently located. The atelierista often assists the classroom teachers with developing many forms of visual communication to highlight the children's learning, such as display panels, binders and books, slide shows, or video presentations. These types of documents help to inform others, both in and outside of the school community, about the work of the school and children's learning experiences.

Further Readings: Cadwell, Louise (1997). *Bringing Reggio home: An innovative approach to early childhood education.* New York: Teachers College Press; Edwards, C., L. Gandini, and G. Forman, eds. (1998). *The hundred languages of children: The Reggio Emilia approach-advanced reflections.* 2nd ed. Westport, CT: Ablex; Gandini, L., L. Hill, L. Cadwell, and C. Schwall, eds. (2005). *In the spirit of the studio: Learning from the Atelier of Reggio Emilia.* New York: Teachers College Press.

Charles Schwall

Attachment

Attachments are emotional bonds that unite people across time and space. The concept of attachment has its roots in an evolutionary approach to early relationships, and can be seen as a lasting emotional tie between people. Attachments form beginning in infancy, where they contribute to human survival by bringing infants, who are dependent on the care of an adult, and their caregivers together. Behavior on the part of both children (i.e., crying, clinging in infants) and caregivers (protection and comforting) results in physical and emotional closeness. Forming attachments to parents or caregivers is seen as a hallmark of socioemotional development in the first year of life.

Typically an infant develops a primary attachment relationship with an important caregiver, usually the mother, but children also form attachment relationships with other people, notably fathers, extended family members, and other caregivers such as child-care providers. Early childhood educators both support parent–child attachments and form their own attachment relationships with children in their care.

Attachment theory has become one of the major organizing frameworks for understanding social and emotional development. After World War II, the **World Health Organization** (WHO), concerned with the welfare of European orphans, asked John **Bowlby,** an eminent British psychiatrist, to review research and clinical work on early relationships. In his comprehensive study of attachment he concluded that a strong relationship with a primary caregiver was essential to healthy development. Mary Ainsworth then developed the research paradigm, "the Strange Situation," to examine the attachment between a child and caregiver, and began the process of characterizing variation in the human attachment system. According to Ainsworth's paradigm, some attachment relationships can be described as "secure" and some as "insecure" (avoidant, resistant, or disorganized). Attachments that are positive and secure provide the basis for trust in self and others, and the confidence to explore and learn new things, knowing that the protection and nurturance of a trusted attachment figure is available if needed. Sometimes, however, infants develop attachments that reflect uncertainty or distrust in the responsiveness of the caregiver.

During the last three decades a large and international body of research on attachment has been conducted. Essential to the concept of attachment is the belief that differences in caregiving yield different attachment patterns. That is, responsive caregiving on the part of the caregiver leads to security on the part of the child. Less responsive, or at the extreme, abusive, care leads to insecure attachments.

Characteristics of attachment relationships are most clearly shown when the child is stressed, since this is when the attachment behavioral system is activated. Some children may seek out a trusted adult for comfort and help when stressed; others may have a difficult time settling in the presence of an attachment figure after an emotional upset; others may not seek out the presence or help of a caregiver when they are stressed. These behaviors say something about the child's *Internal Working Model of Attachment*, or the expectations the child holds that the caregiver will be available (both physically and emotionally) and sensitively responsive when the child is distressed. According to attachment theory, Internal Working Models develop gradually, through a history of interaction with an attachment figure.

Working models, and attachments, can change over time, but these changes are only likely to result from very significant changes in the caregiving environment. For example, consider a one-year-old who has developed an insecure attachment; her caregiver is severely depressed, thus not either physically or emotionally available to attend promptly, consistently, and sensitively to the infant's distress. Research shows that if the caregiving environment changes in significant, positive ways, attachments can become more secure. In this example, if the caregiver's depression was not chronic, and the caregiver became a predictable, sensitive attachment figure, the child might alter the working model toward trust and security.

This example illustrates how attachments are influenced by a caregiver's behavior and life experience, for example, the caregiver's current social support and stress, and their own childhood history. In families where the caregiver has experienced insecure attachments in their own childhood, and the current circumstances make it more difficult to care sensitively for an infant (e.g., marital conflict, unstable living conditions, economic stressors, mental health problems), children are more likely to develop insecure attachments.

Attachments are also associated with children's later development. Longitudinal research has shown that children with secure early attachments are more likely to develop close, positive relationships with other people outside the family, for example with peers and teachers. Attachments are more closely linked with social and emotional development, such as positive social interaction, emotion regulation, and adaptive self understanding, than to intellectual competence. The studies also show that the current life circumstances of the child and the caregivers' sensitivity also have an impact, not simply early attachments.

Attachments seem to be universal across cultures. What varies across culture and context is the particular ways in which attachments are manifest. Children in different cultures may show different patterns of attachment behaviors, relying more or less on close physical contact, for example. Some may rely more on physical contact versus physical proximity. This may indicate that there is no singular model for forming healthy relationships, since children worldwide form secure relationships with their parents. One criticism of attachment theory is based, in part, on the idea that different cultural goals require different caregiving styles and that indicators of secure attachment represent a Western, middle-class bias. In Western cultures, sensitivity is defined by how accessible and emotionally available the caregiver is to understanding the needs of the child, the promptness and timing of response—especially when the child is stressed, and acceptance of the child. A secure one-year-old is one who uses the attachment figure as a "secure base" for exploration, who is able to use the caregiver to help regulate distress effectively, who shows pleasure in the relationship with the attachment figure. Researchers know less about the formation and expression of attachment in non-Western societies, but it is likely that secure and insecure patterns of attachment are related, in part, to different caregiving styles within a culture.

Another criticism of attachment theory comes from those who view attachment behaviors as reflective of innate **temperament** as much as a result of the child's history of caregiving. Research has shown, however, that children with "difficult" temperaments do not necessarily form insecure attachments, since their caregivers can respond appropriately and sensitively to different temperamental characteristics. Similarly, not all children with "easy" temperaments form secure attachments. While a child's attachments may differ with different attachment figures (e.g., secure with mother, insecure with father), a child's temperament remains the same. Temperament may be more closely linked with variations *within* insecure or secure attachments.

Some people used to believe that children "grow out of" attachments; that by the time they are three, children should be independent from their attachment figures. What we now understand is that attachments are lifelong; they change, and the behaviors that are used to express attachments change with age, but attachments do not disappear. Whereas a one-year-old may use physical contact, a three-year-old may be content with proximity and verbal communication when stressed. Older children and adults also maintain attachments, and sometimes just talking with an attachment figure (even by phone) or thinking about them will help to ease distress.

Attachment theory has had a profound effect on early childhood education. Understanding of attachment is seen as essential to supporting children's social-emotional and overall development. This understanding relates to two specific roles for early childhood educators: supporting the relationships of children with their parents and establishing secure relationships with the children themselves.

When caring for and educating other people's children, early childhood educators join a system of care that involves strong emotional ties. Often the emphasis is almost exclusively on the well-being of the child. But that well-being is directly related to the quality of those primary relationships. In working with children, early childhood educators both observe and affect those relationships. Although their role is not to intervene directly, as might a psychologist or clinical social worker, how educators interact with a child and how they support the parent or primary caregiver should be informed by an understanding of healthy attachment. Given a caution about large variation in what healthy attachment looks like, indicators of such attachment in the infant and preschool years include both child and family characteristics. On the part of the child we may see the child showing preference for the attachment figure, wanting physical closeness or proximity when confronting new or stressful situations, using the attachment figure as secure base for exploration, and showing/sharing objects and experiences with the caregiver. On the part of the family we might see mutual pleasure at reunion after separation, adapting family life to include the child, and securing a protective environment for the child. On the other hand, educators are also in a position to observe attachments that are less secure, for example when interactions show that the child expects the caregiver to interfere in activities or tends not to go to the caregiver when upset. Again, such observations need to be made with great caution both because there is a large degree of variation in how secure relationships are formed and because cross-cultural interaction patterns must be considered. Negative judgments about parent–child relationships often affect teacher–parent interactions. Of course, if there are concerns about **child abuse and neglect**, appropriate referrals should be made. However, healthy attachments are not independent of the social support and resources available to families. Early childhood educators can support healthy relationships when they describe the child in a positive manner, point out how the child uses the parent as a secure base, and, in general, see their role as supportive of the primary relationship.

At the same time, educators also form their own attachment relationships with children in their care. Through responsive caregiving, responding to the unique needs of each child, and supporting the child's exploratory activities through curriculum, educators become attachment figures. As with attachment to family members, there is variation in these attachment patterns with some being secure and others insecure, with responsive caregiving relating to the secure pattern, and with secure relationships yielding positive developmental outcomes for children. Children who experience secure attachment with parents tend to do so with their teachers, but this is not always true, with some children forming secure relationships with teachers when the parent–child relationship is seen to be insecure, and vice versa. Good relationships with child-care providers and teachers can help buffer children from insecure attachments at home, by demonstrating to the child that positive, responsive caregiving relationships are possible.

Children are very capable of, and benefit from, multiple attachment relationships. This is true at home, when there is more than one adult with whom the child forms a strong secure relationship, as well as in alternative care settings. Although feelings of competition among adults who care for the same child are natural, teachers must balance their own healthy and appropriate emotional responses to caring for children with the goal of supporting the primary relationship between the parent and the child. When both parents and child-care providers see their goal as a partnership that helps children to thrive through secure, healthy relationships at home, day care, and school, it is rewarding for everyone and provides the strongest foundation for children's development. *See also* Development, Emotional.

Further Readings: Ainsworth, M. D. S., M. C. Blehar, E. Waters, and S. Wall (1978). *Patterns of attachment.* Hillsdale, NJ: Erlbaum; Bowlby, J. (1969/1982). *Attachment and loss.* Vol. 1. New York: Basic (second edition published 1982); Cassidy, J. and Shaver, P. eds. (1999). *Handbook of attachment: Theory, research, and clinical applications.* New York: Guilford Press; Greenberg, M., D. Ciccetti, and M. Cummings, eds. (1990). *Attachment in the preschool years: Theory, research and intervention.* Chicago: University of Chicago Press; Grossman, K., K. Grossman, G. Spangler, G. Suess, and L. Unzner (1985). Maternal sensitivity and newborn's orientation responses as related to quality of attachment in northern Germany. In I. Bretherton and E. Waters, eds. *Growing points of attachment theory and research. Monographs of the society of Research in Child Development.* 50(1-2), 233–256. Hyson, M. (1994). *The emotional development of young children: Building an emotion-centered curriculum.* New York: Teacher's College Press; Partridge, S., S. Brown, D. Devine, J. Hornstein, J. Marsh, and Weil, J. (1990). *AIMS: Developmental indicators of emotional health.* Portland: University of Southern Maine.

M. Ann Easterbrooks and John Hornstein

Attention Deficit Disorder/Attention Deficit Hyperactivity Disorder (ADD/ADHD)

Attention Deficit Hyperactivity Disorder is a syndrome characterized by serious and persistent difficulties in one or more of three specific areas: attention span, impulse control, and hyperactivity. ADD/ADHD is a chronic disorder that can begin in infancy and extend through adulthood, having negative effects on a child's life at home, in school, and within the community. ADD/ADHD presents along a spectrum of severity, and can involve attention problems, primarily hyperactivity, or a combination of the two. It is conservatively estimated that 6–9 percent of the U.S. school-age population is affected by ADHD.

Diagnostic Features

The Diagnostic and Statistical Manual of Mental Disorders (4th ed., revised) identifies three subtypes of ADD/ADHD, each of which requires six or more criteria for diagnosis:

1. Inattentive type
   - Pays little attention to details; makes careless mistakes.
   - Has a short attention span.
   - Does not listen when spoken to directly.
   - Does not follow instructions; fails to finish tasks.
   - Has difficulty organizing tasks.
   - Avoids tasks that require sustained mental effort.
   - Loses things.
   - Is easily distracted
   - Is forgetful in daily activities

2. Hyperactive/impulsive type

Hyperactive symptoms are the following:

- Fidgets; squirms in seat.
- Leaves seat when remaining seated is expected.
- Often runs about or climbs excessively at inappropriate times.
- Has difficulty playing quietly.
- Talks excessively.

Impulsivity symptoms are the following:

- Blurts out answers before answers are completed.
- Has difficulty waiting his/her turn.
- Often interrupts or intrudes on others.

3. Combined type

This category includes children who meet criteria for both the Inattentive and the Hyperactive/Impulsive types.

In addition to the criteria above, to be diagnosed with ADHD a child must: manifest symptoms prior to age 7, present symptoms for at least six months, and present symptoms in more than one setting (school, home, community). Symptomatology must be excessive and functionally impairing beyond what is expected for the child's developmental level or age.

Although it is possible to diagnose this syndrome earlier, most children are not diagnosed with ADHD until they are four- or five-years old, when they first enter a structured setting that requires sustained attention. Most diagnoses of ADHD are made by pediatricians at the request of a parent or as the result of a referral from a teacher or child-care provider. Diagnosis is generally made by parental report and history corroborated by clinical observation. More specific symptom patterns can be identified through standardized testing performed by a psychologist.

ADHD in the Classroom

In the classroom, the young child with ADHD might present in several different ways. The inattentive child is easily distractible, and has greater than typical difficulty staying focused. Such children may often appear dreamy or confused, have trouble starting and completing work, and demonstrate poor time management and organizational skills. The hyperactive/impulsive child often challenges teachers and classmates with disruptive and inappropriate behaviors. These children usually display a need for more physical movement than is tolerated in the typical classroom environment. All of these children are likely to have messy desks and backpacks, lose their papers and school materials, and forget important information or possessions. Given the coincidence of diagnosis with children's early classroom experiences, some critics suggest that the child's behavior is an indication of developmentally inappropriate environments and/or expectations rather than a symptom of a disorder.

There are many useful intervention strategies for optimizing the child's experience in the classroom or child-care setting. The child's seating can be customized to suit their individual requirements. For example, some children benefit from preferential seating close to the teacher, in the front of the classroom, to minimize visual distractions. Other children benefit from seating in the rear of the classroom to enable them to move around freely without disturbing others, and to reduce their impulse to locate the source of distracting sounds. Students can be seated close to more attentive, quieter peers who can serve as role models. The classroom can be organized to ensure a minimum of visual and auditory distractions.

Because children with ADHD have difficulty establishing and maintaining internal structure, they can benefit greatly from increased structure in the environment. Consistent classroom routines, visible indicators of schedules and tasks, clear and simple instructions, and a calm and relaxed classroom tone are generally beneficial. For inattentive children, it is crucial to maintain eye contact and use a variety of strategies to ensure that the child acknowledges and comprehends instructions. Gentle physical reminders to refocus may be useful. Many hyperactive children respond well to breaks that allow for physical movement and deep pressure (carrying heavy objects, doing jumping-jacks, running errands); these kinds of breaks should be incorporated into normal classroom routines as much as possible.

A general rule of thumb for accommodating children with ADHD in the classroom is to identify inappropriate behavior and support children in finding appropriate substitute behavior that satisfies their need for additional movement. For example, a child who repeatedly taps a pencil on a desk could be encouraged to squeeze a squishy ball instead, or a child who spins on the floor during circle time could be offered the opportunity to take a movement break by doing jumping jacks in the hallway or running an errand for the teacher.

Given the behavioral challenges these children present, it is easy to neglect the strengths that they can bring to a group. Often they are among the brightest and most energetic children in a classroom. They may compensate for their lack of organization with a capacity to get physical tasks done. Their distractibility may lead to creative options not considered by others. And their sociability, although often disruptive, may also be important in engaging other children in a project.

ADHD at Home

Young children with ADHD usually require additional patience, practice, and skill from their caregivers. Because multitasking and following sequential instructions is exceptionally difficult for these children, central family routines such as dressing, preparing for bed, and mealtimes at home and in restaurants often become battlegrounds. Sibling relationships can be negatively impacted by the negative attention directed by parents toward the child with ADHD.

Intervention strategies at home may involve behavior modification and methods for enhancing self-esteem. A calm, consistent demeanor affords the child the opportunity to attempt to self-regulate in accordance with environmental demands. Some of the strategies useful in the classroom may also be appropriate at home, for example, empowering the child by creating a list of daily tasks that the child can independently follow and check off. Adults can help children take responsibility for their possessions by setting up systems for storage and easy access to frequently used personal belongings. For hyperactive children, a degree of flexibility in structured daily activities (meals, homework, etc.) can help decrease conflict. Safe and appropriate outlets for physical movement can be tremendously helpful for these children. Parents can help reduce inappropriate behaviors by suggesting alternatives (e.g., jumping on a home trampoline rather than on the couch; running around the yard rather than the living room).

Inattentive children often benefit from taking frequent breaks, or alternating between quiet and active tasks. The environment can be modified to reduce distracting elements, for example by using a white noise machine, turning off the TV, or creating a designated area in the home that is conducive to calming down.

Associated Disorders

ADHD often coexists with other associated features and disorders. Impulse control problems, temper outbursts, behavioral rigidity, poor frustration tolerance, and intense anger are frequently seen in conjunction with ADHD. Children with ADHD are more likely to also display symptoms of other disorders such as Oppositional Defiant Disorder, Conduct Disorder, Mood Disorders, including Anxiety and Depression, Learning and Communication Disorders, and Tourettes Syndrome.

Differential Diagnosis of ADHD

Because inattention and hyperactivity may result from a variety of causes, particularly in young children, differential diagnosis of ADHD is critical. It is necessary to rule out neurological syndromes (particularly absence epilepsy); other psychiatric disorders such as autism, anxiety, and Asperger syndrome; cognitive impairments and learning disabilities, such as Nonverbal Learning Disorder; and processing difficulties, such as Sensory Integration Disorder, Central Auditory Disorder, and visual-processing disorders.

Treatment of ADHD

Treatment of ADHD is multimodal. Pharmacotherapy may incorporate different categories of medication including predominantly stimulants, but also antidepressants, anticonvulsants, or antihypertensives. Psychological interventions may incorporate behavior modification, parental management training, and family as well as individual counseling. Alternative options are also becoming more available from a variety of specialists, with variable results. Some techniques discussed frequently in the literature on ADHD include homeopathy and diet, computer-assisted training, biofeedback, hypnotherapy, mind/body techniques, sensory integration training, and applied kinesiology. Professionals in the field of early childhood special education can also help to identify the extent to which developmentally appropriate classroom routines and curriculum activities might reduce the extent of ADHD-type behaviors.

Treatment of ADHD is most likely to be successful when parents and teachers work together to monitor children's responses to modifications to the classroom or home environment, behavioral interventions, and/or medications. Communication between home and school is particularly helpful in identifying the triggers of problem behaviors, assessing the effects of medication, and evaluating the effectiveness of intervention strategies utilized in the classroom. *See also* Developmentally Appropriate Practice(s).

Further Readings: Barkley, Russell A. (2005). *Attention-deficit hyperactivity disorder, A handbook for diagnosis and treatment.* 3rd ed. New York: The Guilford Press; *Diagnostic and Statistical Manual of Mental Disorders (DSM-IV).* 4th ed. (1994). Washington, DC: American Psychiatric Association; Hallowell, Edward M., and John J. Ratey (1995). *Driven to distraction: Recognizing and coping with attention deficit disorder from childhood through adulthood.* New York: Random House; Hallowell, Edward M., and John J. Ratey (1995). *Delivered from distraction: Getting the most out of life with attention deficit disorder.* New York: Random House; Levine, Mel. (2002). *A mind at a time.* New York: Simon & Schuster; Martin, K., and A. Martin (2005). *Celebrate! ADHD.* Washington, DC: Cantwell-Hamilton; Reiff, M., S. Tippins, A. LeTourneau, eds. (2004). *ADHD: A complete and authoritative guide.* Elk Grove Village, IL: American Academy of Pediatrics.

Rika Alper and Cornelia Santschi

Augmentative and Alternative Communication (AAC)

Augmentative and alternative communication (AAC) refers to methods, other than speech, that are used to communicate with and improve the communication of children with severe speech and language disabilities.

All human beings communicate. In fact, it might be stated that human beings are unable to not communicate. Whether it be with words, other vocalizations, gestures, facial expressions, or different types of body language, we are constantly conveying a stream of messages to others, either knowingly or unwittingly. The primary expressive method of communication used by most members of society involves natural speech. However, some children are unable to rely on speech as a primary method of oral communication either temporarily or permanently. These individuals include children with intellectual disabilities, autism, apraxia, neuromotor problems such as cerebral palsy, traumatic brain injury, and developmental verbal apraxia. Some of these children may also exhibit difficulties with written communication. In such cases, practitioners may see a need to enhance these children's effectiveness of communication, oral or written, by introducing augmentative and alternative communication (AAC).

There are no candidacy requirements for the introduction of AAC. To the contrary, a zero exclusion policy is applied, suggesting children may benefit from these methods regardless of type or severity of disabilities. The key criterion in pursuing AAC for children is not their demonstration of specific prerequisite behaviors but rather a search for effective methods of communication for those whose speech is insufficient in addressing everyday communication needs.

The term "augmentative" suggests the goal is to supplement extant communication methods that are already proving to be effective for the child, even if only marginally. Rather than eliminate these residual skills, the child is encouraged to continue relying on them while turning to AAC as a means of expanding communication options in terms of content, effectiveness, and efficiency.

Some situations call for applying AAC as an alternative method of communication. For example, children may rely on challenging behaviors, such as screaming, hitting, and pinching, to convey basic wants and needs. An educational goal might involve replacing these behaviors with more conventional, socially appropriate messages conveyed via an AAC system. Other children rely on behaviors that are so subtle and idiosyncratic that only the most familiar listeners can guess their intended meanings. AAC may replace such behaviors, providing opportunities to communicate more conventionally and thus effectively with a broader range of conversational partners.

AAC is not merely a thing, but should be perceived of in terms of an entire "system." While the various aided (e.g., computers, speech-generating devices, and communication books) and unaided (e.g., gestures and sign language) methods of communication are important, AAC consists of far more than the method by which communication is carried out. AAC can be depicted in relation to four primary components: symbols, aids, strategies, and techniques.

Symbols

Symbols can be graphic (e.g., photographs and line drawings), auditory (e.g., auditory scanning, where possible choices are presented aurally and the child indicates when she hears the desired message), tactile (e.g., Braille), and gestural (e.g., sign language). The level and complexity of symbols used for a particular child is determined by many factors, including the child's sensory and cognitive skills. For example, a child with severe to profound intellectual disabilities might be found to be a candidate for symbols represented by actual objects or photographs as opposed to line drawings. Another child may be capable of using traditional orthography (e.g., spelling) as a primary symbol set. An important part of an AAC assessment involves determining a child's capabilities to use symbols of increasing complexity and abstractness. Skills in this domain may be targeted as part of a broader effort to enhance literacy skills.

Aids

Aids, whether they are electronic or nonelectronic, are the systems used to transmit and receive messages. They may be something as simple as a page on which a choice of two photographs are affixed, to something as complex as an electronic device containing more than a hundred different symbols that can be combined to formulate an infinite number of messages.

The type of aid selected is based on a highly individualized process that typically employs some type of feature matching between the capabilities (e.g., cultural, academic, language, cognitive, motoric, behavioral, perceptual, sensory, and emotional) of the child and the operational requirements of the particular device. The process proceeds systematically and generally includes the following steps:

1. The child's communication needs and opportunities for communication are identified.
2. Present methods by which the child communicates, and their relative effectiveness, are determined.
3. The child's capabilities, cited above, are assessed.

4. A list of possible AAC options is generated based on the child's capabilities as well as characteristics of people and settings in which the system will be used immediately and in the future.
5. The child field tests equipment considered for adoption.

In most cases, an AAC system will not consist of a single device or method of communication but instead be comprised of multimodal means of communication. Children must learn to recognize when any one particular means of communication is most effective based on experiential and environmental considerations. Their abilities to code switch, moving from one method of communication to another based on partner and setting variables, is viewed as an integral component of their communicative competence.

Many variables must be considered in finding the right match between a child and an aid. In the case of young AAC users, aids should be evaluated in relation to the following factors:

• Flexibility to accommodate children's increasing linguistic abilities over time.
• Extent to which they can be used to foster language and communication development.
• The range of communicative functions (i.e., purposes for communicating such as commenting, answering, requesting information, sharing novel information, requesting objects and actions, requesting clarification, and developing and maintaining social relationships) that can be expressed.
• Ability to address present and future communication needs.
• Number of environments in which they can be used effectively.
• Variety of familiar and unfamiliar communication partners with which they can be used.
• Acceptability to children and their families.
• Cost.
• Maintenance requirements and overall durability.
• Extent to which they enhance the quality of the lives of children and their families.

As indicated above, these various aid characteristics are weighed relative to children's capabilities. Evaluation of the latter requires a multidisciplinary evaluation by an AAC team. Membership on the team can vary depending on the task at hand but often includes parents, teachers, speech–language pathologists, physical therapists, and occupational therapists. Other professionals that may be involved include rehabilitation engineers, administrators, equipment vendors, psychologists, audiologists, and pediatricians.

Strategies

Strategies refer to methods of enhancing the effectiveness or efficiency of message transmission. They include procedures such as word prediction (i.e., activation of each letter results in presentation of a menu of words with the highest probability of following that particular letter or sequence of letters), letter prediction, and dynamic display (where activation of a key opens up a page of additional vocabulary, expanding the range of meanings that can be conveyed). They also include techniques for arranging symbols such as categorizing them in relation to "who", "what," "what doing," "where," "how," and "in what manner," listing items alphabetically, and/or arranging letters to correspond with the typical QWERTY keyboard.

Strategies also incorporate patterns of interaction that foster children's effective uses of their different AAC methods. For example, conversational partners are encouraged to be patient, to give children ample time to formulate and transmit their messages, to provide numerous opportunities and reasons for communication throughout the day, and to model effective uses of AAC and other communication methods.

Techniques

Techniques relate to how messages are accessed and transmitted. The two techniques for activating messages via aided communication are direct selection and scanning. Direct selection involves pointing (whether that is with a finger, head pointer, optical light indicator, or some other source) directly at the desired item. Scanning involves sequential presentations of different items until the desired item is highlighted at which point the communicator typically uses a switch to select the item or continue the scanning pattern.

While the goals of AAC are many and varied, overarching themes include maximizing effectiveness of communication while simultaneously fostering children's participation and inclusion in their schools and communities. Interventions involving AAC are carried out most effectively in children's homes, schools, and other natural settings. They attempt to involve as many communication partners, in as many settings, as is feasible.

Objectives are integrated into curricula, rather than constituting isolated behaviors. For example, rather than teaching choice making in a contrived setting, an SLP might analyze the various environments in which interactions typically occur and recruit natural partners in these same environments to present children with systematic opportunities to make choices using their AAC systems. Children's self-determination can be fostered through this process of role release.

In conclusion, AAC represents a programmatic team response to an existing or projected set of challenges. Effectiveness of AAC is defined in relation to the extent to which it supports enhanced qualities of life for children and their families.

Further Readings: American Speech-Language-Hearing Association (2004). Roles and responsibilities of speech-language pathologists with respect to augmentative and alternative communication: Technical report. ASHA Supplement 24, 1-17; Beukelman, David R., and Pat Mirenda (2005). *Augmentative and alternative communication: Supporting children and adults with complex communication needs.* 3rd ed. Baltimore: Paul H. Brookes; International Society for Augmentative and Alternative Communication (ISAAC). Available online at http://www.isaac-online.org/select_language. html.

Stephen N. Calculator

Autism

In 1943, Dr. Leo Kanner of the Johns Hopkins Hospital first described the syndrome of early infantile autism. His diagnostic criteria were based on a child's inability to relate to others, a characteristic that he described as "extreme aloneness." In the 1960s this disability was thought to have a low incidence. In

2006, the Research Institute and the Centers for Disease Control and Prevention estimate that 1 in 166 children is diagnosed with a form of autism, a ratio that no longer qualifies as a "low incidence." Although much research is being conducted, the cause of this increase, or even the extent to which the increase in numbers diagnosed represents an actual increase, is not yet known. Autism occurs in all racial, ethnic and socioeconomic groups. Again for unknown reasons, three to four times as many boys as girls are diagnosed.

Since 1952, physicians and psychologists have used the *The Diagnostic and Statistics Manual of Mental Disorders* (DSM) for identifying disorders, including autism, and differentiating one from another. This manual, published by the American Psychiatric Association, is revised frequently. The current edition, (DSM-IV-TR), lists the condition of Pervasive Developmental Disorder as an umbrella term under which are included Autistic Disorder, Childhood Disintegrative Disorder, Asperger Disorder, Retts Disorder, and Pervasive Developmental Disorder—Not Otherwise Specified (PDD-NOS). In 1994 the organization **Zero to Three**, the National Center for Infants Toddlers and Families, created the *Diagnostic Classification of Mental Health and Developmental Disorders of Infancy and Early Childhood* to identify and differentiate disorders as they are seen in children from birth through three years of age. A revised edition (DC:0-3R) was released in 2005.

The authors of this book describe Multisystem Developmental Disorder as a disorder of relating and communication resulting from biologically based differences in a variety of interconnected systems including sensory modulation, sensory integration, and motor planning. They liken it to Pervasive Developmental Disorder. The notion of a spectrum of disorders was first described in the early 1980s by Lorna Wing who wrote about a range of related disorders from autism to Asperger. The term Autistic Spectrum Disorders (ASD) is now coming into wide use to clarify that the term autism is not one condition.

At the beginning of this century the United States Office of Special Education Programs requested that the National Research Council of the National Academy of Science undertake a study of what is known about autism relevant to children from birth to eight. The findings are published in a book entitled *Educating Children with Autism* (Lord and McGee, 2001). Echoing the foregoing, the authors write, "The manifestations of autism vary considerably across children and within individual children over time. There is no single behavior that is always typical of autism and no behavior that would automatically exclude an individual child from a diagnosis of autism, even though there are strong and consistent commonalities, especially relative to social deficit."

There is agreement that the core deficits of this spectrum of disorders, when seen in early childhood, include significant impairments in the areas of socialization, communication, and behavior. Some signs and symptoms associated with this spectrum at this age include but are not limited to the following:

• Lack of joint regard or shared attention.
• Impairment in gestural (e.g., pointing) and reciprocal communication.
• Lack of imitative, functional, and pretend play that is appropriate to developmental age.
• Difficulty regulating emotions.

In some children hints of future problems are evident early in infancy but for most children problems with communication and social engagement become evident as the child's skills begin to lag behind other children of the same age. Some children begin to develop normally and then between 18 and 24 months lose language and social skills they had previously acquired. There are other problems that frequently accompany ASD. It is estimated that one in four children with ASD will develop seizures starting in early childhood or adolescence. Sensory problems, including difficulties perceiving and integrating information through the senses, are also common and may explain many of the repetitive or stereotyped behaviors such as hand flapping and rocking.

Theories about the etiology of this complex disability include the influences of genetics, infectious disease, prenatal and postnatal trauma, immune system deficiencies, and metabolic disorders. Recent studies suggest that for families with one child with autism the risk of having another child with autism is as high as 1 in 20 or 5 percent. Although there is general agreement that this is a biologically based disorder, there are currently no biological markers or "tests" that detect autism. Its diagnosis is based upon parental report and the observations of clinicians. There are tools that are used with these observations, for example, the Childhood Autism Rating Scales (CARS) by Schopler et al. and the Modified Checklist for Autism in Toddlers (M-CHAT) by Robins et al. (2001). The items on the latter scale that are most significant in differentially identifying autism in children over 24 months include lack of the following:

- Interest in other children.
- Use of index finger to point in order to indicate interest in something.
- Showing parent or caregiver an object.
- Imitating a familiar adult's expressions and/or actions.
- Responding to his/her name when called.
- Visually following another's point gesture to an object.

Clinicians may also use the Autism Diagnostic Observation Schedule—Generic (ADOS-G) (Lord et al., 2000), a semistructured play-based tool to determine whether a child meets the criteria for autism in the communication, social interaction, and imaginative play domains. No tool should be used in isolation, however, and a diagnosis of autism should be made only as part of a comprehensive assessment.

The early belief that autism was caused by cold or aloof parenting has been discredited. However, because this disorder can affect a child's ability to communicate, form relationships with others and respond appropriately to the external world, it can be disruptive to attachment patterns between children and their primary caregivers. Therefore, seeing families as the primary interveners and professionals as their allies is essential in promoting growth and development in their children. Providers of service to these families should be sensitive to the difficulties parents experience in diagnosing and treating these children. These parents see what looks to be typical development over the first months and even years of life. They also experience a lack of relatedness on the part of the child that affects how they feel as a parent. Although these features may also be true of some other developmental conditions, the predominance of highly intensive interventions and the perception that if the condition is not treated early it will not be ameliorated add additional stresses in the lives of these parents.

Studies have shown that early detection and intervention can have significant effects on the progress and functioning level of children. A wide range of approaches to intervention is currently available. Some focus specifically on and work through the physiology of the disorder (e.g., dietary and pharmacological), others the behavioral manifestations (e.g., applied behavioral analysis), and still others a combination of the biological, psychological, and social elements (e.g., developmental, individual differences, relationship-based approach). While there are several methodologies currently in use, "there are virtually no data on the relative merits of one model over another" (National Research Council, 2001, p. 171), nor is there any apparent association between any particular current intervention and recovery from autism" (p. 43).

Among model comprehensive programs for young children there is, however, agreement about the components of successful intervention (Hurth et al., 1999; National Research Council, 2001).

- Intensity of engagement: Engagement refers to sustained attention to and participation with a person or a developmentally appropriate activity.
- Individualization of services for children and families: Profile of services, outcomes, settings, measurement of progress should be tailored to individual child and family.
- Family involvement: Family is given support in accommodating their child's needs in everyday situations.
- Systematic, planful teaching: Planning includes assurance of developmentally appropriate, functional interventions that have a coherent theoretical basis.
- Specialized curriculum: Curriculum addresses the core deficits of ASD such as communication, social/emotional interaction, play, and problem solving.
- Objective measurements of progress: Objective, observable and anecdotal measurements are used to determine whether a child is benefiting from intervention.
- Opportunities for inclusion with typically developing peers in natural environments: Appropriate supports are provided in home and community settings to promote fully inclusive experiences among peers.
- Earliest possible start to intervention.

In the United States current federal legislation such as **Individuals with Disabilities Education Act** (IDEA) supports **early childhood special education** services for children with autism and other developmental disabilities. The youngest children, defined in each state as either birth through three or birth through five, receive **early intervention** through the state departments of education, health, or human services. These services are provided in inclusive environments that are natural to the child, for example, home, child care, and community settings. While some services are at public expense (e.g., evaluation, development of an **Individual Family Service Plan**), families participate in paying for some services. Services for older children are provided by the state department of education in the "least restrictive" school environment that can provide a free and appropriate public education.

Although ASD is currently viewed as not yet curable, there is treatment available. As there are many treatment options available, there are just as many outcomes. It is important to receive the correct diagnosis. The degree of success of any treatment program will depend on accurate diagnosis, the characteristics of the child, and the extent to which treatment is individualized and based on the child's unique profile. Given these supports and our increasing knowledge, it is reasonable to look to the future with positive expectations. *See also* Inclusion.

Further Readings: Bilken, D. (2005). *Autism and the myth of the person alone.* New York: New York University Press; Greenspan, S. I., G. Degangi, and S. Wieder (2001). *The Functional Emotional Assessment Scale (FEAS) for infancy and early childhood: Clinical and research applications.* Bethesda, MD: Interdisciplinary Council on Developmental and Learning Disorders; Hurth, J., E. Shaw, S. Izeman, K. Whaley, and S. J. Rogers (1999). Areas of agreement abougt effective practices among programs serving young children with autism spectrum disorders. *Infants and Young Children, 12*(2), 17–26. Lord, C., and J. McGee, eds. (2001). *Educating children with autism.* Washington, DC: National Academy Press; Lord, C., S. Risi, L. Lambrecht, E. H. Cook, B. L. Leventhal, P. C. DiLavore, A. Pickles, and M. Rutter (2000). The autism diagnostic observation schedule-generic: A standard measure of social and communication deficits associated with the spectrum of autism. *Journal of Autism and Developmental Disorders* 30, 205–233; National Research Council (2001). *Educating children with autism.* Committee on Educational Interventions for Children with Autism. Catherine Lord and James P. McGee, eds. Division of Behavioral and Social Sciences and Education. Washington, DC: National Academy Press; Robins, D., D. Fein, M. Barton, and J. Green (2001). The Modified Checklist for Autism in Toddlers (M-CHAT): An initial study investigating the early detection of autism and pervasive developmental disorders. *Journal of Autism and Developmental Disorders* 31, 131–144; Shopler E., R. J. Reichler, R. F. DeVellis, and K. Daly (1980). Toward objective classifications of childhood autism: Childhood Autism Rating Scale (CARS). *Journal of Autism and Developmental Disorders* 10, 91–103; Wiseman, N. D. (2006). *Could it be autism?* New York: Broadway Books; ZERO TO THREE (2005). *Diagnostic classification of mental health and developmental disorders of infancy and early childhood: Revised edition (DC:0-3R).* Washington, DC: ZERO TO THREE Press.

Antoinette Spiotta, Corinne G. Catalano, and Sue Fernandez

B

Baker, Katherine Read. *See* Read, Katherine

Bandura, Albert (1925–)

Albert Bandura was born December 4, 1925, in Mundare, northern Canada, of Polish and Ukrainian immigrants. As a teenager, Bandura attended the only high school in town, where he learned the value of self-direction. He obtained his undergraduate degree from the University of British Columbia, Vancouver, in 1949, and his Masters and Ph.D. in Clinical Psychology from the University of Iowa, in 1951 and 1952, respectively. His major advisor was Arthur Benton and he was also highly influenced by the writing of Kenneth Spence. In 1953, he became an assistant professor at Stanford University, where he now is the David Starr Jordan Professor of Social Science in Psychology. Over the course of his long career, Bandura has received over a dozen scientific honors and awards, including awards for lifetime achievements from the American Psychological Association and the American Association of Behavioral Therapy. He has also received honorary degrees from 14 universities worldwide. Bandura married Virginia Varns, a nursing instructor, and has two daughters and several grandchildren.

His major contribution to education, psychology, and other fields was to propose and develop the **social cognitive theory** (previously named the social learning theory). The major premise of this is that people are proactive agents in their own learning and change. They are self-organizing, self-reflecting, and self-regulating (Bandura, 1986), and not merely reactors to external environmental forces. Several major components of this theory are the triadic reciprocal causation model: observational learning and modeling, self-efficacy, and self-regulation (see **Social Cognitive Theory** for more details). Through his social cognitive theory he has influenced education in many ways. His interpretation of children's social development was a specific contribution to the field of early childhood education. Bandura's Bobo doll experiments revealed the power of violence as portrayed by media on children's aggression, and showed methods to diminish aggression, promote prosocial functioning and foster the adoption of moral standards of conduct

(Zimmerman and Schunk, 2003). In the area of children's **cognitive development**, Bandura's studies contradicted the prevalent stage theories, such as **Piaget's**, by emphasizing that children's learning was influenced by their social learning experiences, goals, and development of knowledge and skill. Regarding children's observational learning, Bandura contended that teachers' explanations linked to demonstrations significantly enhance students' conceptual learning. Bandura's work shows that self-efficacy beliefs involve people's self-judgments of performance capabilities in particular domains of functioning. These beliefs not only enhance achievement, they also promote intrinsic motivation and reduce anxiety (Zimmerman and Schunk, 2003). Bandura also explained self-regulation as the degree to which people are able to exert self-regulatory control over their level of functioning and the events in their lives. His theory explains a cyclical process of self-regulation through goal-setting, self-observation, self-judgment, and self-reaction.

Further Readings: Bandura, A. (1986). *Social foundations of thought and action: A social cognitive theory.* Englewood Cliffs, NJ: Prentice-Hall; Pajares, F. (2004). *Albert Bandura: Biographical sketch.* Retrieved 9/06/05, from http://www.emory.edu/EDUCATION/mfp/bandurabio.html; Zimmerman, B. J. and D. H. Schunk (2003). Albert Bandura: The scholar and his contributions to educational psychology. In B. J. Zimmerman and D. H. Schunk, eds. *Educational psychology: A century of contributions.* Mahwah, NJ: Erlbaum.

Srilata Bhattacharyya and Sherri L. Horner

Bank Street

The Bank Street College of Education was founded in 1916 and is considered a leader in child-centered education in the United States. Its mission is to discover the environments in which children can grow and learn to their full potential and to encourage teachers and others to create these environments. Founded by Lucy Sprague **Mitchell** and first known as the Bureau of Educational Experiments, Bank Street has continued to reflect the vision and practice of progressive theorists, educators, and social reformers who believe that we can build a better society through education.

Over the years, Bank Street's education philosophy has been most frequently called either "the Bank Street approach" or the **"developmental-interaction approach."** Although this approach is not unique to Bank Street, the college has been putting the theory behind it into practice for almost 90 years.

The College today comprises an independent, fully accredited Graduate School of Education, serving over 900 students and offering master's degrees in a variety of educational programs; a Division of Children's Programs consisting of a Family Center (a model child-care program for infants, toddlers, and preschool children, as well as a home-based program for 50 infants, toddlers, and preschoolers), a School for Children (serving over 500 students and consisting of a pre-K through 8 demonstration school), and a Head Start program, among others; and a Division of Continuing Education, which offers short-term courses, certificate programs, and staff development to educators and others, as well as direct service programs to children and young adults; major outreach programs, such as New Beginnings, a project to restructure early childhood education in the Newark Public Schools; and the Center for Universal PreKindergarten, which supports educators, improves the quality of Pre-K programs, and, most importantly, achieves positive outcomes for children. Bank Street develops projects, often in conjunction with other educational institutions and communities that address issues arising from the emerging needs of children and families, ranging from literacy to kith and kin care to the introduction of new technologies into the classroom.

Bank Street also has a publications and media group, which publishes books and multimedia materials that over the years have included critically acclaimed and prize-winning products such as *The Voyage of the Mimi* TV series, the *Bank Street Readers* series, and the seventy-two-book *Ready-to-Read* series. Recent collaborations include *Jojo's Circus*, a preschool interactive television show; prekindergarten and **kindergarten** educational materials and teacher curriculum guides. Bank Street also has a Bookstore, which is recognized as New York's best source of material for and about children.

Today Bank Street is one of five institutions of teacher preparation designated as a national resource center for educators by the National Board for Professional Teaching Standards. It is also one of three graduate U.S. teacher-preparation programs to be hailed as exemplary by the National Commission on Teaching and America's Future. In the spring of 2002, the National Council for Accreditation of Teacher Education accredited Bank Street College of Education at the initial teacher preparation and advanced preparation levels. In 2002, the Carnegie Corporation of New York, in partnership with the Annenberg, Ford, and Rockefeller Foundations, selected Bank Street for its ambitious reform initiative, Teachers for a New Era. This project is designed to stimulate construction of excellent teacher preparation programs at selected U.S. colleges and universities.

In today's increasingly technological and multicultural world, Lucy Sprague Mitchell's words and actions continue to inspire us as we seek ways to preserve and strengthen our work in response to the challenges and opportunities that lie ahead. For more information on Bank Street, visit www.bankstreet.edu. *See also* Preschool/Prekindergarten Programs.

Maria Benejan and Toni Porter

Behaviorism

Behaviorism began as a methodological movement in psychology during the early part of the twentieth century. Its founder was John B. **Watson** (1878–1958), who believed that psychology would never become a legitimate scientific discipline until its subject matter was the *behavior* of organisms (both animal and human) and its methods included only objective observations and measures like those used by natural scientists. He rejected the approach of other contemporary psychologists who were using *introspection* to study mental and emotional states, and instead focused on observing how environmental stimuli produced conditioned responses. Although Watson's extreme position about the importance of the environment and learning in shaping human development was rejected, his objective methodological approach has had a major impact through its influence on psychologists such as B. F. Skinner and the eventual widespread application of learning principles to human problems.

Burrhus Frederic Skinner (1904–1990) was the founder of *radical behaviorism*. Like Watson, Skinner carried out his most important experimental work on animals. He did not believe in building theories of behavior; rather, he recommended that scientists generate empirical data from which to draw inductive principles about behavior prediction and control. Skinner called his method the *experimental analysis of behavior*, which was considered "radical" at the time because it accepted states of mind and introspection as existent and worthy of scientific study. However, Skinner did not view mental states as causes of behavior. He saw them as types of verbal behavior and therefore capable of being measured and analyzed.

Skinner created a method of studying behavior that allowed him to control the environment and carefully observe and record its effects. He designed the now famous *Skinner box*, which included a food dispenser and bar connected to another one of his inventions, the *cumulative recorder*. He learned that the rate with which an animal pressed the bar was controlled by stimuli (food pellets) that followed its occurrence, or what Skinner called *contingencies of reinforcement*. He eventually discovered several principles that described how these contingencies worked, namely, positive reinforcement, negative reinforcement, punishment, and extinction. These principles, which describe how consequences affect the future occurrence of behavior, are familiar to anyone who has taken a basic course in psychology, child development, or early childhood education. They are called *operant* principles because they describe what occurs when an organism operates on the environment.

In addition to his operant learning principles, Skinner identified different *schedules of reinforcement* and described the process of *discrimination learning*. Procedures such as *shaping* (reinforcement of successive approximations to the target behavior), *chaining* (reinforcement of simple behaviors that are then strung together to form more complex behavior), and *fading* (the gradual withdrawal of prompts and cues that guide the performance of complex behavior) also emerged from Skinner's experimental work.

In 1938, Skinner published his findings in *The Behavior of Organisms*, which, along with a series of other books and journal articles published in the 1940s and 1950s, formed the conceptual foundation for a group of individuals who established the *Journal of the Experimental Analysis of Behavior* in 1958. It was through this journal as well as professional groups like the Society for the Experimental Analysis of Behavior that like-minded scholars presented and published original research, review articles, and theoretical papers relevant to the behavior of individual organisms.

Another group of scientists, however, was interested in the application of behavioral principles to socially important human problems, many of which involved typically developing children as well as children with disabilities. They did not study behavior in the laboratory; instead, they observed children and their caregivers in natural settings such as homes, preschool programs, and early intervention classrooms, the very places where socially important behaviors were likely to occur. Within these settings, this group of researchers used the inductive approach to research that Skinner used and developed observation methods and research designs that allowed them to conduct experimental analyses of individual child and adult behavior. They called themselves *applied behavior analysts.* More than any other group of behaviorists, it was they who identified the contingencies and contextual features of early education settings that promoted adaptive behaviors in children with and without disabilities. In 1968, the first issue of the *Journal of Applied Behavior Analysis* (JABA) was published. It included an article, "Some Current Dimensions of Applied Behavior Analysis" in which the authors, Donald Baer, Montrose Wolf, and Todd Risley, described the central features of the ABA approach.

Over the course of the next several decades, applied behavior analysts repeatedly demonstrated that procedures based on operant principles, in combination with others such as modeling, could be utilized effectively by parents and early education teachers to address a wide variety of behavior and learning problems. Mild to moderate problems in children with and without disabilities such as high rates of social isolation, opposition, and aggression and low rates of turn taking, sharing, resting during naptime, and following instructions were (among many other behaviors) subject to teacher intervention by the proper application of operant procedures such as differential attention (praise and ignoring), timeout (sit and watch), and prompting, fading, and shaping. One of the goals of this work was to allow children to come under the control of their *natural communities of reinforcement* where they would continue to learn in response to the consequences typically present in teacher-directed and peer-group contexts. Many of these studies were conducted in preschools at the University of Washington, the University of Kansas, and the University of Illinois (where Sidney Bijou directed the Child Behavior Laboratory).

Another area in which applied behavior analysts made a major contribution is in the development of procedures for promoting language, both in typically developing children and children with disabilities. *Incidental teaching*, for example, was used initially to promote more elaborate language in children from low-income families who were attending compensatory preschool programs, and was eventually modified to address the language deficits of children with disabilities. Incidental teaching opportunities occur when a child shows an interest in something, such as a play material, by approaching and reaching for it or asking for help in obtaining it. By showing such interest, the child defines a topic of instruction for the teacher who can then briefly model a new language form or encourage the child to practice an already established one.

Although there is impressive evidence that operant-based procedures have positive effects when used with typically developing children, there is even more evidence for the beneficial effects of these procedures on children with disabilities. A well-known example is the research of Ivar Lovaas who investigated the effects of operant procedures on the behavior of young autistic children. Today, intervention methods based on his approach (discrete trial training) and the work of numerous other researchers who have focused on improving the lives of autistic children and their families are being applied by early childhood educators and parents in nearly every state in the country. Applied behavior analysts also have developed procedures to address adaptive, social-emotional, physical, and cognitive delays in children with a wide range of disabilities that can be found in research journals such as *Topics in Early Childhood Special Education* and the *Journal of Early Intervention.*

Despite the extensive empirical support for the positive effects of operant-based procedures, there remains a persistent devaluation and misunderstanding of this approach among professionals in the fields of early childhood regular and special education. Although the use of sit and watch (timeout) is the most common source of controversy, there also is disagreement about the use of praise, both because of the narrowness of the concept and as a detriment to intrinsic motivation. Common criticisms of the behavioral perspective as it has been applied in early childhood regular and special education can be found in the bibliography and also traced through the URL links listed at the end of this entry.

In addition to developing and evaluating operant-based procedures used in response to child behavior and learning problems, applied behavior analysts brought their research methods to bear on the *environmental contexts* in which children and teachers spend their time, and in which teaching methods from a variety of disciplines are used. The division of space into areas, type and arrangement of play materials, activity schedules, mealtime routines, transition procedures, group size, and location of staff are common physical, programmatic, and social features that characterize all early childhood classrooms. Early educators have known for some time about the importance of these features for ensuring that children productively engage the environment, and some have written extensively about ways the classroom environment should be organized. However, their recommendations have been based largely on theory, teaching experience, and anecdotal accounts of classroom organization.

The experimental analyses of the organizational features of early childhood settings began with the work of Todd Risley and his colleagues who focused on the operation of caregiving environments such as day-care centers, nursing homes, and after-school recreation programs. This work was undertaken for two reasons. First, if a setting is organized to encourage children's engagement and learning and to make it easier for teachers to perform routine care, there will be more time for teachers to play and talk with them as well as teach them. In this type of environment, children will engage in far less disruption, aggression, and noncompliance, reducing the need for operant-based procedures. Thus, the first aim was the promotion of favorable conditions for human development and the prevention of child behavior problems.

The second reason for undertaking such analyses is that well-organized classrooms make it more likely that operant-based procedures will be effective when they do need to be used. Procedures such as modeling, differential attention, sit and watch (time-out), and incidental teaching depend for their optimal effects on a well-organized, stimulating environment. For example, in order for a brief time-out from reinforcement to be effective, the child must want to return to activities that are stimulating and fun and refrain from behaving in ways that result in brief removal from those activities.

The effects of specific ways of organizing classroom space, presenting materials, or scheduling daily events on children's engagement with their surroundings cannot be explained strictly within the framework of Skinner's operant learning principles. It is more useful to think of them as examples of the more recent concept of *setting events*, complex social and environmental conditions that set the occasion for and make it more likely that previously acquired behavior will occur. For example, if meals are served family-style in early childhood classrooms, with bowls of food passed from child to child (rather than full plates simply being handed to children), the environmental and social conditions are present for children and teachers to talk about the food and for children to learn about serving themselves appropriate portions. This context also provides teachers with opportunities to focus on children who require individualized teaching to develop more elaborate language.

The contributions of behaviorism (specifically applied behavior analysis) to early childhood regular and special education range from operant-based teaching strategies and procedures that address behavior problems to experimental demonstrations that behavior and the procedures designed to change it are inseparable from the context in which they occur. Particularly for early childhood special education, this approach has facilitated a focus on the individual child and the natural environment as the appropriate place for intervention, strategies that are consistent with the *principle of normalization.* Applied behavior analysts and others who have adopted their research methods continue to investigate socially important topics of great interest to early childhood educators.

Further Readings: Baer, Donald M., Montrose M. Wolf, and Todd R. Risley (1968). Some current dimensions of applied behavior analysis. *Journal of Applied Behavior Analysis* 1, 91–97; Horowitz, Frances D. (1992). John B. Watson's legacy: Learning and environment. *Developmental Psychology*, 28, 360–367; Nordquist, Vey M., and Sandra Twardosz (1990). Preventing behavior problems in early childhood education classrooms through environmental organization. *Education and Treatment of Children* 13(4), 274–287; Pierce, David W., and Carl D. Cheney (2004). *Behavior analysis and learning.* Mahwah, NJ: Erlbaum; Strain, Phillip S. (1992). Behaviorism in early intervention. *Topics in Early Childhood Special Education* 1, 121–142; Twardosz, Sandra (1984). Environmental organization: The physical, social, and programmatic context of behavior. *Progress in behavior modification.* Vol. 18. Orlando, FL: Academic Press, pp. 123–161; Warren, Stephen F., and Ann P. Kaiser (1986). Incidental language teaching: A critical review. *Journal of Speech and Hearing Disorders* 51, 291–299.

Web Sites: Behavior Analysis, Division 25 of the American Psychological Association. Available online at http://www.apa.org/divisions/div25/; Center on the Social and Emotional Foundations of Early Learning. Available online at http://www.csefel.uiuc. edu; Stanford Encyclopedia of Psychology. Available online at http://plato.stanford.edu/ entries/behaviorism/.

Vey M. Nordquist, Sandra Twardosz, and William Bryan Higgins

Behavior Management and Guidance

In many early childhood settings, the term *behavior management* is no longer in vogue. Like the word *discipline*, which has also fallen largely out of favor, it carries a connotation of the use of power by teachers, a practice that many in the field do not endorse. The more positive term *guidance*—as used in *Developmentally Appropriate Practice in Early Childhood Settings* (Bredekamp and Copple, 1997)—has replaced both terms in the minds of many early childhood educators, reflecting a movement to a more humanistic and constructivist view of child development where the child is an active participant in his own learning and the teacher is seen as a facilitator. That's not to say, however, that there is no longer a need to understand the principles of *behavior management*—now usually reserved for especially difficult and persistent behavior problems for which techniques associated with **behaviorism** are preferred.

Guidance refers to the teacher's efforts to help children behave in ways that will enhance all aspects of their development and learning, both as individuals and as part of a group. This is most effectively achieved when teachers recognize that inappropriate behavior is an opportunity to teach, not punish. Guided by the ecological theory of Urie **Bronfenbrenner,** teachers can draw upon a wide body of knowledge and skills and consider not only the child but also their own expectations and interactions with the child, the physical and socioemotional environment of the child-care setting, the child's family and **culture**, and the broader community. The most effective strategies available to teachers include understanding risk and protective factors for challenging behavior; preventing challenging behavior by developing a positive, caring relationship with each child and creating a warm and welcoming physical environment and social community within the classroom; and utilizing individualized intervention plans to respond to severe and persistent challenging behavior.

An understanding of the risk and protective factors that shape challenging behavior makes it easier to meet children's needs and help them to succeed. Risk factors have a cumulative effect. A child who has just one faces no more risk of developing challenging behavior than a child with none. But a child who has two is dealing with a risk four times as great (Yoshikawa, 1994). The risk factors for challenging behavior fall into two broad categories, biological and environmental.

Biological risk factors include genes (which influence traits associated with aggressive behavior); **temperament** (problems are more likely when the temperament of the child and the expectations of the family or teacher do not coincide); **Attention Deficit Disorder/Attention Deficit Hyperactivity Disorder** (ADD/ADHD); complications of pregnancy and birth; substance abuse during pregnancy; language and cognition disorders (see also **Learning Disability**); and gender (boys are at greater risk for aggressive behavior than are girls).

Environmental risk factors include problems in the parent–child relationship (which acts as a prototype for the child's future relationships) (see also **Attachment**); **poverty**, and the conditions surrounding it; exposure to **violence** through the media or in person (see also **Domestic Violence**); **child care** (researchers have found a link between problem behavior and the number of hours children spend in child care); and cultural dissonance (respect for a child's culture is essential to formation of a positive self-concept; cultural conflicts between home and school culture can cause challenging behavior).

Increasing protective or opportunity factors can buffer the impact of risk factors and improve children's developmental outcome. This ability to cope with adversity is called *resilience*. A child's most important protective factor against risk is a warm, responsive, consistent relationship with an adult. Although families usually provide this support, nurturing relationships with teachers and other community members can also foster resilience.

The best way to stop challenging behavior is to prevent it from occurring. Children are less likely to resort to challenging behavior when the teacher's approach and the physical and social environment meet their physical, cognitive, cultural, emotional, and social needs. It may be necessary to individualize many aspects of care in order to meet the needs of one particular child, but the effort is worthwhile. When he or she is able to play and learn successfully, it becomes possible for all the children to play and learn successfully. Prevention can keep children with aggressive behavior from accumulating risk factors and slipping into a downward spiral where they are rejected by peers and teachers, fail at school, join a gang, abuse alcohol or drugs, or become delinquent. Prevention is more effective when it begins early, continues over a long period, is developmentally appropriate, takes place in a real-life setting, and works on several fronts (such as home and school) simultaneously.

As resilience research has shown, a caring relationship with a child is a teacher's most powerful tool for preventing and decreasing challenging behavior. With a warm, supportive adult as a guide and model, children learn to understand and control their own feelings and behavior, care about and trust other people, and see things from another's perspective. In response to their teachers' sensitive handling of their anxieties and challenging behaviors, children's confidence and self-concept grow, along with their desire to experience more of these positive feelings. A solid relationship with the child's family also strengthens a teacher's relationship with the child and enables teachers and families to work together for the child's benefit (see also **Families, Parents, and Parent Involvement.**)

Because teachers' attitudes and behaviors make a substantial contribution to the way children behave, it is important for them to be aware of how their own emotions, past experiences, temperament, values, and culture influence their expectations and reactions in the classroom. Self-reflection (see also John **Dewey**) enables teachers to increase their self-control, accept and express their feelings, and respond appropriately to children's intense emotions and difficult behavior.

The physical environment can elicit either aggressive or prosocial behavior, depending on how it is arranged (see also **Environmental Assessments in Early Childhood Education**). Children with challenging behaviors often have trouble functioning in a space filled with restrictions, so the arrangement of the room should enable them to move around without reminders. Low bookcases can divide large spaces into uncluttered areas with different functions like dramatic play, messy play, or quiet reading and listening. Learning centers and shelves should be well organized, inviting, and easily accessible. Since crowding can lead to frustration and aggression, it makes sense to limit and control the number of children who can play in each area. Well-marked boundaries and pathways from one spot to another allow children to feel more comfortable and promote cooperative behavior. It may be necessary to reduce the level of stimulation to facilitate the participation of children who find it hard to deal with classroom noise and bustle—for example, those with attention deficit hyperactivity disorder (ADHD), **fetal alcohol syndrome** (FAS), hearing loss, or hyper-sensitive temperaments.

The social climate also exerts a powerful influence on behavior. Children are less likely to act aggressively in a cohesive and friendly community (DeRosier et al., 1994). As the leader and primary role model in the classroom, the teacher is responsible for establishing the social climate and influencing children's attitudes and behaviors toward one another. Structured cooperative activities that emphasize the group rather than individuals enhance cooperation during unstructured times and teach children to empathize, work together, negotiate, problem-solve, share, and support one another.

When planning the **curriculum**, teachers must think not only of the skill they wish to teach but also of the behavior they are trying to encourage. Ever since Friedrich **Froebel** founded the first **kindergarten**, European American theorists have believed that being able to make meaningful choices empowers children, who, as a result, do not have to look for inappropriate ways to assert their independence. The program should be developmentally appropriate on the basis of the belief that, if a task is too difficult, children will do whatever they need to do to avoid participating and failing. A less structured program with open-ended materials and activities engenders social interaction and prosocial behavior. Close supervision enables teachers to help children who need extra structure and guidance.

Children feel more secure and function better when there is a consistent routine; clear, positively stated rules that they have helped to create; and the minimum number of transitions, which present a special challenge for children with challenging behaviors. Transitions run more smoothly when the teacher makes them fun, warns children of the upcoming change, and uses strategies such as allowing children who are slow to adapt to have more time and giving children jobs to perform (e.g., putting ten blocks on the shelf). Whole-group activities, such as circle and story time, also require extra planning; holding them less often and/or providing alternate activities for certain children may be helpful.

The teacher's approach toward the acquisition of social and emotional skills (see also **Curriculum, Emotional Development**)—a major developmental task of early childhood—is also important in creating a positive social climate. Teaching social and emotional skills proactively highlights their value, makes the classroom ambience more cooperative, and offers children who need special assistance a chance to learn that they might not have had otherwise. Often based on the social cognitive learning theory of Albert **Bandura**, formal social and emotional skills programs use a variety of methods, including didactic teaching, modeling, group discussion, and role playing. Their focus is usually on emotional regulation and empathy, impulse control, anger management, social problem solving, friendship skills, and responding assertively. It is also important for teachers and socially competent peers to talk about feelings and model, encourage, and reinforce social and emotional skills in ordinary daily interactions.

Even when educators use preventive methods consistently, some children may exhibit challenging behavior. In response, teachers commonly use a number of guidance and behavior management techniques based on a variety of theoretical perspectives, including humanistic and psychoanalytic thought, social learning theory, behaviorist theory, the work of Alfred Adler, and the work of Carl **Rogers**. Models range considerably in the degree of teacher control they employ, from low (Haim Ginott, Thomas Gordon, Alfie Kohn), through medium (Rudolf

Dreikurs, William Glasser), to high (Lee Canter, Fredric Jones). High-control methods have found more followers in schools than in early childhood settings. Even the behavioral-based interventions used for very difficult behavior problems (functional assessment, positive behavior support) have many humanistic aspects.

Advocates of low-control strategies believe that children are active participants in their own learning who flourish in a supportive and democratic classroom where they can make their own choices and construct their own values. The teacher's role is to facilitate children's development by attending to their feelings, thoughts, and ideas.

Those who prefer medium control may choose techniques that are often referred to as behavior management, such as positive reinforcement and logical consequences. Positive reinforcement—a pleasant response that follows a behavior and increases its frequency or intensity—is perhaps the most basic of all strategies. Drawn from behaviorism and **social cognitive theory**, positive reinforcement can be verbal or physical, social, or tangible (although tangible rewards are not used with children who are developing normally). A child who has the teacher's positive attention will probably behave more positively; a child who fails to receive positive attention is likely to seek negative attention. It is therefore important to watch for and acknowledge acceptable behavior. Positive reinforcement extends the child's capacities and helps to replace inappropriate behavior with appropriate behavior. Positive reinforcement is most effective when it is delivered immediately and consistently, when it clearly describes the action that is being reinforced, and when it is part of an honest, warm relationship between teacher and child.

Positive reinforcement that takes the form of encouragement is preferred over praise. Encouragement emphasizes behavior and process rather than person and product; recognizes effort and improvement rather than achievement; and lets children know that mistakes are part of learning. Praise, critics charge, motivates children to act for extrinsic reasons and dampens their autonomy, creativity, self-control, self-esteem, and pleasure.

Many teachers utilize natural and logical consequences, a technique popularized by Rudolf Dreikurs, who believed that consequences flow not from the power of adults but from the natural or social order of the real world and that children learn from experiencing the consequences of their own behavior. Some consequences occur naturally, but when natural consequences are too remote or dangerous, teachers may create logical or reasonable consequences instead. The teacher should offer options that relate directly, reasonably, and logically to the child's behavior; the consequences must be enforceable and enforced, but not threatening or punitive.

Punishment—a penalty for wrongdoing, imposed by someone in power who intends it to be unpleasant—provides a quick fix, but its results are fleeting. It suppresses the undesirable behavior only in the punisher's presence and must increase in intensity to remain effective. Punishment undermines the relationship between adult and child and creates a distrust of adults. Although in theory educators frown upon punishment, it sometimes creeps into classrooms in the guise of time-out, a technique that has created controversy in the early childhood community. Rooted in social learning theory and behaviorism, it technically means time-out from positive reinforcement and typically involves removing a child from the group to sit in a remote area of the room on a specified chair, for one minute for each year of his age, to think about his behavior. Critics maintain that time-out teaches children that the use of power to control others is acceptable and does not help them learn to behave appropriately. It is also said to damage self-esteem by humiliating children in front of their peers, a dire punishment for those from cultures where being part of the group is paramount.

When a child's challenging behavior is severe and/or persistent, an individualized intervention is called for. Two of the most effective and widely adopted behavior management strategies are often used together: functional assessment and positive behavior support. Developed in the late 1970s and early 1980s in work with persons with developmental disabilities, both methods are derived from applied behavior analysis, an offshoot of behaviorism. Because they are so effective in determining the cause of behavioral problems and formulating positive strategies to address them, functional assessment and positive behavior support are often required under the **Individuals with Disabilities Education Act** (IDEA) Amendments of 1997.

The underlying principle of functional assessment is that every challenging behavior can be thought of as a child's solution to a problem and a form of communication. The technique requires educators to look at the world through the child's eyes, figure out how the behavior benefits the child, and teach an acceptable behavior that can fulfill those needs instead. The focus of a functional assessment is the child's immediate environment, which provides vital clues about where the behavior is coming from, why it is happening at a particular time and place, the logic behind it, and the function it serves for the child. Even if the behavior is inappropriate, the function seldom is.

A functional assessment and positive behavior support plan are best achieved by a team of all those who work with the child—family, teachers, bus drivers, consultants, and so on. The team's first task is to develop a hypothesis about the function of the challenging behavior and the environmental conditions that cause it, drawing on resources such as the child's records, interviews with parents and teachers, and observation using an A-B-C analysis. Teachers and/or other observers note antecedents (A) or events that take place just before the challenging behavior and seem to trigger it; behavior (B) that can be measured and altered; and consequences (C) that occur after the behavior, including the teacher's own responses to it. These observations are systematically recorded until a clear pattern emerges, confirming or negating the hypothesis about the function.

Functional assessment postulates three possible functions:
- *The child gets something* (attention from an adult or a peer, access to object or activity).
- *The child avoids or escapes from something* (unwelcome requests, difficult tasks, activities, peers, or adults).
- *The child changes the level of stimulation* (Karsh et al., 1995).

Once the function is understood, it becomes possible to design a positive behavior support plan to enable the child to meet her needs. An intervention that is effective in teaching a child how to get what she wants through appropriate means usually utilizes three different methods: changing the environment (the antecedents and the consequences) so that the challenging behavior becomes unnecessary; replacing the challenging behavior with appropriate behavior that achieves the same outcome for the child more quickly and with less effort; and ignoring the challenging behavior. As the plan is implemented, the team continues to monitor the child's progress in order to evaluate and revise the plan if necessary.

Teachers frequently depend on more than one strategy. Every child is unique, and each requires an approach that fits his or her state of mind, temperament, developmental stage, and culture. With several strategies at their disposal, teachers can choose one or a combination that suits the circumstances. At the same time, it is important for teachers to believe in the strategy—it is unlikely to work if they do not feel comfortable with it or understand the philosophy behind it. *See also* Constructivism; Gender and Gender Stereotyping in Early Childhood Education.

Further Readings: Bredekamp, Sue, and Carol Copple (1997). *Developmentally appropriate practice in early childhood settings*, Revised ed. Washington, DC: National Association for the Education of Young Children; DeRosier, M. E., A. H. N. Cillessen, J. D. Coie, and K. A. Dodge (1994). Group social context and children's aggressive behavior. *Child Development* 65, 1068-1079; Kaiser, Barbara, and Judy Sklar Rasminsky (2007). *Challenging behavior in young children: Understanding, preventing, and responding effectively,* 2nd ed. Boston: Allyn and Bacon; Karsh, K. G., A. C. Repp, C. M. Dahlquist, and D. Munk (1995). In vivo functional assessment and multi-element interventions for problem behaviors of students with disabilities in classroom settings. *Journal of Behavioral Education* 5, 189-210; National Association for the Education of Young Children (2003). Preventing and responding to behaviors that challenge children and adults [Special issue]. *Young Children* 58(4), 10-57; O'Neill, Robert E., Robert H. Horner, Richard W. Albin, Jeffrey R. Sprague, Keith Storey, and J. Stephen Newton (1997). *Functional assessment and program development for problem behavior: A practical handbook*, 2nd ed. Pacific Grove, CA: Brooks/Cole Publishing; Sandall, Susan, and Michaelene Ostrosky, eds. (1999). *Practical ideas for addressing challenging behaviors.* Longmont and Denver, CO: Sopris West and the Division for Early Childhood of the Council for Exceptional Children; Slaby, Ronald G., Wendy C. Roedell, Diana Arezzo, and Kate Hendrix (1995). *Early violence prevention: Tools for teachers of young children.* Washington, DC: National Association for the Education of Young Children; Yoshikawa, H. (1994). Prevention of cumulative protection: Effects of early family support and education on chronic delinquency and its risks. *Psychological Bulletin* 115, 28-54.

Barbara Kaiser and Judy Sklar Rasminsky

Biculturalism

Biculturalism refers to the process through which individuals enter into contact with a new culture and create a new identity by meshing values, attitudes, and behaviors of their own culture into the new one. In other words, bicultural individuals adapt to ways valued in the new culture while retaining an attachment and identity with their culture of origin. Often, biculturalism has been discussed as a capacity to move from one culture to another with relative ease and learning how to navigate and participate in both worlds. For most children living in multicultural contexts, the process of biculturalization involves the negotiation of their parents' cultural beliefs and attitudes and those of the dominant society.

Bicultural identity formation is a dynamic process that is constantly shifting and being constructed according to specific circumstances. Bicultural identity has also been defined as intercultural identity. Intercultural identity refers to an identity that works toward integration and meshing of two cultures, rather than separation and division. Understanding the importance of biculturalism is essential in the area of early childhood education, given the high influx of **immigration** taking place in the world (particularly in North American and some European countries), and recent discussions on capacity building within Indigenous communities. By supporting biculturalism, the field of early childhood education is conveying a commitment to the protection and promotion of child well-being while sustaining culture, traditional languages, and community values.

To fully understand biculturalism, it is important to distinguish it from processes of acculturation. Acculturation is defined as the process through which individuals change the attitudes, values, beliefs and behaviors associated with their culture of origin and replace them with those of the mainstream society. At the extreme, acculturation involves abandoning old identities and embracing those of the dominant society. The process of acculturation has been linked to a variety of problematic situations (e.g., high-risk behaviors in adolescence such as violence and drug use) that can be attributed to a lack of connection with the culture of origin, a lack of understanding of mainstream society, and/or the absence of opportunities to interact with the dominant culture in meaningful ways. Acculturation is also associated with children's feeling as though they have little connection with their cultural origins. This lack of connection might be related to the fact that children often feel a need to belong to the dominant culture and yearn for acceptance without undue attention to cultural differences. This need for belonging is a complex issue that is enmeshed within the challenges brought on by racism, discrimination, and **poverty,** which are experienced by many immigrant, minority, and Indigenous groups. When biculturalism has been viewed from a perspective of acculturation, it has been defined as successful or additive acculturation. In general, the negative effects of extreme acculturation are not reflected in the process of biculturalization, which is linked to positive adjustment for minority children.

Biculturalism has also been analyzed from a resilience perspective. From this approach, it is maintained that "biculturalism is a resilient outcome because it implies a set of values, behaviors, and social service availability that allows positive adaptation despite the constraints given by poverty and discrimination" (Infante and Lamond, 2003, p. 169). It is often argued that some minority groups have high resilience in spite of the adversity they have faced. Some of the factors that may contribute to higher resilience might include social skills, support networks, strong family relationships and cultural attachment. This way "as the child is exposed to the acculturation or biculturation process, the child has a strong foundation and can accept some different ways of thinking and behaving" (p. 184).

Bicultural development has also been closely linked to bilingual competence (see **bilingual education**). Language and culture are closely intertwined, and participation in a culture is accomplished in part through learning the language and thereby being able to participate in communal activities and communication practices. In the case of children, bilingualism allows them to maintain family ties and relationships with family members, thereby providing a conduit to learn about cultural values firsthand.

Early childhood programs represent an essential institution in working toward the facilitation of a bicultural identity development for minority and Indigenous children as well as in supporting families in the bicultural development of their children. Early childhood educators could play an integral role in supporting a bicultural identity among children. By starting the process of supporting the development and well-being of minority and Indigenous children, educators could ensure that these children eventually participate more successfully in the mainstream society. While bilingual development is often recognized in training programs for early childhood practitioners, biculturalism is not widely understood or proactively supported.

To advance biculturalism, there are a number of requirements for early childhood professionals. First, a thorough understanding of bicultural development is essential—one that involves attention to issues of race, discrimination, and power. Second, a respectful understanding of the children's and families' background is highly beneficial for early childhood educators. Third, early childhood educators would benefit from a thorough understanding of the dynamics of the mainstream culture within which the program they are delivering is embedded. In other words, educators need to understand the source and significance of the values on which their programs rest and the impact that the program has on the development of biculturalism among these particular children. Fourth, early childhood practitioners need to be able to work in partnership with families so they can successfully support the needs of the family, specifically with regard to biculturalism.

In spite of the numerous challenges to supporting biculturalism in early childhood educational programs, there are successful examples both in the United States and abroad. In the United States, the Kamehameha Early Education Program (KEEP), implemented in Hawaii with Hawaiian children and on a Navajo Reservation in Arizona, provided insights into the incorporation of cultural knowledge into mainstream education. Researchers involved in this program concluded that "if children need to be educated in ways that are compatible with their cultures, then solutions to educational needs and problems need to be developed locally, with and for the different populations and communities that schools are trying to serve" (Jordan, 1995, p. 97). In Aotearoa/New Zealand, an early childhood education program (Te Whariki) has been developed with a strong commitment to the development of biculturalism (Ritchie, 2003). Through this program, Maori children are perceived as bicultural and their own cultural knowledge is validated within the broader society. The program challenges ideas of assimilation of Indigenous peoples into dominant society and allows for the development of a society that supports social justice through the acknowledgment of the importance of raising bicultural children.

Biculturalism is considered a predictor of positive adjustment and psychological well-being of immigrant and Indigenous children (Suarez-Orozco and Suarez-Orozco, 2001). Moreover, biculturalism is an essential element of a society focused on social justice since it encourages members from minority ethnic, racial, and religious groups to preserve their own values, beliefs, traditions, ways of being;

while at the same time allowing them to become active members of the host society. As defined by the United Nation's *Convention on the Rights of the Child*, being and becoming bicultural is a basic right of children. Moreover, it is a necessity in today's global society. *See also* Race and Ethnicity in Early Childhood Education.

Further Readings: Ballenger, C. (1992). Because you like us: The language of control. *Harvard Educational Review* 2(2), 199–208; Ballenger, C. (1999). *Teaching other people's children: Literacy and learning in a bilingual classroom.* New York: Teachers College Press; Infante, Francisca, and Alexandra Lamond (2003). Resilience and biculturalism: The Latino experience in the United States. In Edith Grotberg, ed. *Resilience for today: Gaining strength from adversity.* Westport, CT: Praeger, pp. 161–188; Jordan, C. (1995). Creating cultures of schooling: Historical and conceptual background of the KEEP/Rough Rock collaboration. *The Bilingual Research Journal* 19(1), 83–100; Knight, Ann (1994). Pragmatic biculturalism and the primary school teacher. In Adrian Blackledge, ed. *Teaching bilingual children.* Staffordshire, UK: Trentham Books, pp. 101–111; Ritchie, Jenny (2003). Bicultural development within an early childhood teacher education programme. *International Journal of Early Years Education* 11(1), 43–56; Soto, Lourdes D. (1999). The multicultural worlds of childhood in postmodern America. In Carol Seefeldt, ed. *The early childhood curriculum: Current findings in theory and practice.* New York: Teachers College Press, pp. 218–242; Suarez-Orozco, Carola, and Marcelo Suarez-Orozco (2001). *Children of immigration.* Cambridge, MA: Harvard University Press; Tharp, R., and R. Gallimore (1988). *Rousing minds to life: Teaching, learning, and schooling in social context.* Cambridge, UK: Cambridge University Press.

Veronica Pacini-Ketchabaw

Bilingual Education

Bilingual education in the United States has traditionally referred to the education of children whose home language is not English. Typically, the goal of bilingual programs has been to raise the English fluency of the students to a level that will allow them to function in English language classrooms. Once they are judged to be sufficiently fluent in English (usually through a mixture of academic achievement and language fluency testing), the students are transitioned to English-only instruction. Rarely is the goal to promote high levels of proficiency in two languages, but rather to provide sufficient instruction and support that allows the child to exit from the bilingual program as quickly as possible with no ongoing support for the home language. Thus, the term bilingual education is a misnomer in light of the actual goals and program practices in most U.S. educational settings.

Currently, it is estimated that about 20 percent of the school age population in the United States speaks a language other than English at home; between 14 and 16 percent of children speak Spanish as their home language (Reyes and Moll, 2004), and another 4–6 percent speak something other than Spanish. Bilingualism, or nearly equal proficiency in two languages, has been studied and debated for decades in this country. In 1968, the Bilingual Education Act was passed, which required teachers and schools to meet the cultural and linguistic needs of children who did not speak English. This led to the proliferation of bilingual programs in school districts, followed by many studies evaluating the effectiveness of different approaches to bilingual education. Disagreements over the value of bilingualism in the context of U.S. social policies has resulted in an English-only movement that has severely restricted bilingual education programs in some states. With the enactment of the federal **No Child Left Behind Act** in 2001, current policies emphasize the rapid acquisition of English without explicit attention to the role of the home language in long-term academic achievement. In fact several states have adopted English-only policies and many more repeatedly submit to voters English-only ballot initiatives that would require English only in all spheres of public life.

Children whose home language is not English are considered *English-language learners* (ELLs). They are also frequently described as *linguistic minority students* or more recently as *linguistically diverse students*. As children acquire a second language, one language may be more dominant because they are using that language more than the other at a particular point in time. Frequently children demonstrate a *language imbalance* as they progress toward bilingualism. During this time, children may not perform as well as native speakers in either language. This is a normal and most often temporary phase of emergent bilingualism (see **Second Language Acquisition in Early Childhood**). It is rare for young children to achieve a balanced bilingualism without special assistance, but most can achieve it given sufficient exposure, opportunities, and motivation for use. For this reason, it is important to assess bilingual children on both their first language and English to monitor the progress of their bilingualism.

There are several models for early childhood bilingual education in the United States. Bilingual Education programs are generally expected to divide classroom interaction between English and the child's first/home language. However, the percentage of time actually devoted to native language versus English varies enormously depending on the language fluency of the teaching staff and the goals of the program. Bilingual programs must have at least one teacher who is fluent in the child's first language. Examples of bilingual programs include dual-language classes (which include minority-language and English-speaking children), maintenance bilingual education, transitional bilingual education, English submersion with native language and ESL support, and integrated bilingual education. The goals of such programs vary from transitioning into English as quickly as possible, maintaining and supporting home language development while simultaneously supporting English acquisition, or promoting second language development for both English speakers and non-English speakers, that is, dual language programs.

Dual language programs are increasingly found in the United States. There are a variety of terms used to describe these programs: Two-way immersion, two-way bilingual education, developmental bilingual education, and dual language education. Dual language classrooms contain an approximate balance of language minority and native English-speaking children. Both languages are used throughout the curriculum in approximately equal amounts so that all children will become bilingual and eventually biliterate and multicultural. English-language learners are expected to become proficient in their home language as well as English. Native English speakers are expected to develop language and literacy skills in a second language while making normal progress in English.

A second approach to bilingual education is through Primary/Native Language Programs. In these programs all or most interactions are in the child's first or primary language. In these settings, the teachers must be fluent in the child's home language. The goals include development and support for the child's first language with little or no systematic exposure to English during the early phases. The child's home language is used for the majority of classroom time with the justification being that the concepts, skills, and knowledge will transfer from the first language into English. The home language is promoted to support cognitive and literacy development in a language the child understands, and to preserve cultural identity. One such program—the Carpenteria Preschool Program, a Spanish language preschool in California—has been studied and evaluated to determine the long-term effects of first language instruction during the preschool years on future language and literacy skills. Researchers concluded that first language instruction during the preschool years fostered both native language and English language fluency (Campos and Rosemberg, 1995).

English Immersion is another common approach to bilingual education. Immersion simply means that students learn everything in English. The extreme case of this is described as a "sink or swim" approach to learning English. However, teachers using immersion programs generally strive to deliver lessons in simple and understandable language that allows students to internalize English while experiencing the typical educational opportunities in the preschool or kindergarten curriculum. Sometimes students are pulled out for "English as a Second Language (ESL)" programs, which provide them with instruction—again in English— geared for language acquisition. The goals of English-only classrooms include development of English, but not development or maintenance of the child's first language.

Transitional bilingual programs are increasingly the predominant model in most U.S. school-age programs. The purpose of this approach is to achieve enough English language proficiency to move quickly into the English-only mainstream. In early childhood settings, although the research is limited, there is some evidence that this model is also the most common one, particularly when multiple languages are represented in the child population and/or the primary-grade classrooms are English-only. This approach typically provides one or two years of support for the home language while children transition into English-only classrooms. The goal is to increase the use of English while decreasing the child's reliance on the home language for communication and instructional activities. Early childhood programs that explicitly use this model are presumed to be helping the child transition quickly into English and become assimilated into the majority culture. The amount of support for home language development and culture varies according to multiple program and community factors.

Historically, research on the effectiveness of bilingual education programs has produced mixed results, in part because program evaluation studies—featuring appropriate comparison groups and random assignment of subjects or controls for preexisting differences—are extremely difficult to design. Moreover, there is considerable variation among the instructional approaches, settings, children, and communities being compared in such studies. While numerous studies have documented the benefits of bilingual programs, much of this research has faced methodological criticisms—as noted by a recent expert panel of the National Research Council (August and Hakuta, 1997).

When designing and evaluating the effectiveness of bilingual versus monolingual approaches in preschool, it is important to consider the distinctions between preschool and elementary school. During the early childhood years, children are actively acquiring a first language that will form the base for future cognitive and academic development. They are just developing the basic language skills necessary for benefiting from formal instruction; young children are also highly responsive to their social and language environment, and they are intricately embedded in their family culture, values, and language patterns. For these reasons and others, preschool is an ideal time for young children to learn two languages— their own as well as that of the dominant culture.

Recent program evaluations have tended to favor models that allow children to develop their native language skills to high levels of proficiency while they are learning English. The results of preschool program evaluations have demonstrated that native language instruction can confer long-term language and literacy advantages; and that high-quality preschool bilingual programs can promote both home language and English acquisition. In contrast, well-designed and carefully implemented English immersion programs for ELLs can lead to short-term gains in English acquisition (Rice and Wilcox, 1995), but children in these programs tended to lose their native language fluency over time (Oller and Eilers, 2002).

Recent research has linked loss of home language with poor long-term academic outcomes. R. Slavin and A. Cheung (2005) reviewed all the experimental studies on reading instruction for English language learners and concluded that teaching reading in the child's home language and English at different times of the day leads to the best reading outcomes. Thus, early instruction in both languages can promote both goals and can also be used as the foundation of a two-way bilingual program that promotes Spanish acquisition for English-only children in addition to English fluency for ELL children.

Other researchers (Oller and Eilers, 2002) have also found that for Spanish speaking children learning English, two-way education as opposed to English Immersion showed few if any long-term advantages or disadvantages with regard to language and literacy in English, but that two-way education *(dual language)* showed significant advantages for bilingual children in acquisition of language and literacy in Spanish. An unexpected finding of their research was that children who speak Spanish at home quickly come to prefer to speak in English and that by third grade, many ELL children had lost fluency in their home language.

Lily Wong Fillmore (1996) has also documented the loss of language and cultural patterns among U.S. immigrant populations. She describes the pain and personal sense of loss that she experienced as a Chinese immigrant when she lost the ability to communicate with family members and the sense of shame associated with their cultural practices.

The important point to keep in mind for young ELL children is that their home language and cultural practices are fragile and susceptible to dominance by the English language and mainstream culture. The consequences of learning

English too early without systematic support for the home language are certainly detrimental socially, culturally, and recent evidence points to negative long-term academic outcomes.

The literature on bilingual education has repeatedly reported linguistic, cognitive, metalinguistic, and early literacy advantages for children who successfully become bilingual over monolinguals. It is clear that many conceptual, literacy, and language skills transfer from the child's first language to English. However, there are many unanswered questions around the impact of social class and bilingual education for very young children who have not yet developed proficiency in their first language. When ELL children from low SES families enter our early childhood programs, what are the costs of adding English when their native language abilities are significantly delayed? How much native language fluency is necessary before adding a second language? Does this vary by individual child characteristics and the resources of the program? While there are clearly social, economic, and cultural benefits to becoming bilingual and biliterate, the research has yet to conclusively describe the methods for achieving this goal.

Nevertheless, a consensus of researchers in bilingual education and language acquisition recognizes that the following propositions have strong empirical support and implications for early childhood: Native-language instruction does not retard the acquisition of English; Well-developed skills in the child's home language are associated with high levels of long-term academic achievement; Bilingualism is a valuable skill, for individuals and for the country. *See also* Language Diversity; Literacy.

Further Readings: Bialystok, E. (2001). Bilingualism in development: Language, literacy and cognition. Cambridge, UK: Cambridge University Press; Espinosa, L. (2006). The social, cultural, and linguistic components of school readiness in young Latino children. In L. M. Beaulieu, ed. *The social-emotional development of young children from diverse backgrounds.* Baltimore: National Black Child Development Institute Press; Espinosa, L., and S. Burns (2003). Early literacy for young children and English-language learners. In C. Howes, ed. *Teaching 4-8 year-olds literacy, math, multiculturalism, and classroom community.* Baltimore: Paul H. Brookes, pp. 47–69; Garcia, E. E. (2005). *Teaching and learning in two languages: Bilingualism and schooling in the United States.* New York: Teachers College Press; Genesee, F., J. Raradis, and M. Crago (2004). *Dual language development and disorders: A handbook on bilingualism and second language learning.* Baltimore: Paul H. Brookes; Oller, D. K. and R. Eilers, R., eds. (2002). *Language and literacy in bilingual children.* Clevedon, UK: Multilingual Matters; Rodriguez, J. L., D. Duran, R. M. Diaz, and L. Espinosa (1995). The impact of bilingual preschool education on the language development of Spanish-speaking children. *Early Childhood Research Quarterly* 10, 475–490; Slavin, R., and M. Calderon (2005). Succeeding in reading with English language learners. ASCD Audio CD; Tabors, P. (1997). *One child, two languages: A guide for preschool educators of children learning English as a second language.* Baltimore, MD: Paul H. Brookes; Winsler, A., R. M. Diaz, L. Espinosa, and J. L. Rodriguez (1999). When learning a second language does not mean losing the first: Bilingual language development in low-income, Spanish-speaking children attending bilingual preschool. *Child Development* 70(2), 349–362.

Linda M. Espinosa

Binet, Alfred (1857–1911)

Alfred Binet was a French psychologist who studied and researched a wide variety of topics dealing with the mental capacity of humans. His work has impacted the field of education primarily in regard to intelligence testing, albeit a small example of his contributions to general psychology. Many of his findings were anticipatory of future research in psychology. Throughout his lifetime, Binet published extensive works on topics ranging from psychophysics to creativity and launched the publication of *L'Année Psychologique*, which remains a prominent psychology journal in France today.

Alfred Binet was born in July 1857, in Nice, France. His physician father and artistic mother separated when Alfred was young and from then on his mother took responsibility for his upbringing. At fifteen years of age, he studied at the prestigious Louis-le-Grand and was rewarded for his exemplary capabilities in literary composition and translation. He studied both law and medicine, and while he held a degree in law, did not continue either vocation. In his twenties he was granted permission as a reader at the Bibliothèque Nationale, wherein he began to read about developments in psychology.

The works of both Théodule Ribot and John Stuart Mill intrigued a young Binet and piqued his interest in sensory and associationistic psychology. In the 1880s he was introduced to Jean-Martin Charcot at the Salpêtrière Hospital, during which time he observed, experimented, and published extensively on hypnosis and hysteria. In defending a controversial theory and questionable experimentation, Binet gradually came to understand the effect of suggestibility on psychological experimentation.

Binet married Laure Balbiani in 1884 and their two daughters, Madeleine and Alice, were born in 1885 and 1887, respectively. Binet left the Salpêtrière in 1890 and conducted home experiments with his daughters, systematically observing their behavior and responses. His published works detailing these experiments suggest a budding interest in individual differences and measuring intelligence. Binet's test of his daughter's ability to differentiate the relative size of collections prefaced conservation studies by Jean **Piaget**.

Soon afterwards, Binet took a volunteer position at the Laboratory of Experimental Psychology at the Sorbonne, which led to a position as director in 1894. Along with Henry Beaunis he established the psychology journal *L'Année Psychologique* in this first year; many of his collaborative works with Théodore Simon on intelligence were published through this journal. This publication is arguably his most significant contribution to psychology.

Binet's experimental research extended to schoolchildren and Victor Henri briefly assisted him on investigations of visual memory and inquiry into individual psychology. Binet's writings reflected a growing understanding that intelligence could be measured as well as of the individual differences in intelligence. Toward the end of the century he joined La Societé Libre pour l'Étude Psychologique de l'Enfant (the Free Society for the Psychological Study of the Child) and was selected to a Commission on the Education of Retarded Children by the French government in 1904. This affiliation as well as the addition of Théodore Simon to the laboratory at the Sorbonne gave way to the development of **intelligence tests** for which he is known.

Motivated by the desire to identify deficiencies that determine mental subnormality, Binet and Simon set out to design an instrument to aid in this process. Their work culminated in a series of age-related items indicating the child's mental abilities. While Binet consistently favored classifying rather than quantifying intelligence, future uses and revisions of the original Binet–Simon intelligence tests have given rise to a number of scoring systems such as the **intelligence quotient** (IQ).

Within his lifetime, Alfred Binet foreshadowed many modern research topics in experimental psychology. His multitudinous literary contributions offer preliminary insight into a vast array of subjects relating to the workings of the human mind. His research emphasis on the variable intelligence of children provided an initial framework for measuring and understanding the individual differences of both typically and atypically developing children.

Further Readings: Binet, Alfred, and Theodore Simon (1980). *The development of intelligence in children.* Nashville, TN: Williams Printing Company; Binet, Alfred (1915). *A method of measuring the intelligence of young children.* Chicago, IL: Chicago Medical Book Company; Kimble, Gregory A., and Michael Wertheimer (1991). *Portraits of pioneers in psychology,* Vol. 3. Mahwah, NJ: Erlbaum; Palmer, Joy A. (2001). *Fifty major thinkers on education: From Confucius to Dewey.* London: Routledge; Wolf, Theta H. (1973). *Alfred Binet.* Chicago: University of Chicago Press.

Sia Haralampus

Black Caucus (NAEYC)

The Black Caucus of the **National Association for the Education of Young Children** (NAEYC) was founded in 1969 during an NAEYC national conference held in Salt Lake City, Utah. Upon arrival, blacks and other people of color were openly discouraged from attending not only the conference, but also the opening session held at the Mormon Tabernacle. Four Black Board members—Evangeline Ward, the NAEYC president, Ira Gibbons, Canary Girardeau, and Carrie Cheek—approached J. D. Andrews, an NAEYC staff member, to help organize a meeting to discuss the present situation and how blacks could become more active and prominent within the organization, giving them a chance to influence decisions and make policy through the conference and throughout NAEYC's vast affiliate network.

As a result, the conference format was reorganized into committee meetings designed to discuss the treatment of citizens of color in this country who were working in the early childhood education field. NAEYC also decided that it would never again hold its conference in a city where people of color experienced such blatant discrimination, and the Black Caucus was officially formed. According to someone who attended the seminar, the Salt Lake City conference was a turning point for NAEYC to break away from its past of exclusion and begin its efforts to reach out to people of color.

Each year since its founding, the Black Caucus has met during the NAEYC annual conference and has sponsored either an event or meeting open to anyone concerned about the welfare of black children. Because of the commitment that NAEYC staff leaders Marilyn Smith and J. D. Andrews had to diversity within the organization and within the field, the Black Caucus, under their leadership, has had strong support for maintaining its identity. In addition to arranging meeting space during its annual conference, NAEYC has also been receptive to the recommendations the Caucus has made to the association.

Through the years, the Black Caucus has been concerned with issues affecting the status of African American children and African American leaders within the association and in field of early childhood education. Caucus members have weighed in on controversial topics such as Ebonics (the language of the black community), cultural dimensions of **developmentally appropriate practices**, center accreditation policies, **parent involvement**, teacher training and professional development, and **bilingual education**. The Caucus has recruited members to run for Board seats and to serve on major committees within the association. Always vigilant to represent perspectives from the black community, the Black Caucus has held many spirited meetings and each year participants look forward to the opportunity to network and meet new colleagues in the early childhood education field. The Black Caucus has also sponsored powerful and memorable conference sessions focused on the black child, drawing upon such national experts as Drs. Evangeline Ward, Barbara Bowman, Asa Hilliard and Hector Myers, Betty Shabazz, Janice Hale, Evelyn Moore, and Jack Daniel. The Black Caucus has also served as a study and support group for blacks in this field. It has provided not only a community of support to these individuals but has also been responsible for the development of leadership in black educators and members of the organization.

A chairman who is selected by the group and serves for a term averaging from three to five years leads the Black Caucus. Past chairmen have included Canary Girardeau, Carrie Cheek, Barbara Ferguson Kamara, Dwayne A. Crompton, Carol Brunson (Phillips) Day, Gayle Cunningham, Marci Young, and Shyrelle Eubanks.

In 2000, the Black Caucus became known as the NAEYC Black Caucus Interest Group. In addition to holding its annual gathering, the organization has also begun to participate with several other NAEYC interest groups in a celebration of diversity. Beginning in 2002, the Black Caucus Interest Group began presenting a Leadership for Children Award for excellence in serving children and families. Dwayne A. Crompton, Edward M. Greene, Barbara Bowman and Carol Brunson Day are past recipients of the award.

Carol Brunson Day

Blow, Susan Elizabeth (1843–1916)

Susan Elizabeth Blow was born in St. Louis, Missouri, in 1843 and is credited with establishing the first public, continuous kindergarten in the United States. Known as the "Mother of the Kindergarten," Blow was recognized by her father for her intelligence and was supported by him throughout her life. She served as his secretary when he was Ambassador to Brazil and accompanied him on a tour of Europe in 1871. During that tour she was impressed by her observations of German kindergartens established by Friedrich **Froebel**. Trained in New York as a teacher at Miss Henrietta Haines's private school, Blow was eager to return to St. Louis and establish a similar program for young children in the United States.

Blow used her family's influence to convince the Superintendent of St. Louis Public Schools to open a **kindergarten**, based on the theory and practice of Frederick Froebel, in the new Des Peres Elementary School. That first kindergarten class in St. Louis met in the mornings during the 1873–1874 school year, with sixty-eight children, one paid teacher, and three volunteers. Blow made sure the tables and benches from the Froebel kindergartens that she had seen in Europe were duplicated for the classrooms in St. Louis. The reports of the first kindergarten classrooms indicated that children were better prepared to enter regular elementary school if they participated in the program run by Susan Blow. More kindergarten classrooms were added and a teacher training program was implemented to help prepare kindergarten teachers for St. Louis Public Schools and for schools across the United States.

Susan Blow soon returned to Miss Haines's school in New York to study with Maria Boelte, a teacher who had studied under Froebel, and brought his philosophy and ideas to her work at Haines's school. In 1985, Blow began taking her kindergarten method to other parts of the United States and into other countries. A special teaching certification was developed and issued by the St. Louis Public Schools for teachers completing the kindergarten training program. Teachers came from all over the United States to train with Blow and returned to their towns to establish kindergarten programs.

By 1884, in poor health with Graves Disease, Susan Blow left St. Louis to recuperate in Cazenovia, New York. In her later life, she wrote five books to discuss Froebel's work and its application to the kindergartens she established in the United States. She continued her work as a member of the Advisory Board of the International Kindergarten Union and a lecturer on contemporary Kindergarten thought. She began lecturing at Columbia Teacher's College in 1898, continuing until within three weeks of her death in 1916.

The Carondelt Historical Center in St. Louis, Missouri, maintains the Des Peres Elementary School as a museum featuring a kindergarten classroom with replicas of the benches, tables, and materials used to teach children enrolled in the kindergarten classes of 1873. Families donated samples of materials that their relatives created as students in the kindergartens directed by Susan Blow, including needle work, folded paper, and notebooks of children's work. All twenty of the "gifts" in Froebel's theory for the education of young children are represented in the display cases at the museum. In addition, diaries of Susan Blow and workbooks from apprentice teachers are displayed. There are also two stained glass windows, one of Froebel and one of Blow, originally made for display in the nearby Shepard Elementary School. Several of the schools used today still have evidence of the large rooms intended for use as kindergartens, proportioned to accommodate the large wooden tables that Blow had built for the classrooms. Wilkinson Elementary, built in 1922, has the original stained glass created to identify the kindergarten classrooms.

Further Readings: Harris, Nini (1983). *The Carondelet Historic Center and Susan E. Blow: Preserving kindergarten history childhood education* 59(5), 336–338; Menius, Joseph M. (1993). *Susan Blow "mother of the kindergarten" Gateway to education: A pioneer in early childhood education.* St. Clair, MO: Page One.

Susan Catapano

Bowlby, John (1907–1990)

John Bowlby is widely considered to be the "father" of **attachment** theory. In a lifetime devoted to understanding the importance of the relationship between the child and his or her primary caregiver, Bowlby developed a theory that has generated more research and writing than any other topic in the socioemotional realm. An important later development to the theory of relevance to early childhood educators was the recognition that children also develop attachments to adults other than the parent, particularly to day-care providers, early childhood teachers, and others with whom they spend time.

John Mostyn Bowlby was born in London in1907, the fourth of six children. He was raised by a beloved nanny, which was the custom in upper-middle-class England at the time, but she left the family just before young John turned four. As was also typical, he was sent to boarding school at age 7, and it was very difficult for him. Undoubtedly these two experiences affected him deeply and influenced his interest in separation and loss.

Bowlby attended the University of Cambridge in 1928 where he studied what we now call developmental psychology. Just after graduating, he volunteered at a school for "maladjusted" children, and he began to watch them closely and with great interest. It is likely as a result of these experiences that Bowlby set about to become a child psychiatrist. In addition to studying medicine and psychiatry, he was trained as a child psychoanalyst by Melanie Klein at the British Psychoanalytic Institute. While Klein's training greatly influenced Bowlby, he parted ways with her theory in its interpretation of family interactions as not particularly important to understanding the child. Instead, Bowlby began to recognize the primary relationship between the child and caregiver, namely the mother. In 1938, Bowlby married Ursula Longstaff, and over the course of the next decade he fathered four children. In 1945, following World War II, he became head of the Children's Department at the Tavistock Clinic, where children with serious emotional problems were treated. There, he began to focus on the parent–child relationship in both healthy and pathological circumstances. At Tavistock, Bowlby was greatly influenced by James Robertson, who helped him closely observe and film the behavior of children who had been separated from their parents due to hospitalization.

In 1950, Bowlby was asked by the **World Health Organization** (WHO) to examine the mental health of children who had been orphaned by World War II. This gave him a chance to gather all information available and, importantly, to talk with other experts on this topic. He was influenced by the work of Konrad Lorenz, Robert Hinde, and their field of ethology, which emphasized the existence of critical periods in development. By bringing together information about child development, psychoanalysis, and ethology, Bowlby's report to the WHO set forth the primary thesis of attachment theory. The report was so influential that it was eventually translated into 14 languages and sold 400,000 copies in its initial edition. While the language of the report was still very psychoanalytic in origin, Bowlby's main conclusion set the course of attachment theory: "What is believed to be essential for mental health is that the infant and young child should experience a warm, intimate, and continuous relationship with his mother (or permanent mother-substitute) in which both find satisfaction and enjoyment" (Bowlby, 1969, p. xi). Later, Bowlby was joined by other influential colleagues, notably Mary (Salter) Ainsworth, who traveled to Uganda to observe children's separations and reunions from caregivers in naturalistic settings. Her Uganda research led to the development of reliable ways to measure the attachment relationship, an essential step to conducting empirical research. Bowlby's ability to learn from others and to collaborate with them, particularly others from a wide array of professional disciplines, was notable and gave him the broad perspective that led to a remarkably generative theory.

Bowlby presented his first work on attachment theory in the late 1950s and early 1960s to the British Psychoanalytic Society in London in three papers that have become classics in the field: "The nature of the child's tie to his mother," "Separation anxiety," and "Grief and mourning in infancy and early childhood." These were followed by significant research by Bowlby and colleagues and resulted in Bowlby's enormously influential three-volume series: *Attachment* (Bowlby, 1969), *Separation* (Bowlby, 1973), and *Loss* (Bowlby, 1980).

Further Readings: Ainsworth, M. D. A. (1967). *Infancy in Uganda: Infant care and the growth of love.* Baltimore: Johns Hopkins University Press; Bowlby, J. (1958). The nature of the child's tie to his mother. *International Journal of Psycho-Analysis* 39, 350–373; Bowlby, J. (1959). Separation anxiety. *International Journal of Psycho-Analysis* 41, 89–113; Bowlby, J. (1960). Grief and mourning in infancy and early childhood. *The Psychoanalytic Study of the Child* 15, 9–52; Bowlby, J. (1969/1982). *Attachment and loss, Vol. I: Attachment.* London: Hogarth Press; Bowlby, J. (1973/1980). *Attachment and loss, Vol. II, Separation: Anxiety and anger.* London: Hogarth Press; Bowlby, J. (1980). *Attachment and loss, Vol. III, Loss: Sadness and depression.* London: Hogarth Press; Bretherton, Inge (1992). The origins of attachment theory: John Bowlby and Mary Ainsworth. *Developmental Psychology* 28, 759–775.

Martha Pott

Bronfenbrenner, Urie (1917–2005)

Urie Bronfenbrenner is widely regarded as one of the world's leading scholars in developmental psychology, child-rearing, and the **ecology of human development**. He spent most of his professional career at Cornell University, where he was the Jacob Gould Sherman Professor of Human Development and of Psychology. Born in Moscow, Russia, in 1917, Bronfenbrenner came to the United States at the age of six. After graduating from high school in Haverstraw, New York, he received a bachelor's degree from Cornell in 1938, completing a double major in psychology and music. He went on to do graduate work in developmental psychology, completing an M.A. at Harvard followed by a Ph.D. at the University of Michigan in 1942. The day after receiving his doctorate he was inducted into the Army where he served as a psychologist in the Air Corps and the Office of Strategic Services. Following demobilization, he served briefly as the Assistant Chief Clinical Psychologist for Research in the new VA Clinical Psychology Training Program, and then did a two-year stint as an assistant professor of psychology at the University of Michigan. He joined the Cornell faculty in 1948.

From the very beginning of his scholarly work, Bronfenbrenner pursued three mutually reinforcing themes: (1) developing theory and research designs at the frontiers of developmental science; (2) laying out the implications and applications of developmental research for policy and practice; and (3) communicating—through articles, lectures, and discussions—the findings of developmental research to students, to the general public, and to policymakers, both in the private and public sector.

Bronfenbrenner's 1979 book, *The Ecology of Human Development: Experiments by Nature and Design*, was hailed as groundbreaking, establishing his place at the forefront of developmental psychology. His ecological theory, and his ability to translate it into operational research models and effective social policies, contributed to the creation of **Head Start**, the federal child development program for low-income children and their families.

Bronfenbrenner's theoretical model transformed the way many social and behavioral scientists approached the study of human beings and their environments. His starting point was the observation that historically the study of early development had been conducted "out of context," that is, in the laboratory rather than in the environments within which children grow and develop (what he called the study of the strange behavior of children in strange situations with strange adults for the briefest period of time). He maintained that development needs to be understood in ecological context, as "the progressive, mutual accommodation between an active, growing human being and the changing properties of the immediate settings in which the developing person lives, as this process is affected by the relations between those settings, and by the larger contexts in which those settings are embedded."

Bronfenbrenner pointed out that the environments shaping development can be specified as systems, and that the properties of those systems can be identified. In his 1979 book he laid out four systems levels, conceived as nested, one within the next, like a set of Russian dolls: *microsystems* (patterns of activities, roles, and interpersonal relations experienced by the child directly); *mesosystems* (the interrelations between two or more such microsettings); *exosystems* (settings that affect or are affected by the developing child, but do not involve the child as an active participant); and *macrosystems* (the beliefs and values found at the level of culture, society, or subculture that manifest themselves as consistencies in the form and content of the other three environmental systems—the "blueprint," so to speak). Bronfenbrenner understood that a complete understanding of societal characteristics and dynamics requires comparison with other societies, which he pursued through extensive cross-cultural ecosystem comparison. His *Two Worlds of Childhood: U.S. and U.S.S.R.*, written in 1970 at the height of the

Cold War, provided unique insights into the ways that societal values are (or are not) transferred from one generation to the next. (For more on the ecology of human development perspective, see that entry.)

As a developmental psychologist Bronfenbrenner was as interested in the changing nature of the developing person as he was in the environmental systems that shape that development. In his view the developing person, through maturation and interactive experience, becomes increasingly capable of altering the environmental "niche" that it occupies. Thus Bronfenbrenner's theoretical perspective was "optimistic," in the sense that it included a belief in the power of influence by the developing person to modify the surrounding environment through active engagement and increasing personal control. In his view the social structural forces of society (class, gender, race, socioeconomic status) were not immutable in shaping individual destinies, but could be modified to some extent by developmentally competent persons. Richard Lerner points out that this optimism was manifest in Bronfenbrenner's conviction, based on scientific evidence, that "applications of developmental science may improve the course and contexts of human life."

Later in his career, Bronfenbrenner extended his ecological theory, adding the prefix "bio" to "ecological" in recognition of his long-held view that biological resources are important to understanding human development. But for him, biological potential was just that—potential. Whether it was brought to fruition depended on the presence of environmental systems that promoted enduring, reciprocal, highly interactive processes between a developing organism and other individuals or objects in the environment.

Bronfenbrenner has had and continues to have considerable influence within the field of early childhood education, both within the United States and abroad. His emphasis on the power of reciprocal relations (adult–child, child–child) as the "engines" of development reinforces much previous and contemporary theory and practice in early childhood education. In an influential paper written in 1976 for the Office of Child Development of the U.S. Department of Health, Education, and Welfare, he documented the importance of an explicit emphasis on the parent–child dyad in the design **of early intervention** programs, thereby shifting the programmatic focus beyond the individual child to include the parent or other significant adult. This insight, supported with empirical evidence, underscored the general importance of parent involvement in early education programs, and anticipated the shift to "two-generation" programming that has increasingly become the norm in the twenty-first century (**Early Head Start** is a prime example). Perhaps his most unique and enduring contribution to the field has been in helping policy-makers, practitioners, and academics track the ways that public policies developed and implemented at the national or state level shape the major institutions of society (work-places, schools, child-care settings) to affect the development of children through interactions with significant adults and peers.

Bronfenbrenner's active involvement with public policy in early childhood was during a twenty-year period between 1965 and 1985, beginning with his service on the National Planning Committee for Project Head Start. He worked closely with staff of the national Office of Child Development (including Dr. Edward Zigler) during the 1970s, and was an advisor to Senator and then

Vice-President Walter Mondale throughout that decade. In the late 1970s and early 1980s Bronfenbrenner codirected the Family Matters Project (with Moncrieff Cochran and William Cross Jr.), a five-country longitudinal study of stresses and supports in the lives of families that included (in the United States) development, implementation, and evaluation of a family support program (home visiting and peer support). The findings from that effort to understand and augment natural helping systems in the lives of American families helped to shape the national family support movement.

In his later years Urie Bronfenbrenner spoke and wrote often of his fear that the processes central to healthy human development are breaking down as disruptive economic and social trends in American society bring insecurity and violence into the lives of America's families and children. "The hectic pace of modern life poses a threat to our children second only to poverty and unemployment," he said. "We are depriving millions of children—and thereby our country—of their birthright . . . virtues, such as honesty, responsibility, integrity and compassion." The gravity of the crisis, he warned, threatens the competence and character of the next generation of adults—those destined to be the first leaders of the twenty-first century. "The signs of this breakdown are all around us in the ever growing rates of alienation, apathy, rebellion, delinquency and violence among American youth," he wrote. Yet, he added: "It is still possible to avoid that fate. We now know what it takes to enable families to work the magic that only they can perform. The question is, are we willing to make the sacrifices and the investment necessary to enable them to do so?"

Further Readings: Bronfenbrenner, U. (1974). Developmental research, public policy, and the ecology of childhood. *Child Development* 45, 1–5; Bronfenbrenner, U. (1976). Is early intervention effective? Facts and principles of early intervention. In A. M. Clark and A. D. B. Clark, eds. *Early experience: Myth and evidence.* London: Open Books; Bronfenbrenner, U. (1979). *The ecology of human development: Experiments by nature and design.* Cambridge, MA: Harvard University Press; Bronfenbrenner, U. (1992). Ecological systems theory. In R. Vasta, ed. *Six theories of child development: Revised formulations and current issues.* London: Jessica Kingsley, pp. 187–249; Bronfenbrenner, U., ed. (2005). *Making human beings human: Bioecological perspectives on human development.* Thousand Oaks, CA: Sage; Lerner, R., (2005). Foreword. In U. Bronfenbrenner, ed. *Making human beings human: Bioecological perspectives on human development.* Thousand Oaks, CA: Sage.

Moncrieff Cochran and Stephen Ceci

Bruner, Jerome (1915–)

Jerome Bruner is a cognitive psychologist who has been a major influence on educational theory and practice for over half a century. As one of the key figures in the "cognitive revolution" of the 1950s, Bruner was one of the first interpreters of Lev **Vygotsky**'s work in the United States and Western Europe. More recently he has become critical of the direction educational theory and practice has taken since the cognitive revolution of the 1950s and he now espouses a cultural view of education (1996). His interest and influence go well beyond psychology into the humanities and law.

Bruner was born in 1915 in New York City and at the age of two he had an eye surgery to correct a vision impairment. His early years were marked by frequent moves, often changing schools. In 1937, he received a B.A. degree from Duke University and in 1941 was awarded a Ph.D. in Psychology at Harvard, where he eventually served as a professor of psychology (1952–1972). He served on the President's Science Advisory Committee during the Kennedy and Johnson administrations and was instrumental in the development of the **Head Start** program. He moved to England in 1972 as the Watts Professor of Psychology at Oxford University (1972–1980). Bruner has had numerous academic positions, the most recent of which is as a senior research fellow at the New York University School of Law.

Bruner's long career runs parallel to the evolution of cognitive psychology and education in the second half of the twentieth century and remains at the center of progressive education at the beginning of the twenty-first. He began his career studying the mechanisms of thought and learning. In the 1950s, he was at the forefront of the effort to establish cognitive psychology as an alternative to the mechanistic approaches suggested by behaviorism. Indeed, throughout his career Bruner has been concerned with meaning making. This began with a research program describing the mental processes involved in cognition (e.g., spatial awareness, abstract reasoning). This focus on the active processes in the development of thinking marks Bruner as one of the earliest constructivists. The child is an active contributor to the development of his thinking, and as with Jean **Piaget**, the starting place for learning is with the processes that the child has built to that point in development. According to this view, construction of individual mental abilities is done in active encounters with the real world. Such active learning is a central theme guiding contemporary U.S. perspectives on developmentally appropriate practice in early childhood education.

In the 1960s, Bruner (1966) brought his work on cognition directly into the discussion of educational practice (*Toward A Theory of Instruction*). In this and other works, he encourages teachers to help children build upon their current knowledge through the discovery of principles that underlie an understanding of the physical and social world. He recommends curriculum that is organized in a spiral, in which understandings are built upon what the child currently knows. In line with these views are principles of instruction that take into account the characteristics of the children and that are focused on engaging them in a process of discovery.

In the 1970s, Bruner began examining the role of scaffolding in the learning process. With David Wood and Gail Ross he examined how adults support children in problem-solving tasks. This notion of scaffolding has become a central concept in contemporary discussions of social constructivist theory as well as the early childhood curriculum (Berk and Winsler, 1995). Bruner's work on early language acquisition, also initiated in the 1970s, examines the social environment that leads to meaningful communication. That is, for Bruner, the use of language is not simply the result of an inborn language acquisition device but requires interactions with key people in which it becomes functional. As with his earlier work on mental processes, the emphasis is on active meaning-making in a practical context.

Bruner's criticism of the cognitive revolution is articulated in *Acts of Meaning* (1990), in which he describes how inquiry into how children create meaning was supplanted in psychological and educational research by a mechanistic effort to describe how information is processed. In this and subsequent work he outlines the role of culture in providing a framework for meaning-making as well as children's use of **narrative** as a means of organizing their understandings of the world and their place in the world. He expands on this central role for narrative in *The Culture of Education* (1996) and describes schools as places where culture is transmitted and created.

The broad range of Bruner's work touches on many aspects of early childhood education. In the analysis of specific instructional strategies, he has helped articulate the notions of discovery learning and scaffolding. His emphasis on the pragmatic aspects of early language learning has informed the current discussion of early literacy. His influence is acknowledged among progressive early childhood programs internationally, including those of **Reggio Emilia**. In the broader arena of educational practice he has asked for a re-evaluation of education systems that test for fragmented knowledge rather than the construction of meaning. In the area of public policy, he has more recently engaged in a critique of the national **No Child Left Behind Act**. *See also* Development, Language, Second Language Acquisition in Early Childhood.

Further Readings: Berk, L., and A. Winsler (1995). *Scaffolding children's learning: Vygotsky and early childhood education.* Washington, DC: NAEYC; Bruner, J. (1960). *The process of education.* Cambridge, MA: Harvard University Press; Bruner, J. (1966). *Toward a theory of instruction.* Cambridge, MA: Harvard University Press; Bruner, J. (1983). *Child's talk: Learning to use language.* New York: Norton; Bruner, J. (1990). *Acts of meaning.* Cambridge, MA: Harvard University Press; Bruner, J. (1996). *The culture of education.* Cambridge, MA: Harvard University Press.

John Hornstein

Bullying

Bullying is a type of relational aggression directed intentionally against an individual by one or more other individuals. Bullying behavior has been documented in cultures around the world, though there is evidence that it may be more prevalent in some countries than in others. In one survey of American high-school students, over 60 percent reported that they had, at some time in their school career, been a victim of bullying. Similar percentages have been reported in studies from Europe and Asia. Despite the prevalence of bullying, there is no single agreed-upon definition of the phenomenon. Some scholars emphasize that bullying should be defined as *repeated* aggression directed toward an individual (Olweus, 1993), others emphasize the malicious *intent* of perpetrators as the most important component of bullying (Randall, 1997; Tattum and Tattum, 1992), while other scholars highlight the role that imbalances of *power* and *social position* play in bullying (Smith and Sharp, 1994). Bullying can encompass a range of behaviors including physical, verbal, and psychological aggression. Bullying may be overt (e.g., physical or verbal aggression) or covert (e.g., social aggression).

Bullying in Developmental Perspective

Aggression, like other aspects of children's socioemotional development, passes through various developmental stages. A developmental examination of bullying must also recognize that its development is dependent on linguistic, cognitive, and socioemotional development. Moreover, it must be acknowledged that all development occurs within the context of culture and hence, definitions and manifestations of bullying vary among cultures.

The earliest signs of aggressive behavior have been documented in children as young as seven months of age. From 18 months until 2 years, there is an increase in the frequency of children's aggressive behavior. As children's linguistic development progresses, they increasingly use verbal means to negotiate social tension, and, consequently, name-calling becomes the most frequent form of bullying behavior that has been documented in young children. There is a concomitant decrease in physical aggression.

Between the ages of 3 and 5, there is a marked decrease in the percentage of physical aggression, combined with an increase in the amount of time that children are able to socially interact without physical or verbal aggression. During these years, children may go through a period of what some scholars call "potty mouth": deliberate use of taboo language in order to provoke a reaction from recipients. Specialists in language development view this phase as an outcome of children's pragmatic development as children gain the insight that language can be wielded in the service of power. In fact, young children may not know the meaning of the taboo words they utter, but they do recognize that they are powerful and provocative. As children begin to internalize their culture's social norms, bullying becomes more covert and children may attempt to hide their bullying behavior from adults in their environment.

In the preschool years, children's teasing and name-calling reflects the developmental concerns common to children of this age: control of emotions, bodily functions, and adherence to gender normative behaviors. In the United States, the most common names that young children use to tease each other (e.g., *poo-poo head*, *crybaby*, and *baby*) reflect these developmental concerns. It is rare in the preschool years for children to use language that is overtly linked to social ideologies such as sexism, racism, or homophobia. However, as children internalize the attitudes of their culture, their name-calling comes to reflect the norms and values of the broader culture. For example, in America, where fat is highly stigmatized, it has been documented that children as young as eight will use "fat" as a slur when bullying other children.

In middle childhood, there is a marked increase in the frequency of bullying. This may be due to the fact that, in middle school, peer relationships become increasingly central to preadolescents and bullying may play a central role in establishing and negotiating social hierarchies in the middle school (Pellegrini, 2002). It is during the middle-school years that "social category names" (e.g., *geek*, *dork*, *nerd*, *stoner*, etc.) become frequently used. Use of such slurs serves two purposes: (1) it defines *oneself* by defining *others* and (2), it establishes a sense of group membership and group norms. It is during the middle-school years as well that the use of racist, sexist, and homophobic slurs increases. Indeed, studies of American middle-school children suggest that sexist (e.g., *bitch*, *slut*) and homophobic (e.g., *fag*, *queer*, *homo*) are the most frequent verbal taunts used by middle-school children. These gender-related slurs serve multiple functions: they enforce normative gender behavior while simultaneously stigmatizing perceived infractions of gender norms.

Though bullying behaviors can persist into adulthood (Moffitt, 1993; Randall, 1997), by the time most children reach late adolescence, the amount of bullying decreases sharply when compared to middle school. Bullying becomes less socially acceptable to older adolescents, and it may become more covert.

Gender Differences in Bullying

Although both boys and girls bully, research suggests that they do so in gender-specific ways. Research supports the idea that boys are, on the whole, more aggressive than girls, independent of other variables such as culture and socioeconomic status. Moreover, boys are more likely than girls to engage in physical aggression. Recent scholarship focusing on girls' bullying has found that girls are more likely to engage in social aggression: aggression where the intent is to cause harm to another's self-esteem or social standing.

Implications for Early Childhood Educators

Bullying occurs most often in school contexts, especially at times and in locations where there is minimal adult supervision (e.g., during recess or in the lunchroom). Teachers and other school personnel, therefore, are in a unique position to combat bullying. Scholars and educators (see Olweus, 1993) generally agree that effective antibullying policies must work on multiple levels: school-wide, within individual classrooms, and amongst individual students (both children who bully and those who are bullied). School-wide actions might include the formulation and dissemination of explicit policies and codes of behavior on bullying that delimit the bounds of appropriate language use by students and teachers, and set up clear and unambiguous consequences for infractions. At the classroom level, teachers must be trained to recognize bullying behavior and they must be equipped with the skills needed to intervene effectively. On the level of individuals, educators stress the importance of avoiding labels such as *"bully"* or *"victim"* inasmuch as most children can and do play both roles at some time in their social interactions. Any intervention must involve the child (or children) who bully, as well as the child who is the recipient of bullying. Students themselves must be provided with the social and linguistic tools to intervene in bullying behavior, especially if they are not directly involved; research suggests that by-standers who witness bullying feel as much anxiety as those who are the victims of bullying. If schools establish a clear set of policies and procedures, the incidence of bullying can be dramatically decreased. *See also* Development, Language; Peer Culture; Peers and Friends.

Further Readings: Espelage, D. L., and S. M. Swearer, eds. (2001). *Bullying in American schools: A social-ecological perspective on prevention and intervention*. Mahwah,

NJ: Erlbaum; Moffitt, T. E. (1993). Adolescent-limited and life-course-persistent antisocial behavior: A developmental taxonomy. *Psychological Review* 100, 674–701; Olweus, D. (1993). *Bullying in schools: What we know and what we can do*. New York: Blackwell; Pellegrini, A. D. (2002). Bullying and victimization in middle school: A dominance relations perspective. *Educational Psychologist* 37, 151–163; Pellegrini, A. D., and J. Long (2002). A longitudinal study of bullying, dominance, and victimization during the transition from primary to secondary school. *British Journal of Developmental Psychology* 20, 259–280; Randall, P. (1997). *Adult bullying: Perpetrators and victims*. New York: Routledge; Smith, P. K., and S. Sharp (1994). *School bullying*. London: Routledge; Swearer, S. M., and B. Doll (2001). Bullying in schools: An ecological framework. *Journal of Emotional Abuse* 2, 7–23; Tattum, D. P., and E. Tattum (1992). Bullying: A whole school response. In N. Jones and E. Baglin Jones, eds. *Learning to behave*. London: Kogan Page.

Calvin Gidney

C

Carolina Abecedarian Project. *See* Abecedarian Program

CCDF. *See* Child Care and Development Fund

CCW. *See* Center for the Child Care Workforce

CDA. *See* Child Development Associate (CDA) National Credentialing Program

CDF. *See* Children's Defense Fund

CDGM. *See* Child Development Group of Mississippi

CEC. *See* Council for Exceptional Children

Center for the Child Care Workforce (CCW)

The Center for the Child Care Workforce (CCW) is a nonprofit research, education, and advocacy organization committed to improving early childhood education quality by upgrading the compensation, working conditions, and training of teaching and care-giving professionals. The Center is now a project of the American Federation of Teachers Educational Foundation (CCW/AFTEF).

CCW was founded in 1978 in Berkeley, California, as the Child Care Employee Project (CCEP). Formed by a group of preschool teachers concerned about the poor compensation and low status characteristic of their profession, CCEP began conducting independent research on the early childhood education workforce, building a national network of peers with similar concerns, and developing research, policy, and organizing resources for the field. The organization moved its headquarters to Washington, DC, in 1994, and became the Center for the Child Care Workforce in 1997. In 2002, CCW merged with the American Federation of Teachers (AFT), the nation's largest growing union of professionals representing pre-K–12 grade teachers; paraprofessionals and other school-related personnel;

higher education faculty and professional staff; nurses, and healthcare workers; and federal, state, and local government employees.

The group's landmark research project, *The National Child Care Staffing Study* (1989), was the first to document the status of the early childhood education workforce nationwide, and established a clear link between the quality of care and education that young children receive and the compensation and stability of their teachers. Other key research includes *Then and Now: Changes in Child Care Staffing, 1994–2000,* the first longitudinal study of staffing and stability in child-care centers.

Several publications and training models developed by CCW are now widely used by educators, advocates, and others in the field to enhance the leadership and organizing skills of early childhood education practitioners. *Taking on Turnover* offers strategies for improving child-care center staff retention; *Creating Better Child Care Jobs* provides an assessment framework for home-based and center-based programs on the quality of the adult work environment. CCW's *Leadership Empowerment Action Project (LEAP)* model has been replicated in communities across the country, helping front-line teaching staff work more effectively for improvements in compensation and working conditions.

From 1991 to 1999, CCW served as national coordinator of the **Worthy Wage Campaign**, a national grassroots effort to empower the workforce itself to press for staffing solutions. The campaign was instrumental in raising public awareness of early childhood education workforce issues and promoting activism, policy initiatives and legislative activity at the federal, state and local levels. CCW has also been instrumental in developing solutions to problems in the field, cofounding the California Early Childhood Mentor Program in 1988, and creating the California CARES model, an initiative that provides stipends to early childhood educators who make a commitment to staying in the field by pursuing professional development.

As a project of the AFTEF, CCW/AFTEF has broadened the scope of its public policy work by establishing a new link between early childhood educators and teachers in elementary and secondary schools. For more information, visit www.ccw.org.

Dori Mornan and Marci Young

Cerebral Palsy (CP)

Cerebral palsy (CP) is a term used to describe a group of chronic disorders that impair control of movement. The term can describe impairment such as paralysis, weakness, loss of coordination, or functional abnormality of the motor system due to brain pathology. This disorder was initially known as Little's Disease after an English surgeon John Little from the nineteenth century. Winthrop Phelps, M.D, later coined "cerebral palsy" and in 1937 founded the first treatment facility in the United States (located in Baltimore, MD) dedicated to children with CP. Presently, the center is known as the Kennedy Krieger Institute.

Data from the National Health Interview Survey—Child Health Supplement (1988) reports that 23 of 10,000 children seventeen years of age and under had CP within the United States. In recent figures, the prevalence rate of CP remains the same, occurring in 2–2.5 per 1,000 live births, which makes it the most common severe physical disability affecting children. Disabilities ranging from CP as well as other learning disabilities have a substantial impact on the educational and health functioning of the individual children. These children have 1.5 times more doctor visits, 3.5 times more hospital days, twice the number of missed school days, and an increased likelihood of repeating a grade in school in comparison to children without these conditions (Boyle, Decoufle, and Yeargin-Allsopp, 1994).

There are three types of CP identified by the type of movement problems: spastic, athetoid, and ataxic. Spastic CP accounts for 70–80 percent of the cases in the United States. A child with spastic CP can have stiff muscles or may be unable to relax his muscles. Atheoid CP accounts for 10–20 percent of all CP cases. With this type, children have difficulty controlling the muscles of the body. Ataxic CP accounts for 5–10 percent of all cases within the country. A child with ataxic cerebral palsy has problems with balance and coordination. The various cases can also be broken down according to the body part involved: hemiplegia, diplegia, and quadriplegia. Hemiplegia is a type of CP that affects one arm and one leg on the same side of the body. Diplegia, on the other hand, primarily involves reduced functionality in both legs. Quadriplegia refers to CP that affects all four extremities as well as the trunk and neck muscles.

CP can be congenital as a result of either pre- or perinatal trauma and injury or acquired after birth. Certain causes of CP are preventable or treatable, such as head injury, contraction of rubella (German measles) by the pregnant mother, Rh incompatibility, meningitis, or jaundice. Although symptoms can change over time, CP is not a progressive disorder that increases impairment within the child over time. Different symptoms of CP will arise dependent upon the part of the brain that has been injured. Children diagnosed with CP may demonstrate a variety of symptoms such as difficulty with fine motor tasks (e.g., writing), difficulty maintaining balance or walking, and involuntary movements. The early signs of CP appear usually before the age of three. Often, physicians can diagnose a child by eighteen months due to lags in attaining developmental milestones. Infants with this disability can be slow to attain developmental milestones such as rolling over, sitting, crawling, smiling, or walking.

There is currently no cure for CP. However, treatment can improve the individual's quality of life. Treatment can include: physical therapy and occupational therapy to improve the individual's motor coordination and balance; medication to help reduce spasms and involuntary muscle movements; surgeries; and braces to increase functionality in the family, school, and work settings. Many state- and federally funded programs are in place to improve the lives of children with disabilities. The Rehabilitation Act of 1973, the **Individuals with Disabilities Education Act (IDEA)**, and the Americans with Disabilities Act are in place to guarantee that Americans with disabilities will not face discrimination in receiving federal financial assistance in schools, workplace, and in other public settings.

States are required to provide assistance for families who take responsibility for children with CP. For children up to the age of three, **early intervention** provides assistance to families. Staff work with the family to develop an **Individualized Family Service Plan (IFSP)** to describe the child's individual needs and the services the child will receive in order to address those needs. For school-aged children, special education services will be provided through the school system. The staff will work with the family to formulate an **Individualized Education Plan (IEP)** to meet the needs of the child. In addition to therapy services, children with CP may need assistive technology (e.g., communication devices or computer technology) to improve quality of life. Early childhood educators can play a critical role in creating a supportive, inclusive environment for children with CP. By catering to the child's individual needs, educators and family can collaborate to provide both an appropriate learning and social environment conducive to productivity.

Further Readings: Boyle, C. A., P. Decoufle, and M. Yeargin-Allsopp (1994). Prevalence and health impact of developmental disabilities in US children. *Pediatrics* 93(3), 399–403; McDonald, E. T., and B. Chance Jr. (1964). *Cerebral palsy.* Englewood Cliffs, NJ: Prentice-Hall.

Web Sites: Centers for Disease Control and Prevention. Cerebral Palsy. Available online at http://www.cdc.gov/NCBDDD/dd/ddcp.htm; Kennedy Krieger Institute. Phelps Center for Cerebral Palsy and Neurodevelopmental Medicine. Available online at http://www.kennedykrieger.org/.

Sonia Susan Issac

Child Abuse and Neglect

Child abuse and neglect is a serious problem that affects millions of children throughout the United States. Early childhood educators are concerned about child abuse and neglect because they are committed to nurturing the healthy development of children and to helping prevent problems that can impede a child's ability to fulfill his or her potential. Very young children—a growing number of whom spend significant time in early education and child-care settings—are the most vulnerable to the damaging impact of maltreatment. Early childhood professionals are uniquely well positioned to build relationships with parents and other caregivers, to observe and respond to problems that can place children at risk of maltreatment, and to help families before abuse or neglect occurs. In addition, individuals who work directly with children, including teachers and other staff members in early education programs, are mandatory reporters of suspected child abuse and neglect (see Child Abuse and Neglect, Prevention of). Survey research indicates that awareness of the problem of child maltreatment among early childhood professionals has increased dramatically from 10 percent in the mid-1970s to more than 90 percent today.

Definition

Federal legislation—specifically the Child Abuse Prevention and Treatment Act (CAPTA) amended by the Keeping Children and Families Safe Act of 2003—defines child abuse and neglect as follows:

- Any recent act or failure to act on the part of a parent of caretaker that results in death, serious physical, or emotional harm, sexual abuse, or exploitation.
- An act or failure to act that presents an imminent risk of serious harm.

Each state establishes its own, more specific definition of maltreatment that generally includes standards for physical abuse (e.g., injury caused by hitting, kicking, shaking), sexual abuse (e.g., fondling, indecent exposure, incest, rape), emotional abuse (e.g., behavior that impairs a child's emotional development or sense of self-worth), and neglect (e.g. failure to provide adequate food, shelter, medical treatment, or supervision). (National Clearinghouse on Child Abuse and Neglect Information).

Scope of the Problem

In 2003, across the United States, child protective services—the public agencies responsible for responding to child abuse and neglect—received 2.9 million reports alleging abuse or neglect involving 5.5 million children. One-third of the reports were "screened out" because they did not meet a state's standard for maltreatment. State and local child protective services agencies conducted an investigation or assessment on two-thirds of the total number of reports received, and, based on these investigations, 906,000 children were determined to be victims of abuse and neglect in 2003. (This figure represents approximately 1.2 percent of the total population of children in the United States, which was 73,043,506 in 2003.) Fifteen percent of children who are found to be abused or neglected are removed from their homes and placed in foster care (U.S. Department of Health, 2005).

The rate of victimization per 1,000 children in the national population has dropped from 13.4 children in 1990 to 12.4 children in 2003. Neglect is the most common form of maltreatment constituting 60 percent of substantiated cases, followed by physical abuse (almost 20%), sexual abuse (10%), and emotional abuse (10%). Parents or other caretakers are most frequently the perpetrators of maltreatment (U.S. Department of Health and Human Services, 2005).

Abuse and neglect occurs within all racial and ethnic groups: half of all victims are white; one-quarter are African American; and one-tenth are Hispanic. Pacific Islander, American Indian, Alaskan Native, and African American children have the highest rates of victimization. Girls are slightly more likely to be victims (51.7%) than boys (48.3%) (U.S. Department of Health and Human Services, 2005).

Victimization is inversely related to age. The youngest children are more likely to be abused and neglected and also suffer the greatest consequences in terms of injuries and fatalities. Children from birth to five years constitute 41 percent of victims of maltreatment. More than three-quarters of the 1,500 children who died from abuse and neglect in 2003 were younger than four years (U.S. Department of Health and Human Services, 2005).

Because of the high volume of reports, high staff turnover, and large caseloads, many child-welfare systems struggle to respond to many families' needs and are often criticized for failing to keep children safe. Because of the number of reports that are screened out, cases that are unsubstantiated, and lack of resources, the majority of families reported for abuse and neglect do not receive services. Many child-welfare systems are trying to improve their ability to assess and serve families and are building partnerships with community organizations in an effort to provide higher quality services to children.

Impact of Maltreatment

Many research studies document the negative impact of abuse and neglect on children, including long-term harm to children's physical, emotional, cognitive, and behavioral development. Maltreatment has also been associated with increased risk for poor school performance and learning difficulties, drug and alcohol problems, juvenile delinquency, and adult criminality. For example, the Adverse Childhood Experiences Study reveals a powerful relationship between a traumatic experience in childhood (such as abuse) and physical and mental health problems in adulthood. New brain-imaging techniques reveal that child abuse can cause permanent changes to the neural structure and function of the developing brain. Beyond the individual hardships that result from maltreatment, child abuse, and neglect takes an enormous toll on society as a whole in terms of the tremendous costs associated with expenditures on child welfare, health, mental health, special education, and criminal justice systems, as well as lost wages.

Not all children who are abused or neglected experience these negative outcomes. Many children and families are resilient despite difficult circumstances. For example, children who have been maltreated are five times more likely than nonmaltreated children to become abusive or neglectful parents when they grow up. However, the majority of abused/neglected children, 70 percent, do *not* maltreat their children when they become parents. Research has shown that the presence of a caring adult who is responsive to a child's needs can help mitigate the effects of maltreatment and other problems.

Risk Factors

The causes of child maltreatment are complex. Current ecological theories posit that a mix of factors related to the individual child, family, community, and social context can increase or decrease the risk of abuse or neglect. Children with disabilities or special needs, for example, are more likely to be abused. Family characteristics that are linked with child maltreatment include mental health problems, isolation, substance abuse, domestic violence, and lack of parenting skills. Community-level variables that are linked with maltreatment include **poverty**, which is linked particularly to neglect, as well as high levels of unemployment and violence.

Protective Factors

Through close involvement with young children and frequent contact with parents and other caregivers, early childhood programs can effectively incorporate strategies that promote protective factors in families and guard against maltreatment. Key protective factors include (1) increasing parental resilience, (2) building the social connections of parents, (3) increasing knowledge of parenting and child development, (4) providing concrete support in times of need, and (5) supporting the social and emotional development of children (Horton, 2005).

Responses to Child Abuse and Neglect

Responses to child maltreatment are characterized as forms of primary prevention, **early intervention**, and, in extreme cases, early intervention and protection. Primary prevention is associated with large scale-efforts aimed at a broad, general audience that seek to raise public awareness and understanding of child abuse and neglect such as public education campaigns (e.g., public service announcements); information provided to all new parents (e.g., materials advising parents never to shake a baby or the "Back to Sleep" campaign), education programs for children (e.g., Safe Touch programs to prevent sexual abuse); and a range of community-based, early education, and social services programs that provide a variety of resources and supports to families.

Early intervention refers to those programs and services that target groups at risk of abuse or neglect such as home visiting programs, parenting classes, self-help groups, and supports for teenage parents. Long-term research studies of the Nurse Family Partnership (a home visiting program that targets low-income, first-time mothers) and the Chicago Child–Parent Centers (an enriched early childhood program with services and supports for parents) are two examples of programs that have proven effective in preventing abuse and neglect. Some researchers also point to the small decline in child victimization rates as encouraging evidence that early intervention and prevention efforts may be having an impact on child abuse and neglect.

Child Protection and Treatment Programs respond to abuse and neglect once it is reported, such as public child protection agencies charged with investigating and responding to allegations of abuse and neglect; child welfare agencies provide family preservation, case management, and foster care services; family and criminal courts handle the legal issues that result from maltreatment; child advocacy centers streamline the interview and evidence-collecting process and provide support to victims and their families; and mental health services such as programs that provide treatment to children who have witnessed violence and help families cope with the aftermath of maltreatment. *See also* Child Abuse and Neglect, Prevention of; Domestic Violence.

Further Readings: Anda, Robert, and Vincent J. Felitti (2003). *The adverse childhood experience study.* Available online at http://www.acestudy.org/; Horton, Carol (2005). Protective factors literature review: Early care and education programs and the prevention of Child Abuse and Neglect. Available online at http://www.cssp.org; National Association for the Education of Young Children (NAEYC) (2003). *Early Childhood Educators and Child Abuse Prevention: NAEYC's Perspective, Research Findings, and Future Actions.* Washington, DC: NAEYC. Available online at www.naeyc.org/profdev/support_teachers/ ddreporta.pdf; National Clearinghouse on Child Abuse and Neglect Information (2005). Available online at http://nccanch.acf.hhs.gov; Reynolds, Arthur J., and Dylan L. Robertson (2003). School-base early intervention and later child maltreatment in the Chicago Longitudinal Study. *Child Development* 74(1) 3–26; Teicher, Martin H. (2002). Scars that won't heal: The neurobiology of child abuse. *Scientific American*; U.S. Department of Health and Human Services, Administration on Children, Youth and Families (2005). *Child maltreatment 2003.* Washington, DC: Government Printing Office.

Francie Zimmerman

Child Abuse and Neglect, Prevention of

Early childhood professionals and programs play an important role in preventing—not just reporting—**child abuse and neglect**. Most child abuse is perpetrated by family members (U.S. Department of Health and Human Services, 2003); much less frequently, abuse also occurs in out-of-home settings such as schools, child-care settings, foster care, or organized youth activities. The **National Association for the Education of Young Children** (NAEYC)—the nation's largest organization of early childhood professionals and others dedicated to improving the quality of early childhood programs—clearly outlines in numerous publications early childhood programs' and professionals' roles, responsibilities, and strategies to prevent abuse and neglect both in early childhood settings and in the home. Early childhood programs and professionals are advised to undertake the six actions described below.

1. *Promote standards of excellence for early childhood programs.* High-quality care and education helps to strengthen families and promote healthy social and emotional development, as well as preparing children for later school success. Programs should use developmentally appropriate practices and pursue NAEYC accreditation, which requires a rigorous self-study process and an independent external assessment to determine whether high standards are met. Early childhood professionals should also inform the public about the need for and benefits of high-quality early childhood programs (NAEYC, 1996).

   Staff–child ratios for groups of infants, toddlers, preschoolers, kindergartners, and primary-grade children recommended by developmentally appropriate practices and NAEYC accreditation criteria are examples of how these standards of excellence help prevent abuse. Limiting the overall group size helps staff to better meet the individual needs of each child, and teachers are better able to recognize signs or changes in behavior that may indicate the possibility of abuse. Smaller groups may be necessary for children with certain emotional or behavioral problems who require more intensive and direct supervision.

   These standards of excellence also provide recommendations about the design of indoor and outdoor program environment to reduce the possibility of private, hidden locations. Young children need opportunities for solitude and quiet play throughout the day, but all early childhood program spaces should be regarded as public. Both indoor and outdoor space can be set up to provide opportunities for solitude while allowing for unobtrusive adult supervision. Likewise, the program environment should be designed to reduce the likelihood that adults have opportunities for hidden interactions with children.

2. *Adopt policies and practices that promote close partnerships with families.* Close partnerships with families can reduce the potential for child abuse by family members and misunderstandings about staff actions. For example, programs should continue to value touch in children's healthy development. No-touch policies are misguided efforts that fail to recognize the importance of warm, responsive touch, especially for infants and toddlers. Careful, open communication between programs and families about the value of touch in children's development can help

achieve consensus as to acceptable ways for adults to show their respect and support for children.

Communicating with families, especially about difficult topics, is crucial if educators are to provide support to families. Early childhood programs can provide information and support to families regarding child development and effective strategies for responding to children's behavior (NAEYC, 1996, 2003). This kind of communication is much easier when a supportive, reciprocal relationship already exists. Early childhood professionals should also do the following:

- acknowledge and build upon family strengths and competencies;
- respect the dignity of each family and its culture, language, customs, and beliefs; and
- help families understand and appreciate each child's progress within a developmental perspective;
- help family members enhance their parenting skills; and
- build support networks for families by providing opportunities for interaction with program staff, other families, community resources, and professional services (NAEYC, 1997).

3. *Provide a variety of supportive services to families.* In addition to knowing the signs of abuse and neglect, early childhood professionals should be able to recognize situations that may place children at risk. When working with families who are in those situations, professionals should provide appropriate information and referrals to community services, and follow up to ensure that services have been provided (NAEYC, 1996, 1997). Families' access to health care, housing, income support, and other social services may help protect children from abuse and neglect.

4. *Advocate for children, families, and teachers in community and society.* Early childhood educators, as individuals and as a profession, should participate in the policy-making process by doing the following:
- advocating for well-designed, sufficiently funded, and effectively implemented public regulations, programs, and community support services that meet the individual needs of children and families and promote their well-being;
- cooperating with other individuals and groups in advocacy efforts; and
- opposing policies that impair child and family well-being (NAEYC, 1997).

5. *Collaborate with other helping professionals in the community.* The early childhood community should work with other professionals concerned with the welfare of young children and families (NAEYC, 1997). Collaboration with other agencies and disciplines promotes understanding of child development, supports and empowers families, and strengthens advocacy efforts (NAEYC, 1996).

6. *Understand the ethical obligation to recognize and report suspicions of abuse.* All program staff, substitutes, and volunteers should receive preservice and refresher training regarding the appropriate discipline and guidance of children and child abuse and neglect. Early childhood professionals should do the following:

- be familiar with the symptoms of child abuse and neglect, including physical, sexual, verbal, and emotional abuse;
- know and follow state laws and community procedures that protect children against abuse and neglect; and

- report suspected child abuse or neglect to the appropriate community agency and follow up to ensure that appropriate action has been taken. When appropriate, educators should inform parents or guardians that a referral has been made (NAEYC, 1997).

In 2002, NAEYC embarked on *Supporting Teachers, Strengthening Families,* an initiative to help early childhood professionals and families prevent abuse and neglect. Additional information about this effort and the roles and responsibilities of early childhood programs and educators to prevent child abuse and neglect is available online at www.naeyc.org/profdev/support_teachers/default.asp. The Doris Duke Charitable Foundation generously supports this work. *See also* Domestic Violence; Families.

Further Readings: NAEYC (1996). *Position Statement. Prevention of child abuse in early childhood programs and the responsibilities of early childhood professionals to prevent child abuse.* Available online at www.naeyc.org/resources/position_statements/pschab98.pdf;NAEYC (1997). *Code of ethical conduct and statement of commitment.* Rev. ed. Brochure. Washington, DC: NAEYC. Available online at www.naeyc.org/resources/position_statements/pseth98.pdf;NAEYC (2003). *Early childhood educators and child abuse prevention: NAEYC's perspective, research findings, and future actions.* Washington, DC: NAEYC. Available online at www.naeyc.org/profdev/support_teachers/ddreporta.pdf;U.S. Department of Health and Human Services, Administration on Children, Youth and Families (2003). *Child maltreatment 2001.* Washington, DC: Government Printing Office.

Maril Olson

Child Art

The drawings, paintings, and constructions made by young children have long intrigued artists, educators, psychologists, historians, philosophers, and parents. Over the past century, each group, viewing the same activity from their own unique perspective, has seen and interpreted child art differently. Many early researchers were impressed by the remarkable similarities among drawings made by children of the same age living in different parts of the world. These observers suggested that artistic development was a universal process through which children learn to make increasingly realistic representations as they pass through predictable stages. The evolution of drawn and modeled forms appeared to be closely aligned to other aspects of children's development. Researchers such as Florence Goodenough and Dale Harris, for example, proposed that children's drawings could serve as measures of intellectual maturity, while psychologists such as Karen Machover believed that they revealed emotional distress or well-being.

The apparent universality of children's drawings has been regarded by some as evidence of the powerful influence of principles of image-making also found in the work of mature artists who have not been taught other ways of constructing images or objects. Other contemporary scholars suggest that culture and education play far more decisive roles, earlier than once imagined, in the evolution of children's drawings, spurring their acquisition of multiple drawing systems within a larger repertoire of representational possibilities or languages.

Traces of these diverse orientations toward child art persist in contemporary teaching, research, and popular imagination, as reflected in ongoing discussions of the impact of adults, peers, and the surrounding culture on the process of early artistic learning. A growing number of students of children's art now share the view, as noted several decades ago by one scholar, "If we are to understand child art we must look at what the child has represented and expressed, the conditions under which child art is made, and ourselves and others in the act of studying it" (Wilson, 1997, p. 83).

Stages of Artistic Development

Though it is likely that children have always engaged in playful markmaking and graphic representation, child art was "discovered" late in the nineteenth century, when artists and scholars began to notice children making marks and images on the walls of European cities. Adult observers were immediately fascinated by the differences in complexity and realism between the drawings made by the children tall enough to reach the upper surfaces of the walls and the vigorous scribbled marks that appeared closer to the bottom. The study of child art turned quickly from the spontaneously made images produced by children as part of their play, toward the analysis of drawings on paper purposely collected by adults, often from large groups of children whose work could be compared with others of their age, nationality, and sometimes gender. Researchers found striking similarities in composition and structure of the individual components of these drawings that seemed to change with the age of the children and to persist across cultures. These characteristics were presented as developmental stages, which varied from one writer to the next in number, name, or details, but largely agreed in identifying certain landmarks of developmental progress and universal patterns of change in children's drawings.

Among the most enduring and influential descriptions of children's artistic development was that formulated by Viktor **Lowenfeld** and popularized in his book, *Creative and Mental Growth,* first published in 1947, with an 8th edition published in 1987. Lowenfeld described six stages of development—scribbling (ages 2–4); preschematic (ages 4–7); schematic (ages 7–9); dawning realism (ages 9–11); pseudonaturalistic (ages 11–14); and adolescence (ages 14 through 17). He believed that children's art making was intertwined with intellectual, emotional, social, perceptual, physical, and aesthetic growth, with art as both a reflection of, and an impetus for, continued development of each of these capacities in children. Lowenfeld emphasized that children use art to construct meaning, to examine, and to represent their experiences and understandings. Thus, in describing the scribbling stage, Lowenfeld paid particular attention to the third substage of scribbling in his taxonomy, the point at which children begin to name their scribbles, noting some resemblance between marks they have made through vigorous motion and some object or event they had previously experienced. The significance of this shift in attention from the purely physical gesture of scribbling to an interest in the representational possibilities of marks also intrigued scholars from Lev **Vygotsky** to Merleau Ponty to Howard Gardner, each of whom shared Lowenfeld's recognition of the naming of scribbles as harbinger of an emergent understanding of symbolism. And yet other scholars, notably Rhoda Kellogg, who studied scribbling and its relationship to the evolution of form in the drawings of preschool children, believed that the intensity and the appearance of young children's image-making could be explained solely in terms of their interest in creating balanced abstract designs.

From the beginning of the study of child art, there has been far less agreement on the meaning and the mechanism of the changes that can be observed in children's drawings than about the basic proposition that children's drawings *do* tend to change over time. Certain characteristics seem to be perennially typical of young children's image-making. The emergence of the figure known as the "tadpole man," a first representation of a human resembling a potato sprouting arms and legs from an area encircling an undifferentiated head and torso, is one of these characteristics. The accumulation of figures and objects apparently floating on the page, oblivious to the force of gravity, is a very common way for young children to construct the visual narratives that mirror the free associations of their verbal accounts. Among children in the early primary years, the division of the drawing page into bands of sky and earth, with air in between, providing a narrow stage on which to place houses, trees, dogs, and people, is seen the world over, providing a logical way of depicting their sense of order in the universe of their drawings, and, perhaps, of their experiences as well. These landmarks appear frequently enough to suggest that maturation does play an important role in the acquisition of drawing skills and strategies, while individual differences among children point to the impact of experience with art media, gendered and idiosyncratic interests, and the availability of adult support and cultural models. Many of those who amassed large collections of child art early in the last century, in the midst of significant political turmoil, hoped that they had discovered the beginnings of a universal language in the ubiquitous symbols of child art. In order to preserve this innocent language, they urged parents and teachers to allow child art to unfold unfettered by adult influence or intervention. This advice was offered with great urgency in regard to the art of young children. In recent years, a substantial shift has occurred, as researchers have come to notice and value the cultural and individual differences that exist in children's drawings, and as the focus of research has gravitated increasingly toward the process of drawing, particularly as a process that occurs for many young children in the intensely active social contexts of classrooms and communities.

Attitudes toward Child Art

Jo Alice Leeds (1989) suggested that attitudes toward child art change in response to changes in pervasive cultural beliefs about art and about children. When galleries were filled with large Abstract Expressionist canvases, for example, preschoolers were encouraged to paint freely at easels with large brushes and the exuberant paintings that resulted were highly prized. Wilson (1997, 2004) attributes the current retreat from the certainties of developmental stage theory as symptomatic of a larger cultural shift from the reliance on an encompassing "grand narrative" that characterized Modernist thought, to a more postmodern comfort with modest explanations, small stories that may contradict one another, but may, in doing so, reveal complexities that the grand narrative could not articulate.

Contemporary Perspectives on Young Children's Art

After years in which the matter of child art seemed to be relatively well understood, its progress described in sufficient detail to guide both pedagogy and parenting, there is a resurgence of interest in understanding art in contemporary childhood. Classification of children's drawings according to the complexity of their structure—looking, for example, at the placement of the baseline in landscapes, or the number of details in human figures—has come to seem less important and less useful as a source of knowledge than the information that can be gleaned from the content of their work.

Children's drawings are now recognized across disciplines as important social documents, sources of information about children's interpretations of their experiences, and ways of eliciting conversation about their interests and ideas.

With this renewed interest in the content of children's drawings has come increased attention to the contexts, cultures, and circumstances in which children make art and the influences that come into play in that process. The recognition that drawing, for young children, is an immediate, ephemeral, and social act, and that finished drawings sometimes mask the competence of the child and the complexity of the process that brought the drawing about, recommend close observation and careful documentation of drawing events. This understanding of the importance of the conversations, gestures, and sequences of actions and decisions surrounding children's engagement in art making informs much current theory and practice on early childhood art.

Currently, adults interested in the ways children make meaning through image-making pay increasing attention to the social and performative context that surrounds young children's artistic productions and also consider children's agency as producers and critics of culture, rather than mere consumers. While children's drawings have been the focus of most research and theoretical attention, newly expanded images of children's capabilities as artists and audiences for cultural materials, including traditional art forms and contemporary visual culture, provide a broader understanding of children's participation in the visual arts. Children's video works, their performances, the choices they make in clothing, toys, music, and movies—artifacts of the visual and material culture of childhood—have come to be considered as sites where children make choices and meaning through visual means. This interest in the cultural context of childhood has led to interest in the kinds of art that children produce on their own or with peers, for their own purposes, beyond the work expressly sanctioned by adults in the public space of the classroom.

Practices that challenge established assumptions of how children develop in art—for example, the highly sophisticated art works that children in the preschools of **Reggio Emilia** routinely produce—have prompted scholars in the fields of education and developmental psychology to reconsider how and when children develop in and through making art-like things. The developmental questions have not been abandoned, but rather reframed through compound lenses that offer multiple points of view that promise to inform our understanding of how and when development happens. Despite these changes, interest in children's drawings remains high, since young children's drawings continue to serve as places where children strive to construct and communicate meaning through visual languages. *See also* Language Diversity; Symbolic Languages.

Further Readings: Bresler, Liora, and Christine Marmé Thompson, eds. (2002). *The arts in children's lives: Context, culture, and curriculum.* Boston: Kluwer; Kellogg, Rhoda (1970). *Analyzing children's art.* Palo Alto, CA: National Press Books; Kindler, Anna M., ed. (1997). *Child development in art.* Reston, VA: National Art Education Association; Leeds, Jo Alice (1989). The history of attitudes toward child art. *Studies in Art Education* 30(2), 93–103; Lowenfeld, Viktor (1957). *Creative and mental growth.* 3rd ed. New York: Macmillan; Wilson, Brent (2004). Child art after modernism: Visual culture and new narratives. In Elliot W. Eisner and Michael D. Day, eds. *Handbook of research and policy in art education.* Mahwah, NJ: Erlbaum, pp. 299–328; Wilson, Brent (1997). Child art, multiple interpretations, and conflicts of interest. In A.M. Kindler (ed.), *Child development in art.* Reston, VA: National Art Education Association, pp. 81–94.

Christine Marmé Thompson and Marissa McClure Vollrath

Child Care

Child care is a broad term that encompasses services that protect the health, safety, and well-being of children who require custodial care by adults other than their own parents for a temporary period of time. Child care can provide a number of important services, including the provision of nurturance and learning opportunities for children, support for employed parents, respite care in child welfare cases, access to supplemental services (e.g., vision and hearing screening, developmental testing, feeding programs), and parent support and **literacy** programs (National Research Council and Institute of Medicine, 2000; National Research Council, 2001).

The most common understanding of child care is one of community-based child care in which a child development program is provided for infants or children, away from home, for less than twenty-four hours per day for each infant or child. Child care is typically a full-working day service that provides supervision, nurturance, and learning opportunities to children of job-holding parents, or parents who attend school or job training. Child care is delivered in the private nonprofit, private for-profit, and public sectors in programs known as child-care centers, child development centers, family child-care homes, or infant care centers. The prevailing definition of child-care does not include public or private elementary or secondary schools engaged in legally required educational and related functions. For children with extremely unstable family circumstances, states have developed institutional child-care services that provide a safe and nurturing environment for children in residential facilities, day treatment centers, and child placement agencies.

While child care is increasingly seen as an important component of a broader system of early care and education that includes half-day prekindergarten, part-day

Head Start, and half-day **kindergarten**, there are important distinctions between current U.S. interpretations of child care and these "early education" programs. In particular, child care is explicitly intended to support working parents and, therefore, is offered for extended hours during the day. Even though the term "day care" is frequently used interchangeably with "child care," it is an inadequate synonym. Day care is increasingly regarded as an inappropriate term not only because child-care services are often provided during evening hours and overnight to meet the needs of parents who work nontraditional and shifting hours, but also because children are cared for, not days.

Child Care Delivery

During the 1990s, federal child-care assistance programs began to focus on parents as consumers. As a result, an increasing amount of child-care subsidy funding is now provided in the form of vouchers that parents may use to secure child care in a range of legal settings. Administering programs in this manner allows parents increased choice.

Child-care providers can be broadly classified as being relatives or nonrelatives of children. *Relatives* include mothers, fathers, siblings, grandparents, and *other relatives* such as aunts, uncles, and cousins. Relative care is often referred to as kith and kin care. *Nonrelatives* include in-home babysitters, neighbors, friends, and other nonrelatives providing care either in the child's or the provider's home, in addition to *family child-care providers* who are nonrelatives who care for one or more unrelated children in the provider's home. An *organized child-care facility* is a child-care center, nursery school, or preschool. Child-care facilities can be public, private, religious, secular, home-based, or center-based.

Quality of Child Care

In general, both parents and researchers agree that there are three broad categories of variables they want to see in a high-quality child-care program: (1) a sensitive and nurturing child–provider relationship; (2) manageable and monitored structural features of care (e.g., child to staff ratios, group size); and (3) supportive financing, regulatory, and staff development contexts (National Research Council and Institute of Medicine, 2000). Research has shown that these interrelated areas have a significant impact on the outcomes for young children in child care. In general, young children whose caregivers are attentive, supportive, provide ample verbal and cognitive stimulation, and who are sensitive and responsive are more developmentally advanced than children who do not have caregivers with these attributes (NICHD Early Child Care Research Network and National Institute of Child Health and Human Development, 2005).

Child care as a profession, though, is unstable. According to the U.S. Department of Labor, turnover rates among them (including those who move from one child-care program to another as well as those who leave the field altogether) range from 25 to 40 percent annually across the nation, among the highest of any profession. Exacerbating this are the low wages and minimal employment benefits offered to child-care workers (see, e.g., Center for the Child Care Workforce, 2004).

Child care is administered at both the federal and state levels primarily through departments of human or social services. States set minimum requirements for child-care programs to protect children from injury, unsafe buildings and equipment, fire, and infectious disease. All states regulate child-care centers and some family child-care homes through a licensing or registration procedure, although some centers and many homes are exempt from regulation. Exemptions vary based on what a state decides to regulate. For example, some states do not regulate part-day programs or programs associated with religious organizations. There is, however, general agreement in most states that they do not license the following situations as family child care:

- parents caring for their own children;
- relatives caring for only related children;
- foster parents caring only for foster children;
- care provided only while parents are on the premises; and
- care that is not regularly scheduled or is offered for only a few hours a week. (Morgan et al., 2001)

Beyond basic health and safety requirements, child-care rules and regulations also define a baseline of minimum quality that varies from state to state. The primary structural aspects of child care that are regulated by states' licensing rules are child to staff ratios, maximum group sizes, and staff qualifications and ongoing training.

With both changes to the welfare system and changing patterns of workforce participation of women, there has been a growing demand for child care and an increased recognition of the need for more funding for child-care services. Taking account of the entire child-care industry, families pay approximately 60 percent of total estimated annual expenditures for child care in the United States. Government (federal, state, and local) pays most of the balance (39%) through directly subsidizing all or part of child-care tuition fees or through tax credits. The private business and philanthropic sectors contribute less than 1 percent.

Many families are limited in what they can afford to pay, although they often spend a significant portion of their income on child care. According to Census Bureau figures, low-income families spend approximately 18 percent of their income on child care, compared with nonpoor families who spend 7 percent. Child-care affordability is a serious consideration for both parents and policymakers.

Child-care Policy History

On the basis of the values of industry, independence, religious freedom and toleration, and the belief that the family has primary responsibility for nurturing and educating children, social services in the United States were primarily designed to serve as institutions of last resort when personal and family supports failed. Child care is no different; its history is one of social welfare and services to the poor. While the dominant form of care and education for young children has traditionally been care by parents, out-of home care was first established in the early nineteenth century with the establishment of charitable infant and nursery schools to serve children of the indigent, providing what their parents could not or did not. Child care received heightened federal attention and funding during national times of crisis such as the Great Depression when large numbers of American families faced poverty, and World War II when increasing numbers of mothers were required to enter the workforce (Michel, 1996).

During the 1960s, child care became linked to welfare reform when Congress decided to help welfare mothers into the workforce by supporting targeted child care through block grants to states. A coalition of feminists, labor, and children's professionals supported an effort to federally legislate universal child-care provisions in 1971 with the Comprehensive Child Development Act. President Nixon vetoed the Act and, today, the United States remains as one of the few advanced industrial societies that lacks a comprehensive government-supported system of child care (Organisation for Economic Co-Operation and Development, 2001).

Within the context of welfare reform, the federal Family Support Act of 1988 required welfare recipients to work or participate in federally funded job training programs and states were to guarantee child-care services. Fewer than half of the states ultimately complied and advocates seized the opportunity to reopen a national debate about child care. As a result, in 1990, the **Child Care and Development Block Grant** (**CCDBG**) was signed into federal law, providing funding to states to provide child-care services primarily to low-income families. The Personal Responsibility and Work Opportunity Reconciliation Act of 1996 blended CCDBG with other funding streams, creating the **Child Care and Development Fund** (CCDF). CCDF is the major source of federal funding available to states, territories, and tribes to assist low-income families, families receiving temporary public assistance, and those transitioning from public assistance in obtaining child care so they can work or attend training/education.

Child Care Today

While the policy history of child care is dominated by a social welfare perspective, demographic changes in American family life since the 1950s have made child care an important issue for more than just low-income families. According to the Bureau of Labor Statistics, in 2004, nearly 62 percent of mothers with children under the age of six and 53 percent of mothers of children younger than a year old were in the labor force. Whether these mothers need to work—because they are heads of households or single parents—or whether these mothers want to work, they are in the workforce and they often require child care. Child care has become an important issue for families of all economic levels and social sectors of the United States.

Furthermore, child care is no longer viewed simply as a support for working families, but increasingly as a means to provide children with early learning opportunities. In any high-quality early learning setting (e.g., child care, prekindergarten, Head Start), care and education are delivered hand-in-hand, meeting the developmental and experiential needs of young children. Child care is one means not only for providing children with a safe environment, but also for nurturing children's physical, social, emotional, and cognitive development. *See also* Child Care Subsidies and Tax Provisions; Preschool/Prekindergartern Programs.

Further Readings: Center for the Child Care Workforce (2004). Current data on the salaries and benefits of the U.S. early childhood education workforce. Washington, DC: American Federation of Teachers Educational Foundation; Michel, Sonya (1996).

Children's interests/mothers' rights: The shaping of American child care policy. New Haven, CT: Yale University Press; Morgan, Gwen, Kim Elliott, Christine Beaudette, and Sheri Azer (2001). *Non-licensed forms of child care in homes: Issues and recommendations for state support.* National Child Care Information Center. Available online at http://www.nccic.org/pubs/nonlic-wheelock.html; National Research Council (2001). *Eager to learn: Educating our preschoolers.* B. T. Bowman, M. S. Donovan, and M. S. Burns, eds. Commission on behavioral and social sciences and education. Washington, DC: National Academy Press; National Research Council and Institute of Medicine (2000). *From neurons to neighborhoods: The science of early childhood development.* In J. P. Shonkoff and D. A. Phillips, eds. Committee on integrating the science of early childhood development. Washington, DC: National Academy Press; NICHD Early Child Care Research Network and National Institute of Child Health and Human Development, eds. (2005). *Child care and child development: Results from the NICHD study of early child care and youth development.* New York: Guilford; Organisation for Economic Co-Operation and Development (2001). *Starting strong: Early childhood education and care.* Paris: OECD.

Kristie Kauerz

Child Care and Development Fund (CCDF)

The Child Care and Development Fund (CCDF) is the primary federal child-care program in the United States. Using block-grants to states, the CCDF provides approximately $4.8 billion annually to assist low-income families and families who are receiving or transitioning from temporary public assistance to obtain child care so they can work or attend training or education programs. The children served by the CCDF range from birth to thirteen years and are cared for in child-care centers, public schools, family child-care homes, as well as in more informal care arrangements with family members, friends, or neighbors. In fiscal year 2004, the CCDF served 1.7 million children. The majority of these children (63%) were under six years of age, had working parents (81%), and were cared for in center-based arrangements (59%) (U.S. House of Representatives, 2004). In addition, the CCDF appropriation includes additional funding for specific purposes: nearly $172 million for quality expansion, $100 million to improve the quality of care for infants and toddlers, and $19 million to improve school-age care and Child Care Resource and Referral Services.

The CCDF was created in 1996 as part of a major restructuring of Federal welfare programs. The restructuring ended the welfare entitlement for low-income mothers and replaced it with a time-limited, work-focused program (see Cohen, 2001, for historical account). To provide child-care assistance to low-income, working mothers, the CCDF was created to consolidate and expand other federal child-care programs in effect at the time. With the aim of streamlining programs that had different foci and conflicting rules regarding eligibility, time limits, and work requirements, the newly created CCDF combined the multiple funding streams into one flexible block-grant administered by the states. States determine which families are eligible, the size of payments provided to the child-care providers, and other important elements of the child-care programs. In addition, states must use at least 4 percent of their block-grant to improve the quality or availability of child care but may choose to invest those dollars as they see fit. Thus states vary in their investment in such services as resource and referral counseling for parents and **professional development** for providers.

As states have responded to the flexibility offered to them under the CCDF, the result has been significant variation among state child-care assistance policies that affect the availability, affordability, and quality of child-care provided to low-income children. For example, in 2002, states' eligibility levels for a family of three ranged from $15,020 (in New Mexico) to $46,248 (in Alaska). Monthly child-care copayments for a family in poverty ranged from $0 in nine states to $435 a month (in Texas). Monthly reimbursement rates for full-time preschool care ranged from $330 (in Louisiana) to $903 (in New York) (CDF, 2003). This policy variation shapes the level and nature of assistance available to low-income families and leads child-care advocates to call for carefully monitoring to assess equity in the provision of services across states.

Further Readings: Child Care Bureau (June 2004). *The child care and development fund (Fiscal Years 2002-2003).* Available online at: www.acf.hhs.gov/programs/ccb/geninfo/ccdf02_03desc.htm; Children's Defense Fund (2003). *Key facts in child care, early education, and school-age care.* Washington, DC: Children's Defense Fund; Cohen, S. S. (2001). *Championing child care.* New York: Columbia University Press; National Child Care Information Center (June 2004). *Information products: CCDF.* Available online at www.nccic.org; U.S. House of Representatives, Committee on Ways and Means (2004). *Green book: Background material and data on programs within the jurisdiction of the committee on ways and means.* Washington, DC: Government Printing Office.

Elizabeth Rigby

Child Care and Early Education *Research Connections*

Child Care and Early Education *Research Connections* is a comprehensive resource for researchers and policymakers to promote high-quality research and inform policy on early care and education. *Research Connections* is based at the **National Center for Children in Poverty** (NCCP), a division of the Mailman School of Public Health at Columbia University.

The central feature of *Research Connections* is its Web site www.childcareresearch.org, which provides easy access to a searchable collection of research drawn from over fifty disciplines related to child care and early education. Continually updated, the collection currently contains over 7,000 resources. Resources in the collection examine the child care and early education experiences of children from birth through eight years and—when addressing school-age child care—through age 13. Other topics covered include parents and families using child care and early education services, the early childhood and school-age child-care work force, and child care and early education settings, programs, and policies. Resources include original research, syntheses, datasets (to download and to analyze online), instruments and measures (used for data collection), and other research-related materials. Additionally, the site provides guidance on understanding and assessing research quality, policy links on early care and education, and tools to analyze fifty-state data.

In addition to its research collection, *Research Connections* prepares briefs and reviews that synthesize policy-relevant research findings, for example, on child-care subsidies, promoting early language and literacy, and infant and toddler child care. All *Research Connections* publications are available on its Web site. *Research Connections* also undertakes a range of additional activities, which include organizing trainings on data analysis; convening roundtables on emerging issues; sharing materials from collaborations of researchers and policymakers; highlighting events and opportunities in the field; and responding to online research and policy requests. Information about these activities is available on the Web site.

Research Connections is supported by the Child Care Bureau, Administration for Children and Families of the U.S. Department of Health and Human Services through a cooperative agreement with the National Center for Children in Poverty and its partner, the Inter-university Consortium for Political and Social Research, University of Michigan. Access *Research Connections* at www.childcareresearch.org. For more information or assistance, send an e-mail to contact@childcareresearch.org.

Meredith Willa

Child Care Development Block Grant (CCDBG)

When Congress passed the 1996 Personal Responsibility and Work Reconciliation Act (PRWORA), replacing Aid to Families with Dependent Children (AFDC) with **Temporary Assistance for Needy Families** (TANF), thousands of low-income families receiving public assistance were required to participate in the work force. Because of the expected increase in parental employment, especially among single mothers, Congress also raised the federal government's support of nonparental care by expanding the Child Care Development Block Grant (CCDBG). This expansion gave money to the states to provide vouchers for some welfare recipients and child care providers for care of children under age 13 years. The United States Department of Health and Human Services administers the block grant under the name Child Care Development Fund (CCDF).

Originally created in 1990, CCDBG was designed to assist low-income working families that did not usually receive public assistance. The goal of the block grant was to increase child care availability, affordability, and quality and to enable low-income working families to participate in education and training programs. The expanded CCDBG replaced three federal child care programs: AFDC Child Care (geared to AFDC recipient families enrolled in education or training programs), Transitional Child Care (which helped families moving from AFDC to work), and At Risk Child Care (a program for families "at risk" of AFDC).

CCDBG gives states greater flexibility in allocating child care dollars, allowing them to set their own income limits, copayments, work requirements, and other procedures. There are, however, some federally imposed limitations. CCDBG funds can be used for care that is family-, home- or center-based, public or private, or religious or secular. Funding is available for families with incomes up to 85 percent of the state median for its size. Since CCDBG is not an entitlement program, not every family that is income-eligible receives it. According to the Administration for Children and Families, states generally give priority to several groups: teenage parents, especially those without high-school diplomas or GEDs, families on TANF or those transitioning off, families experiencing medical emergencies, parents enrolled in postsecondary education, families in homeless or spousal abuse shelters, children in foster care or protective services, and low-income parents with children seeking before- and after-school care. Further, states must use at least 4 percent of their allocated funds to improve child care quality.

Eligible families usually receive a child care voucher that they may use with any state-regulated provider. Some states, however, contract directly with providers for a limited number of slots; the provider then receives the payment for that slot from the government, up to a state maximum. Families pay a monthly copayment that is established by the government based on factors such as family size and income. Providers accept the voucher (or contracted government rate) as full payment, though these payments do not always cover the total cost of care. When the vouchers do not cover the full cost, some states allow providers to charge the family a fee in addition to their copayment to make up the differences.

While the CCDBG has been helpful to many low-income families, experts suggest that only 15–20 percent of those eligible for the fund receive it, for various reasons. Some families need the services but are unaware that the vouchers are available; others qualify according to the federal regulations, but do not meet the more stringent state policies; for some states funding is inadequate to meet the increasing need for subsidized care; and still others, particularly those living in expensive areas, have a difficult time finding a provider who will accept the vouchers. In an attempt to address these problems and to respond to increases in work requirements for TANF, welfare reform reauthorization has requested an increase in CCDBG of $1 billion over five years. Some policy experts, however, including the Congressional Budget, estimate that in order to cover most of the eligible families under welfare reform reauthorization, states would need an additional $6.1 billion over a five-year span. CCDBG was due to be reauthorized in July 2002, along with PRWORA, but to date, only the House has passed a reauthorization plan, with no Senate action.

Further Readings: The Child Care and Development Block Grant Act of 1990 (42 USC 9801 et seq.), as amended by the Personal Responsibility and Work Opportunity Act of 1996 (Public Law 104-193) and the Balanced Budget Act of 1997 (Public Law PL 105-33); Collins, A. M., J. I. Layzer, J. L. Kreader, A. Werner, and F. B. Glantz (2002). *National study of child care for low-income families: State and community Sub study interim report.* U.S. Department of Health and Human Services, Cambridge, MA: Abt Associates; Gish, M. (2002). *Child care: Funding and spending under federal block grants.* U.S. Department of Health and Human Services. Administration for Children and Families. Available online at http://www.nccic.org/pubs/crsreport.html#2; Long, S. K., and S. J. Clark, S. J. (1997). *The new child care development block grant: State funding choices and their implications.* Number A-12 in Series, "New Federalism: Issues and Options for States." Washington, DC: Urban Institute. Available online at http://www.urban.org/url.cfm?ID=307043; Schumacher, R. (2003). *Increasing the ability to transfer TANF to CCDF in House Welfare Bill (H.R.4) is still not the answer to unmet child care needs.* Washington, DC: Center for Law and Social Policy. Available online at http://www.clasp.org/DMS/Documents/1045149164.99/CC_Transfer.pdf.

Robert Leibson Hawkins

Child Care Information Exchange. *See* Exchange

Child-care Subsidies and Tax Provisions

Making child care affordable and employment possible for parents, while supporting positive development of children, has become an increasingly important public policy goal in the United States since the 1960s. To these ends, the federal and state governments have enacted a succession of legislation to directly subsidize child care and early education, as well as tax provisions to offset child-care costs. Subsidies have typically targeted low-income parents—with children through age 12—who are employed or preparing for employment. Tax provisions have been aimed at working families of all economic levels.

Subsidies take two basic forms. Widespread today are portable public payments that follow children—often called "voucher" payments—to help pay for child-care arrangements eligible families make for their children. The second are publicly financed child-care and early education programs—sometimes known as "contract" centers or family child-care networks. More common in the early decades of child-care subsidies in the United States, these programs are available to eligible families at low or no cost.

The two main child-care tax provisions that benefit families are tax credits for child-care expenses and employer-sponsored accounts of untaxed earnings that employees set aside to reimburse child-care costs.

Child-care Subsidies

Major federal programs that allocate funds to states for child-care subsidies and the primary families they target have included (chronologically) the following:

- Social Services Block Grant (SSBG) (1981–present). For low-income working families.
- Aid to Families with Dependent Children (AFDC)/JOBS Child Care (1988–1996). For families receiving AFDC and employed or participating in approved education, training, work preparation activities.
- Transitional Child Care (1988–1996). For families leaving AFDC for employment, for one year.
- At-Risk Child Care (1990–1996). For families at risk of receiving AFDC cash assistance.
- **Child Care and Development Block Grant (CCDBG)** (1990–1996). For low-income working families.
- **Child Care and Development Fund (CCDF)** (1996–present). Called CCDF by the Department of Health and Human Services, this 1996 amendment to CCDBG combined AFDC/JOBS, Transitional, At-Risk, and CCDBG child care and aimed to serve low-income working parents with and without connections to cash assistance.
- **Temporary Assistance for Needy Families (TANF)** Child Care (1996–present). For families receiving TANF and other needy families working or preparing for work receive direct TANF child-care subsidies. Most states also transfer unspent TANF funds to CCDF; some transfer to SSBG as well.

Two other major federal programs that support child care and early education are the following:

- **Head Start** (1965–present). For families at or below the federal poverty level, with children three years old to kindergarten entry. Designed to help break the cycle of poverty, Head Start provides a free, comprehensive child development program to meet children's emotional, social, health, nutritional, and psychological needs and works closely with parents. The federal government awards grants to local public agencies, private organizations, Indian Tribes, and school systems to operate Head Start programs at the community level. Usually part-day and part-year, Head Start programs help some participating employed parents meet some of their child-care needs. Particularly after the Personal Responsibility and Work Opportunity Reconciliation Act (PRWORA) of 1996 began moving more low-income mothers into the workforce, Head Start programs increasingly looked for ways to extend their service days, sometimes with wrap-around CCDF funding.
- Child and Adult Care Food Program (CACFP) (1968–present). For child-care providers serving children of low- and middle-income families. Participating providers receive reimbursements for the costs of meals and snacks—with higher reimbursements for low-income children, communities, or family child-care providers.

Spending for federal child-care programs increased substantially with the 1988–1990 creation of CCDBG, AFDC/JOBS, Transitional, and At-Risk child care—the last three responding to new work requirements for AFDC recipients. Head Start spending also began growing steadily in the early 1990s. Another, even larger, boost in child care spending came with the passage of CCDF in 1996, companion legislation to PRWORA, which replaced AFDC cash assistance with time-limited TANF benefits. Between 1997 and 2001, total federal and related state spending for CCDF, TANF, SSBG, Head Start, and CACFP rose to 69 percent, from about $11.1 billion to nearly $18.8 billion (in 2002 dollars). Growth slowed starting in 2001, reaching $20.4 billion in 2003—84 percent for the seven-year period (Table 1, U.S. Department of Health and Human Services).

Spending totals for CCDF and TANF child care include state and some county expenditures in maintenance-of-effort and matching funds. A number of states also regularly spend above the amounts required to receive their maximum CCDF allocations from the federal government. A few localities also support child-care subsidies, often serving families with incomes above eligibility cutoffs for state subsidy programs.

In 2003, the CCDF, TANF, SSBG, and Head Start programs paid for care for over 3 million children—CCDF 1.75 million; TANF 475,000; SSBG 38,000; Head Start about 900,000. The CACFP reimbursed meal and snack costs for 2.91 million children, many in child-care centers and homes that also received subsidies for child-care services. Despite these impressive numbers served, many eligible children do not receive subsidies. With the exception of CACFP, none of these programs is an entitlement. (While all licensed and approved providers serving low- and middle-income children are entitled to participate in CACFP, many do not apply or are not approved.)

In the early 1990s, states began establishing prekindergarten programs. Like the contracted centers and family child-care networks established early on with SSBG funding and like Head Starts, prekindergartens are publicly supported programs. In the 1991–1992 school year, pioneering states spent an estimated $700 million on free, part-day, part-year programs, mainly for disadvantaged four-year-old children at risk of low school achievement. By the 2002–2003 school year, thirty-eight states spent about $2.54 billion to serve approximately 740,000 children. Some states were also serving three-year-olds, and five states were moving to universally available services for children of all income levels. Although prekindergarten services are often offered in public schools, twenty-eight states make provision for prekindergarten in community-based child-care settings (National Institute for Early Education Research, 2004). Like Head Start programs, prekindergarten programs help fill some child-care needs for employed parents.

Portable voucher subsidies—not tied to particular programs—came into increasing use with the establishment of the AFDC/JOBS, Transitional, and At-Risk child-care programs and the accompanying expansion of funding. Voucher use grew even more with creation of the CCDF, which emphasizes parent choice of care and charges states to make subsidies available for all legal forms of care that meet basic health and safety requirements. States may exempt otherwise unregulated care by relatives and in children's own homes from these requirements, or they may set up more stringent requirements. Most states make voucher payments directly to child-care providers, though a few make some payments to parents to pass on to caregivers.

CCDF gives states great flexibility on key subsidy policies, issues central to operating any subsidy program within available financial resources:

- Income eligibility: While CCDF sets the maximum income eligibility ceiling at 85 percent of State Median Income (SMI) based on family size, states typically set lower ceilings as they strive to stay within their budgets. In 2002, the average state eligibility ceiling was 62 percent of SMI, and most families served across the county had incomes well below this level.
- Work and training requirements: Unless subsidies are provided for reasons related to child welfare, CCDF requires that participating parents be working or involved in training or education, but gives states broad discretion in defining these activities.
- Service rationing: CCDF gives no categories of families' entitlement to subsidies, as did the predecessor AFDC/JOBS and Transitional programs. Virtually all states, however, continue to guarantee subsidies to families connected to cash assistance. Further, about half the states have a commitment to serve all state-eligible families who apply, although—like all states—they may lower eligibility ceilings in response to budget shortfalls. The remaining states typically maintain waiting lists.
- Provider payment rates: CCDF asks states for evidence that their maximum payment rates give subsidized families access to a major portion of the child-care market in their communities. Though states are required to conduct Child Care Market Rate Surveys, budget limitations often force them to set rates lower than those indicated by the surveys.
- Parent copayments: Subsidized parents pay a portion of the state rate for their care—based on a sliding scale that typically takes into account income, family size, and number of children in care. There are significant state differences among copayment scales and in the percentage of income required for copayments from families at similar income levels. Also, when cost of care exceeds the maximum rate, parents normally pay the difference.

Child-care Tax Provisions

The following two tax mechanisms assist working families with child-care costs:
- Federal and state Child and Dependent Care Tax Credits (1976–present, federal).
- Federal Dependent Care Assistance Plan (1981–present).

The federal Child and Dependent Care Tax Credit reduces the taxes of working families with child-care expenses. Eligible families must incur expenses for the care of a child under age 13—or of an older dependent unable to care for himself or herself—in order to work or look for work. Twice since its enactment in 1976, the credit has been increased and made more progressive. Beginning in 2003, families with incomes up to $15,000 may claim an annual credit of up to $1,050 for one child (35% of a maximum of $3,000 in expenses) and $2,100 for two or more (35% of $6,000 maximum). Families with higher incomes may claim progressively lower percentages of their child-care expenses. At $43,000 and above, the maximum credit for one child is $600 (20% of $3,000) $1,200 for two or more (20% of $6,000). The credit cannot exceed what a family owes in taxes, and no benefit is provided to families whose incomes are so low that they pay no taxes. Thus, low-income families typically do not receive the credit's full benefit (Burman, Maag, and Rohaly, 2005). In federal fiscal year 2003, the U.S. Treasury lost an estimated $2.7 billion in forgone revenue due to the credit, an amount slightly higher than that year's child-care subsidy expenditures from TANF.

By 2004, twenty-seven states also offered a child and dependent care tax credit or tax deduction. Most states' tax credits are structured as a percentage of the federal credit or as a percentage of the care expenses eligible for that credit. Unlike the federal government, thirteen states with child and dependent-care tax provisions offer refundable credits, benefiting even families with incomes too low to owe state income taxes. Maximum annual values for 2004 ranged from $288 to $2,310 for a family with two or more children. Twelve states offered nonrefundable credits, and three offered deductions of child care expenses. (One state offered both.)

The federal Dependent Care Assistance Plan (DCAP) can benefit families of all income levels. Employees whose employers have set up DCAP plans may put aside up to $5,000 of their earnings each year, tax-free. They may then draw up these accounts to reimburse their documented child-care expenses. In federal fiscal year 2003, estimated revenue loss to the Treasury from DCAPs was approximately $577 million.

Although not specifically tied to child-care expenses, federal and state Earned Income Tax Credits and federal Child Tax Credit also extend the resources available to low-income families. *See also* Preschool/Prekindergartern Programs.

Further Readings: Blank, Helen, Karen Schulman, and Danielle Ewen (1999). *Seeds of success: State prekindergarten initiatives, 1998-1999.* Washington, DC: Children's Defense Fund; Burman, Leonard E., Elaine Maag, and Jeffrey Rohaly (2005). *Tax subsidies to help low-income families pay for child care,* Discussion Paper No. 23. Washington, DC: Tax Policy Center; Collins, Ann M., Jean I. Layzer, J. Lee Kreader, Alan Werner, and Fred B. Glantz (2000). *National study of child care for low-income families: State and community substudy interim report.* Cambridge, MA: Abt Associates; National Center for Children in Poverty. Federal Child and Dependent Care Tax Credit. November 2005. Available online at http://www.nccp.org/policy_index_14.html: National Center for Children in Poverty. State Child and Dependent Care Tax Credit. November 2005. Available online at http://www.nccp.org/policy_index_15.html; National Institute for Early Education Research (2004). *The state of preschool: 2004 State preschool yearbook.* New Brunswick, NJ: The State University of New Jersey, Rutgers; Schulman, Karen, and Helen Blank (2005). *Child care assistance policies 2005: States fail to make up lost ground, families continue to lack critical support.* Washington, DC: National Women's Law Center; U.S. Department of Health and Human Services, Administration for Children, Youth and Families, Administration for Children and Families (August 2005). *Federal and State child care expenditures (1997-2003): Rapid growth followed by steady spending.* Maryland: University of Maryland Foundation.

Lee Kreader

Child Development Associate (CDA) National Credentialing Program

The Child Development Associate (CDA) National Credentialing Program is a competency-based assessment system that offers early childhood professionals the opportunity to develop and demonstrate competence in their work with children ages 5 and younger. Originally developed in 1975 as a collaborative effort between the U.S. Department of Health and Human Services, Head Start Bureau, and the early childhood field, the CDA program has provided a nationally recognized system that has stimulated early childhood training and education opportunities for teachers of young children in every state in the country and on military bases worldwide. The credential is recognized nationwide in state regulations for licensed centers as a qualification for teachers, directors, and/or family child-care providers. The standards for performance that this program has established are used as a basis for professional development across the field of early childhood education.

The CDA program offers credentials to educators in four types of settings: (1) center-based programs for preschoolers, (2) center-based programs for infants/toddlers, (3) family child-care homes, and (4) home visitor programs. Regardless of setting, all CDAs must demonstrate their ability to provide competent care and early education practice in thirteen skill areas organized into six competency areas, which are outlined in the table below. Evidence of ability is collected from a variety of sources including first-hand observational evidence of the CDA candidate's performance with children and families, and this evidence is weighed against national standards. The CDA national office sets the standards for competent performance and monitors this assessment process so that it is uniform throughout the country.

By 2004, nearly 200,000 individuals had received the CDA Credential, with the vast majority (over 80%) prepared to work in centers with three- and four-year-old children. Research studies have found that CDAs have a very high rate of retention in the field, move upwards in terms of salaries and positions, and tend to continue their formal education toward college degrees (Day, 2004). Research studies have also shown that the CDA credential has a strong correlation with classroom quality and outcomes for young children (Raikes and Midwest Child Care Research Group, 2003).

The CDA Competency Standards

Competency Goals	Functional Areas
Goal I. To establish and maintain a safe, healthy learning environment.	1. Safe 2. Healthy 3. Learning Environment
Goal II. To advance physical and intellectual competence.	4. Physical 5. Cognitive 6. Communication 7. Creative
Goal III. To support social and emotional development and to provide positive guidance.	8. Self 9. Social 10. Guidance
Goal IV. To establish positive and productive relationships with families.	11. Families
Goal V. To ensure a well-run, purposeful program responsive to participants needs.	12. Program management
Goal VI. To maintain a commitment to professionalism.	13. Professionalism

People who become CDAs are individuals who want careers in early education and who work in any type of early education setting, including public schools, privately funded child-care centers, church-based preschools, Head Start programs, and family child-care homes. Anyone who is eighteen years old and holds a high-school diploma is eligible. However, prior to application for assessment, individuals must acquire the required competencies by participating in some sort of professional preparation. Many two-year colleges, early childhood agencies and organizations, and some employers offer such CDA education and training programs. Scholarships to participate are also offered in many states, and since the CDA preparation often articulates with college-based programs general financial support for higher education is often available to CDA candidates. As it continues to grow in size and scope, the CDA program is playing a major role in enhancing the quality of education for young children.

For more information on the CDA Program, model curriculum materials for the preparation of CDAs, and other resources, visit the Council's Web site at www.cdacouncil.org. The Council also published a history of the first ten years of the CDA program entitled *The Child Development Associate National Program: The Early Years and Pioneers by* Roberta Wong Bouverat and Harlene Lichter Galen, 1994.

Further Readings: Day, Carol Brunson (2004). *CDA survey.* Washington, DC: Council for Professional Recognition; Raikes, Helen and Midwest Child Care Research Group (2003). *Child Care Quality and Workforce Characteristics in Four Midwestern States.* Lincoln, Nebraska: The Gallup Organization.

Carol Brunson Day

Child Development Group of Mississippi (CDGM)

The Child Development Group of Mississippi (CDGM) was unquestionably the most famous Head Start program in Project Head Start's early years. It was created in the spring of 1965, the first season of the national Head Start program's existence, when, in every state and hundreds of localities, centers were being hastily developed. CDGM is still referenced and written about four decades later. It provides an excellent model for those wishing to reach and inspire very low-income parents of young children, particularly in areas here and abroad where there is an extreme shortage of professionals.

R. Sargent Shriver has often said, at the time and ever since, that CDGM was the most important Head Start in the country. Frequently called the Poverty Tsar, Shriver was the Director of the nation's entire poverty program, which emanated from The Economic Opportunity Act of 1964 and the newly established federal agency called the Office of Economic Opportunity (OEO). Sargent Shriver proposed Head Start to President Lyndon B. Johnson, although it was not mandated in the law, as one of OEO's many antipoverty programs. Shriver approved and signed every Head Start grant given in the United States during his tenure (1965-1970), Head Start's first five years.

CDGM was a visible federal investment because it was the epitome of what Shriver and OEO's Community Action staff wanted Head Start to be for children and families living in poverty, and because it represented traditional democratic values: human rights, health care, education, opportunity, jobs, and adequate wages for everyone. The segregationist wing of the Democratic Party (the Dixiecrats), which had controlled the state for many decades, did not share these values. For these reasons, CDGM was funded as the second biggest Head Start program in the country. For its first summer alone, CDGM was given a $1.3 million grant (in 2006 dollars, this equals about $5 million) to serve 12,000 children. Shriver considered CDGM so exceptional because it represented "maximum feasible participation of the poor." Although those not directly involved were proclaiming CDGM dead by the end of its first year, it has survived to the present under names such as Mary Holmes College Community Extension and Friends of the Children of Mississippi. CDGM and its descendents have served hundreds upon hundreds of thousands of children and had, by 1990, already received a billion federal dollars.

The CDGM was conceptualized and actualized by founding director Dr. Tom Levin, a New York psychoanalyst; the Reverend Arthur Thomas, who lived in Mississippi as Director of the Delta Ministry; and Polly Greenberg, Shriver's Senior Program Analyst for Head Start in the Southeast Region. Greenberg knew of Shriver's dream for the true community action program that Head Start could be and she urged Levin and Thomas to apply for a Head Start grant. The Delta Ministry was the National Council of Churches' Mississippi ministry and for two years had been doing voter registration; supporting race-related demonstrations; supplying legal advice and bail for jailed rights workers; operating a freedom information service; distributing tons of food, clothing, and books collected by church groups in the North; and other projects. Poor people knew and had faith in Tom and Art. Without the Delta Ministry's trusted community organizers, CDGM could not have happened. Trusted community organizers are essential to the replication of this Head Start model.

The thousands of children and families who participated in CDGM's Head Start program were black. Most lived in shacks and shanties in a desolate part of the state known as the Delta; most were the grandchildren or great grandchildren of field slaves. White families were too terrified of Ku Klux Klan reprisals even to talk to CDGM's organizers. There are many books about the reign of terror in this regrettable period of Mississippi's history. The documentary "Emmett Till" and two Hollywood films—"Color Purple" and "Mississippi Burning"—illustrate the context in which CDGM was launched. Historians point out that in 1965 Mississippi was the most racially violent, fiercely segregated, and poorest state in the union; it was a caricature of the South.

The Delta covers more than 7,000 square miles, and includes many counties from which no one had applied for a Head Start grant. The most minimal health care, such as immunizations, was not available within sixty miles of many families, most of whom had no transportation. At that time, there were no public kindergartens in the state, not to mention the Delta. Many families lived in Delta communities of ten or fifteen cabins (without plumbing). Obviously, there were no preschools, day-care centers, or early childhood professionals! Most CDGM children were destined to attend some of the worst public schools in the United States, where many of their future elementary teachers could read only at the third-grade level and there was sometimes only one copy of one book in the classroom—a basal reader. Facts about this widely reported phase of the state's history can be obtained from the U.S. Department of Health and Human Services, the Department of Education, numerous articles, books, and documentary films. National Public Radio and Public Broadcasting System websites are also good sources.

Those who became CDGM families lacked just about everything except generosity and courage. Their level of poverty was extreme—many families' incomes averaged $400 annually. Yet they organized sixty-four CDGM Head Start centers and opened the doors to 12,000 children in dozens of counties, all in eight weeks. To underscore the dangerous context of this astonishing feat, it took place one year after three young people who were helping black residents in Philadelphia, Mississippi register to vote were beaten to death with chains.

In most ways, CDGM centers were like all other Head Start centers in Head Start's earliest years. As guidelines explained, the focus was on children learning to play together, eating nutritious food, and enjoying broadly educational experiences at "school." Health care, social services, and parent participation were as valued as was early childhood education. However, in what many regard as the most important ways, CDGM was eye openingly different. The chief difference was CDGM's three originators' philosophy and the confluence of resources they brought together to implement it.

First, Tom Levin understood how permanently crippling disempowerment of parents is to their children. CDGM's three architects further believed that what happens in the classroom in a brief preschool program, regardless of how good the curriculum, has far less impact upon a child's lifelong trajectory than does what happens in his spirit and sense of possibilities when he watches the enormously disempowered parents with whom he is profoundly identified become competent and confident in bringing him happy days, and in initiating fundamental change in the community and greater society in which he is growing up. They knew that a livable income helps parents do better by their children—jobs would be at the core of this project. Crucial in CDGM's creation and character was that literally thousands of local, very low-income black leaders and parents in Mississippi, such as the famed freedom fighter Fannie Lou Hamer, passionately shared the philosophy, and quickly became forceful CDGM advocates. Dr. Levin, a specialist in psychological dynamics, considered a major role for poor parents such an overwhelming priority in helping their children that he structured the entire project to implement this principle.

As a result of this fundamental orientation to parents, there were no centers unless parents and their peers organized them. Through Delta Ministry and Student Nonviolent Coordinating Committee (SNCC) volunteers, most of the latter local black Mississippians, the word was spread across dozens of counties. They explained Head Start guidelines, and that each group of extremely poor residents would need to form a committee to act as the tiny cross-roads community's "school board," find and fix a facility, sign up eligible children by name and address, and hire potential staff if the locality chose to be part of CDGM's grant application. No grant was guaranteed. As just stated, the people's response was immediate and overwhelming. Even the overall Governing Board was two-thirds very poor people. There were four other members, one of whom was CDGM's eloquent spokeswoman and lawyer, the remarkable Marian Wright (Edelman), who had been living in the state in considerable jeopardy for several years handling school desegregation cases for NAACP's Legal Defense Fund.

Secondly, CDGM differed from other Head Start programs because, at great personal risk, participants attempted to implement one of the early national Head Start program's greatest emphases—motivating communities to activate local public health and social services departments and public schools; and to energize volunteers from the most and least powerful sectors, certainly from among the poor themselves, on behalf of low-income families and their children. This was Sargent Shriver's definition of "community action." His mantra was "What if all segments of each community mobilized to reduce poverty?"

Three weeks after CDGM Head Start centers opened, the white power structure at Mississippi's highest levels attacked it as "Communist" and "fiscally irresponsible." In response, poor people and the handful of professionals employed (at $50 a week) on their central staff and Governing Board members lobbied national leaders of the freedom movement such as Martin Luther King, the National Council of Churches, and the AFL-CIO's Citizen's Crusade Against Poverty. They also sought support from other liberal politicians and leading early childhood educators from many states, the northern press, and sympathetic OEO officials. They advocated so successfully that CDGM received many more Head Start grants. This was the kind of mobilization of middle class and professional communities that Shriver sought.

A third difference between CDGM and other Head Start programs was that it pushed to the limit the emphasis on "new careers for the poor" (especially for mothers), always one of Head Start's extraordinary features nationwide. In most Head Start centers some people learn their jobs as they go along, but key positions in each staff—teachers and directors—are held by individuals with some degree of postsecondary education and/or specialized training. There was no dispute about the value of training, but in CDGM it was believed to be of utmost importance for all children to participate in Head Start along with parents, relatives, and neighbors who were also learning. With only two exceptions statewide, no center staff members, including teachers, started out trained. The week before centers opened, Polly Greenberg left the federal government to work for CDGM in Mississippi. She designed a teacher development and training of trainers program, which she conducted across the state for two years to ensure that the program for children met Head Start requirements.

As a result of this emphasis on careers for the poor, every child saw one or more of her close relatives and well-known neighbors becoming cooks, drivers, social service workers, health workers, teachers, administrators, or members of a hiring and firing committee. They had seen nothing like this before! Children were not the only ones who were motivated. Several times during its first two years when between grants, poor people continued to operate their full scale Head Start programs for as much as six months without any funding. Within national guidelines, Head Start centers are almost always controlled by members of the middleclass and professionals. Within national guidelines, CDGM centers were controlled by the poor. This distinction was missed by no parent, although it has proven difficult for those lacking direct experience with CDGM to grasp.

The fourth difference between CDGM and most Head Starts was the role of professionals. There were none working directly within the centers. Instead, the handful of central staff professionals in each dimension of the program (administration, health services, early childhood education) provided technical assistance through an each-one-teach-one approach, aiming at enabling indigenous people to replace them within a year or less. Typically, CDGM had two or three professionals per 1,100 job holders and 12,000 children. The role of professionals included helping poor people organize, discuss, discover, and connect to sources and resources of all kinds, from learning to write grant applications to contacting influential people. It included being allies and advocates to the people's grassroots "movement" for children.

CDGM represents one of two very different streams of thought about the purposes of Head Start, the role of parents, and the role of professionals. For CDGM, the focus was not on every "student's" academic progress, or even on the child's social development, though certainly no one would have assailed these goals. CDGM's focus was on actualizing the belief that every human being, including children's parents, matters; and not just during the Head Start year, but throughout their lives. CDGM advocates and other like-minded people believe that substantial social change is required if our wish to help poor children "succeed" is authentic. They believe, further, that if activists don't work for it while developing educational programs, their motives can be considered disingenuous at best and possibly unconsciously protective of class privilege. CDGM's greatest lesson is that poor people, with allies, have great potential to press for change so that they find fewer obstacles and more opportunities to help themselves and their children move out of poverty.

Further Readings: Gillette, M. L. (1996). *Launching the war on poverty: An oral history.* Twayne, NY: An imprint of Simon & Schuster Macmillan; Greenberg, P. (1969/1990). *The devil has slippery shoes: A biased biography of the Child Development Group of Mississippi (CDGM)—A story of maximum feasible poor parent participation.* Washington, DC: Youth Policy Institute (originally MacMillan); Greenberg, P. (1990). Head Start—Part of a multi-pronged anti-poverty effort for children and their families. Before the beginning: A participant's view. *Young Children* 45(6), 40–52; Greenberg, P. (2004). Three core concepts of the War on Poverty: Their origins and significance in Head Start. In E. Zigler and S. Styfco, eds. *The Head Start debates.* Baltimore, MD: Paul H. Brookes; Harrington, M. (1962). *The other America.* New York: MacMillan; Matusow, A. J. (1984). *The unraveling of America: A history of liberalism in the 1960s.* New York: Harper and Row; Valentine, C. A. (1968). *Culture and poverty: Critique and counter proposals.* Chicago: University of Chicago Press; Zigler, E, and Valentine, J., eds. (1979). *Project Head Start: A legacy of the war on poverty.* New York: Free Press, pp. 61–83.

Polly Greenberg

Children's Defense Fund (CDF)

The Children's Defense Fund (CDF) is a private, nonprofit organization with an extensive track record of research and action on behalf of children. Founded in 1973 by Marian Wright Edelman, CDF has served as a catalyst for effective change on behalf of all American children. Offering a unique approach to improving conditions for children that combines research, public education, policy development, and advocacy activities, CDF has become an important advocate for the nation's most vulnerable children and families.

The Children's Defense Fund's Leave No Child Behind mission is to ensure every child a *Healthy Start,* a *Head Start,* a *Fair Start,* a *Safe Start,* and a *Moral Start* in life and successful passage to adulthood with the help of caring families and communities. CDF provides a strong, effective voice for all American children who cannot vote, lobby, or speak for themselves, paying particular attention to the needs of poor and minority children and those with disabilities. CDF educates the nation about children's needs and encourages preventative investment before children get sick, into trouble, drop out of school, or suffer family breakdown.

The Children's Defense Fund brings together the national, state, and local infrastructure; networks; experience; and expertise necessary to develop and implement a comprehensive nationwide approach to overcoming obstacles for working families and children. The national and state Children's Defense Fund offices throughout the country have developed working relationships with social service organizations, religious institutions, and schools and local governments to help eradicate poverty and make children's issues a priority.

The Children's Defense Fund helps the United States keep its promise to bring about better choices for children through education, research, advocacy, and organizing. Recent projects include visiting 500 adult prisons to document abuses suffered by children in adult jails, and advocating for changes in penal laws for children. The Children's Defense Fund also played a major role in generating recognition of and laws for children with special needs. CDF members knocked on 8,500 doors nationwide to report the tragic circumstances of two million children out of school, which led to the **Individuals with Disabilities Education Act** (IDEA).

CDF's research and advocacy continue to put a child's face on poverty, discrimination, and gun violence. The CDF's *Children's Defense Budgets* and *State of America's Children* yearbooks help activists stop unwise block grants and budget cuts and push for reforms and expansions in critical services like **Head Start,** housing, Medicaid, and nutrition programs for low-income mothers and their babies. Important laws that CDF has help to pass or are currently supporting include the landmark State Children's Health Insurance Program (CHIP), the Vaccines for Children Program, the **Child Care and Development Block Grant**, and the Earned Income and Child Tax Credits.

Each and every year, through direct tax preparation and in partnership with faith-based and other community groups, CDF enables thousands of low-income working families to claim the tax credits to which they are entitled. In one year alone, CDF helped families collect more than $65 million that went directly into their pockets and then back into local economies. CDF Freedom Schools are partnerships between the Children's Defense Fund and local community organizations, churches, universities, and schools to provide **literacy**-rich summer programs.

The Children's Defense Fund achieves its goals through the efforts of the organization's divisions and a variety of activities. CDF's Programs and Policy Department includes Child Health, Family Income, Child Welfare and Mental Health, Early Childhood Development, and Education and Youth Development, which engage in ongoing policy and communications efforts. The work of these departments includes speaking at national conferences and at Capitol Hill briefings and other influential forums; producing strategic reports; informing and engaging advocates through coalitions, regular updates, action alerts, and listservs; preparing press releases and editorials; and contributing to testimony, floor speeches, and pending legislation in Congress and in states.

Further Readings: Children's Defense Fund Web Site: http://childrensdefense.org.

Yasmine Daniel

Children's Media

Children's media is a popular topic in many fields, including early childhood education, child development, psychology, sociology, technology, and media studies. As a term, children's media has been interpreted in different ways, including media connected to books, television, music, movies, theater, computers, videogames, and the Internet that are produced for and engaged by children. Children's media is often a controversial topic within the popular discourse due to the attention it has been given by the political, educational, familial, and other community sectors. As children spend an increasing amount of their day engaged with media and finances are channeled to expand this industry, concerns have been raised regarding the media's effects on children as well as the messages being conveyed to children.

Research on media has primarily examined the media's effects on children from a developmental perspective with a psychological focus on the correlation or causal variables between the media and children's behavior. Despite this dominant point of view, there are other perspectives on children's media. Sociocultural perspectives examine how children's media is situated contextually in social, cultural, historical, and political contexts. Poststructural perspectives are also interested in the media contextually, but emphasize how children and the media interact with each other. Each of these multiple perspectives will be examined to provide a broader view of children's media.

From the *developmental perspective*, researchers are interested in how a given phenomenon, such as the media, affects children's development. Studies from this perspective are often referred to as "effect studies." Albert **Bandura's** (1973) social learning theory hypothesizes that people acquire behaviors through observations and subsequent modeling of other people's behavior. He was particularly interested in understanding aggression and how people acquire aggressive behaviors. He conducted a meta-analysis of research studies examining the relationship between television viewing and aggression, finding that there is a strong correlational relationship between viewing violence on television and the expression of aggressive behaviors both in the short- and long term. Many researchers have used Bandura's social learning theory to examine how different forms of media, particularly television, influence children's behavior. The popular press often reports on these types of studies, which in turn raise strong concerns among parents and educators. Many policies and regulations have been based upon this perspective, including ratings for movies, music, computer and videogames, the V-chip for cable television, and bans on books.

Adult concerns were further heightened when the Federal Communications Commission deregulated children's television in 1984. This legislation increased advertising minutes and the opportunity for children's toys to be marketed together with children's television programs. There were many concerns that the direct marketing of products related to television programs would negatively influence children's behaviors and in turn their families. Indeed, there was a significant increase in the amount of products available and purchased in connection to television programming. In response to this increase in children's media, many teachers found media-related toys or references to children's media inundated within the classroom. Frequently, teachers banned guns, superhero, and **war play** from the classroom due to the perceived connection to violence and aggression. These concerns are rooted in the developmental perspective and personal beliefs that the media is having a negative influence on children's behavior.

A *sociocultural perspective* differs from the developmental perspective because it situates the media in social, cultural, historical, and political contexts. Thus, this perspective is less focused on the effects of the media on children, but rather in how children interact with, respond to, and construct understanding about the media in cultural contexts such as their homes, classrooms, and in their peer culture groups. A sociocultural perspective often includes a focus on understanding children's perspectives, which is absent in a developmental framework that emphasizes adults' concerns and perspectives on child development.

Like many adults in the early 1980s, Nancy Carlsson-Paige and Diane Levin (1987) were concerned about the consequences of deregulation of children's television. In their work, they specifically address teachers' concerns about children and the influences of the media. Their sociopolitical theory emphasizes the importance of engaging children in discussions about media-inspired play and they recommend that teachers focus on trying to understand children's use of media within the context of their learning. They argue that parents and teachers should express their concerns directly with marketing companies, television agencies, and governmental bodies, rather than banning this play or these toys from the children.

William Corsaro (1985) extended the study of children's media by understanding children's daily lives through his theory of **peer culture**. Through long-term studies, he immersed himself in children's lives and found that children used popular culture texts ranging from literature, movies, and television to construct their own peer culture themes and texts. For example, a group of researchers who studied children's peer cultures in a classroom setting found that superheroes were important to the peer culture group. The children used artifacts related to superheroes to show their affiliation as a group of peers. The children were not simply imitating or repeating thematic ideas from the media; rather these media references were important to the children socially (Kantor and Fernie, 2003).

Vivian Paley (2004) has written prolifically about her interest in understanding children's perspectives and how they construct meaning within her classroom. In many of her writings, she discusses children's interest in the media and how it is brought into their play. Paley believes that fantasy play is an essential part of children's lives. She believes teachers should listen and learn from the children as they construct meaning together through their own storytelling, often around media texts ranging from *Little Red Riding Hood* to *Star Wars*.

Poststructural theorists interested in children's media examine the complex interplay between the reader/viewer and the media. In this perspective, children are viewed as simultaneously having agency while not being completely free from the knowledge and power of the media. In Henry Giroux's oft-cited text, "Are Disney Movies Good for Your Kids?" he conducts a critical analysis of the Disney empire, including its movies, theme parks, and the constructed residential community, Celebration (1997). Giroux believes that children are not passive consumers of the media, but argues that Disney is extremely large and influential and as such holds a large amount of power and influence on children.

Joseph Tobin (2000) argues for the use of children's voices and perceptions in examining children's media. In his book, *Good guys don't wear hats: Children's talk about the media*, Tobin uses a poststructual lens to analyze children's interactions with the media. He selected specific media clips and had the children view and discuss the clips with each other and with him through interviews. He argues that children's "talk" about the media is not solely their individual perspective, but rather is situated with societal concepts and views of the larger society within which they participate.

Similarly, through her ethnographic study of a primary grade classroom, Anne Haas Dyson (1997) analyzed how children incorporate the media into their classroom texts. She examined the infusion of popular culture both in the "official world" of the classroom and in the "unofficial world" of their peer culture groups. In the "official world" the teacher recognized the children's interests in the media, including superheroes, and incorporated these interests into the classroom, such as through their writing. Through integrating the children's media interests into the classroom context, she and the children analyzed their texts and made connections to societal constructions of racism, sexism, and classism. She utilized their written texts and drawings to examine, name, and critique these constructions within their stories, their classroom, and society. Through this, she was acknowledging the complex interplay of knowledge construction between the media and the children's constructed texts.

The study of children's media continues to be a complex and emotionally charged topic. Extending research perspectives will assist families, educators, and legislators to better understand how to address and monitor the potential impact of the media on children's lives. *See also* Play as Storytelling; Technology Curriculum.

Further Readings: Bandura, A. (1973). *Aggression: A social learning analysis.* Englewood Cliffs, NJ: Prentice-Hall; Carlsson-Paige, N., and D. E. Levin (1987). *The war play dilemma: Balancing needs and values in the early childhood classroom.* New York: Teachers College Press; Corsaro, W. A. (1985). *Friendship and peer culture in the early years.* Upper Saddle River, NJ: Ablex; Dyson, A. H. (1997). *Writing superheroes: Contemporary childhood, popular culture, and classroom literacy.* New York: Teachers College Press; Giroux, H. (1997). Are Disney movies good for your kids? In S. R. Steinberg and J. L. Kincheloe, eds. *Kinderculture: The corporate construction of childhood.* Boulder, CO: Westview, pp. 53–68; Kantor, R., and D. Fernie (2003). *Early childhood classroom processes.* Cresskill, NJ: Hampton Press; Paley, V. G. (2004). *A child's work: The importance of fantasy play.* Chicago: The University of Chicago Press; Tobin, J. (2000). *"Good guys don't wear hats": Children's talk about the media.* New York: Teachers College Press.

Jeanne Galbraith and Laurie Katz

Children's Museums

The Association of Children's Museums (ACM) envisions that these institutions "bring children and families together in a new kind of town-square where play inspires lifelong learning." Children's museums over the past twenty years have been evolving into a respite of multicultural play spaces in an era of increasing efforts to quantify and assess children's learning. With explicit goals to use play to stimulate children's curiosity, motivate children to learn, and to enrich communities, children's museums now work with multiple generations and reach across social class, racial and language boundaries to build community partnerships and extend their accessibility.

Children's museums have changed dramatically since the first museum for children was launched in Brooklyn, New York, in 1899. For about the first 70 years, children's museums served an audience of predominantly school-aged and young adolescent visitors. Exhibits and programming were largely focused on Americana, world cultures, natural history, science, and art. Many of the earliest children's museums held rich collections of artifacts ranging from souvenir dolls, dollhouses and early American household objects, to stuffed birds, shells and rocks. To further their learning, neighborhood children participated in a range of club activities from bell ringing and bird watching to diorama making and stamp collecting. Then, in the mid 1960s, Michael Spock, Director of the Boston Children's Museum, launched a new era in children's museums with the introduction of hands-on and interactive learning. In addition to viewing objects in exhibit cases, young visitors could explore the insides of many household and neighborhood items from washing machines to manholes

In spite of their long history, the growth of children's museums is a relatively recent phenomenon. Over 75 percent of ACM member museums opened in just the past twenty years. In 1975 there were approximately thirty-eight children's museums in the United States; eighty new museums opened between 1976 and 1990. An additional 100 have opened since 1990, with many serving as flagships in downtown revitalization projects. In 2001 over 31 million children and families visited ACM member museums. As of June 30, 2004, there were about 220 children's museums in the United States with about eighty in some stage of development. There are children's museums in 45 states, the District of Columbia and Puerto Rico. Only Alaska, South Dakota, Idaho, Vermont, and Delaware do not have a children's museum. Approximately 73 percent of U.S. children's museums are located in urban communities, with 20 percent in suburban, and 7 percent in rural settings.

Young children have always visited children's museum with their older siblings and families; beginning in the 1960s museums began to see an increase in the number of young children (ages 0–5) as the primary child visitor. In 1976, the Please Touch Museum opened in Philadelphia as the first early childhood museum designed for visitors aged 1–7. In 1978, the Boston Children's Museum opened the nation's first "PlaySpace," a parent and child exhibit area especially for children four years and under (Quinn and Robinson, 1984). By the late 1990s, encouraged partly by research on brain development, there was a strong resurgence of interest in the development of an early childhood museum focus, with a number of new spaces, serving children from birth to three years, developed since 2000. Today 78 percent of the children's museums in the United States have an early childhood space or program.

To accommodate younger visitors and their parents, the physical space of museums has changed significantly. For example, museum amenities now include family bathrooms, nursing areas, snacking, and respite areas. Information in the form of parent graphics, tip sheets and exhibit guides help parents introduce and share exhibit concepts with young children.

With sizes ranging from 500 to 5,000 square feet, content, budget and staffing for children's museum programs vary greatly. For example, exhibits may introduce parents and preschoolers to **literacy** through special exhibits on "Clifford, the Big Red Dog" or "Go Figure," an exhibit that brings five math-related picture books to life; both exhibits were created by the Minnesota Children's Museum. PlaySpace, at the Boston Children's Museum, encourages both parents and children to explore the world of play through special areas established to promote creative art experiences as well as gross and fine motor imaginary, discovery, and dramatic play.

As museum programming has shifted, there has been an increased emphasis on community-based partnerships for both families and professional early educators. During the weekdays, museum audiences are predominantly stay-at-home mothers or nannies and young children. Many museums provide significant outreach to the early childhood education community including preschools, **Head Start** and family or center-based child-care programs. Moreover, "the visit" is only one part of what children's museums offer to the community. With professional early childhood educators on staff, many children's museums also offer professional development training for early educators, resources and programs for parents, special family visits and free family memberships and passes. Outreach programs in ACM member organizations extended to over 3.9 million people in 2000 and to over 6.6 million in 2001.

With adults (most of them parents) making up nearly 50 percent of the visitors, children's museums are in a unique position to provide information and support on child rearing and early education. Museum-sponsored parent programs, such as Families First in Boston and Houston, provide single sessions and series of classes led by experts in family and child development for parents who register and pay a nominal fee.

Even as museums take pride in their accomplishments, recent trends suggest new challenges and possibilities in the twenty-first century. There is a new interest in exploring multicultural and international environments, making the local and international communities a potent classroom. For example, *Boston Black*, an interactive exhibit (at the Boston Children's Museum), allows children to explore the cultural, racial and ethnic diversity of the city. A second trend is tied to changes in museum attendance; as the museum audience has become younger, it is no longer dominated by six- to twelve-year-olds. When museums that traditionally served older children and adults, for example, science museums, began to adopt the successful hands-on, interactive techniques pioneered by children's museums, they increased their appeal to older children. Children's museums are also becoming more widely recognized as a "catalyst for intergenerational learning" and "two generation" programming, given their expanding willingness to provide opportunities for learning and sharing in a supportive environment (Crowley, 2000). In spite of the changing emphases, there is not a strong research base on child and adult learning in museums. Much of what is known comes from short-term problem-solving evaluations and surveys; very few studies have involved young children (Sykes, 1996).

Conclusion

Museums have clearly been transformed into dynamic learning environments where preschool children and their families are welcomed and embraced. In this transformation, significant outreach has occurred to bring museum experiences to children and families in the community. Museums are also increasingly recognized as learning tools for the professional development of early educators. These trends have quickly become institutionalized as part of the children's museum identity (ACM).

Further Readings: Association of Children's Museums. Available online at http://www.childrensmuseums.org; Crowley, K. (2000). Building islands of expertise in everyday family activity: Musing on family learning in and out of museums. *Museum Learning Collaborative Technical Report* [MLC-05], Learning Research & Development Center, University of Pittsburgh, PA; Crowley, K., and M. A. Callanan (1998). Describing and support collaborative scientific thinking in parent-child interactions. *Journal of Museum Education* 17, 12–17; Quinn, P., and J. Robinson (1984). *PlaySpace: Creating family spaces in public places.* Boston: Boston Children's Museum Publication; Sykes, M. (1996). Research review on museum-based learning in early childhood. *Hand to Hand: The Quarterly Journal of the Association of Children's Museums* 10(2).

Jeri Robinson and Valora Washington

Child Study Movement

The child study movement, inspired by Darwin's theory of evolution, began in the United States in the early 1880s. The movement attracted and was supported by the work of such luminaries as G. Stanley **Hall**, John **Dewey**, Arnold **Gesell**, and John **Watson**, as well as a housewife by the name of Cora Bussey Hillis. With the realization that little was scientifically known about how children grow and develop, Hall and Gesell set out to collect a large body of data describing the growth and development of children from infancy to adolescence.

The normative data on children's growth and development collected by Hall and Gesell influenced what parents, teachers, pediatricians, and clinicians came to expect as normal development at each age. The child development research stimulated by the child study movement reinforced the importance of the early childhood years and pointed to the desirability of early childhood programs.

G. Stanley Hall (1844–1924) played a pivotal role in the organization and support of activities of the child study movement. In 1884, Hall became the first professor of psychology in the United States when he was given a professorship at Johns Hopkins and John Dewey was one of Hall's first students. Because Hall believed children progressed through stages of development like flowers unfolding automatically, he thought it was important to observe children under natural conditions to formulate a theory of social development. Children, therefore, became subjects of laboratory study. In 1888 Hall founded the Child Study Association of America, shortly before becoming president of Clark University, a position he held until 1924.

Child study clubs were formed in regions all over the United States and large amounts of data were collected by parents, teachers and academic researchers until the early 1900s. Teachers at the elementary and secondary levels were encouraged to document children's learning and their teaching practices, thus contributing to the developing field of educational psychology. Hall gave extensive questionnaires to large numbers of children of all ages to study "the contents of children's minds." He asked questions regarding interests, fears, shyness, imaginary playmates, dreams, friendships, teasing, bullying, favorite toys, and more. Data from questionnaires was aimed at helping teachers learn what knowledge and experiences children had upon entry to kindergarten. Averages of all the items were taken as typical development. The National Education Association established a Department of Child Study in 1893.

Another major contributor to the Child Study Movement was another of Hall's students, Arnold Gesell (1880-1961). After receiving his Ph.D. in psychology in 1906, Gesell set up a "psycho-clinic" at Yale's New Haven (CT) Dispensary so that he might study every facet of the development of infants and children from white, middle-class families (motor skills, social behavior, and personality characteristics) and then establish "norms" or descriptions of typical development at each age level.

Also in 1906, Cora Bussey Hillis, an Iowa housewife and mother, proposed the idea of a research station at the University of Iowa for the study of children and the improvement of child rearing. She reasoned that if raising hogs and corn could be improved by research so could child rearing. This led to the establishment of the University of Iowa Child Welfare Research Station in 1917. The Iowa facility and the Merrill-Palmer Institute in Detroit became the models for other child development institutes that were set up across the country in the 1920s and 1930s. Because one of the main purposes was the dissemination of information about children to parents, teachers, and college faculty, a number of publications were launched: university monographs, research journals (*Child Development*), and magazines (*Parents' Magazine*). The new research institutes also awarded graduate degrees in child development. Upon graduation, these new professionals found employment in colleges and universities, as well as in a variety of applied settings.

The 1920s were the "golden age" for the study of children in the United States. New private and government funds were forthcoming to support child study and parent education. The Laura Spellman Rockefeller Memorial provided millions to foster child development as a growing field of scientific endeavor. Under the direction of Lawrence **Frank**, funds were awarded to establish major child research centers at the University of California at Berkeley, Columbia University, and the University of Minnesota. Financial support was also provided to existing research centers at Yale and the University of Iowa. Smaller research institutes were launched at the University of Michigan and in Washington, DC, and funds were provided for individual research projects. Reflecting the growing interest in and importance attributed to the study of child development, The Society for Research in Child Development was founded in 1930.

The research contributions of these pioneers in child study were summed up in 1930 by Florence Goodenough (Cairns, 1998).

- Mental testing—All research institutes were investigating mental testing. Iowa documented the effects of an enriched environment on intelligence. Minnesota and Fels studied stability and change in intelligence. Stanford disputed any research claims that intelligence was malleable.
- Longitudinal study—Most researchers believed that longitudinal studies were necessary, but did not have the funding or the guarantee that their institutes were permanent enough to undertake long-term studies. Fels Institute and Berkeley, however, began systematic longitudinal studies.
- Behavioral and emotional development—Johns Hopkins, Columbia, Minnesota, California, and Washington University (St. Louis) studied children's fears, specifically how emotions arise and how fears are learned and unlearned. This was an outgrowth of Watson's research at Johns Hopkins.
- Growth and physical maturation—Early research at Iowa addressed the physical development, care, and feeding of children. Gesell at Yale made graphs of normal development for use in identifying atypical development. The Fels Institute examined relationships between physical and behavioral development.
- Research methods—John Anderson and Goodenough at Minnesota, among others, saw the need for better observational research techniques. Goodenough explored new ways of assessing personality and intelligence (including her Draw-A-Person test).

Most of the work at the newly founded institutes focused on the pragmatic question of how to best raise children and the methodological issues of how to study children. Major theoretical development was left to others.

Further Readings: Brandt, R. (1980). *The child study movement.* Charlottesville, VA: University of Virginia School of Education; Braun, Samuel J., and Esther P. Edwards (1972). *History and theory of early childhood education.* Belmont, CA: Wadsworth; Cairns, Robert B. (1998). The making of developmental psychology. In Richard M. Lerner and

William Damon, eds. *Handbook of child psychology*, Vol. 1, 5th ed. *Theoretical models of human development*. New York: Wiley, pp. 25–105; White, Sheldon H. (1992). G. Stanley Hall: From philosophy to developmental psychology. *Developmental Psychology* 28(1), 25–34.

Carol S. Huntsinger

Classroom Discourse

Classroom discourse is the vehicle through which much of the teaching and learning occurs in educational settings. It consists of the communications system that teachers set up to carry out educational functions and maintain social relationships. The discourse between teachers and children includes spoken language and nonverbal gestures and facial expressions that are connected to each other in the flow of talk. A guiding principle in considering discourse is that teacher and student comments cannot be analyzed in isolation from each other or the larger classroom culture.

Classroom discourse is the means by which children gain access to the **curriculum.** Activities alone cannot help the child construct understandings without accompanying teacher–child interactions that help the child make connections to his or her world of ideas. To learn, students must use what they already know so as to give meaning to new ideas in the curriculum. The young child uses her language to construct her own understanding about what is going on. When children give voice to their ideas, their speech makes their interpretations visible to themselves and others, facilitating their ability to relate new knowledge to old. But this potential new learning depends on how the teacher structures the learning dialogue

Careful examination of classroom discourse magnifies the actual teacher–child encounter and enables the observer to see the dynamic nature of teaching, in which teachers and children influence and become environments for each other and the activity changes from minute to minute as the interaction proceeds. In this way curriculum is much more than or sometimes even different from what teachers plan in advance. Teachers' and children's responses to each other during classroom discourse play a powerful role in determining what is actually taught and what is actually learned.

> The actual (as opposed to the intended) curriculum consists in the meanings enacted or realized by a particular teacher and class ... On the basis of the cues, people in interaction develop an idea of what the context is at the moment; in a sense they define the context. Because in the course of the on-going interaction, the context may change from moment to moment, their definition of context may also change. It is partly because of these momentary definitions that people are able to know and decide what is going on. How they shape their discourse shows what they really understand the task to be: what they do shows they understand what is going on. (Erikson and Schultz, 1981, p. 62)

Curriculum, within this perspective, is an evolving process created through reciprocal interactions as the teacher attempts to make the child a partner in the discourse. Children in early childhood classrooms are struggling to refine their own language, and simultaneously learn how to participate in the classroom dialogue and use that dialogue to understand curriculum content and social relationships.

The study of classroom discourse has its roots in the research on teaching as a linguistic process and the influence of anthropologists on making the study of language relevant to classroom practice. Dell Hymes (1972) was one of the first to highlight the importance of studying language as embedded in the social context of the classroom. Courtney Cazden (1986, 2001) further inspired and shaped this field of study.

Green (1983) offers the following five constructs that characterize classroom discourse:

1. Face to face interactions between teachers and children are governed by context specific rules.
2. Activities in classrooms have participation structures with rights and obligations for participation. Contextualization cues are the verbal and nonverbal cues that signal how utterances are to be understood and inferencing is required for conversational comprehension. Rules for participation are often implicit, conveyed and learned through the interaction itself.
3. Meaning is context specific.
4. Frames of reference are developed over time and guide individual participation.
5. Complex communicative demands are placed on both teachers and students by the diversity of communicative structures.

Teachers establish participation rules specific to their own classrooms. Teachers may communicate rules orally or with the way they look at a child, a gesture (hands on hips, pointing), or by maintaining or breaking eye contact. For children to participate successfully in a classroom dialogue, they need to develop communicative competence—understanding how to participate in that particular setting and the ability to use that knowledge in the process of communicating. For example, children must learn the rules about taking turns, acceptable ways of getting into the discussion (getting the floor) and staying in the conversation (keeping the floor).

These participation rules often change when a child moves to another classroom, as illustrated by the variety of acceptable ways children have of "getting the floor," for example, by nomination (child gets a turn when teacher calls her name), calling out (child allowed to talk when she has an idea about the topic), hand raising (child raises hand and waits until called on), going around the circle or passing a "talk object," or being quiet and sitting still—"I'm waiting to see who's sitting still and being quiet."

Traditional and Nontraditional Discourse

The most commonly practiced discourse pattern remains the IRE (teacher initiation, child responds to teacher, teacher evaluates response as right or wrong). For example:

Teacher: What are the three things a plant needs to grow?
  Child: Sun.
Teacher: Right.

One feature of classroom life highlighted in this discourse pattern is the inequality of power between teachers and children. In traditional classroom discourse the teacher generally does most of the talking and controls *all* talk by deciding who speaks and when, regaining the floor after each student turn. In the traditional pattern the teacher asks for the correct answer (usually one word), and, if given an incorrect answer, corrects the child, moves onto another child, or disapproves the answer in some way, essentially cutting off the discussion after the correct answer is uttered. The teacher can interrupt the child at any time and usually waits only a few seconds for a response. In this discourse pattern, the teacher typically uses a specialized kind of talk that is particular to and may only have meaning in the classroom. This conventionalized way of speaking in classrooms is known as the teacher-talk register. Most teachers employ some or all of this conventional talk form. For example, a teacher says "Excuse me" to control or reprimand a misbehaving child and uses test questions that are not genuine questions because the teacher already knows the answer (see example above). Analyses of teacher talk categorize these questions as lower level questions because they require little thinking or language to answer; they can be answered with one word, often by repeating the teacher's words or reiterating simple facts learned previously.

This discourse style best matches a theory of learning that considers the transmission of facts from teacher to child as the best way for children to acquire knowledge. The goal of the discourse is to get specific words from the curriculum spoken in the "official classroom talk."

In the past three decades teachers (particularly those in early childhood classrooms) have begun to use nontraditional discourse styles, due to the growing awareness of the how classroom discourse style influences knowledge construction. In nontraditional classroom discourse, there is an emphasis on making the student a more significant part of the official learning environment based on the idea that children are shapers of their own knowledge and must have many opportunities to do so in the learning dialogue. Increasingly, teachers share power with the children and attempt to make each child a more equal partner in the discourse. In this form of classroom discourse, the teacher does not continually control who is allowed to speak and expects, and often promotes, more child talk than teacher talk. The children are encouraged to initiate talk and express their own ideas and the teacher builds on the information and experiences of the children as well as provides new information. The teacher accepts alternative answers and children are asked to elaborate on their responses.

In this more contemporary classroom, the teacher tries to implement discourse practices that are intended to create a community of learners which children are asked to listen to and learn from their peers as well as the teacher. With a focus on genuine inquiry (as opposed to test questions), nontraditional discourse resembles discussions where children are invited to contribute ideas and engage in collaborative problem solving; and encouraged, when necessary, to disagree with classmates or the teacher. The potentials of this non-traditional discourse practice are illustrated in the following example as kindergarten children discuss Leo Lionni's book *Tico and the Golden Wings*:

Teacher: I don't think it's fair that Tico has to give up his golden wings.

    Lisa: It is fair. See he was nicer when he didn't have any wings. They didn't like him when he had gold.

   Wally: He thinks he's better if he has golden wings.

   Eddie: He is better.

     Jill: But he's not supposed to be better. The wishing bird was wrong to give him those wings.

Deanna: She has to give him his wings. He's the one who shouldn't have asked for golden wings.

   Wally: He could put black wings on top of the golden wings and try to trick them.

Deanna: They'd just sneak up and see the gold. He should just give every bird one gold feather and keep one for himself.

Teacher: Why can't he decide for himself what wings he wants?

(Cazden, 2001, p. 83)

In this discussion of fairness, the turn taking is managed and initiated by the children without the teacher controlling who speaks. They listen to and build on each others' ideas. The teacher and children coconstruct the text as they present and defend their points of view. In the participation structure established in this classroom the children are free to disagree with the teacher. They are equal partners in determining the direction of the discussion. The teacher promotes cognitive development by putting the children's voices in the foreground and asking them to reflect on and state their own ideas. They become the meaning makers. The teacher gains insight into their ability to understand and analyze the text as well as their skill in using language. Of course these types of conversations also influence children's social development as they learn of and debate the merits of different points of view.

Educational researchers have examined the kinds of questions teachers use in the classroom as they influence cognitive and linguistic demands and learning opportunities. Results of such studies suggest that open ended questions and questions that create discrepancies, pose contradictions, and require shifts of perspective are the more cognitively and communicatively demanding, usually involving evaluation or synthesis of information since there are typically many possible answers to these questions. The kinds of classroom conversations where children are asked to recall experiences outside the educational setting are also important because they require children to distance themselves in time and space from the present. Thinking about past or future events requires a mental presentation of what has happened to the child at an earlier time or of what may happen and thus require more cognitive effort and more complex language than is necessary when describing what is immediately observable.

Form Versus Function and Different Patterns of Language

Two features of nontraditional classroom discourse are (1) the movement from a focus on the form to the function of language and (2) the recognition of the need to address what anthropologist Shirley Brice Heath (1983) calls culturally distinctive "ways with words."

Beginning in the 1970s educators, and sociolinguists focused attention on discourse in preschool classrooms and set the stage for growth in preschool discourse practices (Genishi and Dyson, 1984; Halliday, 1975; Tough, 1976). At the time many early language programs focused teachers primarily on syntax, phonology, morphology—how the language looks and sounds, the *form* of language—rather than on how well a child was able to use language to convey meanings and relate successfully to peers and his teachers—the *functions* of language. Classroom discourse was characterized by correcting children's grammatical errors and by teacher modeling and children repeating linguistic forms based on the premise that their knowledge of language was inadequate. However, studies of three to five-year-olds from low socioeconomic and minority backgrounds found that rather than having an inadequate knowledge of the language (as some educators and linguists assumed), these children were disposed to use language differently Their interactions within family and communities often did not match the ways that language was used in educational settings. The resulting lack of mutual comprehension between the teacher and child in the discourse interferes with the verbal and cognitive growth the teacher may seek and of which the children are capable.

While both form and function are integrated and necessary in communication, these studies suggested that if teachers responded to what children were saying and how they were able to use language in the process of interacting (the functions of language), both children's learning and communication skills would improve. Tough (1976) and others (Genishi and Dyson, 1984; Halliday, 1975) developed tools for assessing language use in the classroom that help teachers to reconceptualize their role in the discourse; and assist children to convey meaning more effectively. Teachers could document the complexity of children's thinking and gain useful information about how young children use their language to interpret experiences. Instead of asking for one-word "labels" for objects or pictures in a book, teachers asked children to use language to perform a variety of functions such as describe what happened in a book, report on their experiences, provide explanations, reflect on reasons or predict outcomes of events.

Current curriculum standards and pedagogical practice in early childhood education builds and expands on these ideas as illustrated in the expectations for early childhood professionals by the **National Association for the Education of Young Children** (NAEYC) and other professional resources. Strategies are offered to help infant/toddler and preschool teachers lay the foundation for conversations, foster peer interactions, and help children become more equal partners in the discourse (Weitzman and Greenberg, 2002*). Standards for Speaking and Listening* (2001) outlines the kinds of talk we should expect from children preschool through the third grade and describes how teachers can help children participate successfully in the classroom dialogue. The National Council of Teachers in Mathematics, a discipline previously noted for its traditional discourse pattern, has also issued guidelines calling for the teacher of math to promote classroom discourse in which students listen to, respond to, and question the teacher and one another, initiate problems and questions, and explain how they arrived at math answers. Reflecting premises of **social constructivism** and **sociocultural theory**, teachers are now asked to co-construct the science curriculum with children, framing the discussion around children's questions and responses. The **Reggio Emilia** program is the most prominent early childhood education approach where the child becomes the meaning maker and the classroom dialogue is used to help children unpack their knowledge so that it is available for review and further symbolic representation.

In classrooms characterized by **teacher research** and portfolio **assessment**, teachers will use transcripts of small group dialogues and children's reasoning in problem-solving tasks to understand their science learning (Gallas, 1995). This form of **documentation** allows educators to gain a better understanding of individual development and the nature of shared knowledge being constructed by children in the classroom. Studying classroom discourse also helps teachers become more reflective practitioners, giving them a valuable tool to study and improve their own practice. "There is no other way that is as honest and powerful as a transcript to take you back to that moment in time, and bring everyone else back to that moment . . . allow an outsider to pay close attention to the words of a particular classroom" (Cazden, 2001, pp. 6, 7). Recording the voices of children within the curriculum discourse also validates children as they come to see that their ideas are valued and play a key role in the curriculum as meaning-makers (Wells, in Cazden, 2001). The growing popularity of the idea of *accountable talk* asks that students make use of specific and accurate knowledge, justify claims, use rational strategies to present arguments and be accountable to each other by listening attentively and asking for clarification (Resnick, in Cazden, 2001). In this sense, respect for children's talk can help children learn to be more respectful and responsible citizens in the classroom.

Most early childhood teachers favor non-traditional discourse styles, although varying degrees of traditional classroom discourse can be still in observed in early education settings. Teachers in public elementary schools and federally funded programs, many of whom feel constrained by the **No Child Left Behind Act** accountability and high-stakes testing, are more prone to employ traditional strategies in their discourse. But classroom discourse in early childhood settings has changed significantly in the past three decades as teachers recognize the importance of creating a space for children to have a voice, to become full partners in classrooms. As more teachers use the educational dialogue to support the dynamic and reciprocal nature of teaching and learning, non-traditional classroom discourse will become the tradition. *See also* Curriculum, Science; Development, Social; Symbolic Languages.

Further Readings: Cazden, C. B. (1986). Classroom discourse. In M. E. Wittrock, ed. *Handbook of research on teaching.* 3rd ed. New York: Macmillan, pp. 432–463; Cazden, C. B. (2001). *Classroom discourse: The language of teaching and learning,* 2nd ed. Portsmouth, NH: Heinemann; Erikson, F., and J. Schultz (1981). When is a context? In J. Green and C. Wallat, eds. *Ethnography and language in educational settings.* Norwood, NJ: Ablex; Hymes, D., C. B. Cazden, and V. P. John (1972). *Functions of language in the classroom.* New York: Teachers College Press; Gallas, K. (1995). *Talking their way to science: Hearing children's questions and theories, responding with curricula.* New York: Teachers College Press; Genishi, C., and A. Dyson (1984). *Language assessment in the early years.* Norwood, NJ: Ablex; Green, J. (1983). Research on teaching as a linguistic process: A state of the art. In E. Gordon, ed. *Review of research in education.* Washington, DC: American Education Research Association, pp. 151–254; Halliday, M. A. K. (1975).

Learning how to mean: Explorations in the development of language. London: Edward Arnold; Heath, S. B. (1983). *Ways with words: Language, life, and work in communities and classrooms.* New York: Cambridge University Press; New Standards. Speaking and Listening Committee (2001). *Speaking and listening for preschool through third grade.* Washington, DC: National Center on Education and the Economy and the University of Pittsburgh; Tough, J. (1976). *Listening to children talking: A guide to the appraisal of children's use of language.* London: Ward Lock Educational for the Schools Council; Weitzman, E., and J. Greenberg (2002). *Learning language and loving it: A guide to promoting children's social, language and literacy development in early childhood settings,* 2nd ed. Toronto: The Hanen Centre.

Gail Perry

Classroom Environments

A classroom environment in early childhood education settings involves a space where young children have opportunities to interact with each other and adults and engage in meaningful activities that nurture aspects of a child's development (i.e., sensori-motor, cognitive, social-emotional, and/or communication development) through the direction of teachers, parents and other adults. This type of environment involves many features. One of these features is the physical structure of the environment; for example, size, walls, flooring, windows, lighting, doors, color and texture. Another feature includes the objects within the space; for example, toys, books, manipulatives, children's works, moveable furniture, plants, and decorative stuff. The final feature is the arrangement and organization of these structures, objects and activities within the space. The space of a classroom environment could be located within a school, center, home, workplace, or a religious setting. Although outside space is considered to be part of the classroom environment, the majority of activities usually occur inside of a physical structure. Greenman (1988) states,

> An environment is a living, changing system. More than the physical space, it indicates the way time is structured and the roles we are expected to play. It conditions how we feel, think, and behave; and it dramatically affects the quality of our lives. (p. 5)

As children spend increasingly more time in classrooms, the quality of these classrooms is critical in strengthening children's foundational development. Greenman calls for putting "childhood" back into the classroom and making it a place for children to fall in love with the world and make sense of life's complexities, mysteries and joys.

Theories and Approaches

Although two classrooms may look alike as to their physical structure, the total classroom environments will be distinct from each other according to their inhabitants and philosophies of the curriculum. In each classroom the children's backgrounds, ages, ethnicity, gender, and developmental levels as well as the teacher's personality and training help to comprise the classroom environment.

Each classroom can be simulated to having its own culture reflected in the customary actions, beliefs, knowledge, and attitudes of the children and teacher(s) as they engage in the everyday life of the classroom (Green, Dixon, and Zaharlick, 2003).

Theories that contribute to diverse classroom environments focus on the qualities and conditions of children's development and learning. These theories potentially influence the organization of the classroom, selection of materials, the curriculum, and teaching approaches. The importance of environment in children's lives is stressed by a wide spectrum of theorists from behaviorism (e.g., B. F. Skinner) to constructivism (e.g., Jean **Piaget**) and social constructivism (e.g., Lev **Vygotsky**). Some classroom environments reflect the use of positive behavioral supports stemming from research conducted in the field of applied behavior analysis. The classroom environment may involve intervention efforts that "minimize and prevent the occurrence of challenging behavior in children through the management of antecedent conditions that occasion these behaviors and through the teaching of alternative behaviors and skills" (Wheeler, 2000, p. 73). Jean Piaget emphasizes the activities and materials within the classroom as a vehicle for children developing their knowledge while Vygotsky focuses on the classroom environment as a space that creates zones of proximal development for children to develop through their play and social interactions with their peers and adults.

Other theorists consider the broader societal context as part of children's learning and development through their contributions of general systems theory and ecological psychology. Dunkin and Biddle (1974) were among the first theorists to conceptualize the classroom as a system consisting of events influenced by specific variables, both in and outside of the classroom, referred to as presage and context variables. Presage variables are associated with teacher characteristics that would be considered part of teacher identity (e.g., teacher preparation program, their formative experiences, and personality). Context variables are associated with the classroom children's backgrounds and abilities as well as the school, community, and classroom contexts. These events presume a causative relationship that produces immediate and long-term outcomes for the children.

More recently, researchers in early childhood education have described quality of early childhood settings in terms of structure and process. Structural quality includes the interrelationship between group size, staff–child ratios, and teacher qualifications—otherwise known as "the iron triangle"—in helping to determine children's development. Social relationships and interactions within the early childhood environment describe process quality. Children are more apt to have positive developmental outcomes with sensitive, trained/educated teachers who know their children's strengths and needs; and how to promote their learning (Kagan and Nevman, 1996).

Bronfenbrenner's theory of the **ecology of human development,** expanded the influences of the societal context and reinterpreted the child's interaction with the environment as an active process. In this model, the child is perceived as part of nested systems that directly or indirectly affect learning and development. The child's immediate surroundings (e.g., family and classroom) are his microsystem. These microsystems in a child's life form a connected network known as the mesosystem. Children are more likely to thrive when families and schools are working together to support their learning. Another layer is the exosystem that includes the parents' workplace, social organizations, and other institutions. These exosystems may have minimal if any contact with the child but they influence the child's microsystem by the type of assistance they provide to families and schools. Exosystems exist within the context of cultural belief systems and behavior patterns known as macrosystems. And finally, the chronosystem represents the patterning of environmental events and transition over the life course (Bronfenbrenner, 1994).

These theoretical interpretations of environmental spaces suggest a number of questions to consider before designing and organizing a setting for children: What are the strengths and needs of the children, their interests, their development levels, their cultural backgrounds (including their family structures, socioeconomic status and ethnicity)? Other questions focus on the learning philosophy of the program or the local community, including specific goals for the children as well as plans for how to incorporate those goals within the curriculum. Content standards, **Individualized Education Plan** (IEP) goals and specific learning initiatives or mandated "best practices" will also influence decisions about the design of the classroom in promoting children's growth and development.

Qualities of Effective and Safe Early Childhood Environments

Although classroom environments will be distinct from each other, shared values from the local and mainstream cultures have contributed to policies and position statements that help to define the quality of classroom environments for young children. Some of these shared values include designing an environment (a) for children of varying developmental levels, (b) where all children are safe and feel secure, (c) that promotes a community of learners, and (d) that nurtures aspects of children's development.

Since the 1970s, there has been a focus on designing a classroom environment for children of diverse developmental levels. In these inclusive classrooms, **children with disabilities** learn alongside their typically developing peers. For example, children may be using wheelchairs while others are walking from one part of the classroom to another; children may be verbal or use gestures as their primary modes of communication with their peers and teachers. Children may be drawing while others are writing their stories. It is an environment where strengths are recognized in each child and children learn at their own pace. A classroom that includes children of approximately the same chronological age who are typically developing as well as those having certified disabilities is described as the child's natural environment in Part C of **Individuals with Disabilities Education Act** Amendments of 1997 (IDEA, 1997).

While having some accommodations, these settings are designed in a manner that is natural or normal for a child's age peers. For example, principles of Universal Design have been used to accommodate children of varying developmental levels. The premise underlying Universal Design is that the physical structure and layout of the classroom, instructional materials and activities, equipment, communications and other resources are designed from the start for maximum usability to the greatest possible extent without the need for adaptation or specialized design. This design seeks to offer a flexible curriculum and learning environment where all children have the opportunity to access the general curriculum and achieve the academic content standards that have been established for all students. Students have a range of options for learning that includes multiple means of (a) presentation of information to students, (b) expression by students, and (c) engagement for students (Bremer et al., 2002).

Another shared value involves designing an environment where each child feels safe and secure to explore materials, use equipment, engage in activities and interact with others in a manner that will prevent undue risk to their physical, mental and social well-being and contribute to their whole development. The floor plan is arranged where there is adequate room for children to freely move around equipment and furniture without having to compete for space with other children. Equipment, furniture and materials/toys are durable, in good repair and inspected for safety features. In this type of space children are free from environmental hazards and have adequate lighting to learn from their setting. Positive social interaction is promoted through a well-designed classroom in order to resolve conflict and protect the interpersonal safety of those present. This type of space allows children to be alone or with others while always being monitored by adults to ensure their safety.

Another shared value reflected in classroom management and overall early childhood curricula involves classrooms being constructed in a manner where children and teachers have a sense of belonging to the classroom as well as to the local community. Creating a welcoming, calming, home-like space that's represented in the selection of furnishings, textures/materials, lighting and colors are important factors in creating a "community of learners." The concept of "community of learners" is an important goal for classroom environments that promotes a positive attitude toward learning, prosocial behavior, and a mutual respect for others. Lists of criteria, guidelines, and assessments established to research and evaluate these and other features of quality classroom environments can be found in a variety of **environmental assessments.** For example, quality measures in the NICHD Study of Early Child Care included the extent to which the classroom space was uncrowded and uncluttered, the environment and equipment were clean and safe, a variety of developmentally appropriate toys and materials were available and play areas were protected and quiet (NICHD, 2005).

While there is broad consensus and empirical support for this list of qualities for an optimal environment for young children, environments for young children reflect more than shared understandings about how and what children should learn. They also reflect the teachers' personal and professional well-being. Teachers have a more pleasant personality when they work in an aesthetically pleasing environment, have space to plan, relax and develop their thinking about children's learning with other teachers and their children's families. In addition, environments reflect the values and beliefs of the adult members of the community about the nature of childhood. Some early childhood classrooms have been inspired by the municipal early childhood schools in the Italian city of **Reggio Emilia,** where each classroom reflects cultural influences through the beautification, the personal space, and materials from the local cultural community. In Reggio Emilia classrooms, the walls include the children's own work—carefully and purposefully displayed drawings, sculptures and mobiles. The classroom environment is viewed as another teacher in the class, such that an appropriate design is like a coach who helps, guides, and serves children, thus facilitating their development (Gandini, 2002). The classroom environment is designed to encourage choices, discoveries, and communication; it is an open environment that facilitates interaction among parents, teachers and children, and supports children's collaborative exploration (New, 2004).

A growing number of early childhood educators in the United States and elsewhere are taking inspiration from Reggio Emilia and other Italian early childhood programs to consider the powerful influence of the image of children and childhood shaping early childhood environments. The relationship between this image and the nature of the environment is readily apparent in U.S. classrooms. For instance, when children are viewed as untrustworthy or mischievous, the environment and classroom materials will likely be arranged differently than when they are seen as eager to learn and deserving to feel powerful in their environment. When the primary focus is on health and safety and school readiness, the environment may have easy-to-clean plastic furniture and easy-to-store commercial learning materials and displays. A belief that children should stay involved and engaged with the natural world might be reflected in more windows, outdoor spaces, and ample use of natural materials and products such as woven baskets, shells and stones on wooden shelves. A belief in children's ideas as being worth sharing and reflecting upon might be expressed through walls covered with feature photo stories of the children's questions and pursuits. A belief in the value of aesthetics and surprise may appear in the form of a new plant or a work of art, additions to the classroom justified by their contributions to the space as a place to be shared by adults and children over the course of many hours each day. Teachers in child-care settings across the United States are now considering the classroom environment as a mirror in which to examine their values and beliefs about children; and to create new designs for living and learning (Curtis and Carter, 2003). Gandini (1984) calls for transforming physical settings into "particular" places that represent the individual voices of its inhabitants and its surrounding community. Within a context of increasing standardization of children's early learning experiences, this interpretation of the environment goes beyond that of protecting and teaching children; the environment takes on an advocacy role for children's rights and adult responsibilities. *See also* Inclusion, Reggio Emilia Approach.

Further Readings: Bremer, Christine D., Ann T. Clapper, Chuck Hitchcock, Tracey Hall, and Mera Kachgal (2002). *Universal design: A strategy to support students' access to the general education curriculum.* Minneapolis, MN: National Center on Secondary Education and Transition; Bronfenbrenner, Urie (1994). Ecological models of human development. In Torsten Husen and T. Neville Postlethwaite, eds. *International Encyclopedia of Education.* Vol. 3, 2nd ed. Oxford: Pergamon Press/Elsevier Science, pp. 1643–1647; Curtis, Deb, and Margie Carter (2003). *Designs for living and learning: Transforming early childhood environments.* St Paul, MN: Redleaf Press; Dunkin, Michael J., and Bruce J. Biddle (1974). *The study of teaching.* Washington, DC: University Press of America; Gandini, L. (1984). Not just anywhere: Making child care centers into "particular" places. *Beginnings* (Spring), pp. 17–20; Gandini, Lella (2002). The story and foundations of the Reggio Emilia approach. In Victoria R. Fu, Andrew J. Stremmel, and

Lynn T. Hill, eds. *Teaching and learning: Collaborative exploration of the Reggio Emilia approach.* Upper Saddle River, NJ: Merrill, pp. 13–21; Green, Judith L., Carol N. Dixon, and Amy Zaharlick (2003). Ethnography as a logic of inquiry. In James Flood, Diane Lapp, James R. Squire, and Julie M. Jensen, eds. *Handbook of research on teaching the English language arts,* 2nd ed. Mahwah, NJ: Erlbaum, pp. 201–224; Greenman, J. (1988). *Caring spaces, learning places: Children's environments that work.* Redmond, WA: Exchange Press; Kagan, Sharon L. and Michelle J. Neuman (1996). The relationship between staff education and training and quality in child care programs. *Child Care Information Exchange* (107, January-February), 65–70. New, R. (2004). The Reggio Emilia approach: Provocations and partnerships with U.S. early childhood educators. In J. Roopnarine and J. Johnson, eds. *Approaches to early childhood education.* Columbus, OH: Merrill/Prentice-Hall; NICHD Early Child Care Research Network (2005). *Child care and child development.* New York: Guilford Press; Office of Special Education and Rehabilitative Services (OSERS) IDEA (1997). Available online at http://www.ed.gov/offices/OSERS/Policy/IDEA/the_law.html; Wheeler, John J. (2000). Principles of positive behavioral supports (PSB). In David Dean Richey, and John J. Wheeler, eds. *Inclusive early childhood education: Merging positive behavioral supports, activity-based intervention, and developmentally appropriate practices.* Albany, NY: Delmar, pp. 72–102.

Laurie Katz and Hatice Zeynep Inan

Comenius, John Amos (1592–1670)

John Amos Comenius (Komensky) was a seventeenth-century religious leader, teacher, scholar, and author. His writings on education anticipated themes evident in the work of Johann **Pestalozzi** and Friedrich **Froebel** in the nineteenth century, stressing the importance of early learning and the need to match **pedagogy** to children's development.

Comenius was born in Bohemia, a region in central Europe that is now part of the Czech Republic. He was a member of a Protestant group called the Unity of Moravian Brethren, and his life and writings were guided by his religious beliefs. He was orphaned at an early age and raised by his aunt. Educated first at a local school organized by the church, an experience he remembered as uninspiring, he later attended university and underwent preparation as a pastor of the Moravian Church. He proceeded to work as a teacher and serve the church until his life was disrupted by the events of the Thirty Years' War. Members of the church including Comenius and his family were driven from Bohemia and his wife and two children died during their exile.

While in exile Comenius was appointed bishop of the Moravian Church and it was during this period that he wrote the major works that comprise his legacy in the field of early childhood education, including *Orbis Pictus* (Comenius, 1968), an illustrated textbook, and *School of Infancy* (Comenius, 1896), which described the home-based and mother-led education of children under the age of six. Comenius described early childhood as a unique life stage. Experience was critical in shaping development, with those under age 6 more malleable than older children. Parents were responsible for educating their children in a rational manner, attending to their spiritual understanding, moral development, and knowledge gained through appropriate experiences. A measure of what was deemed appropriate was found in the study of a child's nature. Parents were encouraged to promote joyful learning through children's inclination to play and to make opportunities for their involvement in daily routines appropriate to their age. Comenius described young children as learning best through direct contact with the world of things. Specific activities were recommended at each age in relation to subject areas, including **mathematics**, geometry, drawing, and writing.

Comenius's views on education, described more expansively in his *Pampaedi* (Comenius, 1986) and the *Great Didactic* (Comenius, 1967*)*, were influenced by his experience as a student and teacher, and by his religious beliefs and panoptic worldview. Knowledge in this case was a unitary expression of science, philosophy, and theology gained through a system of universal education over the lifespan, beginning with a prenatal stage and ending in a school for old age. Education for children over age 6 was envisioned as an orderly undertaking led by efficient pedagogues using a common method and following a set **curriculum**.

Comenius's vision for early childhood education was largely neglected until revived by Froebel in the **kindergarten**, an institution that promoted the developmental aims of education and the religious and moral purpose of early schooling in an out-of-home setting led by female teachers. *See also* Curriculum, Science.

Further Readings: Murphy, Daniel (1995). *Comenius: A critical reassessment of his life and work.* Dublin: Irish Academic Press; Comenius, John Amos (1986). *Comenius's Pampaedia, or: Universal education* (A. M. O. Dobbie, trans). Dover, UK: Buckland; Comenius, John Amos (1896). *Comenius' school of infancy: An essay on the education of youth during the first six years* (edited with an introduction and notes by Will S. Monroe). Boston: D.C. Heath. Froebel Archive Digital Collection, Roehampton Digital Library, University of Surrey, http://wordsworth.roehampton.ac.uk/digital/froarc/index.asp. Comenius, John Amos (1967). *The great didactic of John Amos Comenius* (trans. by M. W. Keatinge). New York: Russell and Russell; Comenius, John Amos (1968). *Orbis Pictus: A facsimile of the first English edition of 1659.* London: Oxford University Press; Orbis Sensualium Pictus Gallery. The virtual museum of education iconics, College of Education and Human Development, University of Minnesota. http://education.umn.edu/EdPA/iconics/

Larry Prochner

Computer and Video Game Play in Early Childhood

Computer and video games are becoming increasingly present in young children's lives. According to a national early childhood study in the United States, 70 percent of children between the ages of four and six years have used a computer, and 56 percent have used a computer without sitting on a parent's lap. Eighteen percent of children age 6 and under use a computer on a daily basis, and 9 percent play video games on a daily basis. This figure includes 11 percent of children age 2 and under who use a computer on a daily basis and 3 percent who play video games on a daily basis (Rideout, Vandewater, and Wartella, 2003).

With most forms of play media, the essence of the game exists in the interactions between the players and the physical media—blocks, sticks, dolls, pinecones, paints, etc. Unlike most forms of play media, the essence of computer and video games exists in the interactions between the players and the nontangible experiences that are facilitated by the hardware and software, rather than the hardware and software themselves (Salonius-Pasternak and Gelfond, 2005). This lack of physical media is of particular interest and concern for young children.

Types of Games

Several category systems exist for describing different types of computer and video games. The following categories are used by game designers and incorporate the language often used by the players themselves:
- Real Time Strategy (RTS)
- First-Person Shooters (FPS)
- Empire Builders
- Simulations
- Role Playing Games (RGP)
- Massively Multiplayer Role Playing Games (MMRPG)
- Sports
- Puzzles
- "Edutainment"

These games can be played on computers, consoles, and smaller mobile devices, that is, phones, PDAs, and dedicated game players like Nintendo's GameBoy (Scarlett et al., 2004).

Electronic Play for Infants and Toddlers

Electronic play is progressively being developed and marketed toward younger children, even infants. Most software designed for infants is referred to as "lapware," which is geared toward parents and infants using the programs together. However, other than the social interaction and physical contact with their parents, it is unclear whether this kind of play has any other value (Scarlett et al., 2004). Most early childhood educators believe that young children benefit from interactions with people and objects that can respond directly to children's initiatives—characteristics that are not easily available in programmed electronics. In addition, the American Academy of Pediatrics (AAP) has stated that children under the age of twenty-four months should not watch television, since crucial aspects of brain development during this time seem to rely on more tangible play experiences. The AAP has also recommended that children over the age of twenty-four months should not be exposed to screen media for more than two hours each day (AAP, 1999).

There is perhaps more potential for toddlers over the age of twenty-four months to experience some benefits from electronic play. Toddlers' cognitive capabilities are expanding to include the ability to use and recognize various forms of symbolic representations. This ability seems to be a basic requirement for electronic play because so much of electronic play has to do with appreciating the meaning of images or symbols. Time will tell whether enhanced programming and design can truly provide special advantages for toddlers. However, right now, there does not seem to be any special advantages of electronic play over traditional types of toddler play. What is clear is that the benefits of sociodramatic and constructive **play** are not easily incorporated into toddlers' electronic play.

In addition, there are concerns that electronic play for toddlers may only serve as a negative distraction. An important developmental task for toddlers is the development of a sense of self, which allows them to recognize that they are separate from others and separate from the world around them. The world of electronic play may be too sophisticated for these young children, who are still unclear about boundaries between themselves and the physical world around them, let alone a world of depicted illusions.

Electronic Play for Preschoolers

Preschool children have the cognitive ability to engage in make-believe, which gives them greater access to the play worlds of computer and video games. They can imitate models that are not present and are theorized to find, in their play, multiple ways to represent the reality of the world around them as well as the inner reality of their interpretations. Their play tends to focus on construction through a variety of play media—building forts with blocks, drawing, or painting pictures of home life—and the use of **narratives** in creating stories using dolls about fairly elaborate fantasy worlds. They can engage in all kinds of play requiring symbolizing, organizing, and planning—both alone and in cooperation with others. These capabilities may begin to allow them access to some of the beneficial aspects of computer and video games.

In spite of this perceived readiness for playful engagement with video games and computers, most of those designed for preschoolers fall into the category of Edutainment and focus on academic aspects of school **readiness**. Although this may be enjoyable or beneficial for some children, it is important to remember that these games do not necessarily include opportunities to construct or create new worlds; nor even to develop motor skills, which is another important area of development for young children. Preschoolers are focusing on developing fine- and gross motor skills through physical exploration, which also helps to facilitate their cognitive development, as they begin to make sense of the world around them. More tangible types of play media, that is, wooden blocks rather than electronic play, may be better suited to these particular goals. While most types of computer or console games provide children with an opportunity to practice hand–eye coordination, they also tend to exclude gross motor skills. In addition, these games may limit children's exploration to specific activities that are determined by the software and input devices, whereas virtually the only factor that limits children's exploration of wooden blocks is their own imagination. Furthermore, some parents and teachers believe that learning important concepts through everyday, "real-life" experiences provides a richer cognitive experience for preschoolers because this learning takes place within a naturally occurring environment. However, a natural environment does not insure a richer cognitive experience any more than a video game entails something less than beneficial. While concerns about excess time spent with computers and video games are real, their potentially negative effects should not be exaggerated. Children typically do not exclusively play video games. Instead, playing video games is typically only one of many activities that children engage in; and thus, video games, when appropriate and controlled, might complement, rather than replace, other types of activities suitable for young children.

Conclusions

In considering both the potential benefits and the possible risks that may be associated with young children playing computer and video games, it is important to note that these forms of technology in the lives of young children represent a relatively new and complex phenomenon. Many of the studies that have been conducted so far in this area of research have found inconclusive or inconsistent results. In addition, debates are frequent among several differing perspectives represented by parents, educators, and researchers. Where there is agreement, it is in the opinion that, although computer use and video games provide some potential benefits, they should not replace other types of children's social, physical, and cognitive activities such as outdoor play, constructive play, and dramatic play. Instead, computers and video games should be among many activities in which children engage, as a complement to rather than substitute for other, more physical and interactive activities. To continue our inquiry and expand our understanding in both research and applied settings, it will be important to keep an open mind to the potentials of children's uses of these and other technologies. It will also be important, when studying young children's use of computer and video games, to consider both individual and contextual factors that may play a role in shaping the influences of electronic play on child development and early learning. *See also* Academics; Symbolic Languages; Curriculum, Technology.

Further Readings: American Academy of Pediatrics (AAP) (1999). Media education. *Pediatrics* 104(2), 341–343; Rideout, Victoria J., Elizabeth A.Vandewater, and Ellen A.Wartella (2003). *Zero to six: Electronic media in the lives of infants, toddlers, and preschoolers.* Menlo Park, CA: The Henry J. Kaiser Family Foundation; Salonius-Pasternak, Dorothy E., and Holly S.Gelfond (2005). The next level of research on electronic play: Potential benefits and contextual influences for children and adolescents. *Human Technology: An Interdisciplinary Journal on Humans in ICT Environments* 1(1), 5–22; Scarlett, W. George, Sophie Naudeau, Dorothy E. Salonius-Pasternak, and Iris C. Ponte (2004). *Children's play.* Thousand Oaks, CA: Sage.

Dorothy E. Warner

Constructionism

During the last thirty years, the role that computers and other computer-based technologies play in education has grown dramatically. Koshmann (1996), borrowing from Kuhn's notion of scientific paradigms, identified four major paradigms in the evolution of educational technologies: computer-assisted instruction, intelligent tutoring systems, constructionism and computer supported collaborative learning (CSCL). Each of these paradigms contains different pedagogical and methodological approaches to conceive and to integrate computer-based technology in the teaching and learning process.

Constructionism might best be defined as a constructivist philosophy for educational technologies. Constructionism asserts that computers are powerful educational technologies when used as tools for supporting the design, the construction, and the programming of personally and epistemologically meaningful projects (Papert, 1980; Resnick et al., 1996). By constructing an external object to reflect upon, people also construct internal knowledge.

Constructionism is situated in the intellectual trajectory started in the 1960s by the MIT Logo Group, under the direction of Seymour Papert, based first at the Artificial Intelligence laboratory at MIT and later at the MIT Media Laboratory. Although the Logo Group members held many different research agendas and goals, the collective vision of the group rested primarily on at least four major pillars (Bers et al., 2002).

First, the group believed in the constructionist approach to education. Strongly based on Piaget's constructivism, Papert's theory of constructionism emphasizes the need for technological environments to help children learn by doing, by actively inquiring, and by playing. The interaction with the technological materials around them provides children the opportunity to design and make meaningful projects to share with a community.

Second, the group understood the importance of objects for supporting the development of concrete ways of thinking and learning about abstract phenomena. In this context, computers acquired a salient role as powerful tools to design, create, and manipulate objects in both the real and the virtual world. The group envisioned this technology existing not only in the form of current desktop computers, but also as tiny computers embedded in Lego-bricks that could be programmed to move and respond to stimulus gathered by touch or light sensors (Bers et al., 2002; Martin et al., 2000).

Third, the group valued the notion that powerful ideas empower the individual. Powerful ideas afford individuals new ways of thinking, new ways of putting knowledge to use, and new ways of making personal and epistemological connections with other domains of knowledge (Papert, 2000). Constructionists envision the computer as a powerful carrier of new ideas and particularly as an agent of educational change.

Fourth, the group embraced the premium of self-reflection. The best learning experiences occur when individuals are encouraged to explore their own thinking process and their intellectual and emotional relationship to knowledge, as well as the personal history that affects the learning experience. Constructionism viewed the programming of a computer as a powerful way to gain new insights into how the mind works and learns (Papert, 1993).

Papert's constructionism became widespread in the world of education in 1980 with the publication of his pioneering book *Mindstorms: Children, computers and powerful ideas* (Papert, 1980). In *Mindstorms*, Papert advocated for providing children with an opportunity to become computer programmers as a way to learn about mathematics and, more importantly, to learn about learning. Papert argued that using a child-friendly version of the programming language LISP, called Logo or the language of the turtle, was an easy and natural way to engage students in programming. Logo allowed students to actively create artifacts in a process of discovery-based learning—a process directly aligned with the cognitive constructivist model of learning. Although Papert was one of the key researchers involved in the first implementations of Logo, the benefits of programming, in Papert's view, would extend far beyond the world of Logo. Through the process of designing and debugging computer programs, students would develop a metacognitive approach toward problem-solving and learning.

By now there is a long-standing constructionist tradition of authoring tools and programming environments that follow the Logo steps. Some of these technological environments are designed for children's learning about mathematics and science (Harel and Papert, 1990; Kafai, 1994; Resnick et al.,1996, 2000), for creating virtual communities to foster peer learning and collaboration (Bruckman, 1998; Resnick et al., 1996), and for designing computational environments to promote positive youth development through storytelling (Bers, 2001). Other constructionist approaches focus on creating social environments in which constructionist types of learning activities using technologies can happen (Resnick, Rusk, and Cooke, 1998).

Constructionism is rooted in Jean **Piaget**'s constructivism, in which learning is best characterized as an individual cognitive process given a social and cultural context. However, while Piaget's theory was developed to explain how knowledge is constructed in our heads, Papert pays particular attention to the role of constructions in the world as a support for those in the head. Thus, constructionism is both a theory of learning and a strategy for education. It offers the framework for developing a technology-rich design-based learning environment, in which learning happens best when learners are engaged in learning by making, creating, programming, discovering, and designing their own "objects to think with" in a playful manner.

Although constructionism has both theoretical and practical limitations, namely the lack of theoretical conceptualization of the role of **sociocultural theory** in designing learning environments and the difficulties of applying constructionism in formal institutions such as schools (Papert and Harel, 1991), more recent developments within the constructionist paradigm, such as social constructionism, cultural constructionism, and sociocultural constructionism extend the notion of constructionism to encompass sociocultural theories.

Contemporary perspectives of constructionism encompass a philosophy and theory of learning that synthesizes the understanding of the learning process as a result of an individual's cognitive self-organization and participation in socially and culturally organized practices. Therefore, a constructionist learning environment is one that gives the individual the freedom to explore natural interests using new technologies, with the support of a community of learners that can facilitate deeper understanding.

Further Readings: Bers, M., I. Ponte, K. Juelich, A. Viera, and J. Schenker (2002). Teachers as designers: Integrating robotics into early childhood education. *Information Technology in Childhood Education* 1, 123–145; Bers, M. (2001). Identity construction environments: Developing personal and moral values through the design of a virtual city. *Journal of the Learning Sciences* 10(4), 365–415; Bruckman, A. (1998). Community support for constructionist learning. *Computer Supported Cooperative Work* 7, 47–86; Harel, I., and S. Papert (1990). Software design as a learning environment. *Interactive Learning Environments* 1(1): 1–32; Kafai, Y. (1994). Learning design by making games: Children's development of design strategies in the creation of a complex computational artifact. In Y. Kafai and M. Resnick, eds. *Constructionism in practice: Designing, thinking and learning in a digital world.* Hillsdale, NJ: Erlbaum, pp. 41–96; Koshmann, T. (1996). *CSCL: Theory of practice of an emerging paradigm.* Hillsdale, NJ: Erlbaum; Martin, F., B. Mikhak, M. Resnick, B. Silverman, and R. Berg (2000). To mindstorms and beyond: Evolution of a construction kit for magical machines. In A. Druin and J. Hendler, eds. *Robots for kids: Exploring new technologies for learning experiences.* New York: Morgan Kaufman, pp. 9–33; Papert, S., and I. Harel (1991). *Constructionism.* New York: Ablex; Papert, S. (1980). *Mindstorms: Children, computers and powerful ideas.* New York: Basic Books; Papert, S. (1993). *The children's machine: Rethinking school in the age of the computer.* New York: Basic Books; Papert, S. (1999). Papert on Piaget. "The century's greatest minds." *Time* March 29, p. 105. http://www.time.com/time/time100/scientist/profile/piaget.html; Papert, S. (2000). What's the big idea: Toward a pedagogy of idea power. *IBM Systems Journal 39*(3/4). http://www.research.ibm.com/journal/sj/393/part2/papert.html; Resnick, M., Bruckman, A., & Martin, F. (1996). Pianos Not Stereos: Creating Computational Construction Kits. *Interactions, 3*(6), 41–50; Resnick, M., Berg, R., & Eisenberg, M. (2000). Beyond Black Boxes: Bringing Transparency and Aesthetics Back to Scientific Investigation. *Journal of the Learning Sciences, 9*(1), 7–30; Resnick, M., N. Rusk, and S. Cooke (1998). The computer clubhouse: Technological fluency in the inner city. In D. Schon, B. Sanyal, and W. Mitchell, eds. *High technology and low-income communities.* Cambridge, MA: MIT Press.

Marina Umaschi Bers

Constructivism

Early childhood educators generally agree that constructivism is a theory of how children learn by building or *constructing* knowledge from the inside rather than by internalizing it directly from the environment. As stated by Bredo (2000, p. 128), however, "constructivism is both diverse and moving. The fact that the term has become so popular and used in such differing and changing ways makes its meaning uncertain." For some people, constructivism is an epistemological theory; for others it is a philosophy of education, or a psychological theory about how children learn. Still others incorporate constructivism into a theory called "social constructivism" that states that knowledge is socially created.

In the field of early childhood education, constructivism can be divided into two broad categories—(a) as a philosophy of education about how best to teach children and (b) as a psychological and/or epistemological theory explaining how children learn (with some also attending to teaching as well as learning). Each of the two categories has something to offer teachers of young children.

Constructivism as a Philosophy of Education

The idea that students build knowledge from within is as old as Socrates. An example of contemporary constructivism as a particular pedagogical approach is outlined in the text, *In Search of Understanding: The Case for Constructivist Classrooms* (Brooks and Brooks, 1999). The authors identify what they describe as constructivist principles of teaching, such as teaching by posing problems of emerging relevance to students, by seeking and valuing students' points of view, and by adapting curriculum to address students' suppositions (p. ix). In support of these principles, many of which are in opposition to traditional transmission models of teaching, the authors cite scholars and philosophers of education such as **Bruner, Dewey,** Eisner, Gardner, Goodlad, Goodman, Graves, David **Hawkins,** Katz and Chard, Loevinger, **Piaget,** Inhelder, Slavin, **Vygotsky,** and others. These authors' philosophies of education differ from the traditional belief in transmitting knowledge to students in ready-made, well-organized form in which good teaching is believed to consist of presenting facts and interpretations, giving exercises, reinforcing correct answers, and correcting incorrect responses.

Constructivism as a philosophy of education appears in the work of many scholars in literacy education, several of whom were constructivists before constructivism became popular. Bissex (1980), Chomsky (1979), Goodman and Goodman (1979), and Smith (1978) are all examples of constructivists who view children's acquisition of knowledge as a process from the inside. Constructivism as a philosophy of education has especially influenced reforms in **mathematics** education as can be seen in *Cognitively Guided Instruction* (Carpenter et al., 1999), *Developing Number Concepts* (Richardson, 1999), and *Developing Mathematical Ideas* (Schifter, Bastable, and Russell, 1999). These educators advocate encouraging children to do their own thinking and to invent their own procedures for solving problems rather than mimicking the algorithms of "carrying" and "borrowing."

Constructivism as a Theory about How Children Learn

For most scholars, constructivism is an epistemological and/or psychological theory explaining the nature of knowledge and how human beings acquire it. Epistemologists and psychologists' task is only to describe and explain knowledge, and the application of their theories to education is beyond the scope of their field. An example of a descriptive epistemological theory is radical constructivism.

Radical constructivism (von Glasersfeld, 1995) states, in essence, that human beings cannot know reality itself because all we can know is what we construct on the basis of our experience, which is limited. Radical constructivists believe that we will therefore never be able to attain truth and that we can attain only knowledge that is "viable." An idea is viable as long as it is useful in accomplishing a task or in achieving a goal. Instead of claiming that knowledge represents a world outside of our experience, radical constructivists thus say that knowledge is a tool that serves the purposes of adaptation. As a philosopher, von Glasersfeld wrote about the implications of radical constructivism for mathematics education, but his interest was mainly in describing and explaining the nature and limits of human knowledge.

The constructivist scholar whose work is best known to early childhood educators in the United States is Jean Piaget. Piaget was interested in describing and explaining the nature of human knowledge. His theory is different from philosophical theories in that it is a scientific theory based on sixty years of systematically collected evidence. He especially studied the centuries-old epistemological debates between empiricists and rationalists and concluded that both camps were correct in some ways and incorrect in other ways. As a scientist trained in biology, he decided that the only way to resolve the centuries-old debates between empiricism and rationalism was to study the origin and development of knowledge scientifically. His study of children was a means to answer such questions as "How do we know what we think we know?"; "How do human beings acquire logic?"; and "What is the nature of number?"

Piaget made a fundamental distinction among three kinds of knowledge according to their ultimate sources—physical knowledge, logico-mathematical knowledge, and social-conventional knowledge (Piaget, 1967). Physical knowledge is knowledge of objects such as liquids, solids, and the noise a rattle makes when a baby shakes it. Examples of social-conventional knowledge are knowledge of languages and etiquette. As the ultimate source of physical knowledge is objects, and the ultimate source of social-conventional knowledge is conventions made by people, these two kinds of knowledge can be said to have sources outside the individual. By contrast, logico-mathematical knowledge consists of mental relationships each individual creates from within.

Our knowledge of number is an example of logico-mathematical knowledge as can be seen in the conservation-of-number task. When children have not constructed a certain level of logic from within, they say that a long line of eight counters has more than a short line of eight counters that they put out before with one-to-one correspondence. Children can see the counters (physical knowledge), but number is logico-mathematical knowledge, which is not empirically observable. When children have constructed a higher level of logic, however, they begin to deduce that the two rows have the same number "because you only moved them."

The distinction among the three kinds of knowledge has far-reaching implications for curriculum for young children. For example, it informs us that learning to speak, read, and write belongs to social knowledge that requires input from people. This need for social transmission, however, does not mean that social knowledge does not have to be constructed from the inside. When babies begin to talk, they begin with one-word utterances like "ball!" and go on to two-word utterances like "ball gone." In **kindergarten**, children speak in complete sentences but often say, "I thinked it in my head." These are examples of the constructive process from within.

The physical sciences are the logico-mathematization of physical knowledge. An example of a good science activity based on Piaget's theory is **play** involving the domino effect. By varying the distance and angle between dominoes, children find out about how force can be transmitted from domino to domino under certain conditions. This is a much better science activity than exploration with a magnet, which is often recommended as a science activity. A magnet attracts certain metals but not others that look exactly the same, and many believe that young children cannot understand magnetism beyond these seemingly random behaviors.

The Importance of a Scientific Explanation of How Children Acquire Knowledge

For centuries, education has been based on opinions called "philosophies." But education began to be influenced by science when it embraced associationism and behaviorism. **Behaviorism** essentially explains learning as a function of rewards and conditioning and is a scientific theory that has been confirmed all over the world.

Piaget's constructivism is another scientific theory that has been evaluated, debated, and examined through cross-cultural research. While variations in the ages of children's acquisition of key mental constructs have been found, the theoretical tenet that knowledge is constructed from within has never been disproved. There is little question but that constructivist theory has had a profound effect on the field of early childhood education. To date, however, educators endlessly argue about the superiority of "this method of teaching" or "that method of teaching." Continued research and applied investigations of constructivism as it explains children's knowledge construction (e.g., Kamii, 2000) will enhance understandings of how human beings acquire knowledge. *See also* Curriculum, Science; Pedagogy.

Further Readings: Bissex, Glenda L. (1980). *GYNS at WRK: A child learns to write and read.* Cambridge, MA: Harvard University Press; Bredo, Eric (2000). Reconsidering social constructivism: The relevance of George Herbert Mead's interactionism. In Denis C. Phillips, ed. *Constructivism in education: Ninety-ninth Yearbook of the National Society for the Study of Education, Part I.* Chicago: University of Chicago Press, pp. 127–157; Brooks, Jacqueline G., and Martin G. Brooks (1999). *In search of understanding: The case for constructivist classrooms.* Alexandria, VA: Association for Supervision and Curriculum Development; Carpenter, Thomas P., Elizabeth Fennema, Megan L. Franke, Linda Levi, and Susan B. Empson (1999). *Children's mathematics: Cognitively Guided Instruction.* Portsmouth, NH: Heinemann; Chomsky, Carol (1979). Approaching reading through invented spelling. In Lauren B. Resnick and Phyllis A. Weaver, eds. *Theory and practice of early reading.* Vol. 2. Hillsdale, NJ: Erlbaum, pp. 43–65; Goodman, Kenneth S., and Yetta M. Goodman (1979). Learning to read is natural. In Lauren B. Resnick and Phyllis A. Weaver, eds. *Theory and practice of early reading.* Vol. 1. Hillsdale, NJ: Erlbaum, pp. 37–54; Kamii, Constance (2000). *Young children reinvent arithmetic.* New York: Teachers College Press; Piaget, Jean (1971). *Biology and knowledge.* Chicago: University of Chicago Press. Originally published in 1967; Richardson, Kathy (1999). *Developing number concepts.* White Plains, NY: Dale Seymour; Schifter, Deborah, Virginia Bastable, and Susan Jo Russell (1999). *Developing mathematical ideas: Number and operations.* Parsippany, NJ: Dale Seymour; Smith, Frank (1978). *Understanding reading,* 2nd ed. New York: Holt, Rinehart and Winston; von Glasersfeld, Ernst (1995). *Radical constructivism: A way of knowing and learning.* London: Falmer Press.

Constance Kamii and Yasuhiko Kato

Contemporary Issues in Early Childhood

Contemporary Issues in Early Childhood (www.triangle.co.uk/ciec) is a fully refereed, international research journal that provides a forum for researchers and professionals who are exploring new and alternative perspectives in their work with young children (from birth to eight years of age) and their families. It aims to present opportunities for scholars to highlight the ways in which the boundaries of early childhood studies and practice are expanding, and for readers to participate in the discussion of emerging issues, contradictions, and possibilities.

Contemporary Issues in Early Childhood incorporates interdisciplinary, cutting edge work, which may include poststructuralist, postmodern, and postcolonial approaches; queer theory, sociology of childhood, alternative viewpoints of child development. The journal articles deal with issues such as language and identity, the discourse of difference, new information technologies, stories and voices, curriculum, culture and pedagogy, or any combination of such ideas.

The primary audience for *Contemporary Issues in Early Childhood* is early childhood students (graduate and undergraduate) and educators as well as those involved in associated family and community services. The multidisciplinary focus ensures that the journal is relevant to professionals from a wide variety of interrelated disciplines that consider issues related to the lives of young children. For example, these may include social workers, allied health professionals, and policymakers as well as professionals who conduct research into the social contexts of education, literacy, and numeracy, the new information technologies, the sciences and the arts. Additionally, it has a broad appeal to teachers and researchers interested in specific aspects and applications of curriculum and social issues related to young children.

Susan Grieshaber and Nicola Yelland

Convention on the Rights of the Child (CRC) (1989)

The Convention on the Rights of the Child (CRC) is a legally binding, nonnegotiable international document unanimously adopted by the General Assembly of the United Nations on November 20, 1989. The CRC was created to ensure every child the right to survival, development, protection, and participation by recognizing and protecting their civil, political, economic, social, and cultural rights. The CRC defines a child as any person below age 18, unless a younger majority age is recognized by national law (Article 1).

The CRC is the most rapidly and universally accepted international human rights treaty in history. It entered into force on September 2, 1990, and has been ratified by 192 countries. Only two countries—the United States and Somalia—have not ratified the CRC, with the latter nation unable to ratify because it currently has no recognized central government authority (UNICEF).

The CRC rests on the following four foundational principles:

1. Nondiscrimination (Article 2).
2. The best interests of the child (Article 3).
3. The child's right to life, survival, and development (Article 6).
4. Respect for the views of the child (Article 12) (BvLF, 2001).

The CRC was built on the consensus of a special working group formed by the United Nations in 1979. The group, representing countries with various traditions, cultural values, religious beliefs, and varied legal and economic systems, carried out an in-depth, 10-year review including preexisting declarations and covenants (UNICEF).

The Convention requires governments to view the child as an individual with rights and freedoms, including the right to a name and nationality at birth; participation in family, cultural, and social life; access to education, health care and nutrition; freedom of opinion, expression and association; and protection from abuse and exploitation (including children with handicaps, orphans, and refugees). The Convention obliges governments to inform children of their rights.

The CRC contains a preamble, fifty-four provisions, and two optional protocols. The preamble recalls the basic principles of the United Nations and specific human rights treaties and proclamations foundational to the CRC. Articles 1–41 detail the minimum rights of all children, without discrimination, including standards by which all governments must aspire to achieve them. Articles 42–54 outline the implementation of the CRC and its entry into force, including the obligation of states to report to a body of independent elected experts every five years (Article 44) (OHCHR). The Optional Protocols were added to strengthen the provisions of the CRC in specific areas. The first protocol addresses the involvement of children in armed conflict; the protocol entered into force on February 12, 2002, and has been signed by 117 countries and ratified by eighty-eight. The second protocol addresses the sale of children, child prostitution, and child pornography; it entered into force on January 18, 2002. To date, 110 countries have signed and eighty-seven have ratified this protocol.

Equally authentic texts of the CRC are available in Arabic, Chinese, English, French, Russian, and Spanish. *See also* United Nations Children's Fund (UNICEF); United Nations Education, Scientific, and Cultural Organization (UNESCO).

Further Readings: Bernard van Leer Foundation (BvLF) (June 2001). The convention on the rights of the child and young children. *Early Childhood Matters* 1998, 8–21. Retrieved from http://www.bernardvanleer.org/downloadFile?uid= 55e95349fe77730650cb53f5e0797486; Office of the United Nations High Commissioner for Human Rights (OHCHR), Committee on the Rights of the Child. "The Rights of the Child" Fact Sheet No. 10 (Rev. 1). Retrieved from http://www.ohchr.org/english/ about/publications/docs/fs10.htm; United Nations Children's Fund (UNICEF). Convention on the rights of the child. Retrieved from http://www.unicef.org/crc/convention.htm; United Nations Children's Fund (UNICEF). Full text of the "convention on the rights of the child." Retrieved from http://www.unicef.org/crc/fulltext.htm.

Hollie Hix-Small

Corporal Punishment

Corporal punishment is the use of physical force with the intention of causing a child to experience pain, but not injury, for the purpose of correction or control of the child's behavior. Examples include slapping a child's hand or buttocks, squeezing a child's arm, and hitting the child on the buttocks with a belt or paddle. Until recently, in all nations except Sweden, parents and teachers were expected and sometimes required to use corporal punishment as a means of controlling and socializing children. In 1929, Sweden became the first to end corporal punishment in schools. Fifty years later, the law prohibiting corporal punishment was extended to parents. The Swedish no-spanking law did not include any criminal penalties. It was intended as a statement of national policy and to authorize funds for educational efforts to bring about the change. Since then, corporal punishment by parents has been banned in thirteen other countries. In June 2006, the United Nations Committee on the Rights of the Child issued a policy statement declaring that it is "the obligation of all States parties to move quickly to prohibit and eliminate all corporal punishment and all other cruel or degrading forms of punishment of children by parents, teachers, and other caregivers."

Prevalence and Chronicity of Corporal Punishment by Parents and Teachers

Corporal punishment of children has been the norm for thousands of years. According to Proverbs 13:24 "He that spareth his rod hateth his son; but he that loveth him chasteneth him betimes." According to Deuteronomy 22;12, corporal punishment in childhood may avoid more serious consequences later. "This son of ours is stubborn and rebellious. He will not obey us. He is a glutton and a drunkard. Then all the men of the town shall stone him to death." In eighteenth-century England, Susanna Wesley wrote to her son John, the founder of the Methodist Church, about how he and his siblings were brought up: "When they turned a year old . . ., they were taught to fear the rod and to cry softly. . . ."

Despite changing attitudes to corporal punishment, its use by parents continues to be prevalent. In modern America, a majority of parents believe that corporal punishment is sometimes necessary, and books that advise parents to spank, such as "To Spank or not to Spank" and "Dare to Discipline," sell millions of copies. Recent research indicates that over a third of American parents hit infants, and over 90 percent hit toddlers, making this form of violent child rearing part of the socialization experience of almost all children, although the severity and frequency varies tremendously. Nevertheless, when corporal punishment is used as a parenting strategy, it is relatively frequent. For toddlers, several studies show an average of about three times a week. Corporal punishment is not limited to the infant–toddler period. To the contrary, children are typically hit by adults for many years. In the United States, corporal punishment continues until the early teens for about a third of children. Opponents of corporal punishment describe this as twelve years of violent socialization. A 2006 study of university students in nineteen nations found that 57 percent recalled frequent corporal punishment before age 12, but the rates varied widely from 13 percent (Leuven, Belgium) to 73 percent (Washington, DC, USA).

Research by Hyman found that corporal punishment by teachers was equally prevalent. In 1979, forty-six of the fifty American states, and almost all other countries, permitted teachers to hit children. Nine U.S states give teachers immunity from civil damages if a child is injured when they use corporal punishment. However, a provision giving such immunity in the federal **No Child Left Behind** legislation of 2001 was removed before passage despite strong pressure from the president.

Although the trend away from corporal punishment is strong and world-wide, it is controversial. The controversy occurs because, except for a small group of children's rights activists, the majority of parents and the majority of child psychologists and parent educators, including those who think that corporal punishment should be avoided, are opposed to banning corporal punishment. This seeming contradiction occurs because they believe that punishment works when other methods do not, and therefore may sometimes be necessary. For example, a 2000 study of clinical child psychologists by Schenck et al. (2000) found that although they were generally opposed to corporal punishment, two-thirds considered it ethical to advise corporal punishment under some circumstances. A 2006 study of university students in thirty-two countries by Straus found that only 26 percent of students in the median university strongly disagreed that "It is sometimes necessary to discipline a child with a good hard spanking." Among American students, only 21 percent strongly disagreed. Only in Sweden did almost all university students (95%) reject the idea that corporal punishment is sometimes necessary. Many fundamentalist Christians believe they have a religious obligation to follow the Old Testament injunctions to use the "rod" to correct misbehavior. On the other hand, many liberal Christians believe "rod" refers to the staff used by shepherds to guide the flock, not to an instrument for hitting.

Research on Effectiveness of Corporal Punishment in U.S. Settings

One of the reasons why corporal punishment continues to be a common practice in many families is a deeply ingrained belief that corporal punishment is more effective than other methods of discipline. Even people who are opposed to using corporal punishment tend to believe it is sometimes necessary when other methods have failed. However, this belief is not supported by any empirical study that compared corporal and noncorporal punishment. A study by Larzelere and Miranda (1994) is particularly important, not only because it clearly shows that corporal punishment is *not* more effective than nonviolent methods of discipline in preventing repetition of the misbehavior but because it also shows the power of commitment to the presumed necessity of sometimes spanking. Despite his own research results, Larzelere continues to support use of corporal punishment, perhaps because studies showing that corporal punishment is not more effective in preventing repetition of the misbehavior can also be interpreted as showing that corporal punishment is just as effective as other methods. Therefore, why not spank? Critics of corporal punishment point to studies, including seven that were longitudinal, which have found that, although in the short run corporal punishment produces compliance by the child, it is counterproductive in the long run, i.e., it is less effective, and has harmful side effects. For a few children, one spanking may end that misbehavior once and for all; just as for a few children one verbal admonition may end the problem once and for all. But on average, although corporal punishment often stops the misbehavior in the immediate situation, the effect in the subsequent weeks and months is to *increase* the subsequent level of misbehavior. In addition, research has found that corporal punishment is associated with subsequent increase in many behavior problems such as antisocial behavior and slower cognitive development; and later in life, with problems such as depression, violence against dating and marital partners, and conviction for committing a serious crime.

A turning point in understanding the effects of corporal punishment occurred in 1997 with the publication of the first longitudinal study that obtained data on *change* in the child's behavior subsequent to spanking. This was a crucial development because none of the previous research on the link between spanking and child behavior problems demonstrated that corporal punishment might actually contribute to the behavior problems. In fact, the pre-1997 research can just as plausibly be interpreted as showing that child behavior problems cause parents to spank. Subsequent longitudinal studies show that, although misbehavior serves as direct incentive for some parents to spank, it is a counterproductive method of correcting misbehavior and is psychologically dangerous to the child. The benefit of the longitudinal studies is associated with the opportunity to examine change in the child's misbehavior subsequent to spanking, allowing determination of whether the spanking was followed by a decrease in misbehavior (as per the cultural belief system) or an increase in misbehavior and behavior problems. Each of these longitudinal studies had results that show spanking to be associated with an increase in antisocial behavior problems two years later.

It is important to acknowledge that the magnitude of the harmful effects of corporal punishment on an individual child is small compared to the effects of other kinds of violent victimization of children, such as physical and sexual abuse. However, the potential cumulative effect on the mental health of the population is significant, given that such a large percent of children experience corporal punishment and because of the high frequency during any one year and the repetition for many years.

These studies suggest three key conclusions: First, although corporal punishment usually "works," it does not work any better than other methods of correction and control even in the immediate situation and, in subsequent months and years, it tends to be less effective. Second, corporal punishment has harmful side effects that other methods do not. Third, given these harmful side effects, standard medical practice requires advising parents to switch to a "medicine" that has the same effectiveness but not the harmful side effects; that is, to noncorporal modes of discipline. However, only a tiny percent of pediatricians and child psychologists follow this standard practice and advise parents to never spank. For example, a review of ten leading child psychology textbooks found none that recommended *never* spanking. Even *Dr. Spock's Book of Baby and Child Care*, instead of advising parents to never spank, advises them to "avoid it if you can." Ironically, that advice almost guarantees that parents will spank if their goal is to teach very young children to control their own behavior. Larzelere and Miranda's study of two-year old children found that half repeated the misbehavior within two hours and 80 percent within the same day, and that this applied to all methods of correction. Thus, when parents follow the advice of "avoid it if you can" and the child repeats the misbehavior after noncorporal modes of correction, they are likely to conclude that they cannot avoid spanking. Thus, to end corporal punishment, the advice needs to be *never* spank.

Never-spanking is a message parents and professionals working with parents find difficult to accept because the belief that corporal punishment works when other methods do not is so firmly embedded in the culture of most societies. It is also hard to accept because it seems to be contradicted by the day-to-day experience of parents who have told a child "no," reasoned or explained, or used time-out, only to have the child repeat the misbehavior. Parents and professionals advising parents do not point out to parents that this happens just as often when toddlers are spanked, and they also do not tell parents to never spank, as they would tell them to never let a child smoke.

An important difference between spanking and other modes of correction is that parents who spank are prepared to do it again and again until the child ceases the misbehavior. But when parents use noncorporal discipline and the child repeats the misbehavior, they are likely to fall back on corporal punishment— the method their culture incorrectly tells them works when other methods have failed. Parents who spank and repeat the spanking as needed are using the right strategy, but with the wrong method. If they were as persistent with noncorporal methods, they would be even more effective, and not put the child at risk of the harmful side effects.

Trends

Aside from legislative changes, there is data on trends for only a few countries, but in every case it reveals substantial decreases in corporal punishment by parents. Perhaps the most dramatic example is Sweden. A study of all children born in a district of Stockholm in 1955 found that at age three, 94 percent of the parents were still using corporal punishment, and a third of them did it "at least daily." By 1994, the percent of parents who spank had dropped to 31 percent. The most complete data is for the United States, although it conveys a more mixed picture. About two thirds of a national sample of parents of thirteen-year-old children reported using corporal punishment in 1975. By 1995 that percentage had decreased to a third, suggesting changing attitudes and practices for older children and adolescents. However, for toddlers, there was no decrease from the over 90% of parents who spanked in 1975, suggesting a continued belief in the efficacy of physical means of socializing the very young child.

Perhaps the most important explanation for the decreasing use of corporal punishment is an acceleration of a centuries-long trend toward a less violent society. Violence, even for socially desirable ends, is becoming less and less acceptable. Sanctioned corporal punishment of wives and of members of the armed services ended in the last quarter of the nineteenth century The death penalty has ended in all countries of the European Union and in many other nations as well. Interwoven with the decrease in interpersonal violence is an expansion in the scope of human rights, as manifested in the end of slavery, voting rights for women, the right to a free public education, and the United Nations charter on human rights. In 1990, the United Nations adopted a **Convention on the Rights of the Child**, which prohibits inhumane treatment of children. As noted previously, the committee implementing the Convention has defined corporal punishment as inhumane and has called on all signatory nations to make it illegal. To date, the Convention has been signed by all nations except Somalia and the United States. These provisions of the Convention and other legal changes are part of what Norbert Elias calls a centuries-long "civilizing process." Ending corporal punishment is one manifestation of that process.

Credit goes to Sweden for initiating this process in the 1920s and prohibiting corporal punishment by teachers, long before empirical evidence of harmful side effects became available. The end of corporal punishment in Swedish schools and the decrease in corporal punishment by Swedish parents thus reflects a change in moral standards more than a response to scientific evidence. Since the 1979 Swedish law, thirteen other countries have also banned sparking by parents. However, the educational effort to implement these laws has varied. Again, Sweden has done the most. For example, after the Swedish parenting law, all milk cartons carried the nonspanking message. A year later, over 90 percent of parents and children knew about it. In Germany, there was also a large educational effort after the legal change in 2000, but it was not specifically directed to children, and a year after the law, only about 30 percent of parents knew about it. Given the recency of most of the legislative changes and the variation in educational effort, the long term effects of prohibiting corporal punishment at this point are best evaluated for Sweden. The Swedish data show that, contrary to warnings that Sweden would become a country with children out of control, the opposite has happened. There have been substantial *decreases* in crime, drug use, and suicide by Swedish children and youth. There are many possible reasons for these decreases and they cannot be attributed to the ending corporal punishment. However, it can be concluded that the fear of uncontrollable children if corporal punishment ended has not been borne out by the change in Sweden to a less violent and more humane mode of child rearing.

Over the past several decades, there has been a world-wide movement to end corporal punishment in schools, and more recently in the home. In the United States, about half the states now prohibit corporal punishment by teachers, and most of the large cities in the remaining half have prohibited corporal punishment even though state legislation or rules permit it. Child psychologists and pediatricians discourage corporal punishment. However, only a small minority explicitly advises parents to never spank, but that group is growing. Early childhood professional organizations such as the **National Association for the Education of Young Children** (NAEYC) also have a specific stance against any form of corporal punishment for young children. Globally, child advocates continue to seek means to ban corporal punishment of children. In addition to the United Nations charter on children's rights, the European Union now requires member nations to end corporal punishment of children. Many child advocates look forward to an end to what some describe as a common and necessary socialization practice and others perceive as unnecessary and the "primordial violence against children."

Further Readings: Elias, Norbert (1978). *The civilizing process.* Vol. 1 and 2. Oxford, UK: Oxford University Press; Gershoff, Thompson Elizabeth (2002). Corporal punishment by parents and associated child behaviors and experiences: A meta-analytic and theoretical review. *Psychological Bulletin* 128, 539–579; Greven, Philip (1990). *Spare the child: The religious roots of punishment and the psychological impact of physical abuse.* New York: Alfred A. Knopf; Hyman, Irwin A. (1990). *Reading, writing, and the hickory stick: The appalling story of physical and psychological abuse in American schools.* Lexington, Massachusetts: D.C. Heath; Larzelere, Robert E. and Jack A. Mirenda (1994). The effectiveness of parental discipline for toddler misbehavior at different levels of child distress. *Family Relations* 43, 480–488; Sears, Robert R., Eleanor C. Maccoby, and Harry Levin (1957). *Patterns of child rearing.* New York: Harper & Row; Straus, Murray A. (2001). *Beating the devil out of them: Corporal punishment in American families and its effects on children.* 2nd ed. New Brunswick, NJ: Transaction; Straus, Murray A. and Rose A. Medeiros (2007). *The primordial violence: Corporal punishment by parents, cognitive development, and crime.* Walnut Creek, CA: Alta Mira.

Murray A. Straus

Council for Exceptional Children (CEC)

The Council for Exceptional Children (CEC) is a professional association dedicated to improving the educational success of children with disabilities and/or gifts and talents. Its nearly 50,000 members include special education teachers and administrators, professors, related service providers, paraprofessionals, and parents. CEC focuses on improving the quality of special and general education. To achieve this goal, the Council works with state and local education districts, the federal government, and other education organizations to find ways to better identify, teach, and care for children with exceptionalities.

In addition to encouraging the professional growth of its members and other special educators, CEC aids in recruiting personnel and promoting high professional standards. It encourages research in the education of children with exceptionalities and assists in the dissemination of research findings. And it engages in lobbying efforts at all levels of government to promote legislation that supports the education of children with special needs.

Disseminating information about the education of children with exceptionalities is one of CEC's major activities. CEC provides information to members and others who work with children with disabilities and/or gifts and talents through conventions, conferences, the CEC Web site, and publications. The Council publishes two professional journals, *TEACHING Exceptional Children*, a professional, practical-based journal, and *Exceptional Children*, a research journal. CEC also publishes C*EC Today*, the organization's newsletter, which covers current trends in special education and CEC activities. In addition, CEC publishes books and videos on special education and instructional strategies, research monographs, reviews of research, and special bulletins.

Another significant aspect of the Council's activities is developing standards for the field. To date, CEC has developed standards for what special education teachers, diagnosticians, administrators, and paraeducators must know to provide effective instruction and service. An important aspect of CEC's standards activities is providing recognition for outstanding special educators, which it accomplishes through its professional awards program.

CEC also engages in extensive **advocacy** activities. The Council cooperates with other education organizations to promote legislation that supports education in general, and special and gifted education in particular. CEC focuses its legislative efforts on ensuring that children with special needs receive a high-quality education and that special and gifted education programs are adequately funded. The Council further works to inform legislators at all levels, as well as the general public of the benefits society receives when children with exceptionalities reach their educational potential.

CEC consists of local, state/provincial, and regional affiliations. CEC's affiliates address state or provincial issues, hold conferences, publish newsletters, and coordinate the activities of the local chapters. The local chapters hold meetings, engage in projects to advance the education of children with exceptionalities, and publish newsletters.

CEC also has seventeen divisions, each of which specializes in a particular area of special education, including a **Division for Early Childhood** (DEC). Other divisions specialize in such areas as **learning disabilities**, mental retardation, and gifted education. Each division holds conferences on its particular area of special education, and produces a journal, Web site, and newsletter. The divisions also provide networking opportunities and support for their members.

CEC's national headquarters are located at 1110 N. Glebe Road, Suite 300, Arlington, VA 22201. Its phone number is 888-232-7733 and Web site is www. cec.sped.org.

Lynda Van Kuren

CP. *See* Cerebral Palsy

CRC. *See* Convention on the Rights of the Child

The Creative Curriculum for Preschool

The Creative Curriculum for Preschool is a comprehensive curriculum that defines for teachers what content to teach, why the designated content and skills are appropriate for young children, and how to teach effectively.

The Creative Curriculum® *for Preschool* is based on six fundamental beliefs:

1. The value of play as a vehicle for learning.
2. The importance of helping children to develop social competence.
3. The vital role of the teacher in connecting content and learning.
4. The benefits of building a partnership with families.
5. A belief that all children, including those with special needs, can thrive in an appropriate classroom.
6. The importance of linking curriculum and assessment.

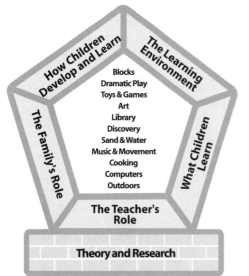

Part 1: The Curriculum Framework

There are five components of the *Creative Curriculum* framework.

How children develop and learn. A preschool child's social/emotional, physical, cognitive, and language development, and his or her characteristics and experiences, make each child unique. Goals and objectives for children are linked to the *Developmental Continuum*, a tool for observing children's development and tracking their progress in relation to Curriculum objectives.

The learning environment. The structure of the classroom that makes it possible for teachers to teach and children to learn. This includes how teachers set up and maintain interest areas in the classroom, establish schedules and routines, organize choice times and small- and large-group times, and create a classroom community where children learn how to get along with others and solve problems peacefully.

What children learn. The body of knowledge included in national and state standards for six content areas—literacy, math, science, social studies, the arts, and technology—and the process skills children use to learn that content. The Creative Curriculum shows how children learn content and skills through daily experiences.

The teacher's role. How careful observations of children lead to a variety of instructional strategies to guide children's learning. The Creative Curriculum explains how teachers interact with children in interest areas and during in-depth studies. It describes a systematic approach to **assessment** that enables teachers to learn about and plan for each child and the group.

The family's role. The benefits of developing a partnership with every family and working together to support children's optimal development and learning. This last component includes getting to know families, welcoming them and communicating with them regularly, partnering on children's learning, and responding to challenging situations.

Part 2: Interest Areas

The five components of *The Creative Curriculum* framework are applied to eleven areas—blocks, dramatic play, toys and games, art, library, discovery, sand and water, music and movement, cooking, computers, and outdoors. The Creative Curriculum describes the materials that meet the developmental needs of young children and enhance learning and teaching. Each interest area description shows the connections between *The Creative Curriculum*'s fifty objectives and academic content and how teachers guide and assess children's learning. Each description ends with a letter to families on ways to support children's learning at school and at home.

Throughout the Creative Curriculum there are examples of how two teachers, Ms. Tory and Mr. Alvarez, work with a group of eighteen preschool children.

A key element of *The Creative Curriculum for Preschool* is the strong link between curriculum and assessment. *The Creative Curriculum* goals and objectives provide the direction for planning the program and a framework for determining what each child knows and how each child is developing.

Each of the fifty objectives is mapped on a continuum of development so that teachers can evaluate and analyze a child's progress and offer strategies and activities to help that child progress to the next level. The following diagram shows an example of one objective of *The Creative Curriculum Developmental Continuum for Ages 3–5*. The nonshaded boxes illustrate typical development of children ages 3–5 on Objective 50, writes letters and words. The shaded box labeled *forerunners* includes examples of emerging skills for children who are not in the typical range of development and lag behind because of lack of experience or a diagnosed disability.

50. Writes letters and words	**Forerunners** Scribbles with crayons Experiments with writing tools such as markers and pencils Draws simple pictures to represent something	Uses scribble writing and letter-like forms	Writes recognizable letters, especially those in own name	Uses letters that represent sounds in writing words

Teachers observe children during their everyday classroom experiences, document what they see and hear, and then make informed decisions regarding a child's development using the *Developmental Continuum.* They use this information to plan activities and experiences tailored to the individual child.

This observation-based, authentic, ongoing assessment system is based on a valid and reliable instrument, *The Developmental Continuum for Ages 3–5.* There are two versions of this system:

- *The Developmental Continuum Assessment Toolkit for Ages 3–5,* the paper version. It includes all the materials and forms needed for a class of twenty-five children, including report forms for parents to be used three times a year.
- *CreativeCurriculum.net,* the online subscription system. Online, teachers enter observational notes and upload photos, scanned images, audio files, and video clips. Each observation is then linked to *The Creative Curriculum* objectives. Teachers refer to these when analyzing and evaluating children's progress on the *Developmental Continuum.* There are more than 500 activities for both home and school, each linked specifically to a developmental step on the Continuum.

The Creative Curriculum® is the title of a series of curriculum and assessment materials that include the following:

- *The Creative Curriculum*® *for Infants & Toddlers*
- *The Creative Curriculum*® *for Preschool*
- *The Creative Curriculum*® Developmental Continuum Assessment System
- *The Creative Curriculum*® *for Family Child Care*
  See also Families.

Diane Trister Dodge

Creativity

Among early childhood educators, belief in the inherent creativity of young children is long standing and pervasive. In the field of creativity studies, however, the subject becomes more complicated. Among creativity scholars, numerous definitions exist that describe the creative person, the creative process, or how a variety of factors interact over time in a particular context to produce a creative product. Studies of extreme cases of creativity may highlight unusual gifts or atypical, sometimes psychotic, behavior. There are also definitions that credit esoteric forces, such as divine power or spirituality, with the occurrence of great creativity. Some even believe that creativity should not be defined—that it is unknown and unknowable.

Two of the most influential theories of development—those of Jean **Piaget** and Lev **Vygotsky**—provide support for the view that children are creative in certain respects. But, as this discussion will show, they also assert that creative contributions of enduring value are only achieved after childhood and early adolescence.

There are many questions about creativity that are of interest to the early childhood educator. Among them are these: How does childhood fit into the puzzle of creativity? Are all young children creative, as is commonly believed, or is creativity a quality of the select few? What roles should teachers and **parents** play, if any, in enhancing creativity? Does it make sense to try to identify creative children and develop their talent, or is the relationship between childhood influences and adult creativity negligible or nonexistent? Although definitive answers to these questions are likely well into the future, the field of creativity studies has contributed to our understanding and, more important for the present purpose, to the relationship between creativity and early childhood education.

This discussion will first trace the belief that all children are creative back to its likely source—the influence of developmental theory on early childhood education over the past century. Next, the discussion will turn to contemporary creativity studies, including an examination of how influential theorists and scholars see the relationship between childhood and adult creativity. The reader will learn that recent definitions of creativity lean away from describing the traits of creative people (children or adults) and toward analyzing the multidimensional aspects of creativity.

Essentially, creativity will be shown to rely on a variety of qualities, skills, and capacities, some of which are partially developed during early childhood. The discussion will also show that a fundamental distinction must be made between those qualities of creative thought that are universal and common to all children, as contrasted with those qualities that vary from child to child. Moreover, context and timing is critical in determining who or what will ultimately be judged creative. The essay will conclude by pointing out that early childhood education serves a vital role in providing optimal conditions for sustaining creativity, a role that may be somewhat different from the one traditionally held.

The Influence of Developmental Theory on Definitions of Childhood Creativity

At least since the **child study movement** of the late 1800s, **progressive** American educators, such as kindergarteners **Patty Smith Hill** and Alice **Temple,** have recognized and celebrated young children's imaginative and expressive tendencies. Rachel and Margaret **McMillan,** famous for founding the nursery school movement in London in 1911, also placed a high value on children's imagination, **play,** and "creativity."

In more recent decades, prominent early childhood educators in America and abroad have carried on the traditions of the child study movement by applying the developmental theories of Arnold **Gesell,** Sigmund **Freud,** Erik **Erikson,** Jean Piaget, and, most recently, Lev Vygotsky. Each of these theorists granted children's creativity a prominent place, although interpretations varied according to each theory. Early childhood educators, in turn, have interpreted theory and research in relation to their existing goals, beliefs, and practices.

Gesell's normative age/stage theory identified a timetable for the emergence of physical, social, emotional, and intellectual characteristics, including manifestations of creativity, such as fantasy and representational play. Freud's psychosexual theory linked early childhood to creativity by emphasizing that children's thought processes are not subject to rules of logic, an important feature of adult creativity, and by establishing a link between cognition and strong emotion, a driving force behind creativity. By stressing the importance of symbolic and fantasy play, during which time children take leave of reality, psychoanalytically oriented theories showed how some of the natural tendencies of young children might play themselves out in adult creativity.

The constructivist theories of Piaget and Vygotsky influence early childhood education today and are often cited in descriptions of **developmentally appropriate**

practice. Piaget's theory of **cognitive development** emphasizes individual constructions of knowledge, while Vygotsky's **sociocultural theory** places more emphasis on social and instructional contributions to development. Both theories, however, emphasize the importance of play (albeit different kinds of play) for promoting cognitive development and preparing for adult creativity.

For Piaget, the emergence of symbolic thought at around age two brings with it an explosion of language and the beginnings of pretend, symbolic play—the quintessence of creative activity during early childhood. As well, Piaget's description of equilibration, the process that drives cognitive development, includes characteristics that associate readily with prevailing definitions of creativity during early childhood—qualities such as curiosity, exploration, and invention.

A more subtle description of Piaget's ideas about creativity involves assimilation, which, along with accommodation, are the two basic processes involved in the equilibration process, that is, the construction of knowledge. Piaget viewed assimilation as relatively more effortless than accommodation in its functioning. For example, Piaget said that symbolic play was the purest form of assimilation—in symbolic play, children make of the world whatever they wish with little regard for reality. In contrast, Piaget called imitation the most obvious form of accommodation, a process that is more cumulative and that builds up knowledge over time.

For Piaget, adult creativity depends on keeping intact the child's powerful tendency to assimilate new experiences to serve her or his own purposes. However, the tendency to assimilate is necessary but not sufficient for creative contributions. Only when the person has acquired a rich and accurate understanding of the known world will she or he be able to transform it productively. Piaget (1972) recognized that some individuals are more talented at doing creative work than others, but why this is so, he acknowledged, is "wrapped in mystery. . ." (Piaget, 1972, p. 221).

Vygotsky also believed that play facilitated creativity, but his focus was on play as it helped children learn what is true in their social world through creation of "imaginary situations" (Vygotsky, 1978). In contrast to Piaget, Vygotsky emphasized the kind of play that facilitates accommodation (although he did not use Piaget's terminology). Through play, Vygotsky maintained, children create their own "zone of proximal development," the most famous of Vygotsky's ideas. The zone of proximal development is the distance between what children can do independently and what they can do with the assistance of more capable others, such as playmates, parents, and teachers. In play, Vygotsky believed, children are always reaching ahead of themselves.

So it is that the influence of at least a century's worth of child development theory, intertwined with a Western **culture** that tends to romanticize children and childhood, has by now produced an orthodoxy on the question of childhood creativity. The conviction that all young children are creative permeates the early childhood literature. None of these developmental theories, however, deals with specific talents and gifts that may portend exceptional development. Their focus is on various aspects of early thought and emotion and the role that these have in achieving normal development. This role is crucial, but it leaves open the question of how to identify and support exceptional promise.

As well, the field has not undertaken systematic empirical work to support the claim that all children are creative, nor has it yet assimilated the subtleties of psychology's most powerful developmental theories. Creativity in the received developmental point of view of early childhood education emphasizes the child's playful, imaginative, spontaneous, expressive, and inventive capabilities, just as one might expect based on the theories briefly reviewed here.

The Field of Creativity Studies

In 1950, J. P. Guilford, outgoing President of the American Psychological Association, launched the field of creativity studies with a daring challenge to psychologists—to broaden their research on **intelligence** to include creativity. Up to that point, psychologists had focused their study of talented adults on **IQ**, an approach that, in Guilford's view, limited scholarship on a topic of critical national importance (Guilford, 1950). Guilford saw creativity as a trait shared to greater or lesser degrees by all individuals and believed that a psychometric test could be constructed that would provide an accurate measure of a person's creative capacity. Guilford's work was with adults, but other scholars, inspired by Guilford's vision, tried to extend creativity testing into the early childhood years. After two decades of research, consensus within the field of creativity studies concluded that the effort to produce valid and reliable psychometric instruments for the assessment of creative potential was on the whole unsuccessful.

Starting in the mid-1970s, the field of creativity studies moved away from testing and toward the study of cognitive, emotional, personal, and cultural aspects of creativity, primarily in adults. The field also embraced the case study method, with several important studies of exceptionally creative individuals (e.g., Darwin, Gandhi, Madame Curie). These studies revealed valuable information about the childhoods of the cases. For example, Darwin was slow to develop as a student and would not have been identified as unusually creative in early childhood. On the other hand, his passion for insects could have been spotted by an astute early childhood educator. This finding suggests that today's teachers might help identify and develop children's specific interests rather than trying to enhance general development. A growing consensus in the field of creativity studies suggests that creativity is domain specific.

Robert Sternberg's (1999, pp. 4–12) *Handbook of Creativity* summarizes the major contemporary perspectives on creativity, none of which is specifically aimed at early childhood. Mystical views of creativity, dating back at least to Plato, credit divine intervention with creative production; although not widespread, mystical views of creativity persist. Indeed, Piaget (1972), quoted earlier, expressed such a view when it comes to individual talent or genius.

In direct contrast, pragmatic approaches, which seem to have a good deal of popular and commercial appeal, attempt to stimulate innovative thinking of the sort identified by Guilford by using training exercises. Pyschodynamic approaches, associated most closely with Sigmund Freud's psychosexual theory, attribute creativity to unconscious drives and rely primarily on case studies of eminent creators; relatively few studies with an explicitly psychodynamic perspective currently appear in the literature.

Psychometric approaches dominated the creativity field from 1950–1970. This approach relied on paper and pencil assessments that tested divergent thinking, cognitive fluency, flexibility, and the originality of a subject's responses. The Torrance Tests of Creative Thinking (Torrance, 1974), for example, were widely used to identify individuals, including children, who were "creative." The tests did not reliably predict a relationship between high scores and real life creativity, however, weakening claims that the tests measured creative potential.

The cognitive approach to the study of creativity uses both human subjects and computer simulations in an attempt to identify the mental representations and processes underlying creative thought. A fundamental belief of this point of view is that creativity can be reduced to ordinary cognitive processes that can in turn be programmed into computers or taught to people.

Personality analyses of creativity have appeared in the literature for decades, with researchers noting time and again that certain personality characteristics tend to describe creative people. These characteristics include independence of judgment, self-confidence, attraction to complexity, aesthetic orientation, and risk-taking. Motivational traits, such as boldness, courage, ambition, and perseverance, also characterize creative people.

The relevance of the social context and of historical events to creativity has also become an active area of research, particularly as the field shifted away from the study of creative persons and toward the creation of more complex models. Simonton (1994), for example, studied creativity over broad spans of time and in diverse cultures to show the impact of society on creative performance. His work considered how variables such as cultural diversity, war, role models, financial support, and the number of competitors in a domain determine who will ultimately achieve creative eminence.

Each of the six approaches discussed in Sternberg's (1999) review (mystical, pragmatic, psychoanalytic, psychometric, cognitive, and personal-social) has contributed to our understanding of creativity, but none offers a completely satisfying solution to the questions that early childhood educators ask about creativity. The field of creativity studies has now moved toward more integrative, multidisciplinary, systemic views of creativity, emphasizing that creative development is more domain-specific than had been previously believed. While still in their formative stages, several of these new approaches offer helpful ideas about the role of teachers and schools in fostering creative development.

Systems Approaches to the Study of Creativity

Systems approaches to the study of creativity maintain that multiple factors must converge for enduring creativity to occur. Howard Gruber's study of Charles Darwin's thought as he constructed his theory of evolution through random variation and natural selection helped launch the evolving-systems point of view about creativity. Gruber's study of Darwin shows that creative contributions of the highest order require sustained effort over long periods of time (at least ten years), coordination of many strands of activity, extensive experience and preparation in the subject matter field, and a powerful vision that guides the work.

Working along similar lines, David Henry Feldman proposed a model of creativity where a "coincidence" of dimensions is involved in instances of creative genius. Feldman's work also revealed that children, even child prodigies, rarely make contributions that can be considered enduringly creative. Mihaly Csikszentmihalyi's systems approach highlights the interaction among the individual, the field, and the domain, and emphasizes that creativity is as much a judgment by society as it is an individual achievement. Howard Gardner, best known for his **multiple intelligences** theory, also works within a systems tradition, focusing his attention on analyzing the lives of indisputably creative individuals. *Changing the World: A Framework for the Study of Creativity* collects the work of these scholars into one volume (Feldman, Csikszentmihalyi, and Gardner, 1994).

Creativity and Young Children

This entry began by raising several questions about creativity and young children. As we have seen, the scholarly field of creativity studies is vital and diverse, but has for the most part not addressed directly the questions of greatest interest to the early childhood community. At the outset, we asked whether all young children are creative, as is commonly believed. Our review has shown that, while all typically developing children display characteristics associated with creativity, such as curiosity, expressiveness, playfulness, attentiveness to the world, generativity, inventiveness, imagination, and spontaneity, these qualities of the early childhood years are quite likely aspects of natural *development* and will not necessarily lead to adult creativity. Childhood creativity is not the creativity of the master, but some of its qualities must be preserved if masterworks are to be achieved. Feldman (2003) alerts us to one of the most challenging questions in the field of both creativity studies and early childhood education: How can we sustain the childlike spark that ignites the creative process through the many challenges to its expression and in a form that can be appreciated by others?

Perhaps the definition of early childhood creativity should be expanded beyond the usual platitudes to include the idea that children should use their exploratory and inventive tendencies *to change the world around them*—to take liberties with reality and to transform natural or artificial materials in an infinite variety of ways. The field of early childhood education has traditionally led the way in providing young children with open-ended materials that invite imaginative use and endless variations on the play themes of childhood, and this effort seems all to the good so far as creativity is concerned. The field should perhaps be as concerned about helping identify remarkable creative potential in children in specific content areas as in sustaining and supporting the natural creative tendencies of all children.

The preschools of **Reggio Emilia,** Italy provide a model that deserves mention in any discussion of childhood creativity (Edwards, Gandini, and Forman, 1995). Loris **Malaguzzi** was adamant that all humans have creative potentials and that schools must nurture this as well as other developing capacities. Lessons from Reggio Emilia suggest strongly that young children need ample time, adequate space, inviting materials, a supportive climate, and, perhaps most important, provocative experiences with challenging subject matter that arouse and sustain their creative impulses. Whether or not these ingredients lead to creative accomplishments in adulthood should not be the main concern, for surely they will lead to healthy development. This may in turn lead to an increase in the number of children who grow up to lead creative lives and enrich their culture through enduring creative achievements. *See also* Constructivism.

Further Readings: Edwards, Carolyn, Lella Gandini, and George Forman, eds. (1993). *The hundred languages of children: The Reggio Emilia approach to early childhood education.* Norwood, NJ: Ablex; Feldman, David Henry (2003). Creativity and children. In R. Keith Sawyer, Vera John Steiner, Seana Moran, Robert J. Sternberg, David Henry Feldman, Jeanne Nakamura, and Mihaly Csikszentmihalyi, eds. *Creativity and development.* New York: Oxford University Press; Feldman, David Henry, Mihaly Csikszentmihalyi, and Howard Gardner (1994). *Changing the world: A framework for the study of creativity.* Westport, CT: Praeger; Guilford, J. P. (1950). Creativity. *American Psychologist* 5, 444–454; Piaget, Jean (1972). Creativity: Moving force of society. Reprinted in Gallagher, J. M., and D. K. Reid (1983). *The learning theory of Piaget and Inhelder.* Monterey, CA: Brooks/Cole, pp. 221–229; Simonton, Keith (1994). *Greatness.* New York: Guilford; Sternberg, Robert J., ed. (1999). *Handbook of creativity.* Cambridge, UK: Cambridge University Press; Torrance, E. Paul (1974). *Torrance tests of creative thinking.* Lexington, KY: Personnel Press; Vygotsky, Lev (1978). *Mind in society.* Cambridge, MA: Harvard University Press.

Ann C. Benjamin and David Henry Feldman

Culture

Culture is an important construct in **early childhood education and care programs** because these are often the first institutional settings in which young children spend time away from their families. Early childhood programs are intergenerational meeting grounds of diversity in which teachers, children, caregivers, and families from different cultural and language backgrounds come together. All of these individuals (including young children) act as cultural agents who bring ways of knowing and being that reflect their culture's traditions and practices. In these settings cultural differences often involve fundamental aspects of meaning, interpersonal communication, norms, assumptions, roles, and models of competence. For example, constructs such as **disability**, **health**, mental health, learning, teaching, **race**, adult roles, and child development all are grounded in particular cultural beliefs. The capacity of early childhood educators or programs to respond effectively to children and families may be hampered by misunderstanding of unexamined cultural values, behaviors, and meanings. Teachers' and caregivers' professional socialization to the culture of early childhood may also influence their interaction with children and **families** from different cultural backgrounds. Further, care and education in early childhood programs may involve practices such as feeding, toileting, sleeping, literacy, and discipline that convey cultural values and beliefs about child competency, identity, and development. In addition, teacher competence in working with children from different cultural and language traditions is thought to be a significant factor in children's educational achievement and development. Research (Knapp et al., 1995) suggests that teachers who use their knowledge of a child's culture and language (e.g., communicate in the child's language regarding educational content; engage children in culturally sensitive ways) are more effective educators than teachers who do not as measured by children's language and mathematics achievement.

Culture includes both *meaning systems* (such as values, beliefs, morality, myths, language) and *activity* (such as customs, practices, roles, rituals) shared by a group. Culture involves dynamic processes that give ordinary and extraordinary human experiences meaning, and is central in all human interaction. It is a complex web of relationships that include changing patterns, social formations, and institutions that adapt to collective experience, individual idiosyncrasies, and ecological conditions. Culture may include constructs and categories that reflect social stratification such as **race**, clan, social class, **disability**, **gender**, and **ethnicity**. Culture shapes individual and group interactions with the world and between children, families, and institutions. The effect of culture on children is not unidirectional—through their activity and engagement they redefine and reconstruct their culture. As they grow and develop, children are a significant source of cultural change. Culture is not a monolith and all members of a culture do not express or adhere to all core values, norms, and behaviors all of the time, or to the same extent. For example, African Americans are often defined as having one culture despite research evidence that cultural discontinuities exist among them (e.g., Anderson, 1999). In addition, children may belong to more than one culture—for example, the culture of their traditional family and community, the culture of school, and the culture of a playgroup—each of which has its own norms, values, and beliefs. In early childhood settings, culture may be expressed through parental goals, expectations, role prescriptions, spiritual beliefs, models of child competence, as well as behavioral expectations, norms, and scripts that define everyday practices (e.g., sleep routines, toileting). In addition, culture involves the public and private settings in which young children are reared, socialized, and educated—schools, child-care programs, playgroups, religious classes, backyards, streets, and living rooms. It is in these everyday settings that young children learn through participation, observation, and conversation with adults and peers the meanings, behaviors, roles, language, communicative behaviors, and prohibitions necessary for cultural fluency.

Defining culture has challenged social scientists and educators. Different definitions reflect differing models of human competence and theories of development. Understanding and interpreting cultural variation in child development, child rearing, parenting, and family functioning across groups has been influenced by the culture (e.g., values, worldview) of interpreters. Western social science has often described culture in terms of dichotomies (e.g., Western versus non-Western, individual versus collective/communal, high versus low, advanced versus primitive) that have reflected American and European developmental theories and ideologies. Research grounded in ethnocentric developmental theories on "culturally diverse" children (e.g., African American, Mexican immigrant, Zuni) that concludes they are "disadvantaged," "deficient," "deviant," or "at-risk" has been criticized for theoretical and methodological biases (Vàldes, 1996). Despite these identified biases, a substantial body of anthropological research has documented distinct rich cultural traditions that exist among racial and ethnic groups within the United States, for example African American (Haight, 2002), Hawaiian, and Navajo (Tharp, 1994).

Historical trends in the evolution of Western social science have influenced the degree to which culture has been considered a central factor in child development. For example, in the mid-twentieth century **Jean Piaget**'s seminal theory and research essentially ignored culture and cast the child as the solo agent of her/his development; whereas in latter decades perspectives of child development, influenced largely by the theory of Lev **Vygotsky**, began to stress the importance of the child's active engagement in practices with informed cultural guides (e.g., adults, peers) (see Rogoff, 2003; Shorr, 1996). In addition, psychological research has too frequently attempted to reduce culture to a single "variable" or "factor" which ignores its essential role as processes inherent in human activity. These limitations have contributed to a general lack of understanding of how child development varies in the many cultures that are represented in modern societies, including the United States.

Interdisciplinary research involving anthropology, psychology, sociolinguistics, sociology, education, history, among other disciplines, has helped explain how culture influences child development. Significant early research (e.g., Margaret Mead, **Beatrice and John Whiting**) helped to establish the importance of understanding development in context, the role of participation in cultural activities as key to child socialization, and parenting as a cultural practice. Researchers influenced by this work contribute to our understanding of age-old questions regarding what is universal and what is particular to a given context, group, and individual. Robert LeVine's influential hierarchy of universal parental goals and his research on child–caregiver interaction among the Gusii of Kenya have richly illustrated models of parenting, child rearing, and child competence that challenge assumptions about optimal child development avowed by Western social science. For example, LeVine et al. (1994) report that Gusii mothers, in contrast to middle-class White American **mothers**, engage in less verbal interaction with young children, keep young children physically close, and carefully monitor expressions of infant distress and discomfort (e.g., infants sleep with their mothers, are carried by mothers, cry very little). In addition, young Gusii children do not commonly play with a variety of commercial toys. Yet despite early developmental experiences that are, by Western middle-class standards, less rich in mother–child language interactions and **play** with objects, activities thought to be associated with educational achievement, Gusii children's educational attainment is age appropriate. Similarly, the work of other researchers (e.g., Kağitçibaşi, 1996) suggests that cultures offer children a variety of successful developmental pathways to child and adult competence.

In early education research and policy, culture has often been used as a proxy for social class and race. Since the 1960s early childhood educators and researchers have attributed observed differences in child outcomes (e.g., school **readiness**, educational attainment) to presumed cultural differences between social elites and socially and educationally marginalized groups (e.g., the poor, African Americans). Terms such as *cultural disadvantage* and *culture of poverty* have been employed to explain why poor children and children of color may need remedial programs (e.g., **Head Start**). In addition, **school culture**, especially when it does not correspond to or show a goodness of fit with "home culture" (that is, the culture of their families and communities), is seen as a factor in the educational failure of some children.

In early childhood programs cultural diversity, including **second language acquisition**, has become a significant issue in **curriculum** development, instructional practices, and professional preparation of early childhood teachers and staff. Programs and practitioners are expected to provide services to culturally and linguistically diverse children and families, and to address perceived inequities that are a reflection of social stratification (e.g., race, social class) and poorer educational outcomes for children of marginalized groups. **Anti-bias, multicultural education** and programs designed for second language learners (e.g., **bilingual education**) have been educational responses intended to address issues of culture, equity, and social justice. Early childhood practitioner development, especially teacher preparation, has been a significant focus of the field. In part this is due to two factors: a recognition that teachers—their training, dispositions, subject knowledge, ability to understand the children, families and communities—are the most important factor in the educational enterprise (Bowman, Donovan, and Burns, 2001); and changing demographics in early childhood programs. It is estimated that, if current demographic trends continue, by the year 2020 the population of children under 18 years of age will be 48 percent non-white and Spanish-speaking, and by mid-century a majority of Americans will live in ethnically diverse families (McAdoo, 1993). Despite these realities, the majority of teachers (78–97%) remain, and will be for the foreseeable future, predominately White, monolingual, and middle-class (Saluja, Early, and Clifford, 2002). Research (Ray, Bowman, and Robbins, 2006) shows that early childhood teacher preparation programs do little to adequately prepare teachers for culturally and linguistically diverse classrooms. In a study of 226 undergraduate programs Ray et al. found that less than 13 percent of professional course requirements addressed any aspects of child diversity, including culture, language, and special needs. In addition, poorly defined and little researched concepts such as *cultural competence* have emerged in practice literature. Generally, cultural competence refers to the presumed capacity of early childhood practitioners to engage and work effectively with children and families from different cultures. Often lacking in this practice literature are descriptions of the processes by which early childhood professionals gain the skills and knowledge necessary for effective work in settings that are increasingly multicultural and multilingual, including assessment strategies for gauging cultural competence and remediation for perceived deficiencies in teacher practice with children and families from diverse cultures and backgrounds.

Further Readings: Anderson, E. (1999). *Code of the street: Decency, violence, and the moral life of the inner city.* New York: W. W. Norton; Bowman, B., S. Donovan, S. Burns (2001). *Eager to learn: Educating our preschoolers.* Washington, DC: National Academy Press; Haight, W. C. (2002). *African-American children at church: A sociocultural perspective.* Cambridge, England: Cambridge University Press; Kağitçibaşi, Ç. (1996). *Family and human development across cultures: A view from the other side.* Mahwah: Lawrence Erlbaum; Knapp, M. S. and Associates (1995). *Teaching for meaning in high-poverty classrooms.* New York: Teachers College Press; LeVine, R., A. Dixon, S. LeVine, A. Richman, P. H. Leiderman, C. H. Keefer, and T. B. Brazelton (1994). *Child care and culture: Lessons from Africa.* Cambridge, England: Cambridge University Press; McAdoo, H. P. (1993). Introduction. In H. P. McAdoo, ed., *Family ethnicity: Strength in diversity.* Newbury Park, CA: Sage, pp. ix–xv; Ray, A., B. Bowman, and J. Robbins (2006). *Preparing early childhood teachers to successfully educate all children: The contribution of four-year undergraduate teacher preparation programs,* Final Report to the Foundation for Child Development. Erikson Institute, Project on Race, Class and Culture in Early Childhood, Chicago, IL; Rogoff, B. (2003). *The cultural nature of human development.* New York: Oxford University Press; Saluja, G., D. M. Early, and R. M. Clifford (2002). Demographic characteristics of early childhood teachers and structural elements of early care and education in the United States. *Early Childhood Research & Practice,* 4, 1–19. Available on-line http://ecrp.uiuc.edu/v4n1/saluja.html; Shorr, B. (1996). *Culture in mind: Cognition, culture, and the problem of meaning.* New York: Oxford University Press; Tharp, R. G. (1994). Intergroup differences among Native Americans in socialization and child cognition: An ethnogenetic analysis. In P. M. Greenfield and R. R. Cocking, eds., *Cross-cultural roots of minority child development.* Hillsdale, NJ: Erlbaum, pp. 87–106; Vàldes, G. (1996). *Con respeto: Bridging the distances between culturally diverse families and schools, An ethnographic portrait.* New York: Teachers College Press.

Aisha Ray and Barbara Bowman

Curriculum

The subject of "curriculum" has produced controversy in all fields of education, but perhaps nowhere more than in early childhood education. The following discussion provides an overview of definitions and sources of curriculum; dimensions on which curriculum may differ; curriculum mandates and implementation; curriculum comparison research; and continuing issues. This discussion creates a context in which to consider more specific curriculum models or approaches.

Definitions of Curriculum

The very definition of curriculum has been controversial. Curriculum is often described as a course of study with a defined scope and sequence; at the other extreme, curriculum has been viewed as everything that happens in the classroom—a perspective more commonly held in early childhood than in elementary and secondary education. A simple definition is that curriculum includes what children should know and how they should be taught. In its early childhood program standards, the **National Association for the Education of Young Children** (NAEYC) describes curriculum as including goals for the knowledge and skills to be acquired by children and the plans for learning experiences through which such knowledge and skills will be achieved.

Because of these definitional issues, there is also disagreement about which models or approaches should be defined as "curricula." For example, some have referred to NAEYC's construct of **developmentally appropriate practice** as a curriculum. However, NAEYC is careful to note that DAP is *not* a curriculum; rather, it consists of a set of guidelines for teaching practices, which could be implemented with many different curriculum models or approaches. Likewise, some have cited **Reggio Emilia** as an example of a curriculum model. The Italian educators, however, emphasize that their approach to early childhood education is not a model—a term that suggests a structured approach to implementation. In fact, they resist defining the approach in this way because it tends to reify what they view as a dynamic, philosophical framework for working with young children and families. Until recently, few would have defined what happens in an infant/toddler program as "curriculum," but today such curricula, often drawing on research supporting the centrality of early relationships, have become widely available and adopted.

Curriculum is also related to, but conceptually distinct from, **pedagogy**, which is generally thought of as the repertoire of methods used by teachers, influenced by their overall philosophy and knowledge base. In other words, curriculum is more the "what" of teaching while pedagogy represents the integration of curriculum content with the "how" and the "why."

Sources of Curriculum

Historically, early childhood curriculum has been derived from child development theory and research; for example, the **High/Scope** curriculum was developed from Jean **Piaget**'s theory of **cognitive development**. However, like pedagogy, curriculum is always a product of multiple influences, not the least of which are social and political forces and dominant values of a particular society, **culture**, and historical period. This is why curriculum is such a contested area, because consciously or unconsciously those who develop, adopt or espouse a particular curriculum see its power to influence what children learn and how they learn it. Critical and postmodern perspectives on curriculum, including early childhood curriculum, have drawn attention to gender-related, cultural, and political biases within the dominant curriculum models. Because early childhood education is commonly viewed as preparation for later schooling, changes in curriculum in the higher grades often influence what is taught in the early years, giving rise to an increasing emphasis on **academics**, or, what has been called "push-down curriculum." This phenomenon has been seen both in the United States and in other countries where curriculum reform and changes in education policy have occurred in primary and secondary education.

Dimensions on Which Curricula May Differ

Whatever the sources of early childhood curriculum, curriculum models (which tend to offer an organized implementation plan) or approaches (which tend to offer an organized framework with considerable flexibility in its implementation) may differ on many dimensions. Some of these are (1) the relative explicitness or structure inherent in the curriculum; (2) comprehensiveness (whether the curriculum is designed to address many areas of development and learning or only one); (3) the relative balance of teacher- and child-initiated activity; (4) the relative focus on subject matter, versus a focus on developmental domains; (5) the relative focus on integration across subject matter or content areas versus subject-specific organization; and (6) the degree to which the curriculum is evidence-based and has been evaluated for effectiveness.

Curriculum Mandates and Implementation

Many countries have adopted a national or state curriculum. These include curricula for children of primary-grade age and older and, increasingly, for early childhood programs, although the curriculum may be implemented in a variety of ways. Indonesia, for example, has a national curriculum for what are called "kindergartens" (mostly private programs for 4–6-year-old children), with specific guidance on weekly topics of study, skills, and concepts to emphasize, and activities. England has introduced a national framework for an early year's curriculum, with specified outcomes and learning goals. New Zealand's early childhood system relies on a curriculum framework called Te Whariki, which includes core principles that may be implemented in a variety of culturally relevant ways (see Volume 4).

The United States differs from many other countries in that there are no federal or state mandates to adopt one specific curriculum. In the United States, however, programs that receive federal or state funds usually are required to adopt some kind of curriculum, with some states providing specific criteria, or with a list of preapproved curricula from which programs may select. Additionally, programs seeking **accreditation** through the National Association for the Education of Young Children must show that they have a written statement of philosophy and use one or more written curricula or curriculum frameworks consistent with their philosophy that address central aspects of child development.

Curriculum Comparison Research

There have been a number of efforts to compare different curriculum models to determine the superiority of one versus another. To date, the results have been inconclusive. Some researchers have claimed that studies support the superiority of child-centered or constructivist models in comparison to didactic, adult-directed curricula. However, the National Research Council's 2001 report, *Eager to Learn: Educating our preschoolers*, did not find the overall evidence compelling. Without endorsing one kind of curriculum over another, what this report and others have emphasized is the value of programs' using some kind of well-defined and intentionally implemented curriculum.

Efforts to validate specific curriculum models or approaches are continuing, consistent with the United States trend toward evidence-based practices and "scientific research" as a basis for educational practice. However, recent research seems to be moving away from efforts to prove the absolute superiority of one curriculum, toward efforts to examine more complex questions, such as which curricula may be effective with which children under which conditions. Several federally funded programs of research in the United States are examining such questions. The research is also beginning to look at some new approaches to "integrated" curricula, for example combining an existing **literacy** curriculum with a curriculum to promote social and emotional competence.

Continuing Issues

Several issues in early childhood curriculum will continue to engage researchers, practitioners, and policymakers in the coming years. The relative merits of a flexible **"emergent" curriculum**, in comparison to a more explicit, preplanned curriculum, have been and will continue to be debated; the forthcoming results from early childhood curriculum research are unlikely to put this debate to rest. As in a number of other areas in early childhood education, the discussion seems to be shifting away from an either–or stance (with a completely open approach to curriculum on the one extreme, and a tightly scripted curriculum at the other) toward recognition of a continuum of valid curriculum approaches. Increasingly in the United States at least, some make a case that "scaffolding" teachers' practice with a relatively preplanned curriculum may be a useful alternative with a workforce characterized by low education and high turnover. Within a developmental perspective, this scaffolding is said to give beginning teachers the opportunity to be successful while increasingly personalizing or modifying the curriculum as they gain experience and pedagogical competence.

The increasing diversity of young children related to demographic shifts, **immigration**, and the inclusion of children with disabilities in early childhood programs, will also pose continuing challenges and questions. Much curriculum research has been conducted with relatively homogeneous samples, leaving open the question of whether curricula need further differentiation to support the learning of children whose home language is not English, or children with physical or cognitive disabilities. In the United States, the recent reauthorization of the **Individuals with Disabilities Education Act** (IDEA) further underscores the right of every child to have access to what is called the "general curriculum." Strategies to ensure this access will continue to be developed and debated.

Increasingly, the early childhood field recognizes that professional development is essential if teachers are to implement curriculum effectively. However, little consensus exists about the most effective content and format for that professional development, and curriculum developers vary in the resources or supports provided. Additionally, different curricula make quite different demands on staff expertise; for example, a "scripted" curriculum may be relatively easier for staff to learn to implement than one that makes higher demands for on-the-spot decision making (e.g., Tools of the Mind, High/Scope, the Reggio Emilia approach, and the **Project Approach**). However, some argue that the value of these more complex approaches to curriculum makes an investment in extended professional development worthwhile. Questions such as these require continued discussion and systematic investigation.

Recommendations of Professional Organizations and Other Bodies about Early Childhood Curriculum

Within these areas of controversy and continuing research, professional bodies have taken positions and created guidelines for early childhood curriculum. For example, in 2003 the National Association for the Education of Young Children and the National Association of Early Childhood Specialists in State Departments of Education developed a position statement and recommendations about early childhood curriculum, assessment, and program evaluation. Specific to curriculum, the document recommends that early childhood programs "Implement curriculum that is thoughtfully planned, challenging, engaging, developmentally appropriate, culturally and linguistically responsive, comprehensive, and likely to promote positive outcomes for all young children" (NAEYC and NAECS/SDE, 2003). Specific indicators of effective curriculum are that children are active and engaged; goals are clear and shared by all; curriculum is evidence-based; valued content is learned through investigation and focused, intentional teaching; curriculum builds on prior learning and experiences; curriculum is comprehensive; professional standards validate the curriculum's subject-matter content; and the curriculum is likely to benefit children.

Additionally, the Council for Exceptional Children's **Division for Early Childhood** (DEC) has created a companion piece to the NAEYC and NAECS/SDE position statement, making more explicit recommendations about curriculum that includes and supports young children with disabilities. The National Institute for Early Education Research (NIEER) has created a policy brief that provides similar guidance to policy-makers and others who are making decisions about adopting or developing curriculum. Together, these recommendations reflect some growing consensus—although not unanimity—about curriculum priorities, at least within the United States early childhood community. The results of continuing curriculum research, as well as the experiences of other countries and changes in education policies, will continue to inform curriculum development and implementation. *See also* Disabilities, Young Children with.

Further Readings: Bowman, B., M. Donovan, and M. Burns, eds. (2001). *Eager to learn: Educating our preschoolers.* Washington, DC: National Academies Press; Bredekamp, S., and C. Copple (1997). *Developmentally appropriate practice in early childhood programs.* Washington, DC: National Association for the Education of Young Children; Frede, E., and D. J. Ackerman (2006). *NIEER Working Paper—Curriculum decision-making: Dimensions to consider.* New Brunswick, NJ: National Institute for Early Education Research. Available online at http://nieer.org/docs/index.php?DocID=142; Goffin, S. G., and C. Wilson (2001). *Curriculum models and early childhood education: Appraising the relationship,* 2nd ed. Upper Saddle River, NJ: Merrill/Prentice-Hall; Hyson, M., C. Copple, and J. Jones (2006). Early childhood development and education. In K. A. Renninger and I. S. Sigel, eds. *Handbook of child psychology, Vol. 4: Child psychology and practice.* 6th ed. New York: Wiley, pp. 3–47; Katz, L. G. (1999). *Curriculum disputes in early childhood education.* ERIC Digest. Champaign, IL: ERIC Clearinghouse on Elementary and Early Childhood Education; Kessler, S., and B. B. Swadener, eds. (1992). *Reconceptualizing the early childhood curriculum: Beginning the dialogue.* New York: Teachers College Press; National Association for the Education of Young Children (NAEYC) (2005). NAEYC Early Childhood Program Standards and Accreditation Criteria. Washington, DC: NAEYC. Available online at http://www.naeyc.org/accreditation/standards/; National Association for the Education of Young Children and National Association of Early Childhood Specialists in State Departments of Education (2003). *Early childhood curriculum, assessment, and program evaluation—Building an effective, accountable system in programs for children birth through age 8.* Washington, DC: NAEYC. Available online at www.naeyc.org/resources/position_statements/pscape.pdf; Schweinhart, L. J., D. P. Weikart, and M. B. Larner (1986). Consequences of the three preschool curriculum models through age 15. *Early Childhood Research Quarterly* 1, 15–45; Saracho, O. N., and B. Spodek, eds. (2001). *Contemporary perspectives on early childhood curriculum.* Greenwich, CT: Information Age; Seefeldt, C., ed. (1999). *The early childhood curriculum: Current findings in theory and practice.* 3rd ed. New York: Teachers College Press.

Marilou Hyson

Curriculum, Emergent

Contemporary interpretations of an *emergent curriculum* draw on the ideals of **progressive education** and **child-centered pedagogy**. The term *emergent curriculum* was introduced to the field of early childhood education by Elizabeth Jones in her introduction to the book *Curriculum Is What Happens* (Dittmann, 1970) and later more completely in the book *Emergent Curriculum* (Jones and Nimmo, 1994). The term served as a container for exiting practices in the field and helped communicate important theoretical and philosophical ideas in a coherent way.

The adoption of the traditional term "curriculum" was intended to shift the frame of reference from teacher-directed, written plans focused on narrow educational objectives to conceptualizing curriculum as all that actually happened in a child's day. An underlying assumption of the approach is that preplanned curriculum can lead to educational standardization and less attention to the diversity of children's experiences and abilities (Jones, Evans, and Stritzel Rencken, 2001). Rather than having curriculum content defined *apriori* by external bodies, experts or frameworks, the emergent approach sees content as virtually infinite for young children. Specific curriculum decisions are negotiated locally by teachers and learners based on their documentation and assessment of the context and through a consideration of the community's educational values.

The foundation of *Emergent Curriculum* in a child-centered pedagogy is best demonstrated in the focus on children's active engagement in **play**. Play is viewed as a context in which young children take the lead in exploring, representing, and solving meaningful problems. While Emergent Curriculum shares many of the tenets of other child-centered approaches by highlighting curriculum content that is designed from children's emerging ideas, questions and problems, the term goes further by acknowledging the significance of other contextual sources for curriculum. These sources include the physical and social environment, serendipitous events, social problems, cultural and community values, and the interests and skills of teachers and other significant adults. In the preface to the Chinese translation of *Emergent Curriculum*, Nimmo, Jones, and Li-Chen (2003) write that children's observations and questions emerge "out of a unique context that speaks to important differences in family, local community, history and culture" (p. 6). In this respect, Emergent Curriculum also shares underlying assumptions with culturally relevant/responsive models (Ladson-Billings, 1994), which emphasize the grounding of curriculum and pedagogy in an understanding of children's prior knowledge, cultural values and history, and learning styles.

Emergent Curriculum has been differentiated from other social constructivist approaches such as the Project Spectrum model (based on the theories of Gardner and Feldman) and the **Reggio Emilia** approach because it has been viewed by some educators as requiring a more passive or minimized role for the teacher (Chen, Krechevsky, and Viens, 1998, p.29). While the term itself grammatically suggests this passive orientation, the associated practice and writings acknowledge the significance of an intentional planning process and the need for negotiation between teachers and learners in determining content and teaching strategies. The terms negotiated curriculum (Forman and Fyfe, 1998) and *progettazione* (Rinaldi, 1998) have been proposed as concepts that more effectively capture this active role of the teacher in curriculum development.

While Emergent Curriculum does not advocate specific pedagogical strategies, there is a clear focus on constructivist and social constructivist practices such as those inspired by the experiences from the schools of Reggio Emilia, Italy, including documentation and collaboration (Rinaldi, 1993). The spontaneity and flexibility of teachers in being able to adapt to and respond to the unexpected and unplanned is viewed as an important pedagogical skill and disposition (Jones, 1986). Emergent Curriculum is complementary to the **Project Approach** (Katz and Chard, 2000) but differs in its emphasis on deriving curriculum from sources that are relevant and meaningful to young children and their context. The specific structures and techniques of the Project Approach, which focus on in-depth projects and an inquiry orientation, can be applied, but the Emergent Curriculum also acknowledges everyday social activity, play, and other isolated classroom experiences that may not be conceptualized as forming specific projects or investigations. *See* Pedagogy, Child-Centered.

Further Readings: Chen, J., M. Krechevsky, and J. Viens (1998). *Building on children's strengths: The experience of Project Zero*. Project Zero frameworks for early childhood education. Vol 1. Series Editors, H. Gardner, D.H. Feldman, and M. Krechevsky. New York: Teachers College Press; Forman, G., and B. Fyfe (1998). Negotiated learning through design, documentation and discourse. In C.P. Edwards, L. Gandini, and G. Forman, eds., *The hundred languages of children: The Reggio Emilia approach—Advanced reflections*. 2nd. ed. Greenwich, CT: Ablex; Jones, E. (1970). Preface. In L. Dittman, ed., *Curriculum is what happens*. Washington, DC: NAEYC; Jones, E. (1986). *Teaching adults: An active learning approach*. Washington, DC: NAEYC; Jones, E., and J. Nimmo (1994). *Emergent curriculum*. Washington, DC: NAEYC; Jones, E., K. Evans, and K. Stritzel Rencken (2001). *The lively kindergarten: Emergent curriculum in action*. Washington, DC: NAEYC; Katz, L.G., and S.C. Chard (2000). *Engaging children's minds: The Project approach*. 2nd ed. Stamford, CT: Ablex; Ladson-Billings, G. (1994). *The dreamkeepers: Successful teachers of African American children*. San Francisco: Jossey-Bass; Nimmo, J., E. Jones, and W. Li-Chen (2004). Preface to the Chinese Language Edition of the book *Emergent Curriculum* by E. Jones and J. Nimmo. Translated by X. Zhou, L. Z. Lu, and B. Wang. Shanghai, China: East China Normal University; Rinaldi, C. (1993). The emergent curriculum and social constructivism. An interview with Lella Gandini. In C. Edwards, L. Gandini, and G. Forman, eds., *The hundred languages of children: The Reggio Emilia approach to early childhood education*. Norwood, NJ: Ablex; Rinaldi, C. (1998). Projected curriculum constructed through documentation-*progettazione*. An interview with Lella Gandini. In C.P. Edwards, L. Gandini, and G. Forman, eds., *The hundred languages of children: The Reggio Emilia approach—Advanced reflections*. 2nd ed. Greenwich, CT: Ablex.

John Nimmo

Curriculum, Emotional Development

Although the place of emotions in early childhood curriculum has been debated, recent child development research provides convincing evidence that young children's emotional competence is key to their later competence, not just in the emotional domain but in social and academic areas as well (Shonkoff and Phillips, 2001). To support positive development and learning, early childhood education programs must therefore implement curriculum that effectively promotes emotional competence, whatever the other goals of the curriculum.

The Emotion-Centered Tradition in Early Childhood Education

In U.S. early childhood education, early childhood programs have traditionally emphasized five components: the emotional nature of teacher–child relationships; activities to meet children's emotional needs; open expression of feelings by children and adults; the development of positive affective states and dispositions; and awareness of children's emotional responses (Hyson, 2003). Although their specific forms have been influenced by cultural contexts, these components have also been prominent in non-U.S. early childhood education programs. Yet this traditional emphasis is at risk. In a social policy report from the Society for Research in Child Development, Raver (2002) concludes that "psychologists' and educators' emphasis on cognition and on children's academic preparedness continues to overshadow the importance of children's social and emotional development for early school readiness" (p. 3). For this reason, many urge that a research-based focus on emotions should permeate the early childhood curriculum.

Focusing on Emotions within the Early Childhood Curriculum

"Emotional curriculum" or "emotion-centered curriculum" does not necessarily require the creation of a separate curriculum about feelings. Indeed, the research on early emotional development suggests that a focus on emotional competence should be infused throughout the curriculum rather than being added on in an isolated or disconnected way. A synthesis of this research would recommend the following as the primary goals of any curriculum that aims to support young children's emotional competence:

1. *Creating a secure emotional environment.* If adults create an emotionally secure climate, children are able to explore and learn.
2. *Helping children to understand emotions.* If adults promote emotional understanding, children have insight into their own and others' feelings, becoming more empathic and socially competent.
3. *Modeling genuine, appropriate emotional responses.* If adults show authentic emotions, and if they are effective models, children are likely to adopt appropriate ways of showing their feelings.
4. *Supporting children's regulation of emotions.* If adults gradually guide children toward self-regulation, children will gain skills that support healthy development in multiple domains.

5. *Recognizing and honoring children's expressive styles.* If adults respect individual differences in emotional expressiveness, while promoting culturally and developmentally appropriate expression, children are nurtured and supported.

6. *Uniting children's learning with positive emotions.* If adults give children many opportunities to experience the joys and overcome the frustrations of new learning experiences, they are better able to persist at tasks and seek out challenges.

Associations between Curriculum Emphases and Emotional Outcomes

Early childhood educators have adopted a variety of curriculum models and approaches to teaching. As summarized in Hyson, Copple, and Jones (2006), several programs of research have examined relationships between the emphasis of a specific early childhood curriculum (especially along the dimensions of teacher-directed vs. child-focused) and the likelihood that the teacher has warm, emotionally positive relationships with children. For example, in studies in which the emotional climate of the preschool classroom was rated along with other features of the curriculum and teaching practices, classrooms with higher levels of adult direction and formal instruction were significantly less likely to be characterized by teacher–child affection and warmth.

In other studies, highly didactic, basic-skills-oriented curricula that emphasized individual success and failure were associated with less teacher warmth and nurturance toward children and less attention to their individual needs than in the more child-focused classrooms. Furthermore, children's motivation suffered in these contexts. Children in these classrooms tended to rate their own academic skills lower than children in classrooms that offered more choice as well as greater acceptance and, when given a choice, they avoided challenging tasks.

Despite these trends, it is impossible to conclude that the only curriculum approach that supports close teacher–child relationships is a strongly child-centered one. It has not been possible to disentangle curriculum approach from emotional climate, since these two variables have been so strongly correlated. There are now a greater number of early childhood programs that cannot neatly be categorized as "child-centered" versus "didactic," including those influenced by Vygotskian and other social-constructivist perspectives, the educational approaches of the Italian **Reggio Emilia** preschools, and revisions to **The National Association for the Education of Young Children's (NAEYC)** guidelines for **developmentally appropriate practices**. These programs place greater emphasis on teachers' active promotion of cognitive and academic competencies through scaffolding, reflection, and representation, while embedding these in first-hand experiences linked to young children's interests and within the context of play and rich social interaction. However, the emotional climate and motivational impact of these curricula have not yet been systematically studied.

Specifically Designed Curricula or Programs to Support Emotional Competence

A number of U.S. researchers have recently developed and attempted to validate specific classroom-level interventions designed to support young children's emotional competence. The following points should be kept in mind when considering or adopting any intervention or prevention program (adapted from Raver, 2002):

- High-quality early education, including a rich, emotion-focused curriculum, provides the foundation to which more specific interventions may be added. Caring, emotionally knowledgeable teachers and a classroom climate that addresses and integrates the broad goals of emotional competence are essential.
- Research indicates that the most effective emotional-competence programs go beyond commercial packages that simply teach children names for feelings and that encourage children to "use words" to resolve conflicts. At least with elementary-age children, such programs are relatively ineffective when used in isolation. Effective programs require investment in professional development; link classroom lessons with games or other activities to build self-control and other skills; and coordinate classroom-level interventions with parent training and support. As compared with more limited interventions, such programs are expensive, but research indicates that the investment is worthwhile.
- An approach that has shown very positive results is to combine universal programs (for all children in a classroom or school) with more intensive intervention, in school and with families, for a smaller number of children who seem to be at greater risk for emotional difficulties.
- Although the programs described below have shown positive results, those who intend to adopt an emotional-competence program should consider whether the evaluations were conducted in settings that were demographically similar to those in which the program has been used and evaluated.
- High-intensity clinical interventions, perhaps using school-based early childhood mental health consultants, are recommended for young children at high risk of serious emotional problems, often because of family adversity. However, researchers emphasize that such interventions must avoid inappropriate labeling or stigmatizing children and must address family needs as well as those of individual children.

Below are three examples of classroom-level interventions designed to support young children's emotional competence. Evaluations have shown at least some positive effects for each of these programs.

Floor Time (program developer: Stanley Greenspan, M.D.). Also termed the Developmental Individual-Difference, Relationship-Based Model (DIR, commonly referred to as the "Floor Time" approach, Greenspan and Weider, 1998), focuses on helping all children, but especially those with disabilities such as autism, develop relationships and emotional communication. The goals of the one-on-one "Floor Time" intervention are to help the child become more alert; take more initiative; become more flexible; tolerate frustration; sequence and execute actions; communicate gesturally and verbally; and take pleasure in learning. Parents and other adults learn how to use individual interactions with a child (with or without disabilities) to support these goals.

The Incredible Years (program developer: Carolyn Webster-Stratton, Ph.D., University of Washington). The "Incredible Years" program provides comprehensive training for parents, teachers, and children ages 3–8, focused on improving children's emotional and behavioral adjustment. Programs include videotapes, activities for parents and children, and other school- and home-based materials. Empathy, problem solving, and anger management are among the areas of emphasis for children. The program has been evaluated in **Head Start** settings (Webster-Stratton, Reid, and Hammond, 2001).

PATHS (providing alternative thinking strategies) (program developer: Mark Greenberg, Ph.D., Penn State Prevention Research Center). This curriculum was originally developed for elementary-age children, adapted for preschool (*Preschool PATHS*), and tested in Head Start programs (Kusche and Greenberg, in press). Using "PATHS characters" and other tools, curriculum units teach self-regulation (the Turtle technique), emotion awareness and communication, problem-solving, positive identity and peer relations. The curriculum also aims to promote a positive classroom atmosphere that supports social emotional learning.

Conclusion

Considerable research supports the importance of incorporating specific emotional competence goals into early childhood curriculum. Two complementary approaches appear to be effective. First is what might be called a universal or broadband approach in which an emphasis on emotions permeates and is integrated into all other aspects of the early childhood curriculum. Second, a number of well-validated interventions may be incorporated into this broadband approach, with the intensity of intervention being influenced by the needs of individual children. *See also* Vygotsky, Lev.

Further Readings: Greenspan, S. I., and S. Weider (1998). *The child with special needs: Encouraging intellectual and emotional growth.* Reading, MA: Addison-Wesley; Hyson, M. (2003). *The emotional development of young children: Building an emotion-centered curriculum.* New York: Teachers College Press; Hyson, M., C. Copple, and J. Jones (2006). Bringing developmental theory and research into the early childhood classroom: Thinking, emotions, and assessment practices. In I. Sigel and K. A. Renninger, eds. *Child psychology in practice, Vol. 4: Handbook of child psychology.* New York: Wiley; Kusche, C. A., and Greenberg, M. T. (in press). PATHS in your classroom: Promoting emotional literacy and alleviating emotional distress. In J. Cohen (Ed.) *Social emotional learning and the elementary school child: A guide for educators.* New York: Teachers College Press; Raver, C. (2002). *Emotions matter: Making the case for the role of young children's emotional development for early school readiness.* SRCD Social Policy Report 16, no. 3. Ann Arbor, MI: Society for Research in Child Development; Shonkoff, J. P., and D. Phillips, eds. (2001). *Neurons to neighborhoods: The science of early childhood development.* National Research Council and Institute of Medicine, Board on Children, Youth, and Families, Commission on Behavioral Sciences and Education. Washington, DC: National Academy Press; Webster-Stratton, C., M. J. Reid, and M. Hammond (2001). Preventing conduct problems, promoting social competence: A parent and teacher training partnership in Head Start. *Journal of Child Clinical Psychology* 30, 283–302.

Marilou Hyson

Curriculum, Literacy

The topic of early literacy curriculum is one that recently has come to the forefront of educational policy decisions in response to concerns about literacy levels in various countries, especially the United States. Research reveals that educational responses to and expectations of young children reflect deeply held cultural values and beliefs, including assumptions about what is normative, necessary, and developmentally appropriate (New, 2001). Conceptions of the how and what of U.S. early childhood education have historically varied as a function of which children are being served and for what purposes. U.S. children of preschool age (3–5 years) continue to be the recipients of diverse and competing interpretations of **curriculum** and **pedagogy**, ranging from programs described as play based and child centered to those characterized by various forms of direct instruction and behavior modification.

While scholars in recent years have contributed a wealth of knowledge about the processes associated with the acquisition of literacy skills and knowledge within children's "social spheres," teachers remain unclear about the nature of developmentally appropriate literacy practices in the classroom. Disagreements over the extent to which literacy instruction is necessary or even appropriate for young children reflect theoretical, political, and cultural interpretations of the purposes of literacy and early childhood education in the lives of young children and families. This eclectic approach to early education not only represents contrasting and changing theoretical interpretations of children's learning. Such program diversity is also directly linked to the pluralistic nature of U.S. society and associated judgments about children's needs as a function of race, income, language, and ability.

When asked what should be taught in early childhood programs, most parents and practitioners would suggest that the early childhood curriculum should address social, emotional, and physical development as well as **cognitive development**. Until recently, few people would have gone much beyond mentioning reading aloud to young children as a specific literacy activity to be included in daily curricular planning. However, literacy development in early childhood has captured significant attention in recent years on the part of teachers, education researchers, families, and politicians. Learning to read and write up until about 1990 was seen as the domain of first and second grade with some preparatory work being done in kindergarten. Proper formation of letters while printing was emphasized, but not until after a child had successfully learned to read. The idea of "reading readiness" dominated the field of education and dictated that literacy learning was clearly a school subject in which instruction focused exclusively on the sequenced mastery of skills while ignoring the functional uses of reading (Teale and Sulzby, 1986).

The concept of reading readiness has been challenged by growing interest and new research conducted within the first few years of life. Studies showing the period from birth through the preschool years as an important period of development played a central role in the deepening understanding of cognitive approaches to issues of learning and development, and validated the premise that literacy understandings develop in the course of every day life (Teale and Sulzby, 1986).

At the turn of the twenty-first century the International Reading Association (IRA) and the **National Association for the Education of Young Children** (NAEYC) published a joint statement, *Learning to Reading and Write: Developmentally Appropriate Practices for Young Children* (Neuman, Copple, and Bredekamp, 2000), which served as a milestone in its recognition of early literacy as a developmental domain in early childhood. This joint statement summarized the research on early literacy and explicated a set of benchmarks for early literacy learning along with broad recommendations for parents, educators, and policy-makers. For the most part, however, this is the point where agreement stops as literacy in early childhood has become a contested topic in politics as well as academics.

It is important within this discussion to clarify the meaning of "literacy." Brian Street (1995) describes two divergent models of literacy learning. In the first, literacy is described as an autonomous set of skills to be mastered that lead to progress, civilization and social mobility. Literacy in this model can be studied in its technical aspects outside of social context. In the second model, literacy is described as ideological in that literacy practices are inextricably linked to cultural and power structures in any given society where any number of standard prac-tices are used by people during literacy "events," which are themselves "situated in broader social contexts and social relations" (Barton, 1994, p. 35). The techni-cal skills and cognitive aspects of literacy are not denied within this model, but cannot be viewed outside of or separately from the social, political, and cultural setting in which they occur. This theoretical understanding helps to explain the successes of some children, such as those from middle-class homes, in acquiring the literacy skills, attitudes, and understandings that prepare them for success in school-base literacy practices. The recognition in recent years that some children are not entering school with the types of linguistic and literacy experiences that prepare them for school success has led to an increased demand for a formal-ized curriculum for early childhood classrooms that can provide the identified necessary experiences. High quality early literacy instruction for all children, but especially for those identified as being "at risk" for school failure, is currently viewed as the necessary preventative measure needed to combat reading failure. This message is prominent in the seminal book *Preventing Reading Difficulties in Young Children* (Snow et al., 1998).

The word "curriculum" can be defined in accordance with the theoretical models of literacy described above. From the autonomous view, curriculum can be described as a course of study, which includes the planned interaction of students with instructional content, materials, and resources to meet certain educational objectives. This course of study can be used by all children in any setting since it is assumed that literacy means the same thing everywhere. Thus, publishing companies are able to develop and sell early literacy curriculum in any school district in this country and assure the local school board that it will meet their needs. From the ideological viewpoint, this does not hold true. Curriculum and the surrounding decisions about what that encompasses would need to be made within a specific social/cultural setting by parents, educators, and policymakers within that setting as they define that nature of early childhood education and the meaning and importance of literacy within that setting.

An examination of reading curriculum used in the primary grades in elementary school for the last few decades reveals the nature of the controversies surrounding literacy learning as it has been enacted in schools across the country. The term "reading wars" describes an educational and political battle that continues to occur between proponents of a phonics emphasis in reading and a whole language emphasis. During the 1950s, reading instruction was dominated by the Dick and Jane basal readers which emphasized a "whole word" approach to teaching reading in which stories with tightly controlled vocabularies repeated words on each page so that, according to behaviorist research, students would eventually remember them. This model for teaching reading was criticized and eventually replaced by curriculum that focused on a "bottom up" approach that emphasized students' phonemic awareness—an understanding of the alphabetic principle that the spelling of words relates to how they sound when spoken. While knowing the rules of phonics helps children to sound out some words, an estimated one-half of the words in the English language cannot be sounded out accurately using these rules. In contrast to this method, the whole language approach to teaching reading was developed, based on the theory of **constructivism**. Within this methodology, emphasis is placed on students constructing meaning from text and teachers providing a literacy rich environment that combines speaking, listening, reading and writing into literacy learning. In this approach, phonics instruction becomes only one component of literacy instruction. Research has clearly established that no one method of instruction is superior for all children, and that approaches that favor some type of systematic code instruction along with meaningful connected reading report children's superior progress in reading (Neuman, Copple, and Bredekamp, 2000). An understanding of how children develop early literacy learning can put a stop to these "reading wars."

Unfortunately, current policies in the U.S. Department of Education such as **No Child Left Behind** and Early Reading First are reflections of an acceptance on the part of policymakers of the autonomous model of literacy learning for young children. The current emphasis on early literacy education as an answer to later school failure problems can be seen in three current federal government initiatives. First, in 1998, the **Head Start** reauthorization changed Head Start's purpose from providing comprehensive developmental services for low-income children to promoting school **readiness** by enhancing the social and cognitive development of low-income children. Changes in Head Start policies reflect an increasing emphasis on language and **literacy.** The 2003 reauthorization describes prereading and language skills as instructional content and specifically mentions the use of scientifically based programs that support school readiness.

The second federal initiative, **Good Start, Grow Smart**, began in 2002 and is an early learning plan designed to address three major areas: strengthening Head Start and other child-care programs, partnering with states to improve early childhood education and providing information to teachers, caregivers, and parents in the areas of early language and literacy learning. One of the objectives of this initiative is the identification of the most effective prereading and language curricula and teaching strategies for early education through rigorous experimental methods. Good Start, Grow Smart has introduced changes in early childhood educational practices by advocating testing of young children's early reading skills, the application of research-based methods in teaching young children, and professional development for teachers in literacy pedagogy.

Finally, Early Reading First, which was established in the No Child Left Behind Act of 2001, was designed as a program to prepare young children at risk of school failure to enter kindergarten with the necessary cognitive, language, and early literacy skills for success in school. This program specifically has as its goal the prevention of later reading difficulties. Preschool programs that are awarded this grant must use a research-based curriculum which includes systematic, intentional instruction in certain identified essential prereading skills—letter recognition;

rhyming, blending and segmenting of sounds; complex vocabulary; and print concepts. Additionally, it requires the use of reliable, valid **assessments** to screen children and to monitor progress in the acquisition of these specific skills. Finally, it requires professional development for teachers in the "scientific approach" to early literacy pedagogy so that teachers are able to implement early literacy curriculum and assessments that have scientifically based reading research as their foundation. Early Reading First is designed to complement the Reading First program whose intent is to incorporate scientifically based reading research to improve and expand reading programs at the primary school level. Reading First has been the subject of ongoing controversy centering on its perceived "overprescriptiveness" as it is administered and allegations of conflicts of interest between consultants to the program and commercial reading and assessment companies. Opponents suggest that schools participating in Reading First have been all but forced to buy textbooks and related materials from a handful of large publishers, several of which have retained top federal advisers as authors, editors or consultants. This same controversy has the potential to spill into Early Reading First if grant applicants are coerced in the application process to select only certain commercially published curricula.

Curriculum decisions in early childhood literacy should include a sound understanding of up-to-date knowledge about how children learn, what the goals of that learning should be, the roles of the teacher and students within the curriculum, descriptions of the learning activities and environment, and the methods of evaluation that will be used to assess student learning. Three learning principles have been suggested in a recent report from the National Research Council (Bowman et al., 2001) which can guide curricular decisions. First, children develop ideas and concepts at very young ages that help them make sense of their world. Curricula should be evaluated on the extent to which they draw out and build on children's existing ideas. Next, developing expertise requires both a foundation of factual knowledge and skills and a conceptual understanding that allows facts to become usable knowledge. Curricula can be judged on the extent to which they promote learning of concepts as well as information and skills. Finally, children can be taught to monitor their thinking in the form of learning strategies, and thus efforts to help children learn more deliberately should be built into curricula.

Other related research in the area of early literacy learning suggests that knowledge of certain skills correlates with success in learning to read, for example, alphabet letter recognition, phonemic awareness, oral language skills (receptive and expressive as well as vocabulary), and concepts of print (Snow, Burns, and Griffin, 1998). Finally, researchers suggest that experiences with storybook reading, discussions about books, listening comprehension, and writing are all crucial in early literacy development. All these factors should guide the development of early literacy curricula that respond to children's developmental and cultural needs. Effective literacy instruction must integrate learning the code of written language with uses and purposes of literacy that are meaningful to the learner. This instructional principle relates directly back to the ideological model of literacy with its context specific definition of literacy.

Writing development has recently been considered a part of early literacy curriculum, a significant change from past policies that limited writing activities to a focus on proper letter formation and spelling after a child had begun to read. Many educators now encourage young children's interest in writing because it serves to foster development of various print concepts such as left-to-right directionality, phonemic awareness as children use invented spellings based on sounding words out, and alphabet letter knowledge even among three-year-olds who endeavor to write their names. Additionally, when young children write, they experience first hand the connections between reading, writing, and oral language as they come to understand the various purposes for these activities. Literacy environments that promote writing development in young children are those that set aside time, space, and materials for children to use. Also important are adults in the classroom who model writing for young children and who plan meaningful ways for children to engage in writing events. From a developmental standpoint, educators currently understand that young children begin to write when they scribble on paper, use gestures to symbolize meaning, and name objects that they have drawn. As with all other literacy activities, it is a socially and culturally situated event.

When planning early literacy curriculum, one aspect of early learning that must be considered is the influence of the environment of the child on this learning. For example, research suggests that families differ in the extent to which the literacy activities provided in the home prepare young children for school-based practices (Heath, 1982; Snow, Hamphil, and Barnes, 1991). The literacy styles found in families from mainstream culture complement the practices used in preschool and primary grades and therefore, children from these homes begin school with the advantage of similarity between life experiences and interactional styles in school and at home (Vernon-Feagans et al., 2001). Since literacy is viewed as activities that are embedded in a social and cultural context, it is obvious that literacy experiences will vary between cultures as parents provide children with opportunities to acquire literacy abilities that are pertinent to their lives. These activities often do not match those found in schools, and this mismatch may lead to difficulties for specific groups of children. An understanding of this issue leads to a realization that a "one size fits all" literacy curriculum will not meet the needs of all children in a diverse society like ours. Instead, by designing literacy curriculum at a local level, teachers can learn about the literacy practices and beliefs of the families they serve and the community in which the children live, and then incorporate these into the classroom to help bridge the children's experiences at home and school. Courtney Cazden's several decades of research (2001), for example, points out the misunderstandings that teachers can have about narrative styles from different cultures, while Anne Dyson's work (1993) suggests the importance of pop culture and peer relations in primary school children's writing development.

Finally, in the consideration of what can be described and included in early literacy curricula, other forms of literacy must be incorporated. For example, various types of video technology as well as computer technology cannot be left out in a time when children begin to use such forms of literacy beginning in infancy. When literacy is viewed through an ideological lens, new forms of literacy can continuously be added to the curricula in response to changes in societies and cultures.

Summary

Literacy learning begins long before children enter school and is a complex and multifaceted process that is strongly influenced by the social and cultural contexts in which it occurs. Curricula that address the needs of early literacy learners must be developed with an understanding of the global developmental learning framework that supports children's growth and the unique cultural settings in which this growth takes place. Additionally, the unique needs of the individual child must be considered. Research has provided broad understandings of the importance of early language interactions and the significance of reading aloud with young children, but these understandings and principles must be interpreted on a local level. Curricular frameworks can be developed to guide well-trained education professionals in planning literacy learning for young children, but a "one size fits all" curriculum cannot successfully meet the learning needs of children in a diverse society. *See also* Curriculum, Physical Development; Development, Emotional; Development, Language; Development, Social; Pedagogy, Activity-Based/Experiential; Pedagogy, Child-Centered; Peers and Friends; Curriculum, Technology.

Further Readings: Barton, D. (1994). *Literacy: An introduction to the ecology of written language.* Oxford: Blackwell; Bowman, B.T., M. S. Donovan, and M. S. Burns (2001). *Eager to learn: educating our preschoolers.* Washington, DC: National Research Council; Cazden, C. B. (2001). *Classroom discourse: The language of teaching and learning.* Portsmouth, NH: Heinemann; Dyson, A. H. (1993). *Social worlds of children learning to write in an urban primary school.* New York: Teachers College Press; Heath, S. B. (1982). What no bedtime story means: Narrative skills at home and at school. *Language and Society* 11, 49–76; Neuman, S.B., C. Copple, and S. Bredekamp (2000). *Learning to read and write: Developmentally appropriate practices for young children.* Washington, DC: National Association for the Education of Young Children; New, R. (2001). Early literacy and developmentally appropriate practice: Rethinking the paradigm. In S. B. Neuman and D. K. Dickinson, eds., *Handbook of early literacy research.* Vol. 1. New York: The Guilford Press, pp. 245–262; Snow, C. E., M. S. Burns, and P. Griffin (1998). *Preventing reading difficulties in young children.* Washington, DC: National Academy Press; Snow, C.E., L. Hamphill, and W.S. Barnes (1991). *Unfulfilled expectations: Home and school influences on literacy.* Cambridge, MA: Harvard University Press; Street, B. (1995). *Social literacies: Critical approaches to literacy in development, ethnography and education.* London: Longman; Teale, W. H., and E. Sulzby (1986). Emergent literacy as a perspective for examining how young children become writers and readers. In W. H. Teale and E. Sulzby, eds., *Emergent literacy: Writing and reading.* Norwood, NJ: Ablex; Vernon-Feagans, L., C. S. Hammer, A. Miccio, and E. Manlove (2001). Early language and literacy skills in low-income African American and Hispanic children. In S. B. Neuman and D. K. Dickinson, eds., *Handbook of early literacy research.* New York: Guilford Press, pp. 192–210.

Kathy Conezio

Curriculum, Mathematics

Mathematics curricula for early childhood is an area of substantial recent research and development activity. For example, re-stimulated by research demonstrating that achievement gaps between children from low- and higher-resource communities begin in the earliest years, developers recently have produced a wide variety of innovative preschool curricula. Such flurries of activity may mislead some people to believe that early childhood mathematics is a new phenomenon. However, history shows that mathematics, as well as conflicts about the type of mathematical experiences that should be provided, have long histories in early education.

Conflicts stemmed from different opinions of the appropriateness of mathematics for young children. Negative opinions usually were based on broad social theories or trends, not observation or study of children. Those who actually worked with young children historically provided a rich mathematics curriculum. For example, mathematics was pervasive in the work of Friedrich **Froebel**, the founder of **kindergarten** (which originally included children from three to seven years of age). Froebel's fundamental gifts were largely mathematical manipulatives and his occupations were mathematical explorations and constructions. As early childhood education was institutionalized, these deep mathematical ideas were largely forgotten or diluted. For example, in the first half of the twentieth century, U.S. psychologist Edward **Thorndike** wrote about learning as associations that were strengthened or weakened by consequences such as rewards. His implications for education was to do things directly. To emphasize health, he suggested replacing the first Froebelian gift (small spheres) with a toothbrush and the first occupation with "sleep." The mathematical foundation of the gifts was thus ignored.

Froebel was a crystallographer. Almost every aspect of his kindergarten crystallized into mathematical forms—the "universal, perfect, alternative language of geometric form." Its ultimate aim was to instill in children an understanding of what an earlier generation would have called "the music of the spheres"—the mathematically generated logic underlying the ebb and flow of creation. Froebel used "gifts" to teach children the geometric language of the universe, moving from solids (spheres, cylinders, cubes) to surfaces, lines, and points, then the moving back again. Cylinders, spheres, cubes, and other materials were arranged and moved to show these geometric relationships. His mathematically oriented occupations with such materials included explorations (e.g., spinning the solids in different orientations, showing how, for example, the spun cube can appear as a cylinder), puzzles, paper folding, and constructions. Structured activities would follow that provided exercises in basic number, arithmetic, and geometry, as well as the beginning of reading. For example, the cubes that children had made into the chairs and stoves would be made into a geometric design on the grid etched into every kindergarten table, and later laid into two rows of four each and expressed as "4 + 4." In this way, connections were key: the "chair" became an aesthetic geometric design, which became part of a number sentence.

Consider several other examples. Children covered the faces of cubes with square tiles, and peeled them away to show parts, properties, and congruence. Many blocks and tiles were in carefully planned shapes that fit in the grid in different ways. "All the blocks and sticks and rings and slats were used in plain view on the ever-present grid of the kindergarten table, arranged and rearranged into shifting, kaleidoscopic patterns or decorative, geometric borders" (Brosterman, 1997, p. 38). Using these materials, Froebel developed skills that had been—and usually remain to this day—reserved for students in higher grades.

Another example of an historical curriculum material that emphasizes mathematics is the building block set. Children create forms and structures that are based on mathematical relationships. For example, children may struggle with length relationships in finishing a wall. Length and equivalence are involved in substituting two shorter blocks for one long block. Children also consider height, area, and volume. The inventor of today's unit blocks, **Caroline Pratt**, tells of children making enough room for a toy horse to fit inside a stable. In Pratt's example, the teacher told preschooler Diana that she could have the horse when she had made a stable for it. Diana and Elizabeth began to build a small construction, but the horse did not fit. Diana had made a large stable with a low roof. After several unsuccessful attempts to get the horse in, she removed the roof, added blocks to the walls to make the roof higher, and replaced the roof. She then tried to put into words what she had done: "Roof too small." The teacher gave her new words, "high" and "low" and she gave a new explanation to the other children. Just building with blocks, children form important ideas. Teachers such as Diana's who discuss these ideas with children, giving words to their actions, can foster such intuitive ideas through constructive **play**. With such materials and through teacher guidance, children can be helped to distinguish between different quantities such as height, area, and volume.

As part of K–12 schools, mathematics education in the primary grades has its own historical path. In the colonial times, counting and simple arithmetic was taught, but not usually to girls. Between 1815 and 1820, U.S. educators revised the teaching of arithmetic in response to the Swiss reformer Joseph **Pestalozzi**. Warren Colburn's text, for example, started with practical examples, used objects (manipulatives) for solutions, and asked students to explain how they solved problems. However, many teachers failed to understand the reform efforts, and routine pedagogy remained common. At this time, "stimulus–response" theory, built on Thorndike, dominated psychology, and its effects were seen in the emphasis on drill procedures in arithmetic textbooks (reflecting a limited understand of even that limited theory).

From the 1920s, social utility theory influenced curricula to focus on those skills needed in everyday life. Emphasis was on practical use, but not on mathematics as a discipline or students' understanding. In the 1930s, Gestalt theory, which focused on insight and relationships, led to recommendations by mathematics educators such as William Brownell that understanding of mathematics principles was a key foundation for learning.

Jean **Piaget**'s research led to a renewed focus on children's thinking about mathematics. Mathematics curricula based on his theories took many forms. Some consisted almost solely on attempting to teach children to correctly respond to Piagetian tasks, such as number conservation, seriation, and classification. Others emphasized the constructivist philosophy of Piaget, and emphasized child-centered exploration. In a more recent extension of that approach, Kamii offers everyday experiences and games that encourage children to construct notions of number, and physical knowledge experiences such as bowling, balancing cubes, and pick-up sticks, for low-achieving young children before they experience any specific mathematical content. Evaluations of these approaches have been positive.

The constructivist theories of Piaget and **Bruner** motivated developers in the mid-twentieth century to incorporate "discovery learning," emphasizing process goals and students' exploration and invention of solution methods. The "space race" led to several different curriculum modifications, from those that emphasized the structure of mathematics itself (e.g., set theory in the "new math") to those that build upon new psychological insights and reform movements to build new types of manipulatives (e.g., the "geoboard" and base ten blocks) and tasks for mathematics education. Thus, there were a variety of curricula through the 1960s and 1970s, although many shared at least some characteristics, such as increased emphasis on mathematical structures and precision, guided discovery approaches, and moving content to lower grade levels. "Laboratory" curriculum materials continued to be developed up to 1980, but excesses of some of these approaches led to some curricula following a "back to basics" approach.

Since that time, two main types of primary-grade curricula have been developed. The first type includes commercially published, traditional text books, which still dominate mathematics curriculum materials in U.S. classrooms and to a great extent determine teaching practices. Ginsberg and others claim that the most influential publishers are a few large conglomerates that often have profit as their main goal, leading them to follow state curriculum frameworks, attempting to meet every objective of every state—especially those that mandate adherence to their framework. They also tend to be eclectic in their teaching approaches. The second type of curricula includes those developed by researchers and innovators, often with external funding and frequently attempting to follow the reform-oriented positions of the National Council of Teachers of Mathematics (see www.nctm.org for this and recent recommendations for Curriculum Focal Points). The resulting innovative primary-grade curricula often provide educational experiences that are simultaneously more child-centered and more challenging. Building on children's mathematical intuitions and problem-solving ability, these curricula ask children to develop their own ideas and strategies, and guide that development toward increasing levels of mathematical sophistication. The curricula develop skills in conjunction with learning the corresponding concepts, because research indicates that learning skills before developing understanding can lead to learning difficulties. Successful innovative curricula and teaching build directly on students' thinking (the understandings and skills they possess), provide opportunities for both invention and practice, and ask children to explain their various strategies. Such programs facilitate conceptual growth and higher-order thinking without sacrificing the learning of skills. They also pose a broader and deeper range of problems in arithmetic and geometry than traditional curricula. However, they also require a more knowledgeable teacher, and are, perhaps, more vulnerable to misconceptions and therefore misuse, such as believing that accuracy is unimportant. Traditional curricula, which still are used in a majority of schools, have been offering more problem-solving opportunities for students in recent years, but often do not reflect all that is known about teaching and learning early mathematics.

Not traditionally part of the elementary school curriculum, preschool mathematics curricula have followed a different, but related course. Originally based on traditions from Froebel, traditional early childhood practices, and then Piaget, curriculum development has recently been influenced by newer theories that put number in a foundational role. Such curricula have shown substantial positive effects. For example, in one study, four-year-old children were randomly assigned to one of three educational conditions for eight weeks: Piagetian logical foundations (classification and seriation), number (counting), and control. The logical foundations group significantly outperformed the control group both on measures of conservation and on number concepts and skills. However, inconsistent with Piagetian theory, the number group also performed significantly better than the control group on classification, multiple classification, and seriation tasks as well as on a wide variety of number tasks. Further, there was no significant difference between the experimental groups on the logical operations test and the number group significantly outperformed the logical foundations group on the number test. Thus, the transfer effect from number to classification and seriation was stronger than the reverse. The areas of classes, series, and number appear to be interdependent but experiences in number have priority.

Recent curriculum development and research in preschool mathematics education has built on these beginnings, as well as the wealth of research on young children's learning of mathematics. For example, contemporary curricula emphasize number, geometry, and to a lesser extent, measurement and patterning, because research shows that young children are endowed with intuitive and informal capabilities in these areas and because these areas form the foundation of later mathematical learning. These curricula have helped children make strong, significant gains in each of these various areas of mathematics in their preschool year. Thus, most recently developed research-based preschool curriculum is based on the notion that children have more capability and interest in mathematical activities than often assumed. They consider children to be active builders of mathematics rather than passive receivers of facts and procedures (see **Constructivism**). They ask children to solve mathematical problems, albeit beginning problems, with understanding and talk about what they have done.

Equity has often been a driving force in creating and studying preschool mathematics curricula (see also **Technology Curriculum**). Research indicates that children from low-resources communities who experience a high-quality mathematics curriculum can learn basic mathematical ideas and skills. For example, they learn the number skills, including number recognition, counting, comparison, and simple arithmetic. This closes the gap between children from low-resource and those from higher-resource communities. The development of geometry and spatial sense are also important. Research on the Agam and building blocks curricula show that rich geometric and spatial activities have multiple benefits. Such activities include finding shapes in the environment, from more obvious examples to embedded shapes; reproducing designs with shapes; composing shapes to make pictures, designs, and other shapes; and forming mental images of shapes. Such curricula increase children's knowledge of geometry and spatial skills, including foundations of the visual arts. In addition, they increase children's arithmetic and writing **readiness** capabilities.

Some of these curricula are more structured than others. Some use whole-group instruction, others small-group instruction, often with games. Most have been successful, if performed in high-quality settings. All approaches have a shared core of concern for children's interest and engagement and content matched to children's cognitive level. Young children benefit from a range of mathematical experiences, from the incidental and informal to the systematic and planned. However, a core of intentional, systematic activities appears to hold particular promise, making unique contributions to children's development.

The ecological perspective suggests that many aspects of the child's environment affect the success of a curriculum. The ecological factor that has most often been identified as influential involves the role of the teacher. Professional development on early mathematics curricula is consistently identified as the main criterion of a high-quality implementation, along with other support for the teacher (see **Interagency Education Research Initiative [IERI]**). Early childhood teachers often lack experiences that develop deep knowledge of the mathematics taught, knowledge of the specific developmental paths of children's learning of that mathematics, and innovative ways of helping children learn mathematics. Indeed, especially for a mainly female group, mathematics is often avoided and viewed as difficult and distasteful. Such knowledge is enhanced when curricula are built around understanding children's development of mathematical ideas and strategies. Family involvement and a classroom environment filled with potential for mathematic explorations are also components of most early mathematics curricula.

In summary, there is a long history of worthwhile mathematics curricula for early childhood, from the preschool years through the primary grades. Achievement gaps between children from low- and higher-resource communities, which begin in the earliest years, lend urgency to building on historical and recent development and research efforts to provide high-quality implementation of innovative curricula to all children.

Further Readings: Balfanz, R. (1999). Why do we teach young children so little mathematics? Some historical considerations. In J. V. Copley, ed. *Mathematics in the early years.* Reston, VA: National Council of Teachers of Mathematics, pp. 3–10; Brosterman, N. (1997). *Inventing kindergarten.* New York: Harry N. Abrams; Carpenter, T. P., E. H. Fennema, M. L. Franke, L. Levi, and S. B. Empson (1999). *Children's mathematics: Cognitively guided instruction.* Portsmouth, NH: Heinemann; Clements, D. H., and J. Sarama (2007). Effects of a preschool mathematics curriculum: Summary research on the *Building Blocks* project. *Journal for Research in Mathematics Education.* Clements, D. H., J. Sarama, and A.-M. DiBiase (2004). *Engaging young children in mathematics: Standards for early childhood mathematics education.* Mahwah, NJ: Erlbaum; Cobb, P., T. Wood, E., Yackel, J. Nicholls, G. Wheatley, B. Trigatti, et al. (1991). Assessment of a problem-centered second-grade mathematics project. *Journal for Research in Mathematics Education* 22(1), 3–29; Ginsburg, H. P., A. Klein, and P. Starkey (1998). The development of children's mathematical thinking: Connecting research with practice. In W. Damon, I. E. Sigel, and K. A. Renninger, eds. *Handbook of child psychology, Vol. 4: Child psychology in practice.* New York: Wiley, pp. 401–476; Gravemeijer, K. P. E. (1994). *Developing realistic mathematics instruction.* Utrecht, The Netherlands: Freudenthal Institute; Griffin, S., and R. Case (1997). Re-thinking the primary school math curriculum: An approach based on cognitive science. *Issues in Education* 3(1), 1–49; Hiebert, J. C. (1999). Relationships between research and the NCTM Standards. *Journal for Research in Mathematics Education* 30, 3–19; Kamii, C. K., J. Rummelsburg, and A. R. Kari (2005). Teaching arithmetic to low-performing, low-SES first graders. *Journal of Mathematical Behavior* 24, 39–50; Mokros, J. R. (2003). Learning to reason numerically: The impact of *Investigations*. In S. Senk, ed. *Standards-based school mathematics curricula. What are they? What do students learn?* Mahwah, NJ: Erlbaum, pp. 109-132; Piaget, J., and A. Szeminska (1952). *The child's conception of number.* London: Routledge and Kegan Paul.

Douglas H. Clements and Julie Sarama

Curriculum, Music

Any educational program designed to promote children's development in the broadest sense of the word must include a music curriculum because music is one of the defining features of the human species. Engaging in musical behavior, whether as a producer or a listener, individual or group member, is something that characterizes contemporary life for many people across the world. Irrespective of culture, ethnicity or language group, people—particularly the young—engage in musical behavior for significant amounts of time each day. In part, this is because our brains are designed to pay particular attention to the sounds around us, to detect similarities and differences, construct patterns and structures, and infer meanings and to be engaged emotionally in the available soundscapes, especially music. Like spoken and written language, music is processed simultaneously in many different parts of the brain. Musical processing is not an option, for without such hardwired capabilities, mastering other aspects of our sound world, such as language, would be difficult. Not only is music fundamental to our biological and neural makeup, it is embedded in and shapes the social and cultural patterning of our worlds. Music plays an important role in the construction of identity, in our communicative processes, and in the ways in which we negotiate meaning with self and others. By inference, therefore, if education is about nurturing, developing, and seeking to maximize every aspect of our human potential, then opportunities must be provided in any curriculum for participants to engage in musical thought, action, and interaction. Without the inclusion of music, we neglect a basic facet of what it means to be human.

Musical features dominate children's earliest experiences from prebirth. From the final trimester of fetal life when the auditory systems begin to function, many of the earliest experiences of a world "outside" are musical. This is because the amniotic fluid that surrounds the fetus transfers the melodic contours, rhythmic patterning, and timbral (sound color), and dynamic (volume) variations of the mother's voice, as well as the musical features of any sounds in her immediate vicinity. Research suggests, for example, that in the first six months, infants are able to recognize musical works heard initially in utero, indicating a sensitivity and awareness of the distinctive musical features of the music that they encounter, and a capacity to recall these over time. After birth, as infants begin to make their own sounds and to make sense of, and imitate, the sounds around them, pitch, dynamic, timbral, and melodic and rhythmic patterns continue to be significant. For example, the sounds that our caregivers offer as they interact with infants over the first year of life are musical, containing many of the features of the dominant musical culture, including melodic contours, rhythmic patterning, changes in dynamics and timbre, as well as consonant and dissonant musical intervals.

Part of our human design is that children are not just receptive to music (what music psychologists term music perception, or music philosophers term music appreciation or aesthetic perception). They are also born with a range of different ways of making music, what music psychologists term "generative" and "performative" skill development. The terms "generative" and "performative" indicate that children are born with innate capabilities to produce certain kinds of musical behaviors. This is not surprising, given the variety of different centers in the brain that are devoted to musical processing and the range of music experience that they encounter from the earliest moments of life. In particular, children can master aspects of the dominant musical culture(s) through their singing and imitative musical play (performative), as well as being able to create through composing and improvising (generative) patterns of sounds that have recognizable musical features. This may occur through the use of 'formal' instruments (including the voice) or other sound-making objects. Importantly, music experience is not solely confined to the auditory: engagement with music in and through movement and dance is a powerful means of developing responsiveness to music and to sensitizing the body and mind to the rhythmic, temporal, and dynamic possibilities of music. In some cultures, the notion of music and movement as separate entities is considered untenable and for many infants their first experiences of music are intimately connected to movement experience as they are rocked to sleep to the accompaniment of a lullaby, or swayed to the pulse of a communal song.

By the time that young children have reached two years of age, they have had considerable enculturated experience of their immediate sound world, alongside many opportunities to make sound as performers and creators. They are also able to notate these musical explorations and creations using written "symbols." Their experiences often embrace a wide variety of different musical styles and genres, particularly if they have been growing up in a modern culture in which music and sound media are omnipresent, whether at home, at child care, in playgroup, at worship and celebrations, when traveling in the car, or shopping in the local mall. The outcome is an emerging mastery of many of the dominant features of their musical culture. For example, through regular exposure, most two-year-olds are capable of reproducing simple musical phrases of songs from the home environment, including those encountered through electronic media, such as TV, CDs, and radio. Some two-year-olds are able to sing complete songs in-tune because of the rich musical experiences that they have shared with their caregivers. They are also capable of generating their own "songs" that draw on features of songs that they have heard. By this age also, they are already able to express a liking for musical sounds and to be particularly attentive to certain pieces of music.

Environment and culture continue to shape musical experience and development across successive months. Cantonese-speaking children in Hong Kong aged two to five years, for example, use the same pitch centers in conversational speech as when singing their favorite songs. In contrast, their English-speaking peers develop increasingly distinct pitch centers, with conversational speech lower than their chosen pitch for singing. Similarly, while at play, Euro-American and Asian children tend to make much use of melody in their singing, whereas the play of Afro-American children tends to contain greater emphasis on rhythmic chants.

Importantly, what constitutes musical experience and development differs across cultural and social groups. Consequently, an understanding of the varying ways in which music experience can be defined, described and valued in different social and cultural settings is crucial for educators.

When given the opportunity to make music using simple instruments, preschool children usually focus on an initial exploration of the sonic possibilities and draw on the characteristic rhythmic, melodic, and dynamic features of their musical cultures. This sound making is intentional as the young child manipulates the chosen instrument in order to make sense of, and enjoy, its particular sonic properties and musical possibilities. Preschool children's invented song-making, a common feature of young children's musical experience, draws on musical and textual themes that they encounter in their daily lives. For example, young children may produce "potpourri" songs where elements of a number of known songs are mixed together with original musical and textual ideas. In later work, children tend to abstract elements of known songs (rhythmic, melodic, structural, dynamic), rather then simply reproducing known elements, to produce original "invented" songs.

As mentioned earlier, when provided with the opportunity, young children are also capable of expressing their creative musical ideas in some form of visual symbolization—their own form of musical notation. Typically, initial "invented" notations appear to be scribble-like, before developing with a focus on one particular feature that is perceptually dominant (e.g., dynamic change). With further experience, this develops into a capacity to notate several different musical features at the same time (such as pitch and rhythm). With appropriate structured experience over a relatively short period (three months), preschoolers are capable of developing their notational skills from "scribbles" to more formal symbols that portray distinctive musical features, such as musical pulse (the "beat") or melodic contour. In preschoolers' notation of songs, both invented and known, words tend to predominate, but greater notational variation is evidenced when they are asked to notate the same music from an instrumental source. The presence of language (as song text) can sometimes distract from musical features. Through invented notation experiences, preschoolers are able to record and retrieve meaning over time, and to reflect on their own and others' music making. Such cognitive work assists in shaping musical thought and action for the young child.

While the preschooler's capacity to "talk" about music may be limited, the lack of a specialized vocabulary does not mean that children are not capable of responding insightfully and appreciatively to music listening experience. Early exposure to, and engaged response with, a range of musical forms and genres provides the building blocks of later musical thought and activity. Through the provision of alternative means of responding other than the verbal, children are able to expand their musical vocabulary and to build incrementally a store of musical patterns and possibilities. Nonverbal responses may include movement and dance, drawing, following music maps visually and kinesthetically, conducting, or tracing the musical contour in the air, on the body, on the ground.

Overall, there is a considerable body of research evidence to indicate that young children are not only able to respond to the music that they encounter, they are also able to reproduce, create, and notate both their own music and components of the music of their dominant musical culture(s). These behaviors are evidenced when opportunities are provided for children to engage in musical exploration and play with a wide range of sound-making artifacts and in a context in which the adults show a keen interest and valuing of children's musical output, acting as "audience" and as comusic-maker, as well as a source of musical ideas and development activities. Young children are not empty vessels that have to be "filled" with music. They are developing musicians who have already acquired considerable skills and understandings informally and who bring to the music learning environment a depth and richness of experience that is often underestimated.

The early music curriculum, therefore, should provide young children with opportunities to explore, play, and engage with a wide variety of musical activities—as composers, improvisers, listeners, movers and dancers, soloists and group members—that build on their early and continuing informal encounters with music. They should be encouraged to create musical narratives that provide evidence to the teacher/caregiver of emergent musical understanding that can then be deepened and developed through further musical engagement. They should be encouraged to engage consciously with a wide range of musical styles and genres as they build the musical vocabulary that will underpin their future musical development. The underlying pedagogical philosophy is for the teacher (or caregiver in non-school contexts) to act as comusic-maker, guide, facilitator and enabler to the richness of musical cultures, rather than assuming a master-apprentice role in which musical knowledge is simply transferred from expert to novice. Children *are* musical!

Further Readings: Barrett, M. S. (2003). Meme engineers: Children as producers of musical culture. *International Journal of Early Years Education* 11(3): 195–212; Barrett, M. S. (2005). Musical communication and children's communities of musical practice. In D. Miell, R. MacDonald, and D. Hargreaves, eds. *Musical communication.* Oxford, UK: Oxford University Press, pp. 261–280; Bresler, L, and C. Marme Thompson, eds. (2002). *The arts in children's lives: Context, culture, and curriculum.* Dordrecht: Kluwer; Deliege, I, and J. Sloboda, eds. (1996). *Musical beginnings.* Oxford, UK: Oxford University Press; McPherson, G. E. (2006). *The child as musician.* Oxford, UK: Oxford University Press; Welch, G. F. (2006). The musical development and education of young children. In B. Spodek and O. Saracho, eds. *Handbook of research on the education of young children.* Mahwah, NJ: Erlbaum, pp. 251–267; Welch, G. F., and Adams, P. (2003). *How is music learning celebrated and developed?* Southwell, England: British Educational Research Association. Available online at http://www.bera.ac.uk/publications/pureviews.php.

Graham F. Welch and Margaret S. Barrett

Curriculum, Physical Development

Although charged with the responsibility of educating the whole child, early childhood professionals have historically focused their efforts on cognitive and social/emotional development (the thinking and feeling child), with physical development (the moving child) receiving much less attention. Preservice training has traditionally done little to prepare teachers to meet children's motor development and fitness requirements; nor, perhaps, has the need to do so been as great in the past as it currently is.

Today, children's physical development is a topic of increasing concern and attention. Factors associated with this new emphasis include **obesity,** now increasing at faster rates among children than among adults; and research that describes children's major at-home activity as being electronically entertained (an average of thirty-three hours a week). As a result, physical fitness has clearly become the responsibility of all who are involved with children. Moreover, because teachers of preschoolers are often more realistic than parents in their assessment of children's physical activity levels and more influential in the prompting of such activity, early childhood professionals can have a significant impact in this area.

The National Association for Sport and Physical Education (NASPE) describes physical fitness as a condition where the body is in a state of well-being and readily able to meet the physical challenges of everyday life. NASPE's (2002) position is that "all children from birth to five years should engage in daily physical activity that promotes health-related fitness and movement skills." Their guidelines for physical activities for young children state that young children should not be sedentary for more than sixty minutes at a time, except when sleeping. NASPE recommends that toddlers accumulate daily at least thirty minutes of structured physical activity and at least sixty minutes (and up to several hours) of unstructured physical activity. Preschoolers should engage in the same amount of unstructured activity but accumulate at least sixty minutes daily of structured physical activity.

The difference between unstructured and structured physical activity is that the former is child-initiated and unplanned. For example, on the playground some children may take advantage of the climbing equipment, while others slide down the slide and swing on the swings. Some children may ride tricycles, while others play tag or simply run around. Structured physical activity, in contrast, is planned by teachers, with specific goals in mind. Teaching children the correct way to perform motor skills such as jumping and hopping is an example of an appropriate goal. And, because motor skills must be taught in early childhood, just as are emerging reading and writing skills and understandings, it is not only an appropriate goal but an important one.

The key word in NASPE's guidelines is *accumulate*. No longer is it considered necessary to perform thirty minutes of uninterrupted aerobic activity to achieve benefits. Rather, new recommendations from such groups as the Centers for Disease Control, the National Institutes of Health, NASPE, and the American Heart Association recommend ten- to fifteen-minute "bouts" of at least moderate-intensity physical activity, adding up to thirty minutes, on most or all days of the week.

To promote physical fitness among young children, early childhood professionals should concentrate on health-related fitness, which includes cardiovascular endurance, muscular strength, muscular endurance, flexibility, and body composition.

Cardiovascular endurance is the ability of the heart and lungs to supply oxygen to the muscles. Someone with great cardiovascular endurance has a strong heart—a heart that is larger and pumps more blood per beat than the heart of an individual who is not fit. Good cardiovascular endurance results when an individual exercises regularly. Typically, aerobic exercise improves cardiovascular fitness. However, aerobic exercise cannot be approached in the same manner in which it is for adults.

Young children, particularly before the age of six, are not ready for long, uninterrupted periods of strenuous activity. Expecting them to perform organized exercises for thirty continuous minutes, as an adult does, is not only unrealistic but also could be physically damaging and could instill an intense dislike of physical activity.

Developmentally appropriate aerobic activities for children include moderate to vigorous play and movement. Moderately intense physical activity, like walking, increases the heart rate and breathing somewhat; vigorously intense movement, like pretending to be an Olympic sprinter, takes more effort and results in a noticeable increase in breathing. Playing tag, marching, riding a tricycle, dancing to moderate- to fast-paced music, and jumping rope are other forms of moderate- to vigorous-intensity exercise for children.

Muscular strength relates to the ability to exert force with a single maximum effort. Muscular endurance is about stamina. Because the two are related, many of the same kinds of activities and exercises benefit both. To build them, children should use their own weight in physical activities like jumping, playing tug-of-war, and pumping higher and higher on a swing.

Flexibility involves the range of motion around joints. When people possess good flexibility, they can bend and stretch without effort or aches and pains, and take part in physical activities without fear of muscle strain, sprain, or spasm. In general, girls tend to be more flexible than boys, who start to lose their flexibility at around age 10. Girls begin to lose flexibility at twelve. However, this doesn't have to happen. If children are physically active, they will remain flexible. They should also be encouraged to work specifically on their flexibility through gentle, static stretches that take a muscle just beyond its usual length (without pain) and are held for at least ten seconds. Such activities as pretending to stretch to climb a ladder, put something on a high shelf, or shoot a basketball through a hoop, or bend to tie shoes, pick flowers, or pet a cat—as well as hanging and swinging from monkey bars—contribute to increased flexibility. Children should work their own limbs through their range of motion, and should be warned against ballistic (bouncing) stretching, as it can cause small tears in the muscle fibers and is not as effective as static stretching.

Body composition, the final component of health-related fitness, relates to the body's makeup in terms of fat, muscle, tissue, and bone or the percentage of lean body tissue to fat. Due to the burgeoning childhood obesity crisis, much attention is currently being focused on body composition. However, weight alone is not a good indicator of body composition. Some children are simply large-boned. Also, muscle weighs more than fat. So it is possible for two children to have the same weight but very different makeups, one possessing very little fat and the other too much. Physical activity, and particularly aerobic and muscle-strengthening movement, is the key to combating body fat.

Given the increasing emphasis in early childhood programs on accountability and **academics**, physical activity is in danger of being eliminated from the early childhood curriculum. Many early childhood professionals admit they have trouble fitting movement and other components of a physical development curriculum into the program because they are too busy preparing children for academic expectations. Indeed, physical education classes and even recess are currently being eliminated from elementary schools in favor of more "academic time." However, academics and physical activity are not mutually exclusive. Researchers have found that regular physical activity contributes to improved school performance. For example, in one study, 500 Canadian students spent an extra hour a day in physical education classes and performed better on tests than children who were less active (Hannaford, 1995). A neurophysiologist, Hannaford states that because movement activates the neural wiring throughout the body, the whole body, and not just the brain, is an instrument of learning. Moreover, brain research has shown us that the mind and body are not separate entities—that the functions of the body contribute to the functions of the mind (Jensen, 2000).

A curriculum for physical development can also contribute to other curriculum goals in early childhood. For example, when children have opportunities to get into high, low, wide, and narrow shapes, they increase their flexibility (one of the five fitness factors). They also learn about **mathematics** and art because these are quantitative ideas (math), and shape is both an art and a mathematics concept. If they practice these shapes with partners, the concept of cooperation, a social studies skill, is added. When children jump like rabbits and kangaroos, they develop muscular strength and endurance and, depending on how continuously they jump, cardiovascular endurance. They explore the concepts of light/heavy, big/small, up/down, and high/low. These are also quantitative math concepts, but physically experiencing and then expressing them enhances language development as well as word comprehension, which contributes to emergent **literacy**.

Regardless of the content area or concept being explored, there is a way for children to experience it physically. Doing so benefits children because they learn best by being actively engaged, and this also promotes physical fitness. Early childhood teachers, therefore, should frequently employ movement across the curriculum. They can also use transitions to promote fitness. Children move from one activity to another during transitions, so they may as well move in ways that are both functional and fun. Flexibility is promoted when children move in tall, straight, or crooked shapes; when tiptoeing; or when moving on three body parts. Muscular strength, muscular endurance, and cardiovascular endurance are enhanced when children hop, skip, or jog lightly.

To further encourage children's active movement, early childhood professionals should arrange the environment to allow for movement, ensuring there is room both indoors and outdoors for physical activity. They should buy classroom and **playground** equipment and props with movement in mind, choosing items like parachutes, plastic hoops, jump ropes, juggling scarves, ribbon sticks, and balls in a variety of shapes, sizes, and textures. Because children learn by watching the important adults in their lives, early childhood professionals can demonstrate enthusiasm for physical activity, giving the children role models and helping them form positive associations with movement. Finally, recognizing why physical activity is necessary promotes a positive attitude toward fitness that will endure beyond childhood. Children should understand why they're being given opportunities to chase bubbles, dance, and pretend to jump like rabbits and kangaroos. They should also have a voice in deciding what physical activity they take part in, as choice is a necessary ingredient in fostering intrinsic motivation; and intrinsic motivation is a contributing factor in ensuring lifelong fitness.

Most people believe children automatically acquire motor skills as their bodies develop—that it is a natural, "magical" process that occurs along with maturation. However, maturation influences only part of the process, allowing a child to execute most movement skills at an immature level. A child whose skill stays at an immature level will lack confidence in her movement abilities and is unlikely to take part in physical activities beyond childhood. The likely end result is an individual who is not physically fit.

The notion of leaving cognitive or social/emotional development to chance is unacceptable. So, too, is the idea that all we need to do is let children play and they will be prepared for all the physical challenges life brings their way. There-fore, just as other skills are taught in early childhood, so too must movement skills have a place in the curriculum. By teaching movement skills and helping children to be more physically active, early childhood professionals can help combat the obesity crisis and promote lifelong physical fitness. *See also* Child Art; Classroom Environments; Development Cognitive; Development, Emotional; Development, Language; Development, Social; Developmentally Appropriate Practice(s); Matu-rationism.

Further Readings: American Association for the Child's Right to Play (IPA/USA). Available online at www.ipausa.org; Hannaford, Carla (1995). *Smart moves: Why learning is not all in your head.* Arlington, VA: Great Ocean; Jensen, Eric (2000). *Learning with the body in mind: The scientific basis for energizers, movement, play, games, and physical education.* San Diego: The Brain Store; Martens, F. L. (1982). Daily physical education—A boon to Canadian elementary schools. *Journal of Physical Education, Recreation, and Dance* 53(3), 55–58; NASPE (National Association for Sport and Physical Education) (2002). *Active start: A statement of physical activity guidelines for children birth to five years.* Reston, VA: NASPE; NASPE (2004). *Moving into the future: National standards for physical education,* 2nd ed. Reston, VA: NASPE; Pica, Rae (2004). *Experiences in movement: Birth to Age 8.* 3rd ed. Clifton Park, NY: Delmar; Pica, Rae (2006). Physical fitness and the early childhood curriculum. *Young Children* 61(3), 12–19; Pica, Rae (2006). *Moving and learning across the curriculum,* 2nd ed. Clifton Park, NY: Delmar.

Rae Pica

Curriculum, Science

Science education is an essential component of the early childhood curriculum because it satisfies children's desire to learn about the everyday world and allows them an opportunity to exercise and further develop their cognitive skills. Young children's high level of engagement in science activities also provides a context within which the early childhood teacher can introduce opportunities for learning other things such as language and early literacy skills.

Science is a cultural and social construct. Ways of referring to science include scientific thinking, scientific facts, the scientific method, and science processes. The goals of science education can include acquiring a body of information, understanding the scientific method as a system of sustained and systematic in-quiry, active participation in this form of inquiry, developing the cognitive pro-cesses used in doing science, and learning to apply scientific understanding to everyday life experiences.

In the United States, science education has typically involved a transmission model whereby the teacher delivered a prescribed body of information to sitting, listening, and perhaps note-taking students who would later be tested on their acquisition and retention of the information. Recent reform efforts in science education have challenged this traditional approach. The American Association for the Advancement of Science (1993) and the National Research Council (1996) concur that science education should focus less on science as a body of facts to be mastered and more on science as a way of thinking and trying to un-derstand the world. Thus, reform in science education calls for students to be involved in the experiences of science inquiry from the very beginning of their education.

The science curriculum within early childhood settings is consistent with many of these recommendations and has a long tradition of what is often called "hand-on" or active engagement. Principles of exploration, manipulation, and hypothesis testing have been seen as vital and natural to young children's science learning. Indeed, Piagetian scholars frequently evoke his imagine of children as "young scientists."

A reform perspective for science education builds on young children's strengths and these traditions. For the most part, children younger than five years depend on their personal experiences as the basis for learning. Although they are actively acquiring language, they are not yet skilled in taking in information through linguistic input alone. Thus, if science is conceived of as a body of knowledge to be transmitted linguistically, it is not suitable for the early childhood classroom. If, on the other hand, science is conceived of as a process of investigating and understanding the natural world, then it is an ideal match for the early childhood classroom because young children continually and actively make meaning of their everyday experiences in their physical and sociocultural environments. Language supplements this experientially based learning. Children use linguistic input from others to assist them in understanding and interpreting their experience and they actively use language to express their understandings and to ask questions that will help them interpret their experiences.

The Components of a Science Curriculum

"Science education" implies moving beyond the young child's natural processes of learning about the everyday world to undertake systematic and sustained in-quiry into phenomena of the natural world. This can lead to three somewhat dis-tinguishable developments that must be considered in designing a science curricu-lum: content knowledge, a "script" for scientific inquiry, and basic cognitive skills.

Content knowledge. Any aspect of the natural world that can be made accessible to the young child can become the content for science education. Young children's reliance on personal experience as the foundation for learning argues for a focus on phenomena that can be perceived by the child—for example, exploring the characteristics of water would be more feasible and appropriate at the early childhood level than would exploring the combination of molecules or the processes of climate change.

Whatever the domain, it is important that it be introduced to children in a structured manner that allows them to build a basic cognitive representation (mental structure) that can form the basis for further learning. Once children have learned, for example, the essential differences between living and nonliving things, that knowledge will influence what they notice and thus what they learn from future experiences. Whatever the domain, it is also important that children be provided with the appropriate tools, including vocabulary to describe their new concepts. Preschoolers who have carried out investigations shining a flashlight at plastic wrap, wax paper, and cardboard have developed some concepts about whether and how light moves through objects. In many cases, if the teacher uses the terms *transparent, translucent,* and *opaque,* the children will spontaneously hear and understand and learn these words and then appropriately extend them to other contexts. Children may also use other forms of representation—such as the graphic representations found in **Reggio Emilia** classrooms—to examine and share their understandings.

Depth and breadth are also important considerations in determining the content of science education. Any topic (e.g., the life cycle, mixing colors) that can be studied at the preschool level is probably sufficiently complex that it can also be studied at the college or graduate level. The topic must be approached at a **developmentally appropriate** level that honors preschoolers' general level of world knowledge and cognitive limitations, yet it should be approached in a way that allows the child to develop a rich and interconnected knowledge base. For example, instead of studying the life cycle of only humans or only green beans, the preschooler could be introduced to the life cycles of several animals and several plants, then helped to describe the similarities and differences in the life cycle of plants and animals. When children have a rich knowledge base, they are better able to engage in higher order cognitive processes such as drawing inferences or drawing analogies. A rich knowledge base also contributes to listening and reading comprehension.

Scientific inquiry. There are methods of inquiry that set science apart from other disciplines. These methods are designed to construct an accurate (e.g., reliable, consistent, and nonarbitrary) representation of natural phenomena and to support or disconfirm explanatory theories. Young children will not use the same methods that adult scientists use, yet science education for young children nevertheless presupposes a systematic process of inquiry. *Benchmarks for Scientific Inquiry* (American Association for the Advancement of Science, 1993) suggests that children K–2[1] acquire understandings such as the following:

- People can often learn about the things around them by just observing those things carefully, but sometimes they can learn more by doing something to the things and noting what happens (p. 10).
- Describing things as accurately as possible is important in science because it enables people to compare their observations with those of others (p. 10).

- When a science investigation is done the way it was done before, we expect to get a very similar result (p. 6).
- Science investigations generally work the same way in different places (p. 6).

There is a consensus among those who focus on science education at the preschool level that it should involve extended investigation within a domain, that it should be hands-on, and that children should be encouraged to ask questions, seek answers, make careful observations, document their findings, and use those findings as the basis for further investigations.

Probably the most explicit guidelines for science inquiry at the preschool level are provided by the *ScienceStart!* curriculum (e.g., Conezio and French, 2003). Teachers using this curriculum to support children in carrying out a science activity each day, following a four-step process described as "Ask and Reflect," "Plan and Predict," "Act and Observe," and "Report and Reflect." While it is expected that the teachers will initially be primarily responsible for implementing these steps, the goal is that preschoolers will gradually internalize and increase their level of participation in this science cycle.

Basic cognitive skills. The early childhood years are a time of rapid development and expansion of basic cognitive skills such as classifying and sequencing. Although developmental psychologists generally believe that these skills develop naturally as the child interacts with the environment, it is also recognized that their development can be enhanced by enriching the child's environment and deliberately providing opportunities for the child to actively use the skills in the service of personally meaningful goals. Conversely, children who are in home and **classroom environments** that provide limited opportunities to use the skills can be assumed to have less experience and thus less expertise in using them.

The basic cognitive skills that are developing during the preschool years are applicable across a variety of domains and are in no way restricted to science inquiries. However, science draws on many of the skills and science education therefore provides an excellent opportunity to foster their development in the young child. The table below shows some of the skills that are developing during the early childhood years along with questions that a teacher might ask to support their use and development.

Cognitive/Science Processes that Develop During the Early Childhood Years	Questions That Can Be Asked During Science Education to Support the Use and Further Development of the Processes
Observing	What do you see here? What just happened?
Comparing	How are these alike? How are they different?
Classifying	Can you put pictures of plants in the first column and pictures of animals in the second column?
Measuring	Can you cut a piece of yarn as long as your jump? Where should it start and end?
Sequencing	Here are pictures of the three bears from the story—can you line them up so the tallest is in the front and the shortest is in the back?
Quantifying	If we have three bears, how may bowls of porridge do we need?

Cognitive/Science Processes that Develop During the Early Childhood Years	Questions That Can Be Asked During Science Education to Support the Use and Further Development of the Processes
Representing data	You each have a picture of a red apple, a green apple, and a yellow apple. And you each have three bites of apple. Taste the different colored apples, then put the picture of your favorite on the tree.
Interpreting representations	Let's look at how people voted for their favorite kind of apple. Which color was the most popular? Which color was the least popular?
Planning	If we want to find out what is our favorite flavor of ice cream, out of chocolate, vanilla and strawberry, what do we need to do?
Predicting	OK, before you taste the ice cream, what do you predict you will like best?
Replicating	If we mix yellow and blue again tomorrow, will we get green again, or could we get a different color?
Reporting	If someone looked at this chart, what would they say was the month with the most birthdays? How could we write that in a sentence?
Defining and controlling variables	So we know now that if we mix yellow and blue food coloring, we get green. What if we mix two drops of blue with one drop of yellow—will that be the same green as if we mix two drops of yellow with one drop of blue?

Developmental psychologists and classroom teachers continue to **document** young children's here-to-fore unrecognized cognitive competencies. However, competence is a complex construct that involves many different components. The younger child's competence is often "fragile" in that it may appear only in a single or very limited range of situations. Expanded opportunities to use a particular skill can increase the flexibility with which it may be used in a variety of situations. For example, the child who is regularly offered opportunities to classify a variety of different sorts of materials and who is talked with regularly about this activity will more rapidly develop stronger and/or more flexible classification skills than the child with limited exposure to activities that involve classification.

Science Activities as a Context for Language and Literacy Development

Language development and early **literacy** development are now a, if not *the*, primary focus of early childhood education throughout the preschool and primary grades. State and federal education agencies are particularly concerned that too many children are entering kindergarten without the foundation in language and literacy needed to support their learning to read. How does science education in early childhood fit in with this emphasis on language and literacy development? Is there really time to include science education in the early childhood curriculum? In fact, science education in early childhood classrooms can provide an ideal context for the development of language and literacy skills.

Language and literacy must be *about* something. Contemporary research on learning has indicated that children learn best when they are engaged in personally meaningful, goal-directed activities. Because of young children's preparedness to learn about the everyday world, they readily engage in hands-on science investigations. The teacher can capitalize on this engagement by embedding language and literacy activities within the science investigations.

The books teachers select to read aloud can be related to the science activities and can provide the basis for the reflecting and developing questions to investigate (for example, after reading *Mouse Paint* aloud, a teacher might invite her students to think about what would happen if they mixed paint themselves). There are many nonfiction books available at the early childhood level that teachers and children can consult as they carry out investigations. For example, they could consult several books on the life-cycle of butterflies when hatching butterflies.

Young children can be encouraged to use writing and other forms of graphic representation to record and analyze their data during science activities. Contributing to making classroom books and charts to demonstrate their findings offers children an authentic opportunity to use their own experiences as the basis for literacy materials they are creating for others. Such writing provides children with meaningful ways to extend their understanding of the alphabetic principle, concepts of print, and writing with an audience in mind.

Language development is enhanced at both the receptive and expressive levels as young children listen to the teacher talk about ongoing science activities and then appropriate some of that language to use as they describe their own activities. Science itself has a specialized vocabulary (tools, prediction, explanation) and the concepts that children acquire in the course of carrying out science activities lead naturally to the acquisition of new vocabulary to describe those concepts (assuming the teacher models the appropriate vocabulary). Science also provides an opportunity for teachers and children to exchange "information-bearing" language as they describe observations, formulate plans, ask questions, and offer explanations. Information bearing language differs from the use of language for behavior management and social exchanges that typically occur in the early childhood classroom and it helps children develop the speaking and listening skills they will need once they enter a formal academic setting.

Resources for Teachers

There are commercially available curricula for teaching science at the kindergarten level and beyond. For the most part, teachers who want to teach science at the preschool level have created their own lesson plans. New materials are being developed, thanks to funding from the National Science Foundation, including The *Young Scientist* series and *ScienceStart!* (see Conezio and French, 2003). There are also a number of reference books available that compile science activities. However, teachers should be cautious in using these activities because they often are teacher demonstrations (rather than hands-on activities) that are not contextualized in terms of an ongoing topic of inquiry and may not be scientifically accurate. One popular activity of this type is arranging a cone over the mouth of a bottle to represent a volcano, then putting baking soda and vinegar into the bottle to create an "eruption" of the volcano—this demonstration does not accurately represent the process of volcanic eruption nor lead to an investigation how the combination of a liquid and a solid could lead to the creation of a gas. It is entertaining, but it is not science.

Summary

Reform efforts are transforming science education from a verbal transmission model to a hands-on inquiry model. This transformation is ideal for young children, who are eager to learn about the everyday world. Young children engage readily in hands-on investigations of natural phenomena. With adult guidance, they are able to engage in systematic and sustained inquiry that leads to the acquisition of a rich scientific knowledge base, the expansion of emerging cognitive skills, and the development of other valuable skills, including language and early literacy.

Note

1. *Benchmarks for Scientific Literacy* (American Association for the Advancement of Science, 1993) describes goals for students' achievement of scientific literacy at various grade spans, beginning at kindergarten through second grade. Many of these goals for grades K-2 are also appropriate for children ranging from three to five, the preschool years.

Further Readings: American Association for the Advancement of Science (1993). *Benchmarks for science literacy*. New York: Oxford University Press; American Association for the Advancement of Science (1999). *Dialogue on early childhood science, mathematics, and technology education*. New York: Oxford University Press; Conezio, Kathleen, and Lucia French (2003). Science in the preschool classroom: Capitalizing on children's fascination with the everyday world to foster language and literacy development. In D. Koralek and L. J. Colker, eds. *Spotlight on young children and science*. Washington, DC: National Association for the Education of Young Children; Czerniak, C., J. Haney, and A. Lumpe (2000). Assessing teachers' beliefs about their science teaching context. *Journal of Research in Science* 37(3), 275-298; Forman, George, and Christopher Landry (1992). Research on early science education. In C. Seefeldt, ed. *The early childhood curriculum: A review of current research*, 2nd ed. New York: Teachers College Press, pp. 175-192; Ginsberg, Herb and Susan Golbeck, eds. (2004). Early learning in math and science. Special issue, *Early Childhood Research Quarterly 19*(1), 1-200; Holt, Bess-Gene (1977). *Science with young children*. Washington, DC: NAEYC; Kilmer, Sally J., and Helenmarie Hofman, (1995). Transforming science curriculum. In Sue Bredekamp and Teresa Rosegrant, eds. *Reaching potentials: Transforming early childhood curriculum and assessment*. Vol. 2. Washington, DC: NAEYC; Koralek, Derry G., and Laura J. Colker, eds. (2003). *Spotlight on Young Children and Science*. Washington, DC: National Association for the Education of Young Children; National Research Council (1996). *National science education standards*. Washington, DC: National Academy Press; National Research Council. (2004). *Mathematical and scientific development in early childhood: A workshop summary*. Washington, DC: National Academy Press; Worth, Karen, and Sharon Grollman (2004). *Worms, shadows, and whirlpools: Science in the early childhood classroom*. Portsmouth, NH: Heinemann.

Lucia French

Curriculum, Social

A *social curriculum* in early childhood education consists of all the things that educators intentionally do to support young children's social learning and development. While every child gains the core of his or her social learning in the family or home setting, nevertheless educators have something important to add. Especially in our complex world today, educators can be key supporters to the family in fostering social development and helping children learn to take their first steps in functioning outside the home and beginning to participate in a diverse society.

Implementing a social curriculum has two main components. The first part involves *creating a learning environment* that promotes a sense of caring and belonging. **Grouping** practices, for example, set the stage for what kind of community can evolve within the classroom. The second part involves the *active teaching of those social skills, concepts, and knowledge* that children need to interact competently with peers and adults and to understand and navigate their social world.

Implementing the social curriculum is closely related to promoting emotional development, but nevertheless, a distinction can be made. Although it also possible to merge social and emotional education into one "social-emotional" domain, the emotional curriculum focuses on helping children develop and maintain healthy attachments to parents and caregivers, trust the security of their environment, understand their own and others' emotions, and gain skills such as empathy, emotional regulation and expression, and kindness and caring. In contrast, the social curriculum builds on those emotional foundations and assists children in getting along with others (*gain social skills*) and learning to understand the rules, roles, relations, and institutions of society (*acquire social/moral knowledge*).

The Social Environment

Research has shown a consistent link between high-quality early childhood environments and positive social and academic outcomes for children. Teachers can foster social development through setting up environments that promote social interaction, dramatic play, sharing, cooperation, and awareness of diversity. In addition, they can forge a caring classroom that communicates respect for others (Stone, 2003) and democratic decision making (Vance and Weaver, 2003). Educators can also dramatically influence classroom social dynamics through grouping practices. Three approaches to arranging the composition of children have received the most attention: mixed-age grouping, looping, and inclusion. Each approach presents different opportunities for children's social learning by providing different relationships with adults and peers.

In **mixed-age grouping**, a classroom is organized to contain children that span two or more years of age. The wider span of ages requires teachers to plan in a more individualized way and create a more differentiated approach to instruction. Studies have shown that multiage grouping allows for more cooperation (less competition), peer modeling and teaching, and increased development of responsibility and perspective taking skills, and that it has beneficial academic and social outcomes for children (Katz, Evangelou, and Hartman, 1990). Findings are particularly strong for low-income children who show benefits in achievement, social development, self-concept ratings, and more positive attitudes toward school when in multiage as opposed to age-segregated settings. Multiage grouping has been used successfully in public schools, preschools, and child-care programs (where it is sometimes called "family grouping"), and is fundamental to the Montessori method, which uses three-year age groupings (under ages 3, 3-6, 6-9, and 9-12).

In looping, a group of children keep their same teacher(s) over a span of years. In the United States, this practice is not widespread but has existed since 1913 under different names: teacher rotation, family-style learning, student–teacher progression, and multiyear instruction. Looping is the norm in many European countries, such as Norway and **Italy**, where the teacher remains with her classroom throughout the entire five or six years of elementary school; and it is also fundamental to the **Waldorf** method. The belief is that teachers thereby know students better and are able to individualize and provide appropriate instruction as well as use more positive approaches to discipline. Looping also saves instructional time because the routines and orientation established in the first year continues in subsequent years but also has social benefits, allowing children more time to develop relationships with teachers and peers. Parents and teachers too develop stronger working relationships that allow them to send consistent expectations to children about the importance of schooling and behavior. Children and parents who need more time to develop connections to school can do so.

Inclusion refers to integrating children with disabilities into the daily life, routines, and social interactions of their natural environments and is conceptualized as a benefit to all children. Social integration in inclusive classrooms tends not to occur unless teacher support is provided, but when teachers are trained and supported, then **young children with disabilities** show more interaction and higher levels of play in inclusive classes as opposed to segregated ones. Typically developing children can become more accepting of human differences, more aware of other children's needs, and more comfortable around children with disabilities. To promote integration, teachers need to coach children in the skills of entering and sustaining play, sharing meaning, attending to verbal and nonverbal cues, and appreciating their similarities and differences—skills that will serve them well the rest of their lives (Diamond and Stacey, 2003).

Teaching Social Skills, Concepts, and Knowledge

A quality early childhood program promotes young children's capacity to learn in a social setting by helping them learn to engage in strong, positive interactions with both adults and peers. Individual differences in children's social competence are readily apparent in groups of young children, and unless these are addressed, children's academic and learning outcomes cannot be maximized. All young children, in particular those from stressful and nonnurturing environments, benefit from a proactive social curriculum.

Dramatic and imaginative play provides children with the best opportunities to learn to notice and appreciate other children's points of view. Ideas and materials have to be negotiated and agreed upon and problems solved as conflicts arise. By encouraging and monitoring children's social play and intervening in a supportive way when necessary, teachers can help young children learn to use words, take turns, lead and follow, and control aggression. To avoid inadvertently widening the gap between different children's social knowledge and skills, teachers must create alternative learning situations for children to practice skills. "Floor time" (Greenspan, 2002) with a trusted adult or peer allows children to become more confident in play. For a child who has particular difficulties with social play, the following are some positive ways to intervene (Landy, 2002, p. 294):

- coach the child in words to use in a situation,
- help the child see the connection between his action and the other child's responses,
- suggest some ways for the child to enter the group and join the play,
- coach the child to respond to other's invitations,
- coach the child to learn and use others' names,
- show the child how to join the flow of the play so as not to disrupt it,
- encourage a rejected child to try again.

Children can also be taught the skills of social problem solving so that they are better able to negotiate, take turns, and solve problems verbally rather than physically. Through direct instruction, stories and formal and informal conversations, teachers can talk about consequences, explain tasks, talk about the sequence of events, and ask questions that help children consider alternatives. In this way, they teach and model the components of social problem solving that become internalized into private speech. Some children, particularly those who have difficulties with attention or impulse control, need intensive support in learning and practicing these skills through such techniques as role-play and structured discussion.

Children demonstrate social skills with adults when they seek information, help, permission and attention in appropriate ways; listen and follow directions; converse, show, and share. The social curriculum includes instruction and guidance in appropriately and consistently using adults as resources.

Education for Social/Moral Knowledge

In primary school, the study of people is called *social studies* and involves looking at how people live and work, now and in past times, how their families and societies are organized, and how people are shaped by their everyday contexts. In preschool, teachers implement the equivalent when they provide experiences, activities, and materials that foster learning about the social world and its organization. When teachers go beyond those basics to teach about rules and conventions, fairness, authority, and welfare, they are enriching the **social studies curriculum** to include a moral domain.

There are many ways for teachers to create topics or themes and sequence their curriculum to help children master social/moral knowledge; different formal curricula offer alternative approaches. For example, the early childhood program known as **Creative Curriculum** organizes the components of "social studies" for preschool children into the four categories: spaces and geography, people and how they live, people and the environment, and people and the past (Dodge, Colker, and Heroman, 2002). These four topics roughly correspond to what, in later grades, will come to be called geography, sociology, ecology, and history. Through these studies, children delve into familiar topics in many preschool and child-care programs, such as their community, maps, families, jobs, school and home rules, caring for the environment, and growth and change over time. The **Montessori** primary level for children aged 3–6 includes a broad "Cultural Curriculum" with many subtopics, including the study of people and cultures in other countries, music, art, world geography, plants, animals, and the solar system. Montessori students always start with the biggest question and the widest scope before moving to more specific questions and topics. They learn about the whole earth before learning about the continents, and then the countries. This approach is intended to teach them to respect other living beings and the earth and to feel connected to the global human family.

A range of approaches to a Social Curriculum can be found in the early learning standards formulated across the United States in recent years in response to federal policies such as the **Head Start** Child Outcome Framework and the **Good Start, Grow Smart** requirements. A comprehensive content analysis of state early learning standards, drawing from the **National Education Goals Panel**'s five dimensions of school **readiness,** categories the curriculum contents into four parts:

- *Physical*—knowledge about the specific properties, characteristics, and facts related to the physical world;
- *Logico-mathematical*—knowledge about mathematics or high-order thinking about relationships, such as same/different, cause and effect, part/whole;
- *Social*—knowledge about roles of persons or groups within society;
- *Social-conventional*—knowledge about the conventions and moral rules of society, the home, classroom, or school.

This analysis revealed that state early learning standards put much less emphasis on the two kinds of social knowledge standards than on either the physical or logico-mathematical areas of knowledge (Scott-Little, Kagan, and Frelow, 2005).

Most early childhood educators believe that young children have intense interests in social and moral knowledge, and that teachers should respond by encouraging them to ask questions, dialogue with others, and think about the reasons underlying social and moral ideas. When teachers approach the teaching and learning of social/moral knowledge in an inquiry-oriented way, children are exposed to rich factual and conceptual information that they can use to construct their own knowledge. In this way, children's thinking grows increasingly abstract and complex with age. For example, young children are interested in the following social and moral concepts that can be featured in the curriculum through books, role plays, dramatic play materials, field trips, and class speakers, which draw attention to the following:

- age categories and relationships,
- gender,
- race (skin color),
- families and kinship,
- friendship,
- ownership and bosses,
- money, buying, and selling,
- social conventions—good manners,
- morality—justice and fairness,
- morality—respect and authority.

In all of these areas, young children at first have simple and concrete ideas about them that may contain "mistakes" by adult standards ("a brother is someone who wears pants with pockets," "I'm a girl, but when I'm four, I'll be a boy") (Edwards, 1986; Edwards, Logue, and Russell, 1983). Children's early social concepts and moral knowledge represent their best approximation of adult knowledge. When adults listen carefully to a child's point of view, encourage discussion, answer questions, and provide stimulating books, social encounters, activities, and thinking games, they can strengthen the child's identification with adults, elicit willing cooperation, and stimulate young children to gradually re-structure their social and moral thinking toward greater maturity.

In summary, teachers support social learning through a social curriculum that includes opportunities for children to do the following:

- learn from each other through play and problem solving,
- model the language and social skills of more competent peers and trusted adults,
- question, discuss, and receive age-appropriate information about the social and moral issues and categories that most concern them,
- participate in setting fair and understandable classroom rules,
- regroup from their mistakes and have enough time and opportunity to practice their emerging skills, and
- master the social skills, concepts, and knowledge that they need to fully participate through multiple pathways.

See also Curriculum, Emotional Development; Development, Emotional; Development, Social.

Further Readings: Diamond, Karen E., and Susan Stacey (2003). The other children at preschool: Experiences of typically developmentally children. In Carol Copple, ed. *Readings on teaching young children in a diverse society*. Washington, DC: NAEYC, pp. 135-139; Dodge, Diane T., Laura J. Colker, and Cate Heroman (2002). *The creative curriculum for preschool.* 4th ed. Washington, DC: Teaching Strategies; Edwards, Carolyn (1986). *Promoting social and moral development in young children: Creative approaches for the classroom*s. New York: Teachers College; Edwards, Carolyn, Mary Ellin Logue, and Anna Russell (1983). Talking with young children about social ideas. *Young Children* 39,12-20. Available online at http://digitalcommons.unl.edu/famconfacpub/12; Greenspan, Stanley, I. (2002). *The secure child: Helping children feel safe and confident in an insecure world.* Cambridge, MA: DaCapo Press; Katz, Lillian., Demetra Evangelou, and Jeanette A. Hartman (1990). *The case for mixed-age grouping in early education.* Washington, DC: NAEYC; Landy, Sarah (2002). *Pathways to Competence: Encouraging Healthy Social and Emotional Development in Young Children.* Baltimore, MD: Paul H. Brookes; Scott-Little, Catherine, Sharon L. Kagan, and Victoria S. Frelow (2005). Inside the content: The breadth and depth of early learning standards. Greensboro, NC: SERVE. Available online at www.serve.org; Stone, Jeannette G. (2003). Communicating respect. In Carol Copple, ed. *Readings on teaching young children in a diverse society*. Washington, DC: NAEYC, pp. 41-42; Vance, Emily, and Patricia J. Weaver (2003). Using class meetings to solve problems. In Carol Copple, ed. *Readings on teaching young children in a diverse society*. Washington, DC: NAEYC, pp. 43-44.

Carolyn Pope Edwards and Mary Ellin Logue

Curriculum, Social Studies

Currently, social studies are defined as the integrated study of the social sciences and humanities with the end goal of promoting civic competence. As an integrated field, social studies involve a myriad of processes and content. The social studies include concepts drawn from anthropology, economics, geography, history, political science, sociology, and many other subject matter areas. While it may seem overwhelming to ask young children to gain all the knowledge and skills implied in this definition, the major goal of today's social studies is to introduce children to the skills, attitudes, and knowledge required of the citizens of a democracy.

There have been a variety of approaches to teaching social studies content and skills to young children over the long history of early childhood education in the United States. Before the 1930s, children memorized facts about history and geography with no thought of relating these facts to the everyday world of the child. In the 1920s and 1930s, theorists and teachers emphasized the social skills of cooperation, sharing, and negotiating, but too often the curriculum was turned into a training program that ignored the complexities of social studies content. The holiday curriculum, still implemented in many schools and sometimes described as a "tourist curriculum," gives children a brief glimpse into some selected cultures. This approach to the social studies also frequently introduces stereotypic and simplistic concepts of these cultures and their beliefs. Children experience a few activities, foods, and clothing and then move on to the next holiday.

Beginning in the 1930s, the emphasis in the social studies curriculum began to shift to a more child-centered and democratic **pedagogy** that emphasized children's firsthand experiences within the community of the classroom. Progressive educators, such as John **Dewey** (1944), emphasized both teaching activities that began with children's daily life experiences and the democratic classroom where children participated in decision making and rule setting. In the early 1960s, Jerome **Bruner** inspired further changes in the social studies curriculum when he advanced the belief that curriculum content should emphasize the structure of a discipline. Many early childhood educators adopted two of Bruner's (1960) basic ideas: (1) introduce the key concepts of a given discipline to children on a developmentally appropriate level; and (2) use inquiry-based teaching strategies to facilitate children's concept acquisition.

Since the 1960s and the Civil Rights Movement, the social studies curricula has expanded to include a strong emphasis on multifaceted, **antibias and multicultural** learning and experiences, akin to a social justice pedagogy. One of the central foci for teachers of this form of social studies curriculum is to create conditions through which children learn to value and respect diversity. Such a curriculum goal is not easy and requires that teachers examine their own values prior to creating experiences for children.

An antibias classroom actively challenges prejudice, stereotyping, bias, and negative decisions made about persons on the basis of race, ethnicity, language, gender, and ability. It introduces children to different family types, religious beliefs, and ways of living. This focus goes far beyond that of introducing children to cultures removed from their everyday experiences; rather, it invites children to explore and respect the diversity of life styles represented in their own neighborhoods and the larger multicultural society. These goals require that teachers also acknowledge the need for children's families to be involved in negotiating an early childhood curriculum.

Contemporary perspectives on social studies curriculum require teachers to make choices about strategy and subject matter as they plan children's experiences. Many of these experiences draw upon ten general themes identified in 1994 by the National Council for the Social Studies (NCSS) for kindergarten and the elementary school. From within this framework, teachers of children in preschool programs may easily create experiences that are developmentally appropriate for their classrooms.

- *Culture.* The study of culture—the art, language, history, and geography of different people—takes place across the total curriculum. To become a citizen of today's global community, children must be exposed early to the universals of human cultures and the ways in which they differ. The teacher of four-year-olds might, for example, display depictions of children by artists from two cultures, and have the children compare color, media, and use of line. Then the children might discuss the artists' diverse interpretations of children. Using the methods of the social sciences, data about diverse cultures and various 'images of the child' could be gathered and presented for discussion.

- *Time, continuity, and change.* Young children should be supported to understand themselves in terms of the passage of time, and to develop the rudimentary skills of the historian. For example, three-year-olds can ask their parents about their physical characteristics as infants; and they can collect images of themselves when they were younger and compare this data with their current lives.

- *People, places, and environments.* Young children are generally eager to learn how to locate themselves in space, to become familiar with landforms in their environment, and to develop a beginning understanding of the human–environment interaction. Four-year-olds, for example, could make maps of their school using blocks and other manipulatives; as well as through other forms of symbolic representation.

- *Individual development and identity.* Children can learn to identify the various forces that shape their identity. How people learn, what they believe, and how people meet their basic needs in the context of culture are part of this theme. The teacher might read a book about an Asian child and help the children to compare that child's beliefs with their own, or share a book such as *My Grandfather's Journey* to illustrate the mixed emotions involved in immigration and acculturation.

- *Individuals, groups, and institutions.* Children have already developed beginning concepts of the role of such institutions as schools and families in their lives. A good teacher builds upon these understandings and forges a strong home–school connection. There are many possibilities for gathering data on families and integrating them into the curriculum. Similarly, five-year-olds might investigate the roles and responsibilities of the persons who work in their school. Findings could be displayed in a class book or other representational forms.

- *Power, authority, and governance.* The emphasis is on beginning experiences in how communities structure themselves to function. Preschool children can make choices about which areas of the classroom they will spend time in during the "free choice" part of the day. When conflict occurs, they will learn to negotiate a solution with the help of the teacher. Young children are also capable of helping to establish rules regarding areas of fairness and safety.

- *Production, distribution, and consumption.* At the basic level, children grasp economic concepts such as labor, wants and needs, and goods and services. The creation of a grocery store in the dramatic play area, the selling of tickets to a puppet show are just two of the many ways in which teachers can help children experience economics in action.

- *Science, technology, and society.* With this curriculum focus, children are introduced to changes in technology, and invited to explore such questions as: "What changes does technology bring to our lives today?" They can also be invited to imagine such changes, for example, how the environment might look if we did not rely on the automobile to get from place to place. Children can become creative environmentalists when asked "What will be the eventual result if we use cars more instead of less?"
- *Global connections.* This curriculum focus is contrary to the views of many parents and teachers of young children, because it advises that children be introduced to topics of great importance in our global society. Some believe that young children cannot comprehend such issues as the global environment, human rights, and economic interdependence. However, with the careful supervision of the teacher, five-year-olds may forge cross-cultural connections, for example, through e-mail and letter writing. They can then ask and answer questions with their peers from other countries.
- *Civic ideals and practices.* Through this theme, children meet the central purpose of the social studies—full participation in a democratic society. According to Seefeldt (2001), more than ever before, children need opportunities to acquire knowledge about what it means to be a citizen; and to gain a basic understanding of the principles of freedom. Without such knowledge, children are ill prepared to assume responsible citizenship in the future and to support freedom wherever it exists or emerges around the world. The early childhood classroom can be an ideal setting in which children gain these dispositions and understandings. "A necessary condition of freedom is the ability to think and make decisions. Decision making is fostered throughout the day, not just at activity center time" (Seefeldt, 1993, p. 7).

Each of the ten themes guides teachers in selecting or deriving content based on children's interests, previous experiences, developmental stages, and skills (Mindes, 2005, p. 14). These social studies themes also include a focus on knowledge, skills, and attitudes and values.

Social Studies Planning and Teaching

Using teaching strategies based on the work of Dewey, Jean **Piaget**, and Lev **Vygotsky**, teachers assist children in constructing their own knowledge through firsthand, meaningful encounters with the environment and with other children and adults. Vygotsky (1978) saw children learning to think and behave in ways that reflect their community's culture by mastering challenging tasks in collaboration with more knowledgeable members of their society. Teachers provide the raw materials for integrated thematic units where children employ the techniques of the social sciences such as gathering, analyzing, discussing, and presenting data. The emphasis is on inquiry and employing problem-solving skills to learn content.

Living in a democracy requires that young children begin the process of building connections to their immediate social group (their peers in the classroom), their school, their neighborhood, and eventually the broader community. According to Dewey (1944, p. 192), "A curriculum that acknowledges the social responsibilities of education must present situations where problems are relevant to the problems of living together, and where observation and information are calculated to develop social insight and interest." Within the small democracy of the preschool or primary classroom, teachers provide children with opportunities to practice respect for the rights of others, promote the common good, participate in making choices and developing class rules, and develop a firm sense of identity and self-efficacy. Key social skills that might result from such social studies experiences include learning how to interact effectively with others, express one's own feelings and empathize and take the perspective of others, develop effective strategies for making and keeping friends, and resolve conflicts effectively. In this sense, a social studies curriculum is similar to a **Social Curriculum,** or a curriculum for social development.

Many early childhood educators believe that a focus on knowledge and skills as they support children's responsible engagement with each other leads to the development of positive attitudes and values. For example, when teachers encourage a group of young children to "adopt" a stream or a playground, children can learn about those spaces; they can also gain a much-needed sense of responsibility and participation in their community. Additional ways to introduce young children to the principles of community responsibility and caring include learning the habits of recycling, visits to a veterinary clinic, carefully facilitated intergenerational contacts, and opportunities to mentor and interact with classmates who have special needs.

In summary, the social studies have evolved from rote learning of facts to a complex marriage of content and process. Today's social studies are based on much more than current theories about how children learn and the wisdom of experts in the content areas. They are also based on beliefs that John Dewey expressed long ago when he described schools as sources for societal change. Of all the content areas in the early childhood curriculum, the social studies curriculum is perhaps the most essential to the changing needs of an increasingly globalized world. As the center of the early childhood curricula, the social studies integrate the disciplines through meaningful age appropriate, hands-on, inquiry-based thematic units, projects and investigations with the end goal of preparing young children to fulfill their role as citizens of a democratic society. "The youngest among us are not expected to assume responsibility for nurturing freedom throughout the world, but the conditions that will enable each to contribute to freedom must be present from the beginning of their educational experiences and continue throughout the course of their schooling" (Seefeldt, 1993, p. 4). *See also* Curriculum, Social Studies; Development, Language; Gender and Gender Stereotyping in Early Childhood Education; Pedagogy, Social Justice/Equity; Race and Ethnicity in Early Childhood Education; Symbolic Languges.

Further Readings: Bruner, Jerome (1960). *The process of education.* Cambridge, MA: Harvard University Press; Copple, Carol, ed. (2003). *A world of difference: Readings on teaching young children in a diverse society.* Washington, DC: National Association for the Education of Young Children; Dewey, John (1944). *Democracy and education.* New York: Free Press; Isenberg, Joan Packer, and Mary Renck Jalongo, eds. (2003). *Major trends and issues in early childhood education.* New York: Teachers College Press; Mindes, Gayle (2005). Social studies in today's early childhood curricula. *Young Children* 60(5) 12–18; National Council for the Social Studies (1994). *Curriculum standards for social studies: Expectations for excellence.* Washington, DC: National Council for the Social Studies; Say, Allen (1994). *My grandfather's journey.* New York: Houghton; Seefeldt, Carol (1993). Social Studies: Learning for freedom. *Young Children* 48(3) 4–9; Seefeldt,

Carol (2001). *Social studies for the preschool/primary child.* Upper Saddle River, NJ: Merrill/Prentice-Hall; Seefeldt, Carol, and Alice Galper (2005). *Active experiences for active children: Social studies.* Upper Saddle River, NJ: Merrill; Vygotsky, Lev (1978). *Thought and language.* Cambridge, MA: MIT Press.

Alice Galper

Curriculum, Technology

People talk of a "technology curriculum" for young children in at least three ways. First, some refer to instruction in "design technology"—an approach involving teaching children as young as kindergartners about science, technology, engineering, and mathematics (STEM) concepts as they design and build things. A second interpretation is that of a technology-*enhanced* curriculum in any subject matter area or combination of areas. A third interpretation refers to a set of ideas or materials for instruction *about* electronic or other technologies, such as teaching children about digital photography, video, or computers. The three meanings vary in their educational goals and approaches, with each making contributions to early childhood education.

"Design technology" can refer to a broad range of curricula that vary from arts and crafts to industrial design. Within the field of early childhood education, design technology describes an interdisciplinary educational approach in which young children engage in design as a process of solving problems. Children's projects provide initial experiences with science and engineering ideas and devices such as wheels, axles, levers pulleys, gears, and forms of energy to create motion. Similarly, children learn ideas and skills from mathematics, literature, and social studies, as well as process skills such as collaboration, trial and error, and evaluation. Youngest children work on the simplest design skills, understanding different media and applying beginning mechanical ideas. For example, kindergartners may be challenged to design and create a bed for a teddy bear or doll.

Design technology is based on the assumptions that such experiences integrate different subject areas, problem solving and higher-order thinking processes; show the application of science and mathematics; teach teamwork; provide an intuitive basis for higher-level mathematics, science, and engineering concepts; and provide a valuable alternative instructional route, especially for children who do not respond well to traditional approaches to academics. As further examples, kindergartners may observe the shape of a cereal box when flattened out and then use what they have learned to design boxes to hold other objects. Not all kindergarten designs have to be "working" models. Some are verbal or pictorial representations of how it "could work." Primary-grade children might explore and design mechanical "function machines," which embody simple multiplication and algebraic relationships—for example, a simple system of gears in which one gear turns around two times each time another gear is turned once. Enhancement of creativity is a main advantage of this approach. Other important specific goals including providing girls with the kind of "tinkering" that enhances spatial, geometric, and mechanical abilities missing in many girls' school and home environments.

The other two interpretations emphasize computer-based technologies. Of course, as the description of design technologies should make clear, technologies have developed for thousands of years. Before computers there were technologies of brushes, paints, pencils, and paper, and before this, children interacted with, and represented, their natural world in different ways. Educators must recognize that every technology may contribute to or attenuate children's development depending on its affordances and applications. We argue that there is little foundation for an a priori decision to expose children only to the technologies of any single era. Similarly, design of materials for early education has hundreds of years of history, but computer-based technologies, emerging in the 1980s, focused the field of instructional design, developed in the 1950s, on extensive curriculum development.

Turning, then, to the second interpretation, technology-enhanced curricula exist in many forms for most subject matter areas. They include technology supplements and complete curriculum including software, print material, and manipulatives. Research literature on these curricula is surprisingly extensive (see Clements and Sarama, 2003). In brief, many technology-enhanced curricula use computers to help children learn to read or write; to acquire knowledge and insight into science, mathematics, and other areas through design; and to support children's expression and development of creativity. They have to be used appropriately to realize the achievements, of course, an ecological issue to which we will return.

Computer-enhanced curricula can also have a positive effect on language development and **literacy**. For example, computer use can facilitate increases in social interaction and use of language, from preschool through the primary grades. Children who use prereading and reading software about ten minutes per day show increases in verbal and language skills, word recognition, phonological awareness, phonics skills, and reading achievement. When used well, computer-based writing also can be successfully integrated into a process-oriented writing program as early as first grade. Even younger students can use computers to explore written language. Computers can facilitate the development of a new view of writing and a new social organization (cooperative learning) that supports young children's writing. In general, children using word processors write more, have fewer fine motor control problems, worry less about making mistakes, and make fewer mechanical errors. Combined with telecommunications, technology also can connect classrooms from across the world together in cooperative writing groups (Clements and Sarama, 2003). As with literacy skills, children can use computer-enhanced curricula to learn mathematics (see **Curriculum, Mathematics**). Computer technology can provide practice-oriented arithmetic processes and foster problem solving and deeper conceptual thinking, including a valuable type of "cognitive play"—playing with mathematics. Children as young as preschool age can learn such skills as sorting and counting. Curricula that use software games and computer manipulatives also extend children's mathematical explorations and learning. They can allow children to save and retrieve work, and thus work on projects over a long period. They might offer a more flexible and manageable manipulative. Moreover, they can connect concrete and symbolic representations, such as showing base-ten blocks dynamically linked to numerals.

Computers can record and replay children's actions, encouraging children's reflection. In a similar vein, computers can help bring geometry to explicit awareness by asking children to consciously choose what mathematical operations (turn, flip, scale) to apply.

Technology-enhanced curricula can make a special contribution to **early intervention** programs and classrooms designed for children with special needs. Whether providing instruction or adaptive devices, technology offers critical benefits to children with disabilities. Software may have unique advantages including being patient and non-judgmental, providing undivided attention, proceeding at the child's pace, providing targeted, individualized instruction, and providing immediate reinforcement. These advantages lead to significant improvements for children with special needs. Augmentative adaptive devices can facilitate communication, movement, and control of the environment. Computer technology can also help teachers work with and track children's progress on IEPs. Children in comprehensive, technology-enhanced programs make progress in all developmental areas, including social-emotional, fine motor, gross motor, communication, cognition, and self-help skills (Hasselbring, 2000 #1955; Hutinger, 2000 #1945; Tinker, 2001 #2195; see http://www.med.unc.edu/ahs/clds/index.html for additional resources).

Several innovative technology-enhanced curricula have demonstrated positive effects in large-scale studies involving diverse populations of children engaging in early literacy, reading, and mathematics curricula (see **Interagency Education Research Initiative** [IERI]). Studies investigating the potential impact of the computer on the social ecology of the classroom indicate that computers enhance, rather than inhibit, existing patterns of positive social participation and interaction. Wise use of computers provides a learning environment that promotes high levels of motivation, discipline, independence, and perseverance. Computers may represent an environment in which both cognitive and social interactions simultaneously are encouraged, each to the benefit of the other. *This is if they are well used;* if they underused or used without knowledge and skill, they will not have such benefits (Cuban, 2001 #2085).

The third and final interpretation of a "technology curriculum" is instruction *about* electronic technologies. Since their birth in the early 1980s, such "technology literacy" curricula teach about the parts of various technologies, from computers to digital cameras; the functions and affordances of these technologies; and their social uses and abuses. Children are interested in such questions, and developing such knowledge is a useful goal. However, few present curricula deal solely with these issues. Instead, they are addressed in context of using technologies to support learning.

Thus, all three interpretations can be valuable. Technology-enhanced curricula are the most important, with wide-ranging potential. Technology literacy programs can be integrated into other curricula in a small but important way. An important exception is that focused media literacy education for *parents* and children can result in young children becoming less vulnerable to the negative aspects of all media and able to make wise choices. Finally, design technologies can make a contribution, as a single, but useful, pedagogical approach to STEM education.

An ecological framework implies that there are many influences on the effects of technology curricula. These may be part of the curriculum, such as features of software, or external to it, such as consideration of child–teacher and child–child interactions. Further, the child's home and cultural environment affect the technologies that are available and how they are used (New, 1999). For example, there remains a "digital divide" in which children from lower-resource communities have less access to computers and the Internet than those from higher-income communities (e.g., Haugland, 1994).

Research suggests that the strongest ecological influence is the teacher. Teachers require substantial professional development to use technology-enhanced curricula well. Some research indicates a harmful effect on children's technological competencies when their teachers have no, or less than ten hours of, professional development, while a positive effect has been found when teachers have more than ten hours. Therefore, single, simple workshops are not recommended.

Research on technology curricula has many implications for the content of professional development (Wang and Ching, 2003). For example, left to their own devices, young children may adopt desirable or undesirable patterns of interaction. Without teacher direction or formal instruction, five- to seven-year-old boys may adopt a turn-taking, competitive approach similar to that used with videogames. With initial guidance, however, young children can learn to collaborate and work independently. Other ecological factors, such as the ratio of computers to children, may also influence social behaviors. With a 22:1 ratio of children to computers, aggressive behavior occurs. In contrast, with a ratio of 12:1 or less, there is substantially less negative behavior. Thus, a 10:1 or better ratio should encourage computer use, cooperation, and equal access to girls and boys.

Equally important is the computer software used. This most directly affects child achievement gains. Educators should insist on complete research evaluations of any media (see Haugland and Wright, 1997, and journals such as *Children's Technology Review*, http://www.childrenssoftware.com/). In addition, the type of computer software influences the types of cooperative interactions in which children engage. Children working in open-ended environments like Logo computer programming are more likely to engage in self-directed work and resolve conflicts successfully. In contrast, those working mainly with drill-and-practice software may give only limited verbal explanations for their work. Those working in cooperative computer-assisted instruction environments display more teaching interactions.

In summary, technology curricula include quite distinct approaches and materials. Each can play a role in providing high-quality early education. Whether creating things to meet a design need or using technology-based curricula, research is available to help educators made informed decisions to enhance the learning of young children about and through technology. *See also* Augmentative and Alternative Communication; Development, Language; Disabilities, Young Children with.

Further Readings: Clements, D., and J. Sarama (2002). Teaching with computers in early childhood education: Strategies and professional development. *Journal of Early Childhood Teacher Education* 23, 215–226; Clements, D. H., and J. Sarama (2003). Strip mining for gold: Research and policy in educational technology—A response to "Fool's Gold,"

Educational Technology Review 11, pp. 7–69; Haugland, S. W. (1994). Computer accessibility: Who's using the computer in early childhood classrooms. Computers and young children. *Day Care and Early Education* 22(2), 45–46; Haugland, S. W., and J. L. Wright (1997). *Young children and technology: A world of discovery*. Boston: Allyn and Bacon; New, R. (1999). Playing fair and square: Issues in equity in early childhood mathematics, science, and technology. In George D. Nelson, ed. *Dialogue on early childhood science, mathematics, and technology education*. Washington, DC: American Association for the Advancement of Science, pp. 138–156; Reiser, R. A. (2001). A history of instructional design and technology: Part II: A history of instructional design *ETR&D* 49(2), 57–67; Yelland, N. J. (1998). Making sense of gender issues in mathematics and technology. In N. J. Yelland, ed. *Gender in early childhood*. London: Routledge, pp. 249–273; Wang, X. C., and C. C. Ching (2003). Social construction of computer experience in a first-grade classroom: Social processes and mediating artifacts. *Early Education and Development* 14(3), 335–361; Wright, J. L., and D. D. Shade, eds. *Young children: Active learners in a technological age*. Washington, DC: National Association for the Education of Young Children, pp. 77–91.

Douglas H. Clements and Julie Sarama

Curriculum, Visual Art

Visual art curriculum has held a central role in the United States early childhood curriculum since its inception for most of its history. Although theories and practices of what constitutes an appropriate art curriculum for young children have changed over time, most early childhood programs have encouraged young children to explore materials and create artwork using a variety of art media. Individual teachers draw upon a variety of art theories and recommendations in their work with children, resulting in the broad spectrum of practices seen in early childhood classrooms today. As U.S. teachers experience an increased need for accountability to meet state-wide and national standards, some may question how art can be integrated into the daily life of the classroom. New light has recently been brought to the subject of visual arts in the early years by the world-recognized accomplishments of **Reggio Emilia**.

Historical Background

The tradition of emphasizing art in early childhood curriculum may have begun in the Frobelian **kindergarten**, where children were encouraged to create practical items such as woven placemats and punched paper designs (see **Froebel, Friedrich**). Nursery-school teachers of the early 1900s encouraged children to represent their ideas using a variety of basic materials such as crayons, clay, and paint in order to foster children's freedom of expression, thereby benefiting development. In the 1930s, John **Dewey's** influential contribution to aesthetic theory, *Art as Experience*, argued that art plays a critical role in society. Dewey argued that art illuminates common human experience and that every citizen deserves the right to aesthetic experience. During the 1940s and 1950s, Viktor **Lowenfeld**'s (1947) *Creative and Mental Growth* outlined a developmental stage approach to children's artistic development that was influential in keeping the arts central in early childhood curriculum while keeping the role of the teacher limited to the provider of space, time, encouragement, and materials.

In the 1960s, work by Howard Gardner and the Project Zero researchers outlined the relationship between children's art and cognition and confirmed the importance of fostering children's creative thought and expression. Continued support meant that the arts at this time were more valued in some classrooms for young children. During the 1980s and 1990s, however, increasing emphasis on achievement in isolated academic skills resulted in shifting interpretations of the role of the arts in early learning environments. This trend is apparent in the rise of state and national curriculum standards, frameworks, and increased standardized testing. These changes in curriculum focus have directed attention away from the arts in higher grades, and have affected the early childhood curriculum as well. Nevertheless, visual arts continue to be an integral part of most curricula for young children.

Theories of Children's Artistic Development

Theories on children's artistic development have informed the development and implementation of art curriculum throughout the twentieth century. There are currently four widely recognized theories which account for children's artistic development: developmental, cognitive, psychoanalytic, and perceptual.

Developmental theorists posit that children develop artistic skills by proceeding through a predetermined linear series of stages. During the 1940s, Lowenfeld described five stages of artistic development as the unfolding of a genetic process, thereby discounting the ability of the teacher to further artistic growth in children. Rather, the teacher was viewed as a guide. Wolfe and Perry refined the idea of developmental stages in art during the 1980s, defining each stage by drawing systems with distinct characteristics and purposes. However, developmental theories have received extensive criticism for their failure to account for individual and cultural differences. Golomb has criticized the lack of cultural context considered when assessing children's artwork in developmental stages, and developmental theorists have also been criticized for their "hands-off" interpretation of the teacher's role.

Cognitive theorists, such as Goodenough and Harris, argued that children draw what they know and that therefore, the creation of art is dependent upon concept formation rather than the developmental level of the child. Gardner's theory of **multiple intelligences** supports cognitive theory by linking children's symbolic representation with cognitive development. During the 1960s, the *Goodenough Harris Draw-A-Person Test* was founded upon cognitive theory. In this test, children's drawings of people were scored based on the inclusion of detail and realism; scores were found to correlate highly with other standardized tests of achievement.

The psychoanalytic theory of artistic development is grounded on the Freudian concept of the subconscious (see **Freud, Anna; Freud, Sigmund**). According to this theory, children draw what they feel. Psychoanalysts believe that children's artwork reflects their inner struggles and desires. As with developmental theory, psychoanalytic theory supports the idea that teachers can merely guide a child to express him or herself through art. Psychoanalytic theory is currently used in the realm of art therapy, in which exploration of various art materials have been found to help children to cope with separation anxiety and offer safer ways for children to express feelings.

The fourth theory of art is known as the perceptual, or perceptual-spatial, theory. This theory argues that children draw what they see. For example, a child may draw a figure as a head with arms sprouting from it because these are the most salient characteristics necessary to represent a person. June McFee, in her book *Preparation for Art* (1970), expands the idea of a perceptual theory, suggesting that children's art is based on multiple factors, including perception, the readiness of the child to consider visual elements, the psychological environment in which children work, cognitive abilities, and developmental skills such as fine motor control.

Current Curriculum Practices

Stake-holders in the education of young children draw upon these art theories when designing and implementing art curriculum. As individuals interpret the merits of these theories differently, curriculum has become diverse in implementation. Art curriculum in early childhood in U.S. classrooms tends to fall on a continuum from more open-ended art experiences to more focused and directed activities.

Open-ended, process-based curriculum. Some teachers want children to explore and manipulate materials independently in an open-ended setting. A teacher implementing this type of curriculum presents children with a variety of art materials with multiple uses, such as pieces of tissue paper and glue, and invites them to explore and create whatever they wish using the materials. In this "hands-off" approach, no formal instruction is provided and there is little emphasis on complete products. The teacher does not want to interrupt the children's natural development of forms or self-expression. A teacher using this open-ended approach may support a developmental or psychoanalytic theory of children's art, and takes a more passive role as children engage in art processes. Some teachers following this curriculum believe that children should be free to be creative in their artistic work, rather than imitating and following a teacher's instructions. A potential drawback of this approach is that teachers often prioritize the importance of providing new materials for children to explore; as a result, children do not spend enough time with a given material to gain confidence or experience in using it. This approach has also been criticized for not directly teaching children the skills and techniques necessary to successfully use specific materials to achieve visual expressive goals.

Teacher-directed curriculum. Other teachers believe that children can gain skills in the arts through more explicit teacher instruction. Mona Brookes, founder of the Monart schools, upholds that teaching children a specific set of forms gives them tools they can learn to apply to representational drawing situations. This approach, rationalized by Betty Edward's *Drawing on the Right Side of the Brain* (1979), encourages children to draw representationally, and rests on the principle that children learn drawing skills by copying a teacher or master. Some art curricula in early childhood classrooms rely heavily on workbooks, repetition, and copying adult drawings. Although the children's work in programs such as these may yield high results in representational drawing, this approach is criticized for ignoring children's interests, restricting their creative processes, and interfering in the natural progression of development.

Teacher and child as partners in learning. Some contemporary early learning environments use a combination of child-centered and teacher-directed art experiences in the classroom. Teachers may use a variety of methods in order to motivate children's engagement, including both teacher- and child-directed experiences. Teachers might make art materials available as a fixed component of the classroom environment. Placed at the child's level, these are materials that the child can retrieve for her/himself. Another approach would be to set out materials as a "planned experience," or center that children may choose to participate in during a choice period. Materials may also be presented as the basis for a planned activity, and further motivated by the teacher's engagement and guidance in the activity. For example, a teacher might display prints of Matisse paper cutouts along with a variety of papers and scissors, as motivation for the children to experiment with paper cutout designs and collage. Content for these activities might develop from both the classroom curriculum at large, as well as the specific work the children are producing.

Role of the Teacher

The role of the teacher in planning art experiences involves understanding the elements of design, setting goals for the children, and setting the environment to motivate the art experience through materials or tasks. There are a number of disciplines within the visual arts that can be implemented in a classroom with young children, such as painting, sculpting, or weaving. An early child-care teacher can facilitate an art activity through these disciplines through diverse art processes such as applying, forming, or interlacing.

Teachers may facilitate art experiences for young children to address local, state, and national standards for art, or to connect with emergent themes in the children's play. Teachers also may use art activities to address other curriculum standards in math, science, and literacy. Art experiences are used in early childhood classrooms today to promote healthy personal/social development, give children opportunities for self-expression, build skills in problem solving, and encourage creative thinking. Teachers often want children to be exposed to and gain experience with materials, as well as begin to understand symbol systems.

Planning lessons and learning Encounters. When a teacher chooses an activity in the classroom, she/he considers what activity and materials best fit the goals for the children, in terms of both the classroom context and the standards addressed. The teacher also takes into account the experience and development of the children involved. Teachers may plan lessons aimed to (1) increase observation skills and perceptual-spatial awareness of details, (2) encourage expressivity, work from feelings, and identify emotional states through symbols, (3) encourage an awareness of artistic elements, physical knowledge of materials, and techniques, (4) encourage creativity, cultivate imagination and novel thinking, and encourage new ways of perceiving (Feinburg and Mindess, 1994). A specific art activity may address more than one of these goals.

Materials. In designing art activities, the teacher whose curriculum is both child-centered and teacher-directed chooses materials purposefully. Before setting up an activity, the teacher first experiments with the materials her/himself to understand what particular qualities might best work in an activity. Qualities of the material, such as size, shape, and scale of the materials, are considered in terms of what they might afford to the particular children and the goals of the activity. Materials can range from more traditional art materials, such as paint, to natural or found objects like leaves or buttons. In choosing materials and setting up the activity, the teacher takes into account what interests the children have and what might motivate their artwork. For instance, in order to encourage more active children to engage in visual art choices, a teacher might set out a box filled with marbles and several colors of fresh paint. The teacher would invite children to lift the box and move the marbles in different ways to mix the paint. The motion of the marbles and the more social aspect of the art activity might encourage members of the class to become more involved in the art area.

Environment. The teacher also takes into consideration the environment when setting an art activity. In creating a space for art within the classroom, the teacher includes as much natural light as possible, and organizes materials so that they are easily accessible and visible to all children. Different environmental juxtapositions of materials within the space, that is, when the child draws on big pieces of paper on the floor versus on smaller sheets of paper on a tabletop, might afford different results in terms of an activity. Changes in the environment, such as including novel environmental elements, doing an art activity in a new place, and restricting or limiting materials can be particularly motivating for children.

Creative process. In early childhood educational settings, teachers tend to give children time to use materials and get comfortable with the technical skills of holding scissors or squeezing glue, before they focus on the product. As children gain experience with materials, they gain confidence in their artwork. The creative process usually begins with exploring materials. The process then evolves as children focus their work, produce a creation, stop their activity, and evaluate or re-work their product. As children engage in the creative process, they may experiment spontaneously, move back and forth between exploring and producing, or work in-depth on a project. Based on the nature of the activity, the children may work independently or as a group. To keep children engaged in art activities, the teacher works to continually motivate children to think, feel, and perceive. Dialogue, objects, words, or images may be used as stimulation or motivators for projects. Teachers may consider the concept of Lev **Vygotsky**'s Zone of Proximal Development to help individual children gain the most from art activities. The teacher provides constructive comments that value the children's work, for example by pointing out particular elements of the process, or making comments that draw attention to the elements of art. The materials, environment, and teacher's comments all contribute to making artwork in the classroom purposeful.

Art and technology. A growing trend to incorporate technology into the early childhood curriculum has meant that an increasing number of classrooms for young children have computers, digital cameras, and other technological equipment. Many of these technologies have potential uses in the art curriculum, and some teachers choose to use them in their classrooms. For example, computer software programs such as KidPix and Microsoft Microworlds give young children digital formats for drawing, editing, and manipulating digital photographs, or creating virtual worlds with illustrations, music, and animation. The inclusion of technology in an art curriculum has expanded the medium through which children can create and appreciate art. The availability of a rapidly developing range of technology and software promises to make this area of art a dynamic playground for growth and exploration in years to come.

Inclusion. In many classrooms in the United States today, children with special needs and typically developing children play and learn together in the same classroom. As different learning styles and individual characteristics are being acknowledged and appreciated, art may provide a way to interest or motivate children who might not otherwise participate. These trends demand that additional attention be paid to art curriculum planning, to ensure that projects and materials are made accessible and engaging to all children involved.

Inclusion means that teachers and specialists may substitute certain materials, spaces, or motivations for others during an art activity, in order to support individual children in the activity at hand. Frequently, specialists and therapists can serve as resources for teachers in determining which types of adaptations are appropriate for a specific child.

New Understandings

As more pressure has been put on teachers to meet standards in the areas of math and reading, the value and goals of art curriculum in the United States have been called into question. Although art has had a strong presence in the early childhood curriculum, the strikingly complex children's artwork that has emerged in the municipally funded preprimary centers of **Reggio Emilia**, Italy, has envoked dialogue regarding current conceptions of the capabilities of young children. The centers in Reggio Emilia integrate art within the curriculum and employ *atelieristi*, faculty who specialize in different areas of art. The *atelieristi* collaborate and co-organize materials, projects, and space with teachers. Reggio Emilia centers provide studio space, called the *atelier*, for work to be done in and outside the classroom. The children in these Reggio Emilian classrooms play an active part in the planning of curriculum. Children spend time each day using art media to represent their ideas, observations, theories, and dreams in graphic **"symbolic languages."** Art is heavily integrated into the curriculum through problem-solving activities and teachers take great care to **document** their shared experiences as well as children's symbolic representations of their plans, hypotheses, and emerging understandings. Reggio Emilia's approach to children's art builds upon theories of the relationship between cognition and **creativity** and emphasizes the potentials of drawing to learn as well as learning to draw. The philosophies of Reggio Emilia have become popular in the United States, and have begun to be integrated into "Reggio Emilia inspired" schools.

In addition to the influence of Reggio Emilia, philosopher Maxine Greene and scholar Eliot Eisner suggest a need to place more value on art in our current educational system. Greene states that art is essential for children to make meaning, think critically, and acknowledge the multiple realities that currently exist in society. Eisner upholds the critical value that art plays in our increasingly symbolic and visual world, honoring multiple perspectives and subtleties. Eisner also stresses the importance of art as it teaches children problem-solving skills that may yield more than one solution.

Conclusion

Exposure to the arts seems to be valued in U.S. classrooms, and teachers across the country are integrating art experiences in meaningful ways. By giving children diverse ways to order, interpret, and describe their world, teachers offer children more possibilities and entry points into the life of the class. Classroom art activities are not only a place for self-expression and tool use, but also a place to think symbolically, make connections between contexts, see multiple perspectives, and solve problems. *See also* Assessment, Visual Art; Child Art.

Further Readings: Davis, Jessica, and Howard Gardner (1993). The arts and early childhood education: A cognitive developmental portrait of the young child as Artist. In Bernard Spodek, ed. *Handbook of research on the education of young children*. New York: Macmillan, pp. 191–206; Dewey, John (1934). *Art as experience*. New York: Penguin Putnam; Edwards, Betty (1979). *Drawing on the right side of the brain*. Los Angeles, CA: J. P. Tarcher; Eisner, Elliot (2003). *What the arts teach and how it shows*. In E. Eisner, *The arts and the creation of mind*. New Haven, CT: Yale University Press, pp.70–92; Feinburg, Sylvia, and Mary Mindess (1994). *Eliciting children's full potential: Designing and evaluating developmentally based programs for young children*. Pacific Grove, CA: Brooks/Cole; Forman, George (1996). A child constructs an understanding of a water wheel in five media. *Childhood Education* 72.5, 269–273; Gandini, Lella, Lynn Hill, Louise Cadwell, and Charles Schwall, eds. (2005). *In the spirit of the studio: Learning from the Atelier of Reggio Emilia*. New York: Teachers College Press; Greene, Maxine (1997). Metaphors and multiples: Representation, the arts, and history. *Phi Delta Kappan* 78, 387–394; Lasky, Lila, and Rose Mukerji-Bergeson (2003). *Art: Basic For young children*. Washington DC: NAEYC; Lowenfeld, Viktor, and W. Lambert Brittain (1987). *Creative and mental growth*, 8th ed. New York: Macmillan; McFee, June K. (1970). *Preparation for art*. 2nd ed. Belmont, CA: Wadsworth Publishing; McWhinnie, Harold J. (1992). Art in early childhood education. In Carol Seefeldt, ed. *The early childhood curriculum: A review of current research*, 2nd ed. New York: Teachers College Press, pp. 264–285; Seefeldt, Carol (1999). Art for young children. In Carol Seefeldt, ed. *The early childhood curriculum: Current findings in theory and practice*. 3rd ed. New York: Teachers College Press, pp. 201–217.

Maggie Beneke and Megina Baker

D

DAP. *See* Developmentally Appropriate Practice(s)

Day Nurseries

References to "day nurseries" or the "day nursery movement" vary depending upon what country is being described. For example, the history of day nurseries in the United States is not the same as in the United Kingdom and the terms have a different "life" and meaning in those two countries. For the most part, day nurseries of the nineteenth and early twentieth centuries can be understood as day-care centers from the perspective of late twentieth-century terminology. Both were originally created to serve predominantly lower income families where the mother was employed outside of her own home. Today, these terms refer to the care of children whose mothers are employed, regardless of level of income. The terms and their associated activities can be described within the broad field of early childhood education, care, and development (ECECD, to utilize a broadly encompassing acronym).

Day nurseries are caught in the awkward nomenclature problems associated with the larger field of ECECD. In the United States, a multitude of terms have been used to describe ECECD programs and services. In a few cases these terms have, or have had, a reasonably "precise" reference (e.g., Montessori and Froebelian programs in their early histories tended to have a fairly specific identity), but in many other cases calling a program a child-care center, day care, nursery, day nursery, or even an infant school or kindergarten did not, and does not, necessarily provide insight into what such a program looked like or hoped to achieve. This lack of precision in ECECD labeling is further distorted by historical preferences for certain terms that often take on different meanings at other periods of time.

Day nurseries emerged at a point in U.S. history when nonmaternal care of young children was in social disfavor (a phenomenon that emerged in the 1830s, tolling the death knell for the 1820s Infant School movement). The earliest programs to describe themselves as day nurseries appeared in the 1850s and such self-described programs persisted in substantial numbers through the first half the twentieth century (although in increasing disfavor as a name from approximately the turn of the century on). Various forms of what used to be called day nurseries persist into the twenty-first century, despite social support for **Head Start** programs commencing in the 1960s and the phenomenal growth of alternative forms of child care beginning in the 1970s and continuing to the present. Day Nurseries, like Child Care (a later twentieth-century term), have been stigmatized as a threat to the more socially valued role of "Mother Care" (see Pence, 1989). As programs that were designed specifically for the children of lower income (regarded by some as lower class) families, participation in such programs was stigmatized, and the provision of such programs was largely the undertaking of a variety of philanthropic, social welfare, and religious organizations.

One of the first day nurseries to open in the United States was the Nursery and Children's Hospital of New York City. Incorporated in 1854, the nursery provided care for children from six weeks to six years, between the hours of 5:30 A.M. to 7:30 P.M., for "the daily charge of infants whose parents labor away from home." (Dodge, 1897). By 1904 the Federation of Day Nurseries listed over 250 member programs in over 100 cities in the United States. The great expansion of day nurseries, particularly in the period 1880–1900, was a reflection of changing social and economic conditions that witnessed a wave of over 9,000,000 immigrants, a related doubling in the total population of the United Sates, a shift from a largely rural to a primarily urban-based population, and an increase in the percentage of women in the workforce from 10 percent in 1860 to 20 percent in 1900.

These changes in the U.S. population and in its labor force characteristics did not go unnoticed by popular writers of the period who deplored this "new departure . . . [as] calculated, by thwarting nature's evident design in making her child-bearer, child trainer, and house mother, to rob her of special gifts of grace, beauty and tenderness" (Meyer, 1891).

Most labor movements were similarly unsupportive of women's role in the out-of-home workforce, with the American Federation of Labor asking at the time: "Is it a pleasing indication of progress to see the father, the brother and the son displaced as the bread winner by the mother, sister and daughter? The growing demand for female labor . . . is an insidious assault upon the home, it is the knife of the assassin, aimed at the family circle—the divine injunction" (Brownlee and Brownlee, 1976).

The power of the mother-care ethic in the United States was not lost on the promoters of a second key ECECD program to emerge later in the nineteenth century—the **Kindergarten** Movement, initially associated with Frederich **Froebel**. Elizabeth **Peabody**, foremost advocate of the earliest Froebelian Kindergartens in the United States (and herself a teacher in an infant school in the 1830s—a fact she seldom acknowledged in her writings and presentations), worked to obscure any connection between kindergartens and forms of "child care." However, the stigma associated with the day nurseries was difficult to avoid. Nina Vandewalker, late nineteenth- and early twentieth-century kindergarten historian, noted the dilemma programs such as kindergartens faced when they became too closely associated with what would today be called "child care" or "day care": "One of the disadvantages [from the adoption of the kindergarten as a philanthropic agency] arises from the close connection that has been established in the public mind between the kindergarten and the crèche or day nursery. The two have frequently been established together, both serving a philanthropic service. In consequence the kindergarten is regarded by thousands as being little if anything more than an advanced form of the day nursery, whose purpose is served if the children are kept clean, happy and off the streets" (Vandewalker, 1908).

An exception to the more general pattern of child care and day nursery stigmatization can be found from the mid-nineteenth century through the twentieth century, during the war years. In particular, child care and day nurseries had a more positive social status during the period of the World War II when women in large numbers were recruited into various "war industries." As part of the "war effort" federal funds were made available to such programs as the two "model" Kaiser shipyard child-care programs in Portland, Oregon. During their two years of operation over 3,800 children received care in these federally sponsored and funded programs (Gordon and Browne, 1996).

With the exception of the war years, however, the jostling, competitive dynamic of day nurseries, crèches and kindergartens, described by Vandewalker in 1908, remained common in the United States in the late twentieth and early twenty-first centuries. Throughout much of the period from 1950 to the present, only those kindergartens and nursery schools that operated on a part-time basis (and were therefore "supplements" to effective mothering, and not "replacements") were considered in the public mind as "good." On the other hand, full-time child-care and day-care programs specifically designed to care for the children of working mothers have generally been regarded as poor substitutes for maternal child care. The mother-care ethos, expounded in the press and from the pulpit from the 1830s onward, remains a potent force at the end of the twentieth and beginning of the twenty-first century—over 170 years after its initial declaration.

The history of the day nurseries, regardless of the programs themselves and their claims to or lack of "quality," exists in the shadow of an ethos of mother care. Day nurseries, like their descendents "child care" and "day care," were and remain a class-based phenomenon—programs laboring on the far-side of respectability.

Further Readings: Brownlee, W. E., and M. Brownlee (1976). *Women in the American economy: A documentary history, 1675-1929.* New Haven, CT: Yale University Press; Dodge, A. M. (May 1, 1897). Development of the day nursery idea. *The Outlook,* 56, 66–67; Gordon, A., and K. W. Browne (1996). *Beginnings and beyond.* Albany, NY: Delmar; Meyer, Annie Nathan (Ed.). (1891). *Woman's work in America.* New York: Henry Holt and Co.; Pence, A. R. (1989). In the shadow of mother-care: Contexts for an understanding of child day care in Canada. *Canadian Psychology,* 30(2), 140–147; Vandewalker, Nina C. (1908). *The kindergarten in American education.* New York: The Macmillan Co.

Alan Pence

Deaf Children

Some 5,000 American families experience the birth of a deaf infant each year (Thompson et al., 2001). These children will experience the world differently than their hearing peers. Approximately 90 percent of deaf children have hearing parents with little or no previous experience with people who are deaf (Marschark, 1993). Most parents today are aware of and sensitive to the importance of the early years for language acquisition and cognitive, social, and emotional development. The diagnosis of a deaf child raises many questions about how the hearing loss will affect the child's development and learning. Often parents cannot imagine what the future holds for their deaf child; they do not know how they will communicate with their child, how he or she will become part of the family, or how the family's decisions and actions can support their child's individual needs.

Today, the availability of newborn hearing-screening programs throughout the country has made possible the diagnosis of hearing loss within the first few months of a child's life. This is a dramatic change and advantage from just a few years ago when a child's hearing loss may not have been confirmed until the child was two years of age or so. Technology has also made significant improvements with the addition of high-powered digital hearing aids and cochlear implants. Families now have more options early on regarding amplification systems for their child; the decision about whether their child should have a cochlear implant or not is challenging within the family unit and extends even further when the controversy extends into the deaf community. This decision is usually made in the context of another question, and that is, what language and communication method is the family going to use with their child? Is it one that will rely on the visual system (American Sign Language or another sign language system) or on the auditory system (English or the family's primary spoken language), or will they choose to do both and be a bilingual family?

Fortunately, early childhood education programs for deaf children and their families and knowledgeable professionals are available to support the family in their decision-making and provide them with the information and skills to communicate with their child and to adapt the linguistic and social environment to match their child's attributes (Bodner-Johnson and Sass-Lehrer, 2003). Family-centered programming has become the cornerstone of the philosophy and practice of early education for deaf children. This has come about as the result of federal legislation; specifically, The Education for All Handicapped Children Act of 1975 (EAHCA; Public Law 94-142) and the laws that have succeeded it (e.g., Public Law 105-17, **Individuals with Disabilities Education Act** [IDEA] of 1997) dramatically influenced the pattern and delivery of educational services for deaf children and their families in the United States. Also, new knowledge has emerged from data based research that supports reformulating guidelines for the development and provision of early childhood programs for deaf children. For example, children identified with a hearing loss and who enroll in a comprehensive **early intervention** program within the first six months of life have been reported to have significantly better language and communication outcomes than their peers identified at a later age (Apuzzo and Yoshinaga-Itano, 1995; Moeller, 2000; Robinshaw, 1997).

A number of principles and guidelines have been developed that offer a framework for designing and implementing early education programs for deaf children and their families. They are summarized below and presented as foundational characteristics of these programs whether families use an auditory/oral, sign language, or other communication approach to communicate with their deaf child.

Family Centered

The development of the young child can best be understood within an ecological (as outlined by **Bronfenbrenner**) and family social system (Minuchin, 1974) theoretical context. The ecological perspective locates individual behavior in its social context; the child develops within the family and the broader contexts of the community and school. Both child and context shape and accommodate to one another as they interact; development relies on the child's ability to understand and shape their world and to communicate effectively with those in their environment. **Family systems theory** points out that interrelationships among family members, more so than individual members, are central to understanding the complexity and diversity of each family. This framework sets the stage for developing programs and practices that establish the well-being of the family as a priority goal and one integral to planning for the child who is deaf. A family-centered approach addresses the family's strengths and concerns, is sensitive to family complexity and supports caregiving behavior that promotes the learning and development of the child (Shonkoff and Meisels, 2000).

Collaborative

Early childhood professionals who establish effective relationships with **families,** and join with them by demonstrating trust and understanding, can significantly enhance the family's ability to boost the development of a child who is deaf (Kelly and Barnard, 1999). Collaboration emphasizes the parents' role as decision maker with the early childhood professional and promotes the self-efficacy of the family. Family-professional partnerships facilitate family participation at all levels of the program. Families are able to make well-informed decisions when they have full access to complete and unbiased information; collaboration with families takes place in ways that are culturally appropriate and consistent with the family's desires.

Developmentally Appropriate Practice

Contemporary interpretations of **developmentally appropriate practice** serve as a guide to programs to develop a philosophy and work with children who are deaf on the basis of what we know about child development and family, community and cultural values. The child's individual learning and development patterns and the family's complexities and perspectives are considered for program planning. Developmentally appropriate practice programs construct experiences for children to learn through **play** and welcoming environments that promote ample opportunities for play (Gestwicki, 1999). Developmentally appropriate practice applies also to how adults work together. Professionals working with parents benefit from understanding the principles of adult development and learning in their work with parents as well as with other professionals and members of the community who are involved in program provision.

Transdisciplinary, Integrated, and Comprehensive

For most deaf children, the focus of their early childhood program is on the acquisition of language and communication skills. American Sign Language falls on one side of the continuum, while the reliance on speech and hearing (an oral/auditory approach) falls on the opposite side of the continuum. In between the two are other communication options for the deaf, including: Cued Speech, Signed Exact English (SEE), Simultaneous Communication, and the Total Communication Philosophy. While communication and language is often a critical need area, professionals and parents involved in planning should be aware of the importance of a comprehensive and cohesive program, including transdisciplinary child **assessments,** appropriate consultative services and full implementation of an **Individualized Family Service Plan** (IFSP). The IFSP is a process through which families and professionals identify a child's needs and strengths and the family's priorities and resources in order to develop a plan for services. Professionals from various fields, such as medicine, social work, speech and hearing, and mental health, as well as individuals from the child's community (e.g., child development center staff, deaf adults) commit to working collaboratively as a team to achieve common goals for the child and family. For example, today the deaf community and deaf culture is recognized as an important resource to the family and to the deaf child throughout his/her lifetime. A comprehensive approach to service provision recognizes the complex developmental needs of the young deaf child and supports an integrated model that emphasizes strengthening all areas of development, (e.g., cognitive, social-emotional, motor, cultural as well as communication and language.)

Assessment Based

Early childhood assessment aims to acquire information and understanding in order to facilitate the deaf child's development and learning within the family and community. Primary among the principles of assessment for infants and young children who are deaf—and for all children—are the following, which reflect a family-centered, transdisciplinary, play-based assessment model (TPBA) (Linder, 1993):

- An assessment that is developmental, transdisciplinary, holistic, and dynamic.
- The assessment should be flexible in structure to meet the needs of the child and family.
- It assesses developmental skills, as well as learning style, interaction patterns, and underlying developmental processes.
- Parents and various professionals from different disciplines observe the child together in a natural environment, where the child is encouraged to demonstrate skills through play.

- Results are used for the development of an individualized education program (IEP) or an individualized family services plan (IFSP) and become objectives and strategies for services provided by the early childhood program.

Parents have a key role and responsibility in working with professionals during the assessment process to provide information about their child's development and learning and the family's priorities and values.

Community-Based and Culturally Responsive

An individual family's perspective regarding their child's abilities, a family's child-rearing practices, their relationships with professionals and their involvement in their child's program are a reflection of the family's particular values and beliefs and should be understood within the family's cultural, ethnic, and linguistic contexts. When a program recognizes cultural diversity in the families they work with, it is more apt to offer greater choices and flexibility in the content as well as the delivery of services.

An individual family's community is a wealth of potential support for the family; their personal social network (e.g., relatives, friends, fellow religious peers, neighbors) and the organizations and programs in their locality (e.g., child-care programs, parent education programs, colleges, various medical facilities) are all resources that parents and professionals can tap into for information, collegiality, and assistance for specific need areas, such as respite care. Identifying and locating these community services could be a shared goal for the professional and parents but should be guided by the parents who indicate the need for certain supports.

Using Sign Language with Deaf and Hearing Children

Language development. An ongoing controversial topic that continues today is the best way to communicate and educate a deaf child. The most natural form of communication for a child with a hearing loss is one that relies on the visual system. In the United States, American Sign Language (ASL) has been studied by linguists and is recognized as a natural language that exhibits all the same features as spoken languages, using a modality other than speech (Valli and Lucas, 2000). It is recognized as the language of the deaf community in America and most of Canada. In the past it was often thought that a child who first learns sign language will lose the ability or motivation to learn to use speech as a way to communicate. On the contrary, deaf children—like all children—need to have a native language in order to provide a foundation to learn a second language. Once deaf children have a foundation and understanding of the "rules" of language in their native language, they more easily can pick-up a second language, whether it is in the spoken form or in the form of early literacy.

A practice gaining popularity today based on its success is the use of sign language to support language development with young hearing children. Research suggests that typical hearing children who are exposed to sign language (whether it is "baby signs" or ASL) are more apt to use signs at an early age rather than spoken language (Acredolo, Goodwyn, and Abrams, 2002). This is mainly attributed to the earlier development of hand muscles and hand, eye coordination before the development of the muscles that are used for speech. These children then tend to "drop" the sign when they begin to speak. This practice is also based on the concept that a child's speech, which provides parents and caregivers with linguistic information to which they respond, is not always sufficiently clear and the opportunity for supporting the child with appropriate input may be lost. When sign language is used alone or simultaneously with speech, the child is able to use the sign expressively, parents understand the sign and communication is successful; causing less frustration on the part of both parent and child. Young children enjoy the action involved in the signing movements and for parents and children, the iconic nature of some signs makes learning the signs easier. For example, the sign "drink" is signed by holding an imaginary cup and drinking from it (www.Sign2me.com).

The use of sign language with hearing infants and toddlers with spoken language delays has also served as a successful strategy for supporting children's transition to spoken language, although not necessarily for all children with language delays.

Early reading. Beyond early language development, parents and teachers are using sign language as part of a multisensory approach to teaching reading. Traditionally, we learn to read by seeing, hearing and saying the word. Because the motor ability required for speech production is more complex for the child than that required for the production of signs, sign language allows the child to feel the word in the action of making the sign. Thus, another sensory avenue (kinesthetic learning) is being used in the learning to read process. In addition, sign language provides teachers with a cost-free tool that does not require additional materials and, again, is enjoyable for the child (Hafer and Wilson, 1986).

Summary

Over the past three decades, legislative and social commitments, theoretical formulations and research on development, learning, and families have come together to support a system of early education program provision that today is most encouraging for children with disabilities and those at risk. For deaf children, the development and widespread availability of newborn hearing screening programs have led to identification of hearing loss at earlier ages—often in the first two months of life. This means that families are able to receive individualized information and support from knowledgeable professionals that matches the particular needs of their child at a crucial time in their child's development. The recognition of ASL as a language and the importance of deaf culture have created new opportunities for deaf children and their families that can lead to bilingual and bicultural learning opportunities. Preschool placements after early intervention for the deaf varies by state, region, and city. In many communities, deaf children who use sign language as their primary means of communication are generally not "mainstreamed" into Head Start or public inclusion preschools because of their need for an interpreter. In most instances, deaf children whose primary communication method is sign language are in preschool settings with other deaf children where the primary language of all the students and teachers is ASL or another sign communication system. In this environment they are able to communicate directly with one another without the use of a third party (interpreter). In some cities, there are residential state schools for the deaf that have preschool programs that local children attend and/or families from outlying areas can choose to have their child bused to and from these schools from their hometowns. There are also other preschools options for the deaf that use a completely auditory–oral approach, or a cued speech approach, or a Total Communication approach. As deaf children become older more options for their educational placement become available depending on their location. In many instances, once children reach elementary school, they are mainstreamed with their hearing peers and placed in a typical classroom with an interpreter and/or assistive technology. There are many different methods and views as to the best way to educate deaf children, and children's individual differences influence the success of any particular approach. Regardless of the method utilized, deaf children are visual learners and need to use their vision to compensate for their hearing loss. Earlier enrollment in a comprehensive and integrated early intervention program presents challenges to the education system to provide appropriate services to younger and younger children and to make sure that professionals have the knowledge and skills to work effectively with these children and their families.

Further Readings: Acredolo, L., S. Goodwyn, and D. Abrams (2002). *Baby Signs.* Chicago: NTC Publishing; Apuzzo, Mah-rya L. and Christine Yoshinaga-Itano (1995). Early identification of infants with significant hearing loss and the Minnesota Child Development Inventory. *Seminars in Hearing* 16(2): 124–139; Bodner-Johnson, Barbara A., and Marilyn Sass-Lehrer, eds. (2003). *The young deaf or hard of hearing child: A family-centered approach to early education.* Baltimore: Paul H. Brookes; Gestwicki, Carol (1999). *Developmentally appropriate practice: Curriculum and development in early education.* Albany, NY: Delmar; Hafer, J. C., and R. Wilson (1986). *Signing for reading success.* Washington, DC: Gallaudet University Press; Kelly, Jean F., and Katherine Barnard (1999). Parent education within a relationship focused model. *Topics in Early Childhood Special Education* 19(9),151–157; Linder, Toni W. (1993). *Transdisciplinary play-based assessment; A functional approach to working with young children.* Baltimore: Paul H. Brookes; Marschark, Marc (1993). *Psychological development of deaf children.* New York: Oxford University Press; Minuchin, Salvador (1974). *Families and family therapy.* Cambridge, MA: Harvard University Press; Moeller, Mary P. (2000). Early intervention and language development in children who are deaf and hard of hearing. *Pediatrics* 106(3), E43; Robinshaw, Helen M. (1997). Early intervention for hearing impairment: Differences in the timing of communicative and linguistic development. *British Journal of Audiology* 29, 315–344; Shonkoff, Jack P., and Samuel Meisels (2000). *Handbook of early childhood intervention.* New York: Cambridge University Press; Thompson, Diane C., Heather McPhillips, Robert L. Davis, Tracy A. Lieu, Charles J. Homer, and Mark Helfand (2001). Universal newborn hearing screening: Summary of evidence. *Journal of the American Medical Association* 286, 2000–2010; Valli, C., and Lucas, C. (2000). *Linguistics of American Sign Language: An Introduction.* Washington, DC: Gallaudet University Press.

Barbara Bodner-Johnson and Michelle Banyai Walsh

DEC. *See* Division for Early Childhood

Department of Defense (DoD) Child Development System

The Department of Defense (DoD) considers care for young children of military members to be a workforce issue with direct impact on the effectiveness and readiness of the force. The demands of military service are many and challenging. The DoD points to the frequent moves, long family separations, and rapid deployments that make quality child care necessary to national defense and vital to military families around the world. The DoD Child Development System, one of the largest employer-sponsored programs in the country, serves over 200,000 children (newborn–twelve years) daily. Each service branch operates within DoD standards to ensure consistent, affordable quality care is offered and programs meet local military command needs.

The goals of the DoD Child Development System are to assist the commander in balancing the needs of the family with the needs of the military mission; to promote the cognitive, social, emotional, and physical development of the child; and to provide each parent with at least one affordable child care option for each child.

Although child care had always been a necessity in the military, it began primarily as hourly care and drop-off services supported by volunteers. The needs of each individual military installation determined the care available. But the demands changed dramatically in the mid-70s with the advent of an all-volunteer force. As the number of families, active duty mothers, and single parents grew, the military realized that in order to have a ready force, it must address the need for child care.

Today, the DoD child development program stands as a model for the nation. This was not always the case, however. Internal focus and investigation revealed the potential dangers and deficiencies of child care lacking adequate funding and oversight. In 1982, the General Accounting Office reported that the program did not meet fire, safety, and health standards and there was no oversight of family child care. At the same time, as has occurred in other child care and development programs, the DoD program experienced several highly publicized child abuse allegations. These events served as a catalyst for Congressional hearings in 1988, and in 1989 Congress passed the Military Child Care Act (MCCA) which became the driving force for change. By implementing these recommendations for change and the wide-reaching requirements of the MCCA, the DoD Child Development Program was able to reinvent itself and form a seamless system of child care for service members.

The MCCA required changes affecting the entire military child care program. Five factors have been key in developing the successful DoD system.

First is the systematic approach to the program. There are four components: child development centers, family child care homes, school-age care, and registration and referral. All components are equal partners in the system. A parent can access all components from one single point of entry. Training standards, inspections, and background clearances are equivalent.

Second is the recognition that a quality program costs more than most parents can afford to pay. The DoD is committed to a prescribed level of funding for all child development programs. On the average, parents pay half the cost of care in other centers. In family child care programs, DoD provides indirect financial support through equipment lending libraries, low or no cost insurance options and training for child care providers. In most instances, DoD also provides direct cash subsidies as incentives for family child care providers to care for infants, children with special needs, and offer extended hours of operation.

The third element is strict oversight of all programs and adherence to standards. There are comprehensive unannounced inspections for all facilities and programs with mandatory correction of deficiencies within ninety days. Noncompliance can, and has, resulted in closure of a center or home. As a result, facilities are in good repair and there is high-quality, institutional-grade equipment that contributes to the positive development of children.

The fourth element directly linked to program quality is the wage and training program for staff. Military caregiver wages average approximately $12.00–18.00 per hour compared to minimum wages in the civilian community and include a range of benefits. Competency-based training is tied to wages and an "up-or-out" personnel policy requires the successful completion of training. After completing training modules based on the thirteen **Child Development Associate** (CDA) competencies, all caregivers must complete twenty-four hours of training annually. Caregivers and trainers work together to determine areas that need strengthening. Low turnover provides children with the continuity of care so vital to their healthy development.

Finally, the commitment by DoD that all military child development centers must meet national **accreditation** standards established by **National Association for the Education of Young Children** (NAEYC) provides DoD an objective evaluation instrument by an outside organization. Because DoD Child Development Programs operate on federal property, they are not subject to state and local child care licensing requirements. However, programs meet comprehensive certification standards established by DoD based on state standards. This certification requires a thorough review of programs with special emphasis on staffing, health and nutrition, safety, and the physical environment. Uniform certification requirements ensure a comparable quality program from one military installation to another, thus providing DoD military and civilian personnel with consistency wherever they may be located. The combination of the DoD certification, equivalent to state licensing, and adherence to national accreditation standards results in a comprehensive review of all center programs.

At the present time, military families with young children have access to a variety of DoD child development options, including Child Development Centers (CDCs) at over 300 locations to provide services for children six weeks to 5 years of age. Most child development centers operate between the hours of 6:00 A.M. and 6:30 p.m., Monday–Friday. Other options include **school-age care** (SAC) programs offered for children (ages 6–12) before and after school, during holidays and summer vacations and family child care (FCC) programs that consist of in-home care provided by certified providers living in government-owned or leased housing. There are more than 9,000 licensed and trained FCC providers. Families rely upon FCC to provide flexible child care for mildly ill children, and night, weekend and nontraditional hourly care for shift work or rotating schedules. Registration and referral (R&R) programs serve as a "one-stop" for parents to gain access to various programs and to obtain referral information about quality child care in the local community.

As an employer-sponsored program, the DoD shares the cost of child care with parents. Parent fees, using a sliding fee scale based on total family income, are established to generate approximately 50 percent of the direct cost of operating the total program. The remainder of the total operating cost of the program is subsidized with government appropriated funds. The average DoD weekly fee was $84.00 in 2004 and did not vary based on the age of the child. In private sector child care, care for infants often costs parents significantly more than for preschoolers. Cost-sharing funds provided by DoD go to the programs, not to the families/patrons. This is a key difference between DoD employer funding and many other government or employer funding approaches.

The DoD occasionally receives additional Emergency Supplemental appropriations during times of war. These funds have been used to provide additional child care services including extended hours, respite for spouses with a deployed military member, and care for children of activated National Guard and Reservists.

The Office of Children and Youth within the Office of the Secretary of Defense is the point of contact for overall policy for child development programs in DoD. Each of the Military Departments (Army, Marine Corps, Navy, and Air Force) and Defense Agencies (National Security Agency and Defense Logistics Agency) issue regulations based on these policies.

Janice Witte

Development, Brain

The brain develops dramatically and rapidly during the period of early childhood (Schore, 2001). At birth the child's brain weighs less than a pound, and triples in weight by the second birthday (Bloom, Nelson, and Lazaroff, 2001). Growth and development in brain structures and functions are reflected in rapid changes in the child's physical, mental, and emotional capacities. Developmental changes in brain structure and function influence and are influenced by the child's experiences and environment, and have dramatic implications for caregiving and education practice during early childhood (see Gallagher, 2005). Recent advances in knowledge about early brain development, including structural and functional aspects of brain development, have implications for early childhood care and education.

Overview: Brain Structure and Function

Described as "plastic" due to its ability to adapt and change, the brain manages, regulates, and responds to information from the body and from the environment. Before birth, the brain develops in orderly stages, beginning with the neural tube, which connects the spinal cord to the base of the brain, the brain stem, in the first four weeks of gestation. As this process is completed, the brain divides into three distinct sections: the forebrain, midbrain, and hindbrain. The forebrain divides into specialized sections: such as the cerebral cortex, the frontal cortex, and the prefrontal cortex. The brain develops in structure (regions of the brain consisting of clusters of brain cells called neurons) and function (activities of the brain, such as sending electronic signals or hormone production and secretion). Structures important to early development and learning include neurons, the cerebral cortex, prefrontal cortex, and the amygdala. Functions include synaptogenesis, myelination, and cortisol production of the HPA (hypothalamic–pituitary–adrenal) system. These structures and functions demonstrate some ways the brain develops in early childhood, and are detailed below.

Neural Development

Neurons are the basic building blocks of the nervous system. Most of the human brain's 100 billion neurons are in place before birth. Through the use of electrical signals, neurons communicate messages within the brain and to and from parts of the body (Kolb and Whishaw, 2001). Information travels between neurons in an orderly fashion, from the dendrites (where electrical impulses are received) to the axon (where impulses are conducted away from the cell body). When information reaches the axon, it travels across a small gap, called a synapse, to another neuron. The synapse is the point of communication between two cells (Shonkoff and Phillips, 2000). Synapses rapidly grow more numerous and dense after birth, in a process known as *synaptogenesis.* A dense network of synapses facilitates transmission of more messages in the brain, affording better processing of cognitive, social, and emotional information.

In infancy, synaptogenesis produces more synapses than needed. Consequently, a one-year-old has approximately one and a half times more synapses than an adult (Bruer, 2004). Though scientists are uncertain why the brain overproduces synaptic connections, it is possible that it is nature's way of preparing children's brains for a variety of possible environmental and social experiences (Shonkoff and Phillips, 2000). Unused or seldom-used neurons slow their synapse production, in a process known as *pruning.* With pruning, neurons remain intact, but unused synapses are eliminated.

Children need a variety of sensory experiences to help neural material develop. When children are deprived of sensory stimulation, they may exhibit developmental delays and disabilities. Certain developmental tasks appear to have *sensitive periods*, or stages at which exposure to certain experiences is essential to developing certain skills. Probably because the brain is highly plastic, there are not many known sensitive periods for humans. Some aspects of language may not develop properly when a child is not exposed to sufficient language before puberty. Research with animals suggests that complex, stimulating environments improve synapse density and structure, but there is not sufficient evidence that complex or stimulating environments increase neural synapse material in humans.

During *myelination* a white, fatty tissue, called myelin, grows around the nerve axons. Myelin protects the nerves, speeds the transmission of electric signals, and prevents signals from firing haphazardly. Many areas in the brain are myelinated in early childhood, but some, such as the frontal cortex (responsible for complex thinking, problem-solving, and regulation) develop later in childhood. Slower signal transmission of neural signals, caused by unmyelinated neurons, is associated with less regulated, disorganized behavior in younger children. Early malnutrition, in particular, insufficient fat intake, is associated with poor myelination (Shonkoff and Phillips, 2000); therefore, quality nutrition is important for optimal brain development.

Cortex Development

The cerebral cortex is the brain's outer layer and is responsible for conscious activity. It has two sides, or hemispheres, which have specialized functions. The right side of the cerebral cortex specializes in processing negative and intense emotions, nonverbal and spatial processing, and creativity (Kolb and Whishaw, 2001). The left side of the cerebral cortex specializes in positive emotions, language development, and interest in new objects and experiences. These brain specializations are highly plastic: they change easily. When an individual has brain damage to one side of the brain, the undamaged area takes over the damaged side's functions (Kolb and Whishaw, 2001). An important consideration for early childhood concerning hemispheric specialization is that the sides of the cerebral cortex develop at different rates. The right side of the cerebral cortex grows more quickly during the first 18 months of life and dominates brain functioning for a child's first three years. This difference in brain hemisphere growth rate emphasizes the role of negative and intense emotion and creativity in a child's very early development.

The frontal lobes of the cerebral cortex are important for emotional development. The frontal lobes of the cortex allow the person to inhibit and control the experience and expression of emotion. The development of the cortex during the early years assists a child in developing self-regulation. At the very front of the frontal lobes, the prefrontal cortex is responsible for executive function, the processes of self-regulation, planning, and organization of behavior (Shonkoff and Phillips, 2000). Executive function is also closely related to, but not the same as, attention and working memory. The prefrontal cortex doesn't independently regulate children's behavior, but it works in concert with other structures of the brain and develops dramatically during early childhood (Schore, 2001).

The Amygdala

Self-regulation in children is dependent on two very closely interconnected areas of the brain, the prefrontal cortex and the amygdala. The amygdala, a small, almond-shaped structure, is believed to be the structure in the brain most connected to emotional and fearful reactions (Blair, 2002). It is interconnected with many areas of the brain, including the prefrontal cortex and neural pathways for vision. It is highly receptive and reactive in nature and is sensitive to environmental stimulation. The location of the amygdala, deep in the center of the brain, has made it difficult to study, but it is accepted that the emotional (amygdala) and executive function (prefrontal cortex) structures of the brain work cooperatively to facilitate self-regulation.

Stress System Development: HPA and Cortisol

One of the most important functions of the brain is to help the individual recognize and respond to danger and stress. The HPA (hypothalamic–pituitary–adrenocortical) system produces the hormone cortisol. Cortisol fluxuates in response to stress, and contributes to the "fight or flight" reflex that helps the body respond to challenging situations (Kolb and Whishaw, 2001). People have a baseline cortisol level that is typical for their own biology and temperament. Cortisol fluctuates throughout the day (usually higher in the morning and lower in the afternoon) and increases in response to stress. In moderate doses cortisol is a good thing—it helps the brain respond to stress and solve problems. But too much cortisol production over a long period of time leads to problems with memory, self-regulation, and anxiety (Gunnar and Cheatham, 2003).

The HPA system and cortisol levels respond to social interactions and are believed to be connected to the child's developing **attachment** system. From animal research, we know that nurturing parenting is important to the offspring's developing HPA system. When mother rats groom their pups frequently, their pups have more stable cortisol levels and react less to stress. When caregivers are sensitive and responsive children have fewer increases in cortisol and are less reactive to stress. Children's cortisol increases when separated from their caregivers, and when experiencing transitions. Children who experience extreme adverse conditions develop patterns of stress reactivity that includes increased cortisol levels, slow growth, cognitive deficits, and behavior problems. However, there is evidence that these patterns can be reversed when the quality of care improves (Gunnar and Cheatham, 2003).

The following are the major implications for caregiving and education:

- *Neural synapses develop rapidly in early childhood, and prune when unused.* Children benefit cognitively, emotionally, and physically from many, varied sensory experiences. More importantly, sensory deprivation can lead to cognitive and emotional problems for children.
- *The right hemisphere of the cerebral cortex, which experiences and manages intense, negative emotion, is dominant in early childhood.* Children benefit from interactions with sensitive, responsive adults who help them to manage strong, negative emotions. These caring relationships are particularly important in the early years.
- *Myelination is important for healthy transmission of neural messages.* Children benefit from nutrition that balances protein, carbohydrates, and fat. Fat intake should not be severely restricted in young children.
- *The HPA (cortisol) system develops patterns in response to intensity and duration of stress the child experiences. Frequent and intense stress in early childhood is associated with cognitive and emotional problems in childhood and into adulthood. Warm, sensitive caregiving is associated with lower cortisol levels and healthier growth, social and emotional development.* Children need protection from some stressors, such as violence and abuse, and benefit from interaction with caring adults who provide support and help the child cope with stressful situations. Early childhood is an important time for learning to establish productive social relationships.

Conclusions

Advances in technology have facilitated increased understanding of brain development in early childhood. As technology continues to develop, information about the brain's structures and functions will provide more insight to children's development. Some key concepts of brain development are supported by research.

The brain is plastic, and changes and adapts in response to experience. Adverse experiences have a lasting effect, but can sometimes be remediated by intervention. Some adverse experiences, such as exposure to toxins, abuse, and malnutrition, are difficult to overcome. Therefore, it is most important to protect children from harmful experiences, and assure that children receive proper nutrition, health care, and sufficient sensory stimulation (Shonkoff and Phillips, 2000).

When children have birth defects or disabilities that prevent them from obtaining quality experiences in typical environments, intense and **early intervention** is necessary to assure that the child has sufficient experiences to compensate for difficulties. Children with sensory impairments, such as vision or hearing impairments, need access to high-quality early intervention. There is substantial evidence that early and intense intervention is effective in remediating some developmental problems for children with disabilities (Shonkoff and Phillips, 2000).

Early relationships are an influential aspect of children's healthy brain development. When caregivers are sensitive and responsive to young children's needs, and provide adequate sensory stimulation, children develop competence in social, emotional, cognitive, and physical abilities. Evidence for this early connection between quality caregiving and relationships is substantiated by research on right hemispheric specialization and dominance (Schore, 2001) and HPA (stress) system development (Gunnar and Cheatham, 2003). Finally, research on brain development provides information about supporting children's development of self-regulation. The neural mechanisms for children's regulation develop through childhood and adult support is essential until those neurological mechanisms (i.e., myelination) are in place. Adults help children manage intense, negative emotions and support language development for children expressing their needs. *See also* Disabilities, Young Children with.

Further Readings: Blair, Clancy (2002). School readiness: Integrating cognition and emotion in a neurobiological conceptualization of children's functioning at school entry. *American Psychologist* 57(2), 111–127; Bloom, Floyd E., Charles A. Nelson, and Arlyne Lazerson (2001). *Brain, mind, and behavior,* 3rd ed. New York: Worth; Bruer, John T. (2004). The brain and child development: Time for some critical thinking. In Edward Zigler and Sally J. Styfco, eds. *The Head Start debates.* Baltimore: Brookes, pp. 423–434; Gallagher, Kathleen Cranley (2005). Brain research and early childhood development: A Primer for DAP. *Young Children* 60(4), 112–120; Gunnar, Megan R., and Carol L. Cheatham (2003). Brain and behavior interfaces: Stress and the developing brain. *Infant Mental Health Journal* 24(3), 195–211; Kolb, Bryan, and Ian Q. Whishaw (2001). *An introduction to brain and behavior.* New York: Worth; Schore, Allan N. (2001). Effects of a secure attachment relationship on right brain development, affect regulation, and infant mental health. *Infant Mental Health Journal* 22(1–2), 7–66; Shonkoff, Jack P., and Deborah A. Phillips, eds.

(2000). *From neurons to neighborhoods: The science of early childhood development.* Washington, DC: National Academy Press.

Web Sites: Brain Facts: A Primer on the Brain and Nervous System. Free download of this 55p document from Society of Neuroscience. Available online at http://www.sfn.org/baw/pdf/brainfacts.pdf; The Brain from Top to Bottom. Available online at http://www.thebrain.mcgill.ca/flash/pop/pop_plan/plan_d.html; Educarer: Early brain development: What parents and caregivers need to know—contains interactive illustrations of brain and neuron. Available online at http://www.educarer.com/brain.htm; PBS: The secret life of the brain—Excellent resource on brain development from infancy to adulthood, including a 3-D tour of the brain. Available online at http://www.pbs.org/wnet/brain/; Zero to Three Brainwonders. Available online at http://www.zerotothree.org/brainwonders/.

Kathleen Cranley Gallagher and Maria Pelzer Bundy

Development, Cognitive

During an interview in the 1950s, newsman and radio personality Art Linkletter tried to catch five-year-old Tommy off guard by pointing out that he was about to interview a woman who was an octogenarian. Looking a bit puzzled, the child asked, "What is an octogenarian?" Linkletter replied that it is someone who is 80 years old. The child thought a bit and then said, "She must be really tall." As Linkletter, the showman, anticipated, the studio audience laughed, charmed by the child's "error."

Lost on the audience was Tommy's remarkable thinking. These types of "errors" whet the appetites of psychologists and educators. Rather than laughing, or at least rather than simply being charmed by a child's insights, developmental scientists and practitioners ask several questions about the nature of Tommy's thinking in this context. First, how is Tommy's thought structured so that he believes that age denotes height? Second, how might Tommy's thinking change over time so as to protect him from inappropriate intuitions in the future? Finally, how do Tommy's interpersonal/intrapersonal realities mutually construct both his inaccurate insight at age 5 as well as move him toward a new, more accurate, representation of the relation of age and growth?

Contemporary theories of cognitive development have much to offer with respect to the three questions attributed to our scientist-practitioner. More precisely, recent theoretical developments coupled with new research provide new understandings of questions that have challenged developmental psychologists for much of the past century: "What is cognition?" "How does cognition develop?" That is, over time, is there a pattern or form to changes in thinking? And, finally, "What are the biological, psychological and social constraints on the nature and development of thought?"

What Is Cognition?

The fact that cognition, as a construct, permeates so many contemporary fields within psychology and education suggests there must be consensus on its meaning. That is not the case. A substantial body of work on cognition examines various theoretical perspectives on cognition, often pitting one against another. Although there is no denying that these theories are incompatible on some, even fundamental, points, it is possible and fruitful to view them as complementary perspectives. Pragmatically, these perspectives provide lenses through which to view the complexity of intellectual life.

For many cognitive developmentalists, Jean **Piaget**'s genetic epistemology is their historical touchstone when addressing the question, "What is cognition?" In fact, it was his training in biology that brought both a scientific orientation to the study of mental life and a conceptualization of psychological functioning as adapting. Adapting entails more than functioning, it implies structure, that is, the functioning of a structured organism. Cognition is an active organizing, indeed, an active constructing, of experience. Piaget coupled his scientific training with his interests in philosophy, and specifically, a fascination with epistemology. He viewed cognition as an epistemological function; thinking is the way in which we come to know or construct our understanding of realities. A more contemporary view of epistemology would recast his goal of specifying the structures that shape knowing as a question of how the mind is designed. Piaget would not be too interested in five-year-old Tommy's specific knowledge of age or growth. Indeed, Piaget and contemporary developmentalists would see through Tommy's conclusion to focus on the logic of Tommy's thinking that functioned as the backdrop to his inference that the 80-year-old woman must be very tall. They see Tommy's insight as a way of making sense of the fact that someone could be 80 years old.

More recently, cognitive sciences, and more specifically those interested in human developmental science, have shifted from cognition as an epistemic function to a metaphysical activity. This view changes our focus from how do we come to know, to what do we know. Rather than looking through Tommy's understanding of age and growth to the study of abstract structures, cognitive scientists of a metaphysical persuasion view aging and growth as ontological or natural categories; more simply put, as basic conceptualizations of theories about what we mean by living things. Focusing on children's conceptualizations of their realities shifts our theoretical focus from cognition as domain general to an analysis of domain-specific cognitive functioning. The goal of metaphysical analyses is to characterize children's "theories" of number, physical and biological realities as well as fundamental interpersonal activities among others. From a metaphysical perspective, Tommy's insight of the height of the 80-year-old woman is guided by his intuitive knowledge of, or intuitive theories about, biological aging and physical growth. Metaphysical theorists would assume that his "errors" were predicated on a theory that "over time, biological things grow" and "to grow means to get taller." Any questions asked by teachers or researchers would try to uncover his "theory of" biological growth.

A third characterization of cognition moves away from epistemology and metaphysics, that is, away from how we come to know or what we know, and toward computer science and information processing. Knowing is processing information, and the computer is the prototypic information processor. The constituent cognitive processes are familiar psychological functions like planning, attention, and memory. A radical application of the computer model reduces RAM to working memory, hard drive to long-term memory, and software or programming to executive function, that is, the mental overseer that coordinates the flow of information between long-term and working memory. A radical information processing model does not capture cognition as human action or as intentional. A less radical model confronts that limitation by incorporating metafunctions. Human planning, attending, or remembering is not hardwired, rather, they are reflective activities that set goals, set strategies and evaluate progress toward that goal. The less radical information processing types would point out that Tommy's asking about the meaning of octogenarian revealed a metacognitive awareness. He knew he did not have critical information, he also knew that his interlocutor had that information. His erroneous insight would be examined in terms of whether, as he encountered people of various ages, he failed to encode the fact that older people are not always taller than those who are younger, or although knowing that, Tommy had failed to access that knowledge. If the latter is the case, did Tommy fail to access that knowledge or was the capacity of his working memory too limited to allow him coordinate all the relevant information?

How Does Cognition Develop? How Does the Way We Think Change Over Time?

The form and even the extent of cognitive development vary significantly from one conceptualization to another. Those assuming an epistemological stance (e.g., Case, 1992; Fischer, 2006; Piaget, 1966) generally view the development of children's thinking as progressive and hierarchically integrated. Case and Fischer were first identified as neo-Piagetians because they constructed theories that resembled Piaget's in fundamental ways; however, their seminal proposals as well as their more mature theories diverge from Piaget's theory on several significant points. Among them are their emphases on development as domain specific and, for Fischer more than Case, the idea that progress is not always linear.

Piaget's studies of cognitive development were grounded in domains: number, geometry, logic and propositional thought. However, he attempted to identify underlying structures, ways of knowing, that were common across these domains. For that reason his theory is referred to by many as domain general. From this perspective, Tommy's insight might be construed as symptomatic of a way of knowing, common to knowing across domains, which bridges his earlier thinking which focuses one dimension, for example, someone who is eighty is very old, to his later thinking, which coordinates three dimensions simultaneously, for example, years, aging and growth.

Fischer and Case would agree that Tommy's thinking is symptomatic of hierarchically integrated way of coordinating dimensions; however, they would not see it as symptomatic of how children are thinking in other domains at that time. They believe that thinking progresses, at different rates across domains, often following varying pathways, yet ultimately reaching a common level of functioning (Fischer, 2006). Thus, domain theorists part with Piaget on the form of development. Piaget and stage theorists in general characterize development as a staircase. They assume that there will be pauses in development as children consolidate their gains. Those pauses do not mask the fact that when there is change it is progressive. By contrast, Fischer abandons the staircase metaphor and adopts a scalloping image of development. As stage theorists, progress in cognitive functioning is progressive over the long haul; however, new developments in thinking are followed by regressions to earlier levels of functioning. These peaks and troughs follow a common cycle of increased activity (IA) leading to reorganization (R) followed by reversals to a previous level (PL) of functioning (IA → R → PL → IA → R → PL ...). The possibility, indeed the reality, of regressing to a lower level of functioning is at the heart of hierarchical development. Lower levels of functioning are built upon or modified, but they are not lost or abandoned. This movement forward with the potential for reversing suggests that cognitive functioning is economical; children work at a level of development set by their ambitions and societal demands.

Beyond the theoretical value of systematically examining the form of cognitive development through childhood, there is a practical value. As descriptions of epistemological functioning, Piaget, Case, and Fischer provide *standards of development* within which we can diagnose levels of cognitive functioning independent of psychological domain. Piaget's logical–mathematical scheme provides a broadban diagnostic tool partitioning development into four stages from birth to adolescence. By comparison, Fischer's skill theory offers a fine-grained scheme composed of ten levels. As Fischer (2006) points out, ordinal scales of measurement of this type allow us to view children holistically, that is, as they are functioning across a variety of significant domains at various levels, without being constrained to an age-specific stage that may not adequately describe their capabilities.

Many of those adopting a metaphysical view of cognition focus on a restricted meaning of domain specificity. Given the fact that infants and children learn at such rapid rates, metaphysical theorists argue and provide empirical evidence that some domains are inherited modules (Carey and Spelke, 1994; Gelman and Brenneman, 1994). Modules are conceptual systems, intuitive ways of knowing that process information specific to a limited set of domains: number, biology, psychology, and physical laws. A significant body of research has focused on validating the claim of modularity of mind as well as describing what infants know about these domains. Research and theory on the manner in which children develop from these initial insights is not as well developed as the schemes identified by epistemological theorists. However, to this point they have identified questions that frame the question of what develops and what sets that development apart from the "what" of epistemological development.

From the metaphysical perspective, development is from an intuitive toward a principled understanding or theories about number, biology, psychology, and physics. From one perspective, progress within one domain is distinctively different from progress in the others because a deeper understanding of **mathematics,** biological, and psychological functioning as well as the laws of mechanics means knowing about categories of things of very different natures. The structure of mathematics is of a different kind than the structure of living organisms. Within this perspective Tommy's error in relating age and physical growth appropriately is predicated on his biological intuitions. Less clear within this perspective on cognition is whether change will occur in Tommy's thinking through the accumulation of more information about biological growth, or through a conceptual revolution that qualitatively reframes his theory of biological growth.

Cognitive modules associated with specific domains of knowing may be supplemented over development. For example, children develop social theories, which, along with biological theories, structure their thinking about gender and race (Hershfeld, 1994). Indeed, these theories compete with each other so that biological theory may override social theory leading children to assume that gender differences are natural; or social theory may override biological theory so that they believe the social segregation of races implies fundamental biological differences (Hirschfeld,1994). Cross-fertilization may not always distort thought; there is the possibility that children may map one domain onto another analogically so that development in one area piggy-backs on advances in another area.

Information processing is directed more toward problem solving than knowing or knowledge. There is a significant amount of research indicating that working memory (RAM) increases with development. The majority of research and theory within development of information processes has focused on changes in strategic thinking, that is, the ways in which executive functioning or metacognitive functioning changes over time (Shonkoff and Phillips, 2000). If there is a common dimension over which to chart a part of development, it would be the increasing reflective capacities of children (Birney et al., 2005; Shonkoff and Phillips, 2000). For example, children's attention becomes more focused so that they tend to pick up less information overall than younger children do. Because attention is guided by expectations, they are more likely to attend to relevant information. Further, information processing theorists postulate that, with time, children become better able to plan and to monitor the effectiveness of those plans, to identify when plans must be modified and in what ways they should be changed to achieve their goal. Tommy's task was as much problem seeking as problem solving. He apparently wondered what it meant to be 80 years old. He framed it as a question of growth. Tommy's inference may be due to his failure to attend to the ways in which age and growth vary in his everyday experience. As he mulled over the relation of age and growth in working memory his information may have been limited or inaccurate. Or he may not have encoded the fact that his empirical experiences do not sustain a belief that there is linear relation between the two. In all likelihood, if he had been introduced to the woman, he would not have been surprised that she was not a giant; rather he may have turned his attention to other inferences on the implication of being 80 years old.

Why Do We Develop Cognitive Capabilities the Way We Do?

Those engaged in analyses of biological and psychological development have moved away from the proposition that organisms emerge from the interaction of nature and nurture or, more specifically, genetic material and environments. For a variety of reasons, various forms of **developmental systems theory** have replaced this two-factor account (Gottlieb, 2003). Psychologists have recoiled from the implication that psychological functioning is the epigenetic product of the joint action of biological systems and the environments that embrace these systems. This explanatory system discredits, if not ignores, the role individual humans play in shaping their physical and social worlds, especially their proximal worlds. In the main, psychologists align themselves with Meacham's (2004) triadic model of human functioning and development; that is, psychological activity entails the coaction of biology, environment, and self. The critical theoretical point of this position is that cognitive activity, as an aspect of self, works in consort with biological and environmental systems to form a *developing system*. More specifically, this dynamic view rejects the possibility that neither our biology nor our environments is a set of fixed and enduring constraints on cognitive activity and its development.

Focusing on cognition is conceptually risky because that isolates it from the biological and environmental aspects of developing systems. The advantage is to allow us to view the nature of cognition and the form of its development that dominates thought in contemporary cognitive development. Within this narrow view, the parameters of agency as determinates of change emerge vividly. For example, Piaget's theory emphasizes the constructive nature of cognitive activity. Cognitive activity both constructs our everyday conscious experience of knowing, or being bewildered, as well as reconstructing our underlying structures of thought. Within *Biology and Knowledge* Piaget (1971) suggests that cognitive activity rewrites biological activity. On one hand this view anticipates Fischer's hypothesis that psychological and biological activity develop in parallel. However, Fischer is more cautious than Piaget; he leaves open the question of how these systems mutually constrain paths of development.

Those adopting a metaphysical approach or information-processing approach to cognition suggest a different relation between psychology and biology. In the main, they hypothesize that cognitive systems are hard wired. These systems launch development; they do not set limits on its paths or extent. Rather, consistent with the triadic view, these seminal systems regulate the way infants act as they are socially engaged, as they respond to changes in stimulation, and how they partition their world in the physical, biological, and psychological kinds. Because the hard wiring is a biological system, it develops as well, changing as infants engage their worlds and as their world responds to them or draws them out.

Thus far in the discussion the social worlds of children have not been examined formally, much less the dynamic relation of child and society. Informally, they have been evident in the hypothetical exchanges between Tommy and inquiring epistemologists, metaphysicians, and information processors. In each case, Tommy's inference provoked hypotheses about why Tommy came to his conclusion and questions about how to proceed to gain evidence pertinent of those hypotheses. These exchanges are structured both by *how* Tommy thinks and *what* we think about that thinking. At a practical level, which theoretical perspective adopted by the adult interlocutor is not critical; that the interlocutor has a perspective is critical because it structures the exchange and the potential path of the child's development. Structured exchanges between an adult and a child need not be an imposition of the elder's beliefs onto the child's. Rather, by encouraging and assisting children to ask good questions (Forman, 1989), the adult nudges and even urges the child to become an active thinker, and move to a new level of understanding (Fischer, 2006).

Too frequently, developmental psychologists have been content with the claim that "context matters." Yet a growing number of researchers now believe that context is not captured adequately by differentiating, for example, cultures into collectivistic or individualistic; or social institutions, like schools, into demographically separate rural, suburban or urban; or social agents like teachers in terms of years of training. More useful information would be to know how these sociological distinctions translate into different opportunities for thinking and learning. Addressing this challenge transforms the importance of "context" as essential to the triadic system of development, to the importance of a decidedly richer construct, culture. Psychologists have begun to embrace the notion by adopting a sociocultural perspective. **Culture,** unlike context, cannot be reduced to something out there or something that contains the child. Rather, it is socially constructed and experienced through our participation. Within this view, cognition is viewed as an interpersonal activity. Returning to our example of Tommy, a sociocultural theorist would say that he is engaged in thinking through conversation with Art Linkletter and that conversation is mediated by language, the primary cultural tool for thinking (Rogoff, 2003). There are different conventions for conversations with preschool children from those characteristic of conversations with older children and these differences are often justified in terms of developmental appropriateness. However, views of when it is appropriate to talk about growth and aging, for example, mediate the opportunities for children to participate in conversations and also structure and delimit opportunities for children to think about human development.

Clearly if we construe cognition as a sociocultural activity, we are moving cognition from an intrapersonal accomplishment and activity to a psychological function that is socially distributed. Tommy's knowledge involves more than an inference about the relation between age and growth. In all likelihood he is aware of this relationship not simply by taking note that older people are taller than he is, but because older people tell him how important this relationship is when they observe, "Tommy, you have grown so much since I last saw you;" or when remarking, "You are so big for a five-year-old!" Tommy learns that height is important and the conversations with him about age give him ways, or symbolic frameworks, of expressing the relation between growth and time or age.

Wedding a sociocultural perspective with those of cognitive development has practical implications and value. Theories of cognitive development are, themselves, culturally constructed and valued within the subculture of developmental psychologists. Scholars have their own kinds of conversations about cognition. They value these conversations and the ways in which they act to demonstrate the validity of claims made by each interlocutor, each theorist. In that sense they inform each other and sustain their culture. However, what is regarded as a theory within one society may be viewed as a tool within another; for example, a society of educators who are committed to the development of thinking. These tools shape the conversations we have with and about children. We ask very different questions when we are trying to guide children to think about *how they know* in contrast to the sorts of questions asked when we expect them to explain their own theories about biology, psychology, religion, society, and the world around them.

There is much more to development through guided participation as emphasized in the sociocultural perspective, but for the purpose of discussing cognitive development within the triadic developmental system, this brief review highlights the complexities of conceptualizing the environmental element of that triad. Cognitive developmentalists who heed the value of this approach must heed the warning that their epistemological trajectories and their metaphysical ontological categories may not be universal. This warning does not deny that there are universal characteristics to cognition, it only alerts us to the need to hold that idea as a hypothesis to be tested both across cultures with different languages and customs as well as within pluralistic societies where languages, customs, and values overlap or are shared. Further, theorists who adhere to each of the perspectives described in this essay must be aware of the strengths and weaknesses of all theories, not just their own. In this sense, developmentalists, and also the reader of this entry, might interpret genetic epistemology, domain theory, metaphysical theory, information processing, and sociocultural theory as complimentary to one another. As such, theorists, researchers, teachers, and the like would understand that each of these theories lends a great deal to the present and future field of cognitive development. *See also* Development, Language; Developmentally Appropriate Practice(s); Sociocultural Theory.

Further Readings: Birney, D. P., J. H. Citron-Pousty, D. J. Lutz, and R. J. Sternberg (2005). The development of cognitive and intellectual abilities. In M. H. Bornstein and M. E. Lamb, eds. *Developmental science: An advanced textbook*, 5th ed. Mahwah, NJ: Erlbaum; Carey, S., and E. Spelke (1994). Domain-specific knowledge and conceptual change. In L. A. Hirschfeld and S. A. Gelman, eds. *Mapping the mind: Domain specificity in cognition and culture*. Cambridge, UK: Cambridge University Press, pp. 169–200; Case, R. (1992). *The mind's staircase*. Hillsdale, NJ: Erlbaum; Fischer, K. W. (2006). Dynamic cycles of cognitive and brain development: Measuring growth in mind, brain, and education. In A. M. Battro and K. W. Fischer, eds. *The educated brain*. Cambridge, UK: Cambridge University Press; Forman, G. (1989). Helping children ask good questions. In B. Neugebauer, ed. *The wonder of it: Exploring how the world works*. Washington, DC: Exchange Press, pp. 21–24; Gelman, R., and K. Brenneman (1994). First principles can support both universal and culture-specific learning about number and music. In L. A. Hirschfeld and S. A. Gelman, eds. *Mapping the mind: Domain specificity in cognition and culture*. Cambridge, UK: Cambridge University Press, pp. 369–390; Gottlieb, G. (2003). On making behavioral genetics truly developmental. *Human Development* 46, 337–355; Hirsch feld, L.A. (1994). Is the acquisition of social categories based on domain-specific competence or on knowledge transfer? In L. A. Hirschfeld and S. A. Gelman, eds. *Mapping the mind: Domain specificity in cognition and culture*. Cambridge, UK: Cambridge University Press, pp. 201–233; Meacham, J. A. (2004). Action, voice, and identity in children's lives. In P. B. Pufall and R. P. Unsworth, eds. *Rethinking childhood*. New Brunswick, NJ: Rutgers University Press, pp. 69–84; Piaget, J. (1966). *Origins of intelligence in children*. New York: International Universities Press; Piaget, J. (1971). *Biology and knowledge*. Chicago: University of Chicago Press; Rogoff, B. (2003). *The cultural nature of human development*. New York: Oxford University Press; Shonkoff, J. P., and Phillips, D. A., eds. (2000). *From neurons to neighborhoods: the science of early childhood development*. Washington, DC: National Academy Press.

Peter B. Pufall and Elizabeth S. Pufall

Development, Emotional

The development of emotion begins at birth and continues across the lifespan. Emotions, and their expressions in face, voice, and gesture, organize and shape human behavior. Most theories of emotion agree that emotions involve a complex process of interaction between cognitive processes in the brain, physiological changes (such as changes in heart rate, body temperature, and endocrine systems), and the environment. Emotions help us to (a) orient, or pay attention; (b) appraise, or assess the situation; and (c) prepare to act. In the fields of psychology, child development and education, emotional development is often defined in conjunction with social development because the two are interrelated. Emotional development is inherently social in that it occurs within a relational context of young children and the people in their environments.

Development of Emotional Expression

Humans are born with the capacity to experience and express emotions from birth. In fact, emotions can be called the "language of infancy" as, even before they have spoken language, infants can experience emotions and communicate them through their facial expressions, cries and other vocal signals, as well as gestures and behaviors. Over the first year of life, babies experience and express a set of emotions which sometimes are referred to as "primary" or "basic" emotions, including fear, anger, disgust, and surprise. These emotions are evident in cultures throughout the world. Newborns, for example, show expressions of interest (by widening the eyes and intently looking) and disgust (by wrinkling the nose, sticking out the tongue, and turning away). By seven months infants display all six primary emotions: interest, joy, fear, sadness, anger and disgust. Infant facial expressions of emotion are comparable to the emotional expressions displayed by adults. Researchers have shown that both caretakers and random observers are able to reliably identify emotional expressions in infants as young as one month. This shows that infant emotion expressions have meaning to adults, and attributions they make about infant emotional states influence their behavior toward them.

Toward the end of the second year, infants begin to display other emotions that are sometimes called "social," "secondary," or "self-conscious" emotions. These emotions, which include embarrassment, envy, empathy, pride, shame, and guilt, are thought to develop as the child becomes more self-aware and cognizant of social conventions and rules. A young child, for example, cannot experience embarrassment until she is aware that her behavior is socially inappropriate. These "self-conscious" emotions do not become stable until the child is older and able to internalize rules and social expectations.

For young children to abide by societal norms of behavior and accomplish their goals, they must first learn how to regulate their emotions. Emotion regulation involves awareness of emotional states and the ability to modify emotional behaviors, sometimes inhibiting or changing the expression of emotions. The caregiver–child relationship is typically the primary context in which children learn to recognize, evaluate, and regulate emotions.

Emotion Regulation

How caregivers respond to an infant's need for emotional or regulatory support plays a role in shaping an infant's emotional and social development. Initially, young infants depend on their caregivers to help regulate or manage their emotional states, for example to swaddle them or pick them up to help them stop crying. Caregivers who are able to read infant cues and sensitively assist infants in regulating their affect help infants learn adaptive ways of regulating their own emotions. Over time, and through many interactions with caregivers, infants learn which of their communication and coping strategies work best and when and how to use them. When children are better able to self-regulate, they can more easily engage with the world around them; they are able to explore their environments and to learn. They become better able to establish and express a more varied and integrated range of emotions.

Of course, not all caregiver–child interactions are positive and seamless; in fact the very process of repairing normal, everyday negative interactions is crucial to the development of successful emotion regulation. However, children are sensitive to others' emotions, and when young children live in environments in which they consistently and repeatedly experience negative interactions with caregivers their emotional development can be put at risk. In cases where a mother is suffering from serious depression, for example, the mother's ability to respond to her child may be diminished by her symptoms, expressed in withdrawal from interaction, or hostile, intrusive kinds of behavior. A depressed caregiver's inability to scaffold and respond in a sensitive manner may result in repeated interactive failures that culminate in negative affect. Over time, a child may begin to see her attempts to engage with others as fruitless and eventually lose the motivation to engage with those around her. As well, in environments of chronic stress or situations of abuse and neglect, young children can develop a lowered sensitivity to stress and fear and maladaptive coping methods and interactional styles that can lead to future social and emotional difficulties.

Emotional Attachments

One of the primary goals of infancy is to establish and maintain relationships with attachment figures. Secure **attachment**, a strong emotional bond between two people, characterized by trust or confidence that the attachment figure will help in times of stress, is thought to be established through readily available, sensitive, and responsive caregiving. Predictable and sensitive caregiving environments increase the infant's opportunities for positive social interactions and experiences. A secure attachment with a primary caregiver provides a foundation for positive emotional development. Children with secure attachments are more effectively able to regulate negative affect.

The development of attachment depends on the "emotional availability" of the caregiver and the infant. The construct of *emotional availability*, which relates to the positive and negative emotional expression and responsiveness of both caregiver and child, is considered central to healthy socioemotional development.

Temperament

Emotion regulation involves the child's temperament, the constitutional predispositions of each individual that influence emotional development. **Temperament** refers to a child's susceptibility to emotional stimuli, how reactive he is to events, and the strength and speed of his response. For example, a two-year-old child may be easily angered by being blocked from a goal, might quickly respond with yelling and kicking, and might be difficult to console. Another child, faced with the same situation, might take longer to get upset, show only mild anger (e.g., fussing), and would more easily and quickly regulate the negative affect. While temperament is thought to be part of our physiological makeup (in part, genetic), the ways in which a child's temperament is expressed can be modified by the environment. The *"goodness of fit"* (or degree of match) between a child's temperament and the caregiving environment is important. For example, a temperamentally shy child may be challenged by a parent who expects and encourages loud, boisterous behavior and easy interaction with strangers. Similarly, an active, uninhibited child may not adapt as well to a highly structured center-based daycare setting where each child must follow a strict schedule.

Understanding Others' Emotions

The ability to recognize and understand emotions is critical for positive social development. Infants as young as six and seven months are able to decipher emotional expressions such as sad expressions from happy ones, but it is not until later in the first year that infants are able to use this information in a meaningful way. One way in which young children begin to take advantage of emotional information is through "social referencing."

Social referencing is the utilization of the emotional responses and expressions of others to gain a better understanding of an environment or an event. An infant, for example, may check a caregiver's emotional expression before approaching a novel toy or person. If a caregiver shows, through his or her emotions (voice, face, and gesture), that an event or object is "okay" or "forbidden," a child will use these cues to guide her behavior (by approaching or avoiding the object). Young children initially rely on the emotional expressions of caregivers to evaluate a situation, but as children get older their use of social referencing extends to others.

Social referencing is one example of the ways in which emotions and their expressions become socialized during childhood. Caregivers show that emotions are acknowledged, accepted, or rejected through their behavior. They may provide emotion labels for children's behavior "you're acting sad," or encourage children to change their emotion states and behavior "come on, let's see a happy smile" or "even when you're mad, it's not okay to hit." Caregivers may encourage children to change the way they express an emotion or they may fail to acknowledge certain emotion states by not talking about them.

During the toddler and preschool years, young children come to recognize that others' emotional states are not necessarily the same as their own. Sometimes they work to change others' emotion states. For example, young children can feel empathy for someone in distress, and share that emotion. Emotions can be a guide to action, and young children who realize that emotion states can be changed might, in this example, bring a "blankie" to another upset child in an attempt to alter the emotion state.

During the preschool years, young children become increasingly sophisticated in their ability to interpret and verbalize their emotions and the emotions of others. The ability to recognize and interpret emotions in self and others, to understand them, and to regulate one's own emotions, is sometimes referred to as "emotional intelligence." These abilities are highly correlated with positive peer interactions and social competency in childhood. *See also* Development, Social.

Further Readings: Crockenberg, Susan C., and Esther Leerkes (2000). Infant social and emotional development in family context. In *Handbook of infant mental health.* Burlington, Vermont: University of Vermont, pp. 60-90; Izard, Carroll E. and Carol Z. Malatesta (1987). Perspectives on emotional development. In *Differential emotions theory of early emotional development.* New York: Wiley, pp. 494-554; Sroufe, Alan (1996). *Emotional development: The organization of emotional life in the early years.* Cambridge, UK: Cambridge University Press; Thompson, Ross A., M. Ann Easterbrooks, and Laura M. Padilla-Walker (2003). Social and emotional development in infancy. In Richard M. Lerner and M. Ann Easterbrooks, eds. *Handbook of psychology: developmental psychology.* New York: Wiley, pp. 91-112.

Joan Riley Driscoll and M. Ann Easterbrooks

Development, Language

The process of language development begins long before children utter their first conventionally formed utterances. In fact, words represent only one of the many communicative resources that are involved. As a result, the major theoretical perspectives in the field include not only a focus on the development of language itself but also a more multimodal view of communication that couches the child's developing language in a complex of representational resources. This essay explores some of the central foci in the field, ranging from the nativist, or biological, requirements for language development to some of its social, cultural, and extraverbal aspects.

From the behaviorist perspective, prevalent by the early 1960s, language development results from the influence of the environment on the child (see **Behaviorism**). The child's language behaviors are thus molded through the positive or negative reinforcement of a progressively narrower selection of target behaviors. Language acquisition is a result of exposure to linguistic stimuli as well as the engagement of the child's own learning capacity. Nonetheless, some sort of neurological hard wiring is necessary to link language input with the language patterning that is recognized, accepted, and used by the speakers of a language. In response, Chomsky (1965) posited the Language Acquisition Device (LAD), an innate mental storehouse of the universals of linguistic structure. The device shapes incoming linguistic experience, or input, into the grammar (i.e., output) of the particular language from which the input derives. More than a catalogue of all possible individual utterances in a given language (Pinker, 1994), LAD accounts for a speaker's ability to generate grammatically new and novel utterances by relating and manipulating the structures operating in a particular language (e.g., *the boy caught the ball* becomes *the ball was caught by the boy*). LAD reflects the view that language development cannot be explained as either the product of cultural exigencies alone (Pinker, 1994) or as the result of simple imitation. Neurolinguistics has more recently aimed to explain precisely how the brain organizes the phonological, syntactic, semantic, and pragmatic systems that enable human communication (e.g., Obler and Gjerlow, 1999).

Utterances, however, also occur in social contexts—real situations in which child participants use language to define, advocate, and accomplish their own purposes. Thus, the interactionist view of language development adds a complementary construct: the Language Acquisition Support System (i.e., LASS) (Bruner, 1983). On this view, the adult world provides a support system for the development of the child's language, a "transactional format" (Bruner, 1983, p. 19) by means of which children can try out and consolidate linguistic changes with others. For example, to construct and manage joint attention between herself and an infant, a mother may introduce objects by interposing them between herself and the infant (e.g., *see the pretty dolly?*) (Bruner, 1983, p. 71). Phonetically consistent forms are integrated into socially well-established games and routines (e.g., "where" and "what" games) that relate linguistic signs to elements of the immediate, nonlinguistic context (Bruner, 1983, p. 77). On the other hand, mothers may follow the child's lead by limiting the semantic content of their speech to those constructions that already occur in the child's repertoire (Snow, 1977). This, in turn, produces the grammatical simplicity of the mothers' speech. On this view, grammar simply works to express meanings that the child already possesses. This means that the teaching and practicing of specific grammatical structures will affect language acquisition " . . . only after the child has independently developed the cognitive basis which allows him to use that structure" (Snow, 1977, P. 48). It is thus the continuing exchange of linguistic and pragmatic knowledge that makes possible the development of discourse patterns that then transfer to other contexts such as picture-book reading, where the exchange is built on non-concrete, pictured topics. The child responds, not just to the form, but also to the intent with a referent, and not simply with a repetition of the adult's language. The operation of LASS and LAD are thus interdependent, the socially generative nature of language as a communicative resource requiring both constructs (Bruner, 1983).

Cultural variance in the ways in which children learn to play appropriate communicative roles has also been explored in several ethnographies that document the ways in which children are socialized into patterns of linguistic as well as communicative competence (e.g., Heath, 1983). These patterns reflect prevalent attitudes toward learning and toward the role of talk itself in various cultural settings. The child is never "in it" alone, but is constantly engaged in highly constructive processes of generating and exchanging meaning with "significant others" who "create the system along with the child" as the child, in turn, "helps the process along" (Halliday, 1980, p. 10). Children help by constructing a "proto-language" beginning at the age of five to seven months by intentionally addressing symbols—sounds or gestures—to others who will "decode" them (Halliday, 1980, p. 9). Pointing, for example, quickly moves from functioning as a simple gesture to designating particular referents (i.e., something needed or wanted). Such a protolanguage communicates meaning but without verbal syntax or vocabulary. The child next needs to turn the proto-language into a three-level system of meanings, wordings, and sound. The adult's function in this process is not to model the language for imitation, but to participate in the process along with the child as an equal partner.

Along these lines, the early work of Elizabeth Bates (1976) explored the child's *intention* to communicate in terms of the development of pragmatic competence—the child's ability to formulate goals and to select suitable means for accomplishing them. In the sensorimotor stage, for example, children engage in the formulation of object-goals and the selection of suitable means to accomplish the "protoimperative" function of recruiting an adult as a means to attain an object or another goal (Bates, 1976, p. 51). The formulation of the goal then combines with "instrumental behaviors" such as reaching, opening and closing the hand, cooing sounds, and gaze (Bates, 1976, p. 55), and this may occur even before there is evidence of a symbolic capacity, according to Bates. Although the child may be unaware of the signal value of these extraverbal elements, the adult interprets and responds as if to a signal. In this way, gestural communication does provide a framework for early language development; however, language does not come to replace gesture; instead, children support their linguistic communication by means of these gestural complexes by the end of the first year (Volterra et al., 1979).

In fact, the rate at which different children develop language can differ by a year or even more; however, vowel sounds and syllable-like consonant–vowel sequences begin to occur between six and twelve months. Although babies can comprehend simple words and intonation as early as ten months, their receptive language capacities tend to outpace their productive capabilities between one and two years of age. Nonetheless, children begin to produce holophrases and one-word utterances not limited to only nouns, but also including social expressions (*bye bye*), verbs (*go*), descriptive vocabulary (*hot*), and locational expressions (*up*) (Lindfors, 1987). At about twenty months, combinatory speech (i.e., using two-word utterances) begins. Vocabulary development speeds up dramatically and by about two years of age, the child possesses a vocabulary of over 200 words, correctly ordered in 95 percent of utterances (Pinker, 1994). Through age 6, the average child's vocabulary increases by as many as ten words per day; additionally, children continue to develop morphosyntactic knowledge even beyond the age of eight (Chomsky, 1969).

Does a critical period exist during which first language (FL) acquisition best takes place? Based on work on brain lateralization by Lenneberg (1967) and evidence from studies of children with **Down Syndrome, deaf children**, and linguistically isolated children, a critical period for language learning was hypothesized to last from about two years of age to puberty after which the process is supposedly neither as rapid nor as successful. Although many accept the view that there is a window for optimal morphemic and syntactic knowledge lasting from birth to age 12 or 14, evidence does exist to counter the critical period hypothesis. Studies of group performance indicate a gradual decline, but not an abrupt drop-off, in the ability to acquire more complex syntactic features but not simpler ones (Bialystok and Hakuta, 1994). In fact, pragmatic, semantic, and vocabulary acquisition capacities may not diminish with age. Thus, the critical period hypothesis remains somewhat controversial and must be considered along with additional factors that are crucial to language development. These include the frequency and richness of the linguistic interaction experienced by the child as well as other social and cultural, rather than solely biological, factors.

Typological differences in various languages do, however, affect children's everyday talk as they develop those languages. Very young German speakers, for example, talk about placement (i.e., causing an inanimate object to move to a place) by relying on the expression of spatial vectors through particles such as *inward*. In contrast, children who are acquiring Hindi or Turkish tend to favor verbs such as *put* or *attach* for talking about placement. While Hindi and Turkish are languages that express the path of motion in the verb, German expresses this by means of a satellite element to the verb such as a suffix or particle. Children none in on these sorts of typological differences very early on in the language development process (Bowerman et al., 2002).

Nonetheless, oral language works as only one of the multimodal mediators by means of which children construct and express the meanings that they recruit to transform their interactional environments. As children develop oral language, it becomes " ... an accompaniment to and an organizer of their symbolic action" in other systems involving print and graphics, for example (Dyson, 1989, p. 6). Neither do children invariably foreground language as a communicative resource; they look instead to find "'best ways' of representing meanings; in some circumstances language may be the best medium; in some a drawing may be; in others color may be the most apt medium for expression" (Kress, 1997, p. 37). Children's communicative development thus makes interdependent use of resources that may be verbal (i.e., the segmental and suprasegmental features of oral language, or texts in written language), visual (e.g., color, texture, line and shape), gestural (e.g., facial expression, hand movements), and actional (i.e., full body movement).

In classrooms, however, teacher talk also mediates the discourse in ways that extend well beyond the transmission of information to enacted definitions of learning, knowledge, communicative competence, and educational equity. Teacher talk thus shapes children's language in both direct and indirect ways; for instance, the use of "inauthentic" questions that require children to merely "display" known information tends to prompt factual, short answers while "authentic" questions that displace the teacher as the sole possessor of knowledge tend to elicit longer and more complex responses because a negotiated space is required (Cazden, 2001, p. 46). Peer talk, too, shapes child language in classroom discourses, but teachers act as reminders (not just as models) of what children can do communicatively. Although peer teaching may be seen to derive, in some sense, from the interactional pattern that the teacher has established in the classroom, children often mirror this in their own language behavior as well as in the kind of social negotiation and problem solving for which the **classroom discourse** makes room.

Teacher talk is also especially critical to providing young children with opportunities to hear and use "challenging vocabulary" or "rare words" that extend beyond basic "school readiness" language such as color term rehearsal (Dickenson, 2001, p. 238). Teachers can enhance children's engagement in higher-order thinking by incorporating into their interactions a wide range of interesting words that children can then contextualize in their **play**. In this way, and by providing interactions that extend across several turns, teachers of three- and four-year-olds can provide conversational space for the development of a range of oral language and print uses that will occur in the **kindergarten**. Children's long-term language growth is also impacted by the total number of words and variety of words used with peers in free play, although free play must be appropriately balanced with more structured activity. Children who, as four-year-olds, have interacted with teachers who reduce the amount of their own talk in favor of lengthening the children's contribution to the conversation also show better kindergarten performance (Dickenson, 2001).

All along the way, language development includes children's engagement in the multimodal discourses that comprise their lives at home and in school. Young communicators do not simply reproduce convention. Teachers can enhance and respond to children's communicative development by creating environments, or sets of contexts, where children can practice questioning, arguing, remembering, and imagining through the orchestration of self-selected combinations of multiple modes—including oral and written language. This enhances language development by linking it to a complex of motivated signs that reflect children's interests as individuals interacting with others (Kress, 1997). Such a multimodal view becomes especially crucial to the integration of verbal, visual, and actional resources in classroom discourse that can no longer be seen as language-centered. On the contrary, language here emerges as one of a range of resources to serve purposes that arise in the moment and recur over time in expansive communicative environments. *See also* Development, Brain; Bruner, Jerome.

Further Readings: Bates, Elizabeth (1976). *Language and context: The acquisition of pragmatics*. New York: Academic Press; Bialystok, Ellen and Kenji Hakuta (1994). *In other words: The science and psychology of second language acquisition*. New York: Basic Books; Bowerman, Melissa, Penelope Brown, Sonja Eisenbeiss, Bhuvana Narasimhan, and Dan Slobin (2002). *Putting things in places: Developmental consequences of linguistic typology*. Stanford University: Symposium, Child Language Research Forum. Available online at http://ihd.berkeley.edu/slobinpapers.htm; Bruner, Jerome (1983). *Child's talk: Learning to use language*. New York: Norton; Cazden, Courtney (2001). *Classroom discourse: The language of teaching and learning*, 2nd ed. Portsmouth, NH: Heinemann; Chomsky, Carol (1969). *The acquisition of syntax in children from 5 to 10*. Cambridge, MA: MIT Press; Chomsky, Noam (1965). *Aspects of the theory of syntax*. Cambridge, MA: MIT Press; Dickenson, David K. (2001). Large-group and free-play times: Conversational settings supporting language and literacy development. In David K. Dickenson and Patton O. Tabors, eds. *Beginning literacy with language: Young children learning at home and school*. Baltimore: Paul H. Brookes, pp. 223–255; Dyson, Anne Haas (1989). *Multiple worlds of child writers: Friends learning to write*. New York: Teachers College Press; Halliday, Michael (1980). Three aspects of children's language development: Learning language, learning through language, learning about language. In Yetta M. Goodman, Myna M. Haussler, and Dorothy S. Strickland, eds. *Oral and written language development research: Impact on the school*. Urbana, IL: National Council of Teachers of English, pp. 7–19; Heath, Shirley Brice. (1983). *Ways with words: Language, life, and work in communities and classrooms*. New York: Cambridge University Press; Kress, Gunther (1997). *Before writing: Rethinking the paths to literacy*. London: Routledge; Lenneberg, Eric. (1967). *Biological foundations of language*. New York: Wiley; Lindfors, Judith

W. (1987). *Children's language and learning,* 2nd ed. Englewood Cliffs, NJ: Prentice-Hall; Obler, Loraine K., and Kris Gjerlow (1999). *Language and the brain.* New York: Cambridge University Press; Pinker, Steven (1994). *The language instinct: How the mind creates language.* New York: HarperCollins; Snow, Catherine E. (1977). Mothers' speech research: From input to interaction. In Catherine E. Snow and Charles A. Ferguson, eds. *Talking to children: Language input and acquisition.* New York: Cambridge University Press, pp. 31–49; Volterra, Virginia, Elizabeth Bates, Laura Benigni, Inge Bretherton, and Luigia Camaioni (1979). First words in language and action: A qualitative look. In Elizabeth Bates, Laura Benigni, Luigia Camaioni, Inge Bretherton, and Virginia Volterra, eds. *The emergence of symbols: Cognition and communication in infancy.* New York: Academic Press, pp. 141–222.

Susan Jane Britsch

Development, Moral

Moral development is the domain in which children grow in their ability to think and act according to their understanding of what is right and wrong. As their moral understanding develops, children are increasingly able to act with the needs of others in mind and resolve moral dilemmas based on ideals of justice, fairness, or caring. Factors in this area of development are children's innate predisposition for empathy, modeling of adults and peers, explicit teaching, transmission of cultural values and their own experiences in interactions with others. Moral development is closely related to cognitive as well as social-emotional development. What we know about young children's development of moral reasoning is based on, first, the cognitively oriented theories of Jean **Piaget** and Lawrence Kohlberg (as modified and extended by later researchers including William Damon, Elliot Turiel, Carol Gilligan, and others); and second, the more emotionally oriented research studies that uncover young children's early capacities for empathy, sympathy, and prosocial behavior as well as shame and guilt in conscience development (for these emotional aspects, see **Development, Emotional, Development, Social,** and **Social Curriculum**). Aspects of current thinking about children's moral development include an emphasis on children's multidimensional moral competence and on recognition of the role of cultural and familial contexts in children's moral development.

Cognitive Stage Theories of Moral Development

In keeping with his theory of stages of **cognitive development**, Piaget also describes stages of moral development. Young children in Piaget's preoperational stage engage *in moral absolutism* and *realism*, a morality of constraint based on simple awe for adult power, concern for concrete rewards and punishment, and unquestioning adherence to outside commands. *Moral relativism* and *autonomy* come later in middle childhood when children develop more elaborate ideas about moral intentionality, extenuating circumstances, mutual parent–child respect, and knowledge about where rules and laws come from and how they can be changed—all associated with concrete or formal operational thinking.

Lawrence Kohlberg extended Piaget's work to develop a stage theory that includes the moral reasoning of adolescents and adults. His six stages are based on the moral judgments that individuals make when grappling with moral dilemmas that involve conflicting issues of right and wrong. To illustrate the differences in reasoning at each stage, he offers a moral dilemma faced by a man he calls Heinz whose wife is dying. The druggist is charging Heinz a great deal of money for the drug that will save his wife. Heinz must decide if he should steal the drug. For Kohlberg, moral development lies in cognitive-structural advances in reasoning about the issues of life, law, property, family roles, authority, crime and punishment that are evoked by the dilemma. (See table for the six stages.) In Kohlberg's theory, young children (about age 6) are typically Stage 1, oriented to simple obedience, but during middle childhood, move to Stage 2, where they make decisions based on tit-for-tat justice, and instrumental rewards and punishment.

Moral Development: Comparison of Theories of Moral Reasoning

Extending Kohlberg's theory, William Damon elaborated Kohlberg's descriptions of younger children's moral thinking based on his studies of their ideas about sharing and other kinds of positive justice, for example, what is right to do when dividing up five cookies among two children, or setting bedtimes for two siblings of different ages. His stages reflect his view of young children's increasing perspective-taking ability and their awareness that adult desires are independent of their own.

Eliot Turiel challenged Kohlberg's inclusion of children's responses to all kinds of "good" and "bad" behavior as parts of morality. Instead, Turiel has focused on reasoning about moral rights and wrongs as separate from *social conventions*. He claims that young children intuitively appreciate a difference in kind between, say, a moral violation of someone's rights (e.g., not to be hurt or to have their property stolen) and a social conventional violation (which concerns rules about the customary, polite, or orderly way of doing things). These intuitions arise out of their own experiences in social interaction.

Challenging another aspect of Kohlberg's theory, Carol Gilligan disputed the emphasis on morality as reasoning about justice and instead focused on morality as reasoning about caring, connectedness, and support for relationships. When thinking about dilemmas, many people (particularly women, Gilligan claims) draw away from absolute decisions separated from contextual and particular issues, but instead seek alternatives that will most strengthen or do least harm to the individual relationships involved. As children grow older, their reasoning about relationships and connections grows more elaborate and fine tuned in a way parallel to but distinct from what happens with their reasoning about justice issues. Gilligan's work points to the impact of gender and possibly other aspects of identity on moral themes that people highlight as they struggle with moral temptations and dilemmas.

Nel Noddings draws on philosophy (not psychology) to support her premise that caring, empathy, and altruism provide a perspective for understanding children's moral actions. She offers a distinctive view on the idea of caring as the *ethic of care,* and describes caring as a reciprocal action that "teaches" or "nurtures" both the one who gives care and the one who receives care. An early childhood environment of active caring with opportunities for children to both provide

Piaget	Kohlberg	Damon	Gilligan
Stages of children's moral development align with stages of cognitive development. *Moral realism:* Children make decisions by following rules as determined by others without questioning authority (preoperational thinking) *Moral relativism:* • Conventional morality. Rule-orientation includes ideas of fairness and equality (concrete operations) • Autonomous morality: Children consider aspects of the situation, such as intention, when making decisions (formal operations)	Additional stages extend to the highest level adult reasoning *Preconventional* Stage 1: Punishment and obedience orientation: Decisions conform with adult authority to avoid punishment Stage 2: Naïve instrumental hedonism: Decisions are based on rewards and self-interest. ***Conventional*** Stage 3: Conformity and approval: Good boy/good girl decisions made to please others Stage 4: Conformity to social order: Decisions follow society's laws and rules *Postconventional* Stage 5: Law as social contract: Laws are made by people who can agree to change them Stage 6: Universal ethical principals: respect for human dignity guides all decision making	Stages describe very young children's moral reasoning *Stage 0A:* Undifferentiated reasoning based on self-orientation; own wishes and needs are satisfied *Stage 0B:* Undifferentiated reasoning based on strict equality, the same for all *Stage 1A:* Differentiated reasoning based on merit. Hard worker deserve more *Stage 1B:* Differentiated reasoning based on need with some consideration of merit and reciprocity	Instead of stages, different perspectives or orientations guide moral reasoning, more aligned with gender than with age Abstract justice and fairness/individual orientation Versus Relationships and caring/other or interpersonal orientation

Adapted from Wheeler, Edyth J. (2004). *Conflict resolution in early childhood: Helping children understand and resolve conflicts.* Upper Saddle River. NJ: Merrill/Prentice-Hall.

and receive care encourages them to think and act in a context of moral understanding. Lisa Goldstein has applied Noddings' work about a caring curriculum in schools to early childhood education.

Implications of Cognitively Oriented Theories

All these theories provide a picture of how both children and adults bring their thinking to bear on moral issues. Reasoning is not consistent across situations and conditions, however. For example, a child may reason at a more mature level about hypothetical issues than about ones that relate to his own self-interest. Furthermore, children are often able to comprehend reasoning at a higher stage with help than they are able to on their own. It is clear that the development of moral judging and reasoning can be stimulated by role-taking opportunities and positive social interaction (e.g., through community service). By providing children with opportunities to practice thinking at a higher stage, adults can facilitate children's moral development. This view is consistent with Lev **Vygotsky's** concept of the zone of proximal development and the practice of scaffolding of learning from an adult or a more capable peer.

Moral Competence of Children

Early childhood professionals have noted that children can sometimes show more competence in their moral thinking and actions than the theories about their moral thinking and perspective-taking typically describe. Consistent with these observations are current beliefs that children are more capable and learn in patterns that differ from those described by stage theories. Young children demonstrate compassion, empathy, kindness, and other aspects of prosocial concern that actually facilitates and nourishes their development of cognitive moral reasoning and action. At times their moral competence rises to the level of true altruism and moral leadership. This extraordinary moral competence is illustrated in the work of Robert Coles whose work offers insights into both what children may seem to know innately and what they learn from observing and listening to adults. He supports the idea that children can be more morally wise and aware than theories would suggest. For example, he records for us the moral strength, wisdom and forgiveness voiced by six-year-old Ruby Bridges as she passes though an angry crowd to enter her newly integrated school in Atlanta in the 1960s.

Cultural Context of Moral Development

Moral development takes place in every cultural community throughout history, but it is hardly an invariant process always looking the same. Quite the contrary. The processes of *moral socialization* have been shown to involve myriad alternative forms depending on how much the parenting figures choose to use physical punishment, verbal reasoning, love withdrawal, strict versus lenient control, involvement of extended kin and nonfamily authority figures, appeals to religion and to the supernatural, and negative sanctions such as ridicule, shaming, threats, and bribes, in their child-rearing techniques. Moreover, cultures vary greatly in their hierarchies of moral beliefs and values, with different groups providing various rankings of such values as honesty, obedience, loyalty, promise-keeping, sacrifice, physical bravery, abstinence, modesty, emotional restraint, and so on, as what is most important for a child to learn. According to critical perspectives in early childhood, children's moral actions take place within a context of **culture** and family as well as community and classroom. It is important, therefore, for teachers to seek to avoid misreading or misinterpreting children's actions when confronting cultural diversity. For example, a teacher may discover that a child has taken more than her share of food as the bowl is passed around the classroom not because she is greedy or disregarding the rules of fairness, but because her parents expect her to try to get food to take home to her brothers and sisters. The moral conflict (for the child) is between the ideals of equality and fairness among school peers and the ideals of equality and fairness among siblings as well as of caring within the family. Implications for practitioners include recognizing conflicting moral expectations that children encounter in different cultural contexts (see also **Language Diversity**).

Implications for Supporting Moral Development

An awareness of the range of theories that explain children's moral thinking and action may help early childhood professionals in supporting children's moral development. Authoritative or democratic parenting and teaching styles allow adults to model moral reasoning (see also **Parenting Education**). Children can extend their moral understanding as adults provide scaffolding of moral reasoning. Both at home and in the classroom, adults can demonstrate perspective-taking, empathy, and caring. In a classroom setting, children can practice an ethic of care through a curriculum centered on themes of caring, such as helping others, or caring for the natural environment. Applying ideas about care-based morality, practitioners may make space for different approaches to moral decision making and integrate relationship concerns into their teaching about rules, justice, and fairness. Further implications include listening carefully to children's reasoning, respecting their moral competence, providing opportunities for expressions of their moral thinking, engaging families, and being responsive to cultural contexts of children's moral development. *See also* Families.

Further Readings: Carlo, Gustavo, and Carolyn Edwards, eds. (2005). *Moral development: Nebraska Symposium on Motivation.* Vol. 51. Lincoln, NE: University of Nebraska Press; Coles, Robert (1986). *The moral life of children.* New York: Atlantic Monthly Press; Damon, William (1990). *The moral child: Nurturing children's natural moral growth.* New York: Macmillan; Delpit, Lisa (1995). *Other people's children: Cultural conflict in the classroom.* New York: The New Press; DeVries, Rheta, and Betty Zan (1994). *Moral classrooms, moral children: Creating a constructivist atmosphere in early education.* New York: Teachers College Press; Gilligan, Carol (1982). *In a different voice: Psychological theory and women's development.* Cambridge, MA: Harvard University Press; Goldstein, Lisa S. (2002). *Reclaiming caring in teaching and teacher education.* New York: Peter Lang; Killen, Melanie, and Judith Smetana, eds. (2006). *Handbook of moral development.* Mahwah, NJ: Erlbaum; Kohlberg, Lawrence (1984). *The psychology of moral development: Essays on moral development.* Vol. II. New York: Harper and Row; Lapsley, Daniel (1996). *Moral psychology.* Boulder, CO: Westview; Noddings, Nel (2002). *Educating moral people.* New York: Teachers College Press; Piaget, Jean (1932). *The moral judgment of the child.* Glencoe, IL: Free Press.

Edyth J. Wheeler and Carolyn Pope Edwards

Development, Social

Fostering children's social development has traditionally been a high priority in early childhood programs. When children enter toddler, preschool, or kindergarten programs, they have to learn to navigate new and complex social situations with both children and adults. Thus, early childhood teachers typically spend a great deal of time and energy helping children learn how to regulate their emotions, understand others' perspectives, and initiate and maintain social contacts and relationships. This emphasis is not misplaced; a number of studies have shown that children with poor peer relationships in early childhood are at risk for later social and emotional problems and academic alienation and failure (Ladd, 1990). Over the past three decades research has identified specific skills and experiences that contribute to the outcomes of children's social development. These factors are associated with numerous implications for early childhood educational practice.

The quality of relationships between children and their teachers and parents plays a crucial role in children's social and emotional development. Those with a secure **attachment** to primary caregivers have the space and support to experience the full range of emotions, to learn culturally appropriate ways to express and regulate them, and to become aware of how other people feel and how relationships work (Sroufe et al., 1984). Conversely, children who are insecurely or ambivalently attached do not have a trusting relationship in which they can freely explore their emotions and fully develop their social awareness and skills. Most research related to attachment has focused on parent–child relationships, but Howes and Ritchie (2002) have shown how young children's attachments with their teachers affect their functioning in school and describe and advocate ways that teachers can foster secure attachments between themselves and their children.

Adults also consciously and unconsciously influence children's views of the social world by engaging in their own social relationships and modeling specific social behaviors (e.g., initiating contacts, resolving conflicts). Children absorb their families' social orientations (e.g., families with very active social lives versus those who are more independent or isolated) and their style of social functioning (e.g., different levels of emotional expressiveness in relationships). Parenting styles—sometimes conceptualized as authoritarian, authoritative, or permissive—may also be a factor. Authoritative parenting styles, which provide warmth, reasoning, and clear expectations and firm parental control, appear to be associated with higher levels of social competence. However, this link may not show up in all groups because economic pressures and specific cultural goals also influence parenting styles and their outcomes.

Aside from personal styles, family demographics, particularly socioeconomic status and racial and ethnic privilege or disadvantage, may also influence children's social development. Living in **poverty** and/or feeling marginalized, in and of itself, does not necessarily impair development, but resulting economic stress sometimes causes parental depression and family tensions which can spill over into conflicts with children and in turn make children more vulnerable to depression, low self-confidence, and poor relationships with **peers and friends** (McLoyd,

1998; Yeung, Linver, Brooks-Gunn, 2002). At the other end of the spectrum, racially privileged children from affluent families may develop attitudes of racial superiority and/or become caught up in competitive consumption, both of which potentially impair their social development. Rather than personal contentment and strong connections with others, privilege and material wealth often lead to a "hankering for more; envy of people with the most perceived successes; and intense emotional isolation spawned by resolute pursuit of personal ambitions" (Luthar and Becker, 2002, p. 1593).

In short, social development occurs in a many-layered context of family, school, community, and larger social and economic values and dynamics. However, within all groups and across many situations, children need to acquire a range of cognitive, emotional, and social skills in order to become socially competent in their particular context. They need to learn to express and regulate their emotions, empathize with others and understand their perspectives, initiate and maintain social interactions, and develop relationships with peers.

In terms of emotional competence, researchers have identified several components linked to **social competence**. First, children who are generally happy and enthusiastic tend have more positive social encounters and are seen as more likeable by their peers. Second, those who understand emotions, both their own and those of others, are able to respond more appropriately and sensitively to peers and adults. Third, children who have a wide range of emotional expressions and are able to modulate them to fit the current situation can both generate excitement among their peers out on the playground (e.g., "help! help! the robbers are coming!!") *and* conform to classroom expectations (e.g., sit quietly at circle time or focus on academic work). In contrast, children who are emotionally "flat" have a difficult time engaging peers; those who are emotionally volatile and unpredictable may frighten their peers and sabotage their interactions (Sroufe et al., 1984).

Fourth, children who understand others' perspectives and empathize with their feelings are also more competent socially. Children go through several phases of empathy development during the early childhood years, although the sequence and timing may vary across social and cultural contexts (Hoffman, 2000). Newborns typically cry reactively when they hear other babies cry, suggesting that humans are born with some innate ability to resonate with others' emotional states. This ability is reflected in toddlers' self-referenced empathy, responsiveness to others' emotions based on the assumption that others feel the same way that they themselves do. As they get older, children learn to differentiate themselves from others and to read more subtle emotions. Preschoolers begin to understand that people may have their own information and ideas and react differently to the same event. Preschoolers also start to see how their own actions affect others (e.g., grabbing a toy makes the other child mad) and begin to learn how to resolve conflicts. As children enter and go through elementary school, they realize that they themselves are the objects of others' ideas and feelings. This development enables children to be more considerate of others and better able to collaborate with other individuals and groups. However, this awareness can also make children self-conscious about what peers think of them, which may lead to rigid conformity to group norms and antagonism toward out-group members.

Teachers can support children's emotional competence by developing practices and activities that emotionally engage children, by encouraging honest and direct emotional expressions, and promoting awareness of others. These practices are sometimes associated with an emotional curriculum. Teachers can foster children's developing capacity to empathize and to understand and care about others' ideas and experiences by engaging them in discussions about how others feel or think whenever the opportunity arises (e.g., watching people engaged in different activities, reading stories that show people reacting to various situations, negotiating with peers about dramatic play roles, materials, and turn taking).

Beyond emotional development, social-skill development also plays into the development of social competence. Learning how to initiate and maintain social interactions and relationships can be a challenge in early childhood classrooms for a number of reasons. Young children tend to have short-term peer interactions and fluid friendships. A child may change "best friends" from day to day and even minute by minute. Early friendships are more likely to orient around shared activities or proximity and only later become contexts for support, intimacy and long-term loyalty and self-disclosure (Schneider, Wiener, and Murphy, 1994). Therefore, young children often have a wide range of casual friendships, particularly at the beginning of the school year.

The fluidity of relationships and the brevity of most interactions mean that children are frequently trying to make contact with peers. A number of studies have examined the effectiveness of different strategies that young children use to enter play situations (e.g., Ramsey, 1996). Collectively, these studies show that children are more successful entering groups if they observe and then fit into the ongoing play than if they explicitly ask to play, demand materials, or try to dominate the scene. Children's entry attempts are also affected by the current situation (e.g., how engrossed the host children are in their play) and the ongoing relationships among the children involved.

After children begin playing together, then they often struggle with maintaining the social interaction. Within the context of an ongoing interaction, children may move up and down among different levels of social participation (defined by **Mildred Parten** [1933] as unoccupied, solitary, parallel, associative, and cooperative). For example, parallel play may evolve into associative play and then shift back to parallel. Toddlers and young preschool children are more likely to engage in solitary or parallel play. Older preschoolers and kindergarteners have the skills to engage in complex and cooperative games and fantasies.

Teachers can support children's attempts to initiate and maintain social interactions through a **social curriculum**. They can help them start conversations with peers and "coach" them on how to initiate and continue interactions. They can also support peer interactions by designing space and selecting materials that are conducive to cooperative play (e.g., group vs. individual projects). Cooperative activities promote children's sense of *inter*dependence, their awareness of others, and their flexibility. Moreover, they potentially foster friendships among children of diverse groups and different abilities (Kemple, 2004). Young children may be limited in their ability to understand others' cognitive perspectives, but they *can* learn how to coordinate their actions with each other in cooperative games. As they mature, children are able to collaborate on puppet shows, plays, art projects, and stories, which require more conscious and sustained coordinated efforts. Many classroom routines can be done cooperatively, such as setting and clearing the snack tables, putting away toys, and putting on outdoor clothes.

Often interactions and relationships are disrupted by conflicts, which are an inevitable part of classroom life. Although often regarded as annoying interruptions, they force children to recognize different perspectives; balance their own wishes with those of others; manage anger and aggression; assess their actions' effects on others; be both assertive and respectful at the same time; and know when and how to compromise. Instead of trying to avoid or quickly resolve conflicts, teachers can use them to help children focus on others' feelings and needs and to work out joint solutions that (at least minimally) satisfy all parties.

Despite all of the efforts to support the development of their social awareness and skills, individual children's social competence varies considerably. Children are born with different characteristics that may affect the course of their social development (e.g., temperamental shyness, poor impulse control). The environment also influences children's social behavior (e.g., contentious vs. harmonious **families**, high/low levels of community violence). Thus, for a variety of reasons, children develop patterns of behaviors that are exhibited over many situations that in turn influence their social roles and how they are viewed by their peers.

A number of researchers (e.g., Asher and Hymel, 1981) identified four distinct social status groups in classrooms: *popular*: attractive, socially, academically, and physically skilled children, who are sought after by their peers; *rejected*: socially awkward or aggressive children who are avoided by their peers; *controversial*: lively high-impact children, who tend to test the limits and are liked by some children and disliked by others; *neglected*: self-contained children, who are content to be by themselves and have very little impact on the social life of the classroom. These categories have been useful for identifying dynamics in groups and individual children's needs. However, they should be used cautiously, because many children do not fit these categories, and all children vary across time and situation.

As these categories illustrate, some children have more successful social lives than others. These disparities often become apparent and entrenched, as social groups become more solidified over time and age. Many children also develop close long-term friendships that provide rich contexts to learn how to manage the ups and downs of peer relationships. However, playing with only one or two children is limiting and puts a lot of pressure on relationships that often fall apart, leaving both parties bereft. Moreover, children's friendships are sometimes exclusionary and often reflect divisions by gender, race, social class, **culture** and language, and abilities (Ramsey, 2004). Thus, a balance of close friends and a wider range of good friends is optimal. Vivian Paley's book *You Can't Say You Can't Play* is a wonderful resource for talking with children about exclusionary behavior, why it happens and how it affects everyone. In particular teachers need to encourage children to learn how to **play** and work with peers who, at first, may seem different (e.g., racially, culturally) from them. By observing these patterns and engaging children in conversations, teachers can encourage children to articulate and challenge the feelings and assumptions that are driving exclusionary and avoidant behaviors.

In sum, social development is a complex process that reflects children's developing cognitive and emotional capabilities and the personal and societal contexts of their lives. To foster this aspect of children's growth, teachers need to carefully observe individual children and the group dynamics in their classrooms and to develop activities and routines that support the capacities and needs of their particular group. Teachers also need to keep in mind how the larger social and economic contexts are influencing this important facet of children's development. *See also* Curriculum, Emotional Development; Development, Emotional; Development, Social; Gender and Gender Stereotyping in Early Childhood Education; Language Diversity; Parenting Education; Race and Ethnicity in Early Childhood Education; Violence and Young Children.

Further Readings: Asher S. R., and S. Hymel (1981). Children's social competence in peer relations: Sociometric and behavioral assessment. In J. D. Wine and D. Smye, eds. *Social competence.* New York: Guilford, pp. 125-157; Hoffman, M. (2000). *Empathy and moral development: Implications for caring and justice.* Cambridge, UK: Cambridge University Press; Howes, C., and S. Ritchie (2002). *A matter of trust: Connecting teachers and learners in early childhood classrooms.* New York: Teachers College Press; Kemple, K. M. (2004). *Let's be friends: Peer competence and social inclusion in early childhood classrooms.* New York: Teachers College Press; Ladd, G. W. (1990). Having friends, keeping friends, making friends, and being liked by peers in the classroom: Predictors of children's early school adjustment? *Child Development* 61, 1081-1100; Ladd, G. W., J. M. Price, and C. H. Hart (1990). Preschoolers' behavioral orientations and patterns of peer contact: Predictive of peer status? In S. R. Asher and J. D. Coie, eds. *Peer rejection in childhood.* New York: Cambridge University Press, pp. 90-115; Luthar, S. S., and B. E. Becker (2002). Privileged but pressured? A study of affluent youth. *Child Development* 73(5): 1593-1610; McLoyd, V. C. (1998). Socioeconomic hardship on black families and children: Psychological distress, parenting, and socioemotional development. *Child Development* 61, 311-346; Ramsey, P. G. (1996). Successful and unsuccessful entries in preschools. *Journal of Applied Developmental Psychology* 17, 135-150; Ramsey, P. G. (2004). *Teaching and learning in a diverse world,* 3rd ed. New York: Teachers College Press; Schneider, B. H., J. Wiener, and K. Murphy (1994). Children's friendships: The great step beyond acceptance. *Journal of Social and Personal Relationships* 11, 323-340; Sroufe, L. A., E. Schork, F. Motti, N. Lawroski, and P. LaFreniere (1984). The role of affect in social competence. In C. E. Izzard, J. Kagan, and R. B. Zajonc, eds. *Emotions, cognition, and behavior.* New York: Cambridge University Press; Yeung, W. J., M. R. Linver, and J. Brooks-Gunn (2002). How money matters for young children's development: Parental investment and family processes. *Child Development* 73(6), 1861-1879.

Patricia G. Ramsey

Developmental Delay

While all children grow and change at their own rate, some children can experience delays in their development. Developmental delay is a descriptive term used in reference to an assessment of delay in infants and young children in one or more of the following areas: **cognitive development**, physical development (which includes fine motor and gross motor), communication development, social development, emotional development, or adaptive development. If a child is slightly or only temporarily lagging behind, that is not considered developmental delay. Developmental delay is recognized by the failure to meet age-appropriate expectations that are based on the typical sequence of child development.

Significant delays in acquisition of developmental milestones in one or more developmental areas would indicate developmental delay and eligibility for **early childhood special education**. Parents usually seek an evaluation for developmental delay once their child fails to meet specific developmental milestones. In early infancy, indicators of developmental delay include a lack of responsiveness, unusual muscle tone or posture, and feeding difficulties. After six months of age, motor delay is the most common complaint. Language and behavior problems are common concerns after eighteen months. Although physical and cognitive delays may occur together, one is not necessarily a sign of the other. In addition, developmental milestones achieved and then lost should also be investigated, as the loss of function could be sign of a degenerative neurological condition.

Each state is responsible for developing more specific definitions of developmental delay, as well as criteria for determining eligibility for services for young children and their families residing in that state. Individual states have defined developmental delay variously as exhibiting a certain percentage of delay in one or more developmental areas, lower functioning than expected for chronological age, informed clinical judgment, atypical development, or a combination of some or all of these definitions. Those criteria measured by standardized assessment instruments are expressed in standard deviations from the mean; percent delay; number of months delay; or a developmental quotient (DQ), similar to an **intelligence quotient** (IQ) score. Criteria that are less quantifiable include atypical development as judged by a trained clinical professional or a multidisciplinary team.

Children who have a high probability of experiencing developmental delays include those who could be considered at established risk, biological risk, and/or environmental risk. Children who have genetic conditions or other medically diagnosed disorders that gives them a high probability of later delays in development have an established risk. Conditions such as **Down syndrome**, muscular dystrophy, and hearing impairment are examples. Children in this category are eligible for special education services by virtue of their diagnosis, regardless of whether a measurable delay is present. Children considered at biological risk have biological histories or conditions that make them more likely to develop a delay than children without the condition. Birth trauma, prematurity, failure to thrive, or complications during pregnancy all put a child at biological risk. The classification of young children who are at environmental risk is intended for children whose environments do not provide for their basic needs, including adequate nutrition, clothing, and shelter to provide psychological and emotional security. Children living in inadequate environments may experience mental, emotional, and/or physical disabilities. Developmental delays and disabilities are most likely to occur when a child is exposed to multiple risk factors, which may be biological, environmental, or both.

The **Individuals with Disabilities Education Act** (IDEA) permits states and schools to use a noncategorical classification such as developmental delay for children ages 3 through 9. This term is used when a definitive diagnosis has not been made, but a child shows persistent delay across domains. In identifying infants and toddlers, a general term such as developmental delay must be used. This law requires that young children with developmental delays receive **early intervention** services as needed. In addition, Part C under IDEA permits, but does not require, states to provide early intervention services for infants and toddlers who are at risk of developmental delays or disabilities but do not display any actual delays or activity limitations. *See also* Development, Emotional; Development, Social.

Further Readings: Division for Early Childhood (DEC). February 2005. Available online at http://www.dec-sped.org; Lerner, Janet W., Lowenthal, Barbara, and Egan, Rosemary W. (2003). *Preschool children with special needs.* Boston: Pearson Education.

Sharon Judge

Developmental Disorders of Infancy and Early Childhood, A Taxonomy of

The following listing *briefly* describes a range of conditions that can affect young children. It should be noted that the perception of disability is a social phenomenon, and that the capacities of an individual child are affected by typical developmental processes, a variety of environmental influences, and biological risk factors. These labels are just that, labels that describe conditions but fail to adequately portray the unique personhood of each child. This taxonomy is organized by underlying conditions rather than by functional categories or environmental risk factors (e.g., lead poisoning, fetal drug, or alcohol exposure). It is intended to provide an overview. For specific diagnostic criteria consult *Diagnostic and Statistics Manual of Mental Disorders* (DSM IV) or the *Diagnostic Classification of Mental Health and Developmental Disorders of Infancy and Early Childhood.* When working with children more detailed information on these conditions is required and should be used in concert with assessment of the child's individual strengths and needs as they relate to parental concerns, developmental domains and real world skills.

Sensory Disorders

Hearing impairment. Hearing impairment ranges from mild hearing loss to *deafness* which is defined as the level of hearing loss at which speech cannot be understood. Conductive hearing loss involves problems with the middle or outer ear often caused by infections such as *otitis media. Sensorineural hearing loss* occurs in the inner ear or auditory nerve and is typically more debilitating than conductive loss.

Visual impairment. Children with a variety of developmental disabilities are at greater risk for visual impairments such as *amblyopia* (lazy eye), *strabismus*—an imbalance of the eye muscles, and *cataracts*—opacity in the lens, as well as more normative conditions like myopia. A number of diseases can cause blindness that can severely affect other areas of development. *Retrolental fibroplasia* has been related to the use of high does of oxygen to premature infants.

Sensorimotor integration disorders. This set of conditions affects a child's ability to integrate sensory input including that from vestibular and proprioceptive systems. *Tactile defensiveness* is an inability to tolerate textures, touch, or stimulation.

Neuromotor Disorders

Cerebral palsy. Cerebral palsy results from brain lesions that result in mild to severe motor problems. A variety of prenatal and perinatal events (e.g., anoxia, RH blood incompatibility, birth complications, and heavy alcohol use) can contribute to the brain damage. Depending upon the location and nature of the lesion upper and lower limbs and sides of the body may or may not be affected.

Spina bifida. Spina bifida results from neural tube defects that interrupt transmission of neural impulses and motor development to the lower part of the body. Due to new surgical techniques the neural openings can now be corrected, limiting the motor disabilities as well as the accumulation of spinal fluid in the brain's ventricles that has the potential to affect cognitive functioning.

Muscular dystrophy. Muscular dystrophy, as opposed to cerebral palsy, is a progressive disorder resulting from a brain lesion. Its mechanisms are less well understood but are linked to a genetically transmitted metabolic disorder. The most common form is Duchenne's, which results in gradual disintegration of muscle cells.

Seizure disorders. Seizure disorders constitute a variety of conditions resulting from abnormal bursts of electrical activity that disrupt brain functioning. *Grand mal* seizures usually involve a loss of consciousness and alternate rigidity and relaxation of muscles. Focal seizures involve localized areas of the brain. *Myoclonic* seizures do not result in loss of consciousness and are characterized by involuntary jerking of the extremities. *Akintetic* seizures are opposite myoclonic in that they involve reduced muscle tone. *Petit mal* seizures are of short duration involving a brief lapse of consciousness without loss of muscle tone. Seizure disorders are often associated with other neurological disorders.

Congenital disorders. Only the most common of many hundreds of congenital disorders are described here.

Genetic Metabolic Disorders

Phenylketonuria is a metabolic disorder that, if left untreated, can cause brain damage and severe mental retardation. It can be identified with routine blood and urine screening at birth. *Cystic fibrosis* is also a metabolic disorder that leads to buildup of mucus in the child's lungs and vulnerability to infections. Death usually occurs by early adulthood. *Galactosemia* results in an enlarged liver. Children are susceptible to mental retardation, cataracts, and infections. *Congenital hyperthyroidism* is a hormone deficiency which, if left untreated, leads to floppy muscle tone and retardation. *Tay-Sachs disease* is a progressive disease of the nervous system that affects infants after about six months of age and leads to severe debilitation and death by age 5.

Chromosomal Disorders

Down syndrome involves mild to severe mental retardation, low muscle tone, and distinctive physical features. In many cases cardiovascular problems are also present. *Cri du chat syndrome* results in microcephaly, smaller than average size, poorly formed ears. Children are usually mentally retarded. *Prader-Willi syndrome* results in moderate retardation, obesity, and low muscle tone. *Fragile-X disease* often results in retardation and behavioral disorders.

Cognitive/Learning Disorders

Mental retardation. Mental retardation is defined as significantly subaverage general intellectual functioning and can be attributed to a broad variety of both biological and environmental factors. Classification is typically arranged by IQ, with IQs of 50/55-70 being considered mild, 35/40-50/55 moderate, 20/25-35/40 severe, and below 20 or unspecified as profound. Labeling also requires evidence of limits on adaptive behavior. Typically in infancy and early childhood developmental delay is referred to, particularly in mild to moderate cases, based on measures of overall developmental functioning to avoid false prediction of retardation as well as stigma.

Learning disabilities. Learning disabilities can affect children of average or above average intelligence. They are characterized by specific inabilities in auditory and visual processes and are rarely diagnosed before school age. There is some evidence that premature and low birth weight babies have a higher incidence of learning disabilities when they reach school age.

Attention deficit disorder. Attention deficit disorder can be categorized in two ways, either with (ADHD) or without (ADD) hyperactivity. The two classifications are characterized by inattention, impulsivity and, in the case of ADHD, by a high activity level.

Social/Emotional Disorders

As with language, these social and emotional disorders may be secondary to other conditions. For example, self-stimulation and self-injurious behavior may characterize the behavior of some children with mental retardation, or social adjustment to a neuromuscular disorder may result in extreme shyness or oppositional behavior. On the other hand, a social-emotional disorder may be a primary disability with an etiology of its own.

Autism. Autism and an associated classification, *pervasive developmental disorder*, are characterized by severe delays of communicative and social development.

Autistic children often engage in repetitive and self-stimulatory behavior and inability to tolerate even small changes in their environment or schedule. Autistic children show a broad range of intelligence and adaptive abilities. Some evidence exists for physiological causes but it is not yet conclusive.

Attachment disorders. Attachment disorders are characterized by behaviors that indicate the lack of a strong emotional tie to a caregiver or caregivers. Such children are seen as avoidant or resistant to forming relationships. These disorders are seen as primarily induced by severe child maltreatment confinement to nonresponsive institutional care.

Behavior disorders. Oppositional and aggressive behaviors in young children are increasing. Typically the child's social environment (e.g., abusive, neglectful, or nonnurturant situations) has been blamed for these behaviors. However, the factors that enter into the equation that result in such disorders may be biophysical and temperamental as well as environmental. Increasingly, a portion of these children are being diagnosed with ADD/ADHD.

Social withdrawal/isolation. Some children are extremely fearful or withdrawn in social situations. Again, a variety of factors, both biological and environmental, can lead to these conditions. Conditions such as social phobias or selective mutism may be identified in the preschool years.

Communication Disorders

Speech and language disability is often associated with many of the other conditions listed here such as retardation, hearing problems, or autism. In some cases, however, language functions seem to be the primary issue of concern. Because of the importance of language functions in development, this primarily functional area is included as a distinct disability category.

Speech or phonological disorders. Speech and phonological disorders involve difficulties with the production of speech sounds. These often include problems with the nerves and muscles of the mouth, vocal cords, and breathing apparatus.

Expressive language disorders. Expressive language disorders are, in some cases, the result of lesions in the motor cortex responsible for language production. They can also be the by-product of a number of other biological and environmental risk factors. They are characterized by difficulty in using words.

Receptive language disorders. Receptive language disorders are those that affect the comprehension and production of language. Receptive aphasias involve damage to temporal language areas. As a result, not only language comprehension but also language production is affected. The understanding and production of language involves a broad set of abilities and hence these problems require assessment that isolates specific areas of skill.

Health-Related Conditions

Failure to thrive. The failure to gain weight within a normal range may be due to a number of factors that may include either an inability to provide sufficient breast milk or digestive problems in the infant. In some instances it has been related to neglect or ignorance of basic parenting practices.

Infections. The incidence of *rubella* is now rare, but in the past German measles during pregnancy resulted in children with sensory and cognitive impairments. Other viral infections such as *cytomegalovirus* and *herpes simplex* can cause severe disabilities. *Meningitis* , an infection of the tissue around the brain and spinal cord, can be due to a virus or bacterial infection and can cause a wide range of neurological problems.

Gastrointestinal. Many children with multiple or severe conditions have difficulty maintaining body weight and meeting basic nutritional needs. In addition they may also have *gastroesphageal reflux*, a condition in which the muscle that prevents food from backing up between the stomach and esophagus is weak. *See also* Attention Deficit Disorder/Attention Deficit Hyperactivity Disorder; Autism; Cerebral Palsy; Fetal Alcohol Syndrome.

Further Readings: Blackman, J. A., ed. (1983). *Medical aspects of developmental disabilities in children birth to three: A resource for special-service providers in the educational setting*. Iowa City: University of Iowa Press; Neisworth J. T., and S. J. Bagnato (1987). *The young exceptional child: Early development and education*. New York: Macmillan; Widerstrom, A. H., B. A. Mowder, and S. R. Sandall (1991). *At-risk and handicapped newborns and infants: Development, assessment, and intervention*. Englewood Cliffs, NJ: Prentice-Hall.

John Hornstein

Developmental-Interaction Approach

The developmental-interaction approach represents a set of beliefs and values about teaching and learning for children as well as the adults who teach them. This approach to early childhood education is identified with **Bank Street** College of Education and is named for its salient concepts, including "the changing patterns of growth, understanding, and response that characterize children and adults as they *develop*; and the dual meaning of *interaction*, as first, the interconnected spheres of thought and emotion, and equally, the importance of engagement with the world of people, materials, and ideas" (Nager and Shapiro, 2000).

Rooted in the early years of the twentieth century, the developmental-interaction approach is associated with **Progressivism** and shares features with a democratic **pedagogy,** including an emphasis on humanist values and the belief that education provides an opportunity to engage in and create a more equitable democratic society. Lucy Sprague **Mitchell**, the founder of Bank Street College (initially known as the Bureau of Educational Experiments), was profoundly influenced by the thinking of John **Dewey** and other early Progressives such as Harriet Johnson, Caroline **Pratt**, and Susan **Isaacs**. In the conceptualization that is now known as the developmental-interaction approach, school and society, democracy and education are inextricably linked. Developmental theorists such as Anna **Freud**, Erik **Erikson**, Heinz Werner, Jean **Piaget**, and Kurt Lewin, who saw development in dynamic terms and in social context, also contributed to the conceptualization of the approach. In more recent years the work of Lev **Vygotsky** and his followers has come to influence the understanding and expression of developmental-interaction.

This approach specifies a set of beliefs about the learner, learning, and teaching. The learner is understood as an active maker of meaning who is curious about the world in which she lives and actively engages with the physical and social world to make sense of it. As an advocate for children, the teacher studies how children learn and grow and strives to understand the communities in which they live. She forges a practice that integrates a deep and sophisticated knowledge of subject matter, an understanding of children and learning, and a passion for social justice. Together the teacher and children create a classroom community that promotes each child's cognitive, linguistic, affective, social, and physical development. The classroom provides a context for becoming a member of a community. School is a major part of children's lives and should provide equitable opportunities for children to build knowledge and skills while they are also experiencing pleasure, enjoying learning, and developing competence. Learning to respect others and resolve conflicts in positive ways are fundamental to the communal learning environment.

These ideas, values and beliefs guide rather than prescribe teaching. They provide a set of principles with which the teacher makes fundamental choices about subject matter content, methodology, and the physical and psychological environment of the classroom. Teaching requires a complex set of knowledge, skills, and dispositions with which to plan, implement, and assess curriculum and children's growth.

In the developmental-interaction approach, **social studies** provide the core of the curriculum. It is selected as a core curriculum because it concerns the relationships between and among people and their environments, both in the present and in the past. It provides an opportunity to integrate knowledge and skills within an experience of democratic living. Bringing her deep understanding of the subject matter together with her understanding of each individual learner, the teacher guides children's learning and the growth of knowledge by asking meaningful questions and selecting learning opportunities such as trips, activities, books, and other materials and resources. Children learn from their experience when they engage directly and actively with the environment and pursue questions that emerge from their observations, interests, and curiosity within a framework of connected opportunities that the teacher provides. The teacher is the key person, guiding children's inquiry, making connections to academic fields of study, and providing continuity in experiences to facilitate and enable learning.

The developmental-interaction classroom is a dynamic environment that encourages active participation, cooperation, and independence. It provides multiple and diverse opportunities for children to represent, express, and communicate their understanding. The individual is valued as a thinker and doer and also as a social and emotional being who is an important part of the community of the classroom, her family, and her larger community. This understanding of the learner generates a broad understanding of **assessment in early childhood**. In the developmental-interaction classroom, assessment reflects an understanding not only of competence in basic skills and knowledge but also of how the learner makes sense of his or her world, the development of analytic capacity, and depth and breadth of knowledge in subject matter areas. Equally important is the teacher's assessment of the attitudes and characteristics of the learner in interaction with the environment, such as the ability to work both independently and collaboratively, to exercise initiative and to be a socially responsible member of the community.

The central tenets of developmental-interaction apply equally to the education of teachers. The **teacher education** program at Bank Street College is based on the conviction that teachers need experiences as learners that parallel the ways they will teach children. Becoming a competent teacher is tied not only to information but also to the ways in which teachers experience, internalize, and construct their growing knowledge and sense of self as a maker of meaning. Some principles that govern the education of teachers include the following:

(1) Education is a vehicle for creating and promoting social justice and encouraging participation in democratic processes.
(2) The teacher has a deep understanding of subject matter areas and is actively engaged in learning through formal study, direct observation and participation.
(3) A sophisticated understanding of the development of children and youth in the context of family, community, and culture is necessary for teaching.
(4) The teacher continues to grow as a person and as a professional.
(5) Underlying practice is a philosophy of education that provides an organized set of principles for teaching and learning.

Developmental-interaction guides both the education of children and teachers. It does not provide a codified set of procedures, but rather presents a framework for the teacher's decision making concerning choice of content, methodology and the physical and psychological environment of the classroom. The teacher has the complex task of expressing these values and principles in planning and implementing curriculum, assessing curriculum and children's growth, and taking on the responsibility of growing as a professional. Together, teachers and children engage actively with the environment, expand their knowledge, and grow as members of caring, intellectually challenging and democratic classrooms. *See also* Advocacy and Leadership in Early Childhood; Classroom Environments; Development, Social.

Further Readings: Cuffaro, Harriet, Nancy Nager, and Edna Shapiro (2005). The developmental-interaction approach at Bank Street College of Education. In Jaipaul L. Roopnarine and James E. Johnson, eds. *Approaches to early childhood education*, 4th ed. Upper Saddle River, NJ: Pearson, pp. 280–295; Nager, Nancy, and Edna Shapiro, eds. (2000). *Revisiting a progressive pedagogy: The developmental-interaction approach.* Albany, NY: State University of New York Press.

Web Site: Bank Street Thinkers. Available online at http://streetcat.bankstreet.edu/essays/main.html.

Nancy Nager

Developmentally Appropriate Practice(s) (DAP)

In the early childhood context the adjective "developmentally appropriate" means varying for or adapting to the age, experience, abilities, and interests of individual children within a given age range. The specific historical origins of the term are unclear, but it is likely that it originated within the field of developmental psychology, which has had considerable influence on the field of early childhood education. Manufacturers of children's toys, clothing, furniture, and other materials regularly make judgments about what is developmentally appropriate when they alert consumers to the age group for which their product is designed. Early childhood educators often use the phrase, "developmentally appropriate," when they describe materials, learning experiences, or expectations of children of varying ages.

Developmentally appropriate practice (sometimes abbreviated as DAP) is a short-hand phrase that has been widely used in the early childhood profession to describe ways of teaching young children that reflect knowledge of child development and learning, and that vary with the age, experience, abilities, interests, needs, and strengths of individual children. The term gained recognition and influence when the **National Association for the Education of Young Children** (NAEYC) first published a position statement promoting such teaching practices (Bredekamp, 1987). Initially, many early childhood educators embraced the concept and the publication became the best-selling book in NAEYC's history with more than 700,000 copies sold.

Within several years, however, the book and the concept of developmentally appropriate practice became the object of considerable criticism and discussion within the profession. The critique in the literature and during public forums created an excellent opportunity for debate within the field. In 1997, after several years of work, NAEYC issued a completely revised edition of the publication that attempted to address many of the critics' concerns as well as more current research and theory (Bredekamp and Copple, 1997). NAEYC's current position states the following:

Developmentally appropriate programs are based on what is known about how children develop and learn; such programs promote the development and enhance the learning of each individual child served.

Developmentally appropriate practices result from the process of professionals making decisions about the well-being and education of children based on at least three important kinds of information or knowledge:

(1) *What is known about child development and learning*—knowledge of age-related human characteristics that permits general predictions within an age range about what activities, materials, interactions, or experiences will be safe, healthy, interesting, achievable, and also challenging to children.

(2) *What is known about the strengths, interests, and needs of each individual child in the group* to be able to adapt for and be responsive to inevitable individual variation.

(3) *Knowledge of the social and cultural contexts in which children live* to ensure that learning experiences are meaningful, relevant, and respectful for the participating children and their families.

Furthermore, each of these dimensions of knowledge—human development and learning, individual characteristics and experiences, and social and cultural contexts—is dynamic and changing, requiring that early childhood teachers remain learners throughout their careers (Bredekamp and Copple, 1997, pp. 8–9).

History of Developmentally Appropriate Practice

All development occurs in social, historical, and political context, including the development of fields of practice and scholarship. The 1987 edition of DAP was written in response to two particular trends occurring in the last part of the twentieth century. First, NAEYC had just launched a national, voluntary **accreditation** system for high-quality early-childhood programs. The phrase "developmentally appropriate" was used throughout the accreditation criteria. Without further definition, the criteria were subject to widely varying interpretations by program personnel and validators making onsite visits for accreditation. A second motivation for the position statement was the trend toward what is referred to as a push-down **curriculum** in which primary-grade academic expectations and teaching practices such as whole-group, teacher-directed instruction were being moved down to **kindergarten** or even preschool. With increasing numbers of public schools serving four-year-olds, association leaders felt strongly that those programs needed guidance about what kinds of practices are developmentally appropriate for that age group.

The concept of developmental appropriateness seemed most relevant to early childhood educators in terms of thinking about the needs and characteristics of different age groups, so NAEYC produced a statement that addressed the issue across the full age-span of birth through eight years. For example, the level of independent functioning or social interaction expected of a two-year-old is, according to most child development research, quite different from that expected of a seven-year-old.

In the 1987 statement, developmental appropriateness was defined as having two dimensions: age-appropriateness, and individual appropriateness. The 1987 statement called for a balance of teacher-directed and child-initiated experiences, and clearly stressed the value of **play** and child initiation. Perhaps most significantly, the document contrasted examples of appropriate and inappropriate practice for each age group. The decision to include negative as well as positive examples was momentous, generating considerable attention to the book. But the dichotomization of appropriate and inappropriate practice also created problems such as oversimplifying the complex act of teaching and leading some practitioners to either/or thinking in place of serious reflection.

Criticisms of the 1987 edition of *Developmentally Appropriate Practice* are well documented (Bredekamp and Copple, 1997; Mallory and New, 1994). To summarize, they include: "1) the either/or oversimplification of practice; 2) overemphasis on child development and underemphasis on curriculum content; 3) the passivity of the teacher's role, the failure to recognize the value of teacher direction; 4) lack of awareness of the significant role of culture in development and learning (white, middle-class bias); 5) lack of application for children with disabilities and special needs; 6) overemphasis on the individual child and underemphasis on relationships and social construction of knowledge; 7) naivete about the significant role of families" (Bredekamp 2001, p. 108).

The 1997 edition of *Developmentally Appropriate Practice* attempted to address many of these concerns. NAEYC also developed a position statement in conjunction with the National Association of Early Childhood Specialists in State Departments of Education on curriculum as a companion piece. In these documents, rather than viewing developmentally appropriate practice as a prescription that is found in a book, teachers are described as professional decision-makers; and the revised position statement includes a set of principles and guidelines for making decisions. The guidelines address the complexity of early childhood practice: creating a caring community of learners; teaching to enhance learning and development; constructing appropriate curriculum; assessing children's learning and development; and establishing reciprocal relationships with families. To reflect the central role of culture in development, the actual definition of what is developmentally appropriate was expanded to include knowledge of the social and cultural context. To go beyond oversimplifications, the document challenges the field to move from *either/or* to *both/and* thinking.

Developmentally Appropriate Practices and Curriculum Content

Shortly after the 1997 edition of Developmentally Appropriate Practice was published, leaders of the **International Reading Association** (IRA) criticized it for failing to reflect current knowledge about the importance of effective early **literacy** instruction in the early years. Noting that the position statement was never intended to outline specific content areas, NAEYC collaborated with members of the IRA and wrote a joint position statement, *Learning to Read and Write: Developmentally Appropriate Practices for Young Children* (Neuman, Copple, and Bredekamp, 2000). This statement applied the definition of developmentally appropriate practices to a specific curriculum area: "Developmentally appropriate practices in reading and writing are ways of teaching that consider (1) what is generally known about children's development and learning to set achievable but challenging goals for literacy learning and to plan learning experiences and teaching strategies that vary with the age and experience of the learners; (2) results of ongoing assessment of individual children's progress in reading and writing to plan next steps or to adapt instruction when children fail to make expected progress or are at advanced levels; and (3) social and cultural contexts in which children live so as to help them make sense of their learning experiences in relation to what they already know and are able to do." The position goes on to say, "To teach in developmentally appropriate ways, teachers must understand *both* the continuum of reading and writing *and* children's individual and cultural variations. Teachers must recognize when variation is within the typical range and when intervention is necessary, because early intervention is more effective and less costly than later remediation" (Neuman, Copple, and Bredekamp 2000, p. 19).

Applying the concept of developmentally appropriate practices to a specific curriculum area, in this case early literacy, provided a model that NAEYC also used for **mathematics** in a joint position with the National Council of Teachers of Mathematics (NCTM). Similar frameworks could be used in all curriculum content areas.

The Future of Developmentally Appropriate Practices

The subject of developmentally appropriate practice continues to be controversial within the field with some people calling for elimination of the term from the early childhood lexicon. Critics continue to challenge the construct's almost total reliance on [improved and more culturally informed] child development theory and oversight of educational and curriculum theories. The concept has become highly politicized as well, with some government entities censoring its use in official publications. A position statement is, by definition, a political statement that addresses an issue of controversy. So it is not surprising that DAP generates controversy just as it attempts to resolve it. NAEYC's leaders will determine the future of Developmentally Appropriate Practice(s) as a position statement and publication. The 1997 edition called for regular review of the concept and revised statements at least every ten years.

The future of developmentally appropriate practice (with lowercase letters) is more certain since it is likely that teachers, parents, and commercial product developers will continue to find it useful to vary experiences and expectations for young children with attention their age, individual characteristics, and cultural and linguistic backgrounds. *See also* Academics; Preschool/Prekindergartern Programs.

Further Readings: Bloch, M. N. (1992). Critical perspectives on the historical relationship between child development and early childhood education research. In S. Kessler and B. B. Swadener, eds. *Reconceptualizing the early childhood curriculum: Beginning the dialogue*, pp. 3–20; Bredekamp, Sue, ed. (1987). *Developmentally appropriate practice in early childhood programs serving children from birth through age 8.* Exp. ed. Washington, DC: National Association for the Education of Young Children; Bredekamp, Sue, ed. (2001). Improving professional practice: A letter to Patty Smith Hill. In *NAEYC at 75: Reflections on the Past, Challenges for the Future*. Washington, DC: National Association for the Education of Young Children, pp. 89–124; Bredekamp, Sue, and Carol Copple, eds. (1997). *Developmentally appropriate practice in early childhood programs.* Rev. ed. Washington, DC: National Association for the Education of Young Children; Dahlberg, Gunilla, Peter Moss, and Alan Pence (1999). *Beyond quality in early childhood education and care: Postmodern perspectives.* London: Falmer Press; Mallory, Bruce L., and Rebecca S. New, eds. (1994). *Diversity and developmentally appropriate practices: Challenges for early childhood education.* New York: Teachers College Press; Neuman, Susan B.,

Carol Copple, and Sue Bredekamp (2000). *Learning to read and write: Developmentally appropriate practices for young children.* Washington, DC: National Association for the Education of Young Children.

Sue Bredekamp

Developmental Systems Theories

Developmental Systems Theories are a family of conceptual models that promote a holistic view of individuals. According to this perspective, development is seen as a dynamic process where all components of the individual and the context interact in mutually influential ways. As such, this theoretical approach views the whole individual as "greater than the sum" of his or her parts. The study of development should not attempt to isolate or disengage individual components of the overall system.

A developmental systems perspective emphasizes the complex relationships that exist between individuals and their ecology, the contribution that people make to their own development, and the importance of viewing a person holistically and in his or her real-life contexts. This perspective has important implications for research and practice in the field of early childhood education and care. According to this theoretical perspective, the relationship between a child and his or her context (e.g. educational program) must be framed by the contribution of the child's unique qualities to his or her development; in turn, the effects of a program have to be understood in the context of the developmental trajectories and the nature of the broader ecology of the children participating in the program. Thus, a developmental systems perspective provides an important framework for researchers and practitioners in the field of early childhood education.

The importance that these theories place on the *relationship* between an individual and the multiple levels that comprise his or her ecology, rather than the individual or the ecology alone, means that a person's development is determined by fused (i.e., inseparable and mutually influential) relations among the multiple levels of the ecology of human development, including variables at the levels of inner biology (e.g., genes, the brain), the individual (e.g., temperament, cognitive style), social relationships (e.g., with peers, teachers, and parents), sociocultural institutions (e.g., educational policies and programs), and history (e.g., normative and non-normative events, such as elections and wars, respectively). The bidirectional relationship between the individual and the context (represented as individual ↔ context), and the multiple levels that are involved in development of this relationship, require that the person ↔ context system be viewed holistically. The continuous interrelation of all levels of the developing system, and how they change, is what constitutes development.

The dynamic (i.e., mutually influential) changes that exist across the developmental system create openness and flexibility in development and thus imply that there is a potential for plasticity (for systematic change) across life. The plasticity of development means that one may be optimistic about the ability to promote positive changes in human life by altering the course of individual ↔ context relations. Furthermore, in comparison to perspectives that regard people as passive recipients of environmental stimulation or of the set of genes acquired at conception, viewing development as a matter of individual ↔ context relations suggests that each person is an important producer of his or her own development. Individuals, through their characteristics of physical, mental, and behavioral individuality, including their setting of goals and the actions they take to pursue their objectives, play an important role in determining the nature of these relationship, and hence, in influencing their own developmental trajectories.

The interaction between an infant and her mother illustrates this active agency of individuals. An infant with an easy temperament (e.g., an ability to rapidly adjust to new events and stimuli, positive mood, and regularity of biological functions such as eating and sleeping) is likely to elicit positive, attentive responses from her parent that in turn, promote further, positive behaviors from the child and ultimately, support a healthy, adaptive parent ↔ child relationship. In this case, the behaviors of both the child and her parent have influenced the behaviors of the other person in the relationship, and the child is coshaping the course of his or her own development. By underscoring the active contribution that each individual has on his or her developmental trajectory, the developmental systems perspective brings the importance of individual differences to the fore. As each individual interacts in a unique way with his or her context, he or she may develop differently from other individuals.

Therefore, from the developmental systems perspective, development is not seen as a simple, linear, cause-and-effect process, but as a complex, flexible process where the actions and intentions of the individual play a causal role. Moreover, this role occurs within the actual ecology of human development. Developmental systems theories place a strong emphasis on ecological validity, that is, the importance of understanding people in settings representative of their real-world settings, as opposed to ecologically unrepresentative laboratory settings.

Thus, a strength of developmental systems theories is that, rather than concentrating on a limited aspect of a person's functioning, or focusing on people in contrived situations, it focuses on the diversity and complexity of human development as it takes place in the contexts within which children actually spend their lives—a focus brought to the fore by six decades of theory and research by Urie **Bronfenbrenner**. Accordingly, from this perspective, educational interventions should seek to change the relationship between the active individual and his or her complex, multilevel context; such work should not seek to enhance the educational process or its outcomes within the contrived laboratory context but, instead, should seek to enhance the positive connections among the classroom, school, family, community, faith institution, and other settings in which children live. Furthermore, such interventions may enter the developmental system at any level of the **ecology of human development**, for example, at the individual, school, family, community, cultural, or social policy level, and still be envisioned to be of potential effectiveness due to the plasticity of the bidirectional relations among all levels of the system.

Thus, developmental systems theories have important implications for early childhood education and care. In particular, given the principle that exists within this perspective about the possibility for positive change, one may maintain that it is feasible to identify individual ↔ context relations that may promote at least some positive transformation in any developmental characteristic. In fact, the ideas of plasticity and of optimism within the developmental systems perspective provide a theoretical foundation for the fundamental goal of educational programs: to promote positive change among all children. Furthermore, given that this perspective suggests that positive change is achieved by fostering a mutually beneficial relationship between the individual and his or her context, programs, educational and otherwise, must remain flexible so that a maximum fit will be created between the diversity (of developmental trajectories) characterizing the children, families, and communities involved in a program. Indeed, to provide the most appropriate services to any specific child, it is important to identify both the individual and more generic characteristics of each child and, as well, to seek understanding of the connections existing between this individuality and the multiple (and themselves diversely constituted) levels of the ecology in which the child is embedded.

Further Readings: Bronfenbrenner, U. (in press). *Making human beings human.* Thousand Oaks, CA: Sage; Ford, D. L., and R. M. Lerner (1992). *Developmental systems theory: An integrative approach.* Newbury Park, CA: Sage; Lerner, R. M. (2002). *Concepts and theories of human development,* 3rd ed. Mahwah, NJ: Erlbaum; Overton, W. F. (1998). Developmental psychology: Philosophy, concepts, and methodology. In W. Damon, series ed. and R. M. Lerner, vol. ed. *Handbook of child psychology, Vol 1: Theoretical models of human development,* 5th ed. New York: Wiley, pp. 107–187; Thelen, E., and L. B. Smith (1998). Dynamic systems theories. In W. Damon, series ed. and R. M. Lerner, vol. ed. *Handbook of child psychology, Vol 1: Theoretical models of human development,* 5th ed. New York: Wiley, pp. 563–633.

Jason Almerigi, Steinunn Gestsdottir, and Richard M. Lerner

Dewey, John (1859–1952)

A leading representative of the progressive movement in the United States and a founder of the philosophical school of Pragmatism, John Dewey was one of the most influential American educational reformers of the last century.

Dewey was born and educated in Vermont. He held several teaching positions between graduation from the University of Vermont in 1879 and entrance to Johns Hopkins University in 1882. After receiving a Ph.D. in 1884, Dewey became a philosophy professor at the University of Michigan, where he married Alice Chipman after she received her doctorate in 1886.

Dewey developed his reputation as a pragmatic innovator while heading the Department of Philosophy, Psychology, and Pedagogy at the University of Chicago between 1894 and 1905. His 1896 establishment of its Laboratory School for children aged four to twelve years, with its curriculum based upon themes and projects, helped pioneer the movement known as **Progressive Education**. Dewey resigned from the University of Chicago in 1904, apparently because of disagreements with its administration. He was then a professor in the Philosophy Department of Columbia University until retirement in 1930.

Dewey's concepts became widely recognized through his books, which included *School and Society* (1899), *The Child and the Curriculum* (1902), *Democracy and Education* (1916), *The Quest for Certainty* (1929), and *Knowing and Education* (1949). After his first philosophical essay in 1882, he had about 150 publications. In addition to articles in professional journals, he contributed to *Harper's, The Nation,* and other popular magazines. He was active in many professional organizations, as an officer and a conference participant. Dewey also traveled and lectured in Europe, Japan, and China.

John Dewey had a significant influence upon today's preschools. When the sub-primary class at the University of Chicago Laboratory School opened in 1896, it was for children aged four to six years and based upon Friedrich **Froebel's** original system. It was not called a **kindergarten** because many American kindergartens had adopted structured activities and abstract symbolism during the previous two decades. Dewey credited Froebel with recognizing that individuals are co-ordinated units from birth onward, taking in experiences from the outer world, organizing them, and relating them to their inner life. His vision of this laboratory class for young children was to test the validity of using activities related to home and community-oriented themes. He took an active role in the kindergarten and child study associations and was elected president of the National Kindergarten Association (1913–1914).

A major contribution to early childhood education was Dewey's mentoring of Patty Smith **Hill**, beginning in the early 1890s and continuing after she took a position at Teachers College in 1904. When she formed the committee that evolved into the **National Association for the Education of Young Children** (NAEYC), he was a supporter. His students included many pioneers in early childhood education, including Lawrence Kelso **Frank,** Lucy Gage, and Alice **Temple.**

John Dewey believed that democratic child-centered classrooms and interaction with their communities would prepare the youngest citizens for living in a democratic society. He established the basic principles of today's early childhood education and of the importance of student-centered education at all grade levels.

Further Readings: Cuffaro, Harriet K. (1995). *Experimenting with the world: John Dewey and the early childhood classroom.* New York: Teachers College Press; Dewey, John (1934). *Art as experience.* New York: Penguin Putnam; Dewey, John (1944). *Democracy and education.* New York: Free Press; Dewey, John (1938). *Experience and education.* New York: Collier Books; Dewey, John (1929). *Experience and nature.* La Salle: Open Court; Dewey, John (1933). *How we think: A restatement of the relation of reflective thinking to the educative process.* Lexington, MA: D.C. Heath; Lascarides, V. Celia, and Blythe F. Hinitz (2000). *History of early childhood education.* New York: Falmer Press, pp. 215–225; Tanner, Laurel N. (1997). *Dewey's school, lessons for today.* New York: Teachers College Press; Weber, Evelyn (1984). *Ideas influencing early childhood education: A theoretical analysis.* New York: Teachers College Press.

Dorothy W. Hewes

Direct Instruction Model

Direct Instruction is both a theory and a model of teaching practice that proposes to accelerate learning through explicitly teaching young children basic skills which then can be generalized to higher-order processes. The model of direct instruction was first developed by Siegfried Engelmann and Carl Bereiter in 1966 through their work on intensive instruction for economically disadvantaged preschoolers; and is based on principles of **behaviorism.** In 1969, Engelmann (and coauthors) contracted with Science Research Associates (SRA) to publish an arithmetic and reading curriculum based on the theories under the brand name DISTAR (Direct Instructional System for Teaching and Remediation). Further dissemination of the model occurred when Engelmann partnered with Wesley Becker and together they created the Engelmann Becker Corporation (also known as the Association of Direct Instruction [ADI]) and the National Institute of Direct Instruction (NIFDI). These organizations continue to research and publish Direct Instruction (DI) materials as well as provide schools with training and program support. Direct Instruction curriculum materials continue to be developed and are marketed through SRA, although the brand name of DISTAR is being used less and less in favor of the simpler Direct Instruction title.

Direct instruction is a teaching model currently designed for use with preschoolers through eighth graders. Curricula have been published for reading, language arts, and **mathematics**, and typically include a sequence of carefully scripted lessons which teachers work through with children in small, ability-based groups. Instruction is generally fast-paced including nine to twelve questions per minute that the children answer in unison. Each lesson lasts about a half hour, and 80 percent of the time is used to review old material with the remaining 20 percent dedicated to introducing new concepts. Information that is under study is constantly tested through oral questioning by the teacher to identify student understandings and repeated to increase the retention of the material.

The approach is based on the assumption that, if explicitly taught specific basic skills, children will generalize these to new learning experiences. For example, instead of teaching the spelling of every word, "children who learned 600 word parts called 'morphographs' and three rules for connecting them could spell 12,000 words. Children rehearse the 600-word parts and three rules to a level of automaticity that allows them to spell the 12,000 words with ease" (Grossen, 2005). The theory also postulates that these skills must be clearly, simply and directly taught in a carefully sequenced manner that breaks bigger skills into smaller component tasks that children can master more quickly. Direct Instruction also holds curriculum constant so as to elucidate what difficulties the student brings and then specifically teaches the missing skills. Lastly the model advocates using scientifically tested curriculums that are designed to anticipate common errors and provide support for a wide range of children.

The program was evaluated as part of the massive federal Follow Through Project that analyzed multiple educational programs for the ability to teach basic skills, cognitive skills, and affective skills. Direct Instruction was the only model in this project to achieve consistently positive results in all three categories. However, the model faces strenuous critique from the teaching community and is often criticized for being too rigid and focusing solely on academic skills. Most recently, current trends toward accountability and high-stakes testing are making the model more attractive for some schools.

Further Readings: Adams, Gary L., and Siegfried Engelmann (1996). *Research on direct instruction: 25 years beyond DISTAR.* Seattle: Educational Achievement Systems; Grossen, Bonnie, University of Oregon (2005). *What is direct instruction?* See University of Oregon, Direct Instruction Model for Middle School Web site: http://darkwing.uoregon.edu/%7Ebgrossen/aftdi.htm; Slocum, Timothy A. (2004). Direct instruction. In Daniel J. Moran and Richard W. Malott, eds. *Evidence-based educational methods.* San Diego: Elsevier Academic Press.

Web Sites: Association for Direct Instruction. Available online at http://www.adihome.org/phpshop/faq/category.php?subject=General&username; National Institute for Direct Instruction. Available online at http://www.nifdi.org/.

Lindsay Barton

Disabilities, Young Children with

According to the CDC (2006), "Developmental disabilities affect approximately 17% of children younger than 18 years of age in the United States." Children typically progress through a series of developmental stages and milestones as they age. Disruption in these stages or a delay in reaching a milestone can be a sign that a child has a developmental delay or disability. Often a parent may wonder if their child has a developmental delay or disability when they notice differences in their child's development. However, because of the variability in rates of development and the relevance of developmental stages and milestones within cultural and ethnic groups, physicians and specialists are often reluctant to label a child as having a disability unless there is an obvious physical difference. In the absence of physical indicators or biological markers of disability, health care professionals depend upon assessment of a child's development, parent reports, behavior, and functional abilities for diagnosis.

There are many diagnostic labels that describe disabilities in young children. Unfortunately, the language used to communicate differences often pathologizes children to the point that they are known by their label rather than by their personalities, preferences, and passions. Many children are identified as having a disability at birth and others are diagnosed later when differences in development become more evident. Birth defects are a primary factor in disabilities in young children. "Birth defects affect about one in every thirty-three babies born in the United States each year. They are the leading cause of infant deaths, accounting for more than 20% of all infant deaths. Babies born with birth defects have a greater chance of illness and long-term disability than babies without birth defects. Developmental disabilities affect approximately 17% of children younger than 18 years of age in the United States" (CDC, 2006). Spina bifida, for example, is present at birth and is generally easily diagnosed based on clear physical indicators.

Other forms of developmental disabilities are not necessarily associated with birth effects. Children with **Autism** Spectrum Disorders (ASD), although being identified earlier, are often not labeled until after the age of three when discrepancies in the quality of motor, communication and social skills are more easily assessed. Likewise Attention Deficit Hyperactivity Disorder (ADHD) is often diagnosed after a child enters school because difficulties with attention and following routines become apparent in the school context. Other disabilities such as **cerebral palsy**, cognitive disabilities, **learning disabilities**, and speech and language delay are diagnosed at different ages depending on the **culture**, child, family, access to health care, and the competency of the health care professionals.

Increasingly children under the age of five are being diagnosed with **mental health** issues. The Substance Abuse and Mental Health Services Administration (SAMSHA) states there are numerous causes: exposure to environmental health risks such as high levels of lead and other toxic substances; exposure to **violence**, such as witnessing or being the victim of physical or sexual abuse, drive-by shootings, muggings, or other disasters; stress related to chronic poverty, discrimination, or other serious hardships; and the loss of important people through death, divorce, or broken relationships (SAMHSA, 2006). Identifying and addressing mental health issues in infants and young children depends upon the competence and knowledge of health care professionals and access to early services and supports.

There are numerous risk factors associated with developmental delays and mental health issues. They include maternal health status, pre- and postnatal history including low birth weight, maternal mental health, **socioeconomic status**, genetics, head trauma, exposure to heavy metals and toxins, and **child abuse and neglect**. If these factors are known by physicians and practitioners, there are several screening and diagnostic instruments and procedures that can document and monitor developmental delay. Given the understanding of the effectiveness of **early intervention** (Guralnick, 2005), there have been numerous efforts to improve early screening and detection of disabilities and/or metabolic disturbances that can lead to disabilities.

Early screening of children occurs in hospitals and physician offices by sampling a child's blood or giving tests specific to sensory and motor systems. The Apgar Scale which is given immediately after birth measures the degree of prenatal asphyxia based on observations of an infant's neuromotor status (Apgar, 1953). A low Apgar score is correlated with poorer developmental outcomes. Newborns are also screened through routine metabolic, endocrine and hearing test. Phenylketonuria (PKU) and hypothyroidism, if untreated, are associated with intellectual disabilities. Research has indicated that (1) there are unacceptable rates of underdetection of common other developmental problems in primary care due to lack of training and information about developmental screening tools; inadequate time; inadequate reimbursement; and unfamiliarity with community resources (e.g., Glascoe, 2003; Pelletier and Abrams, 2002); (2) underdetection of vision problems is a serious concern when 79 percent of preschoolers and even greater numbers of younger children *are not being screened* for amblyopia (American Academy of Pediatrics, 2002), and fewer than half of three-year-olds never have their vision screened using current methods (Hartmann et al., 2000); and (3) early detection of hearing loss is also problematic when only half of children with hearing loss are identified through checklists/questionnaires commonly used by practitioners (AAP, 2003). These gaps in identification frequently result in preventable developmental delays that often impact learning and have lifetime consequences for children and their families.

For children with developmental delays and disabilities, family support should be initiated as well as early services and supports. Early family support is critical for supporting high-quality child–family interactions, family orchestrated experiences that affect language and relationships, play, choice of toys and child care; and health and safety (Dunst, 1995; Guralnick, 2005). Early interventions and supports have proven to be effective in remediating some of the risk factors and preventing the progression of others. Research suggests the earlier the initiation of services and supports, the more positive the child outcomes. Hebb (1949) and Harlow (1958) believed that early experience and education had an impact on the development of the brain and its functions. These theories about the potential of influencing cognition were supported by Vygotsky (1962) who posited the idea that the brain could be influenced by external events. This ongoing process is referred to as neural plasticity.

Once a child has been identified as having a disability or considered at risk, there are several intervention programs available to support the child. **Head Start**, for example, was established in the United States in the 1960's, followed by Early Head Start, as a way to help disadvantaged children and their families overcome the influences of **poverty** and deprivation. It is based on the theory that education and intervention can positively affect child and parent outcomes. There are several major studies that have documented the effectiveness of early intervention. The Milwaukee Project, for example, sought to reduce the impact of "mental retardation" on infants and toddlers and their parents. Mothers who were labeled as intellectually disabled were taught how to stimulate and interact with their babies; and the infants also participated in an early intervention program. At the end of the study, infants in the experimental group scored thirty-five points higher on the Stanford Binet intelligence test. Martin, Ramey and Ramey (1990) reported on the **Abecedarian Project,** which sought to remediate the effects of psychosocial disadvantage. Both children and their parents were involved in the intervention. Children in the experimental group who received intensive (five days per week/all day) intervention had higher test scores at age 3 and were less likely to be retained in school. These gains were retained over time. Children who had mothers who were labeled more significantly disabled had the greatest developmental outcomes. Other studies, including Project Care (Wasik et al. 1990) and the Infant Health and Development Program (Ramey et al., 1992) provided in-home supports and documented that the intensity of involvement in intervention was positively correlated with better developmental outcomes.

In 1987, the U.S. Congress amended the **Individuals with Disabilities Education Act** (IDEA) to encourage states to begin educating infants from birth through three years of age and supporting their families in the natural context of their home. Prior to this amendment, referred to as Part H, state education efforts focused on children from three to twenty-one years. This amendment is now referred to as Early Intervention and is Part C of IDEA. Ramey and Ramey (1996) articulate six principles of Early Intervention that emanate from the research literature. They include the importance of: developmental timing, program intensity, direct versus intermediate provision of learning experiences, program breadth and flexibility, individualized differences in program benefits, and ecological dominion and environmental maintenance for development. In a longitudinal study of families who participated in Part C and received early Intervention programming, Bailey et al. (2004) found that families reported several positive outcomes including parents' improved feelings of competence, improved sense of support and higher expectations for their child's future.

Guralnick (1998) summarized literature on early interventions and commented that early intervention programs generally result in positive outcomes for children. They prevent decline and in many situations improve overall functioning of children. Much of the success depends, as noted by Ramey and Ramey (1998), on the nature of the program and the characteristics and circumstances of the child and family. In sum, developments over the past thirty years in social policy, program design, and research all have created a much stronger context for young children with disabilities, enhancing the likelihood of their optimal development within families and community-based programs alongside their non-disabled peers. Today, such children attend day care with early services and supports; are served in early intervention and **early childhood special education programs** operated by public preschool programs, community agencies, and the public education system. *See also* Attention Deficit Disorder/Attention Deficit Hyperactivity Disorder; Brain Development; Environmental Assessments in Early Childhood Education.

Further Readings: Apgar, V. (1953). A proposal for a new method of evaluation of the newborn infant. *Current Researches in Anesthesia and Analgesia* 32, 260-267; Bailey, D., A. Scarborough, K. Hebbeler, D. Soiker, and S. Mallik (2004). Family outcomes at the end of early intervention. Available online at http://www.sri.com/neils/pdfs/FamilyOutcomesReport_011405.pdf; Brookins, G. K. (1993). Culture, ethnicity, and bicultural competence: Implications for children with chronic illness and disability. *Pediatrics*, 91(5), 1056-1062; Guralnick, M. (1998). Effectiveness of early intervention for vulnerable children: A developmental perspective. *American Journal of Mental Retardation*, 102(4), 319-345; Guralnick, M. (2005). Early intervention for children with intellectual disabilities: Current knowledge and future prospects. *Journal of Applied Research in Intellectual Disabilities* 18, 313-324; Harlow, H. F. (1958). The nature of love. *American Psychologist* 13, 673-685; Hebb, D. O. (1949). *Organization of behavior*. New York: Wiley; Martin, S. L., C. T. Ramey, and S. L. Ramey (1990). The prevention of intellectual impairment in children of impoverished families: Findings of a randomized trial of educational day care. *American Journal of Public Health* 80, 844-847; Ramey, C. and S. Ramey (1992). Early educational intervention with disadvantaged children–to what effect? *Applied and Preventive Psychology*, 1, 131-140; Ramey, C. T., and S. L. Ramey (1996). Early intervention: Optimizing development for children with disabilities and risk conditions. In M. Wolraich, ed. *Disorders of development and learning: A practical guide to assessment and management,* 2nd ed. Philadelphia: Mosby, pp. 141-158; Ramey, C. T., and S. L. Ramey (1998). Early intervention and early experience. *American Psychologist* 53(2), 109-120; Substance Abuse and Mental Health Administration (SAMHSA) (2006). Available online at http://www.mentalhealth.samhsa.gov/publications/allpubs/CA-0004/default.asp; Wasik, B. H., C. T. Ramey, D. M. Bryant, and J. J. Sparling (1990). A longitudinal study of two early intervention strategies: Project CARE. *Child Development* 61, 1682-1696.

Jan Nisbet and Kate Stimmel

Division for Early Childhood (DEC)

The Division for Early Childhood (DEC) of the Council for Exceptional Children is a nonprofit, membership organization designed for individuals who work with or on behalf of children with special needs, from birth through age 8, and their families. Founded in 1973, DEC is dedicated to promoting policies and advancing practices that support families and enhance the optimal development of young children who have, or are at risk for, developmental delays and disabilities.

With 5,000 members worldwide, DEC is the largest professional membership organization dedicated to **early childhood special education**. DEC members are practitioners, administrators, family members, and policymakers. DEC represents a number of disciplines including early childhood special education, **early intervention**, speech therapy, psychology, health care, physical and occupational therapy, and others directly involved in the care and education of young children with disabilities and other special needs.

DEC and its members are committed to advocating for policy, planning and best practice in prevention and intervention. DEC supports full access for young children with special needs and their families to natural settings and service delivery options. Respect for family values, diverse cultural and linguistic backgrounds, and family circumstance are integral considerations in DEC's prevention and intervention efforts and DEC actively promotes parent–professional collaboration in all facets of planning, designing, and implementing early childhood intervention services.

As a membership organization, DEC supports those who work with, or on behalf of, infants and young children with special needs and their families in a variety of settings including preschool special education classrooms, home-based early intervention programs, Head Start and Early Head Start, child-care programs, hospital-based programs, and others. DEC promotes collaboration and communication among organizations, practitioners, and family members, innovations in research and the development of new knowledge, dissemination and use of information about research, resources, best practices and current issues, and professional development through an array of activities and strategies. With a network of more than thirty state and provincial Subdivisions, DEC offers numerous opportunities to network with colleagues and participate in professional development activities in support of early childhood special education.

DEC is a community of professionals, parents and others who are interested in building partnerships at the local, state/provincial, national and international levels to promote high-quality services for young children and their families. Key activities include providing (1) professional development and other training opportunities; (2) two quarterly journals—the *Journal of Early Intervention* and the *Young Exceptional Children*; (3) position statements and concept papers on topics of interest to practitioners, parents, researchers, and policymakers; (4) nearly twenty products including books, monographs, videos, and DEC's most important resource—*DEC Recommended Practices: A Comprehensive Guide for Practical Application*, a resource for identifying evidence-based practices for young children with disabilities and other special needs; (5) an international annual conference; (6) advocacy efforts including a Children's Action Network to communicate with the field and regular policy updates; and (7) opportunities for professionals and parents to share expertise via electronic communication, publications, forums, conference presentations, and journal articles.

Further Readings: DEC Web site: www.dec-sped.org.

Sarah A. Mulligan

Documentation

To "document" is "to support (an assertion or a claim, for example) with evidence or decisive information" (American Heritage Dictionary, 1994). It is this relationship between *assertion* and *evidence* that makes documentation distinct from observation. While many early childhood educators assume that documentation is a new pedagogical practice derived from **Reggio Emilia**, there is actually a long history of documentation in early childhood education in the United States. "Throughout the history of early childhood education in North America, teachers and caregivers have collected evidence of the growth in children's knowledge, skills and dispositions. Lucy Sprague **Mitchell**'s Bureau of Educational Experiments, founded in 1916 and later to become **Bank Street** College, emphasized the importance of teachers not only observing children but also recording children's language, feelings, projects, and daily happenings" (Mitchell, 1950). Early nursery and preschool teachers routinely collected children's drawings and paintings and recorded verbatim children's comments and conversations. These attempts to capture important information about the growth of individual children were used to guide children's experiences. The term documentation appears even earlier in North America when associated with **assessment** and used as evidence for drawing conclusions about performance. The use of the term has become more popular as interpreted and used by the schools of Reggio Emilia, Italy. Teachers *document* by observing, making notes, photographing, recording (audio or video), collecting children's work, and/or taking dictation. The drawings, paintings, writing samples, photographs, anecdotal notes, transcripts, and recordings are called *documentation.*

Today, most early childhood programs do some form of documentation, although its use varies widely. Some programs simply make brief anecdotal notes on children's development; some develop extensive portfolios on children's development; and some use documentation as the primary source for professional dialogue and planning. Regardless of the source behind a particular interpretation of documentation, an important part of the documentation process is the time spent thinking, or reflecting, about the meaning of the evidence. Because of the diversity of documentation in North American it is helpful to use the purposes for documentation as a way to organize thoughts about it. These purposes include guiding instruction, assessing individual children, studying **pedagogy,** and enhancing communication about the educational process. The purpose of the documentation determines how the documentation is collected, thought about, and shared.

Documentation for Guiding Instruction

Documentation used for guiding instruction is typically collected while the learning is happening and reflection on the documentation is usually immediate. Teachers listen, observe carefully, and examine children's work. They may make anecdotal notes, take digital photographs, and collect and carefully examine children's products such as drawings and constructions which are produced during the day or over a short period of time. This documentation is often referred to as raw or unprocessed documentation and has been a common practice in nursery schools and laboratory schools. It is usually not copied, framed, or carefully displayed but used immediately. What the teacher and his or her colleagues gain from this documentation is a sense of where the learning experience might go next, what materials and resources might be helpful to introduce, and how to shape their own interactions with the children. Documentation for guiding instruction enables teachers to be more productive and effective. Teachers may or may not choose to share this raw documentation with others, including parents and members of the school community.

Documentation for Child Assessment

Another purpose of documentation is the assessment of the knowledge, skills, and dispositions of an individual child. Individual child assessment enables the teacher to be sure that each child is progressing. The most appropriate type of assessment for the young child is authentic performance assessment, that is, assessment based on activities in which children engage on a daily basis (Meisels, 1993).

Authentic performance assessment relies on the collection of good quality evidence or documentation. This type of documentation includes children's work samples collected into a portfolio, photographic or video recordings, and observations captured in anecdotal notes. There is often an individual developmental checklist which the teacher uses to document the growth and development of skills over a period of time.

Documentation to provide evidence needed for reliably assessing children's progress, for meeting accountability requirements, or for program evaluation is usually collected as part of a formal process with specific domains or areas of learning documented throughout the year. Teachers examine and discuss the documentation at prescribed intervals and record their conclusions sharing the documentation and their conclusions with parents.

Documentation for Studying Pedagogy

Documentation also provides insight into the teaching and learning process. When documentation is collected and studied for the purpose of understanding this process, it is sometimes called pedagogical documentation (Dahlberg, Moss, and Pence, 1999). Pedagogical documentation is a major component of the philosophy of the schools of Reggio Emilia, where, as shown in the excerpt below, reflection and in-depth documentation shapes their pedagogy and is the major source of professional growth and development.

> ... we place the emphasis of documentation as an integral part of the procedures aimed at fostering learning and for modifying the learning-teaching relationship. (Rinaldi, 2001)

An excellent example of pedagogical documentation in U.S. schools and centers is *Rearview Mirror: Reflections of a Preschool Car Project* by Sallee Beneke (1998). Through this captivating documentation of the exploration of a car by children in a community college child-care center, the reader participates in the reflections of the teachers, the parents, and the automotive center staff where the project took place. The documentation enables the teachers to examine and then convey the pedagogical decisions made during the project and to share the value of the learning experiences with multiple stakeholders, including the children themselves.

In North America there have been a number of research and study projects that have focused on using documentation for studying pedagogy based on the the principles of Reggio Emilia (Cadwell, 2003; Fu, Stremmel and Hill, 2001). One of the most prominent is Making Learning Visible (MLV). The MLV project began in 1997 as a collaboration between Project Zero at the Harvard Graduate School of Education in Cambridge, Massachusetts, and the Municipal Preschools and Infant–toddler Centers of Reggio Emilia, Italy. MLV sought to draw attention to the power of the group as a learning environment and the power of documentation as a way in which students, teachers, parents, administrators, and the community could see how and what children are learning.

Another project which focused on using documentation to inform pedagogy is the Professional Learning Communities Project of the Chicago Metro Association for the Education of Young Children funded by the McCormick Tribune Foundation. This project involved collaboration with early childhood centers to develop professional learning communities within centers and to introduce and support the use documentation as a tool for examining and improving practice.*The Power of Documentation: Children's Learning Revealed*, an exhibit on documentation and professional learning communities in the midwest, was developed by Chicago Children's Museum and is now a traveling exhibit.

Documentation for Communication

Another purpose for documentation is to provide a vehicle for communicating about what is happening in early childhood programs. In fact, one of the primary reasons that many Italian early childhood programs began to utilize documentation strategies was to increase parent interest in contemplating and discussing children's experiences. As practiced in many classrooms in Italy as well as elsewhere, this communication around documentation can occur between staff members, with children, with parents about what is happening in children's classrooms and how their child is learning, and with the members of the greater community to share what is happening in the classroom and to develop respect, understanding, and support of the work that is done there. This use of documentation is becoming more widespread as early childhood programs are becoming more accountable to funding agencies and to parents, each eager for information on the growth in children's knowledge, skills, and dispositions within the early childhood classroom.

Value of Documentation

Documentation requires time and commitment of an early childhood program staff. Although there are many ways to gather evidence about children's learning such as test scores and checklist of performance on specific goals, the open process of documentation as interpreted by many early childhood educators has unique advantages. Documentation provides insight into students' thought processes. An understanding of how a child came to a particular conclusion can show significant learning progress and creative problem solving even when the "answer" is officially wrong. Documentation also gives the audience an appreciation for how children think, and how that thinking is different from adult cognition. Teachers as well as parents and other adults can gain a better understanding of the challenges and questioning that characterize children's thinking. Children's learning dispositions, such as being persistent and curious, can be captured and built upon. Steps in a problem-solving sequence can be recorded. These thought processes and the skills of assessing a problem, designing a solution, trying it out, and persisting to find a better solution are, in fact, a major part of many disciplines of study. Documentation strategies help teachers to directly capture and then reflect upon these thinking processes, alone and with others.

Documentation also encourages teachers to look at knowledge and skills beyond those that can be assessed verbally or in paper and pencil tests. Documentation enables teachers to capture children's learning as they construct models, build in the block area, play in housekeeping, or conduct an experiment in science. Observing and collecting children's work encourages teachers to be open to diverse ways of learning and to focus on unique ways that children approach learning tasks (Gardner, 1993).

Professional Learning Communities

Interest in examining children's work has been the focus of several school improvement movements in public education in North America, including kindergarten and primary school planning. One of these is the professional learning communities (Eaker, Dufour, and Burnett, 2002). Documentation is an integral part of many professional learning communities. A professional learning community is typically defined as a group of teachers at a school or center who meet to examine individual children's work and play, and—based on their observations—create ways to extend each learning. The practice of examining work is an integral part of the teaching-learning process; the children learn more and the teachers become seasoned professionals. In such settings where documentation practices are common, the teaching staff regularly meets to present and share documentation collected from the classrooms; and to debate its significance for their teaching. During this sharing the teacher typically poses questions for brainstorming and discusses the children's interest and skills reflected in the documentation. Other colleagues also share ideas, for example, on how to help the child achieve deeper knowledge or more complex skills in that area and possible next steps. Finally, the group typically incorporates some of the ideas into the following week's curriculum planning. Over time, the group develops a shared set of effective teaching strategies, in effect revealing the contributions of documentation to adult as well as child learning.

Documenting sometimes results in publishing or sharing documentation of the children's work such as a display of a project, a media show, or a book about an experience. These products, however, aren't the primary purpose of documentation but rather a product of the documentation and reflection process. Most programs that use documentation extensively use it to enhance the teaching and learning process.

Further Readings: Beneke, S. (1998). *Rearview mirror: Reflections on the preschool car project.* Champaign, IL: ERIC Clearinghouse on Elementary and Early Childhood Education; Cadwell, L. (2003). *Bringing learning to life: The Reggio Approach to early childhood education.* New York: Teachers College Press; Dahlberg, G., P. Moss, and A. R. Pence (1999). *Beyond quality in early childhood education and care: Postmodern perspectives.* London: Taylor & Francis; Eaker, R., R. Dufour, and R. Burnett (2002). *Getting started: Reculturing schools to become professional learning communities.* Bloomington, IN: National Education Service; Fu, V., A. J. Stremmel, and L. T. Hill (2001). *Teaching and learning: Collaborative exploration of the Reggio Emilia approach.* Englewood Cliffs, NJ: Prentice-Hall; Gardner, H. (1993). *Frames of the mind.* New York: Basic Books; Helm, J. H., S. Beneke, and K. Steinheimer (1998). *Windows on learning: Documenting young children's work.* New York: Teachers College Press; Helm, J. H., and S. Beneke, eds. (2002). *The power of projects: Meeting contemporary challenges in early childhood classrooms—Strategies and solutions.* New York: Teachers College Press, Columbia University; Meisels, S. J. (1993). Remaking classroom assessment with the work sampling system. *Young Children* 48(5), 34–40; Mitchell, L. (1950). *Our children and our schools.* New York: Simon and Schuster; Power of Documentation Exhibit: Children's Learning Revealed, Traveling Exhibit. Chicago: Chicago Children's Museum; Project Zero and Reggio Children (2001). *Making learning visible: Children as individual and group learners.* Reggio Emilia, Italy: Reggio Children; Project Zero, Cambridgeport Children's Center, Cambridgeport School, Ezra H. Baker School, and John Simpkins School (2003). *Making teaching visible: Documenting individual and group learning as professional development.* Cambridge, MA: Project Zero; Rinaldi, C. (2001). Documentation and assessment: What is the relationship? In C. Giudici, C. Rinaldi, and M. Krechevsky, eds. *Making learning visible: Children as individual and group learners.* Reggio Emilia, Italy: Reggio Children, pp. 78–89.

Judy Harris Helm

Domestic Violence

Domestic violence can be defined as abuse or threats of abuse between adults in families. However, many researchers include all types of violence that a child witnesses as domestic violence. Children typically witness domestic violence that occurs between partners, and most often abuse involving a male abusing a female (Groves, 2002; Osofsky, 1997, 2004). Other forms of domestic violence include both partners as aggressors when abuse occurs (Smith Slep and O'Leary, 2005). Research also indicates that when domestic violence involves spousal abuse of the mother, the mother frequently will be abusive toward her children. Children also have often been found to be victims of abuse at the hand of a male when the male is the aggressor toward the female.

Domestic violence has become an increasing problem round the globe with 40 percent of women in many countries reporting spousal or intimate partner abuse (Kishor and Johnson, 2004). An estimated three to eight million children witness violence each year. Every year the incidence increases, and the effects can be devastating for young children (Kearney, 1999). Most aggression consists of pushing, grabbing, shoving, slapping, and hitting. However, some incidents are life threatening. In 2003, the number of domestic violence incidents that resulted in death in the United States was 1,300 in 2003, and internationally this number is not known due to difficulty in calculating and obtaining data.

Witnessing violence or exposure to violence can have a negative impact on all people, but young children are particularly vulnerable (Osofsky, 1997). Many children bear the brunt of not only witnessing violence between adults but also being the victims of domestic violence and living in communities where violence becomes a part of everyday life (Osofsky, 2004). Exposure comes in many forms that include the media, spousal abuse in homes, and violence in neighborhoods. Eventually, for many children violence comes to be seen as the norm.

As a result of witnessing **domestic violence,** infants and toddlers may exhibit limited speech. Other behaviors that develop include regression to behaviors that a child had already mastered, new fears, clinginess, and behavior changes. Infants and toddlers may develop problems with sleeping, temper tantrums, and difficulty separating from caregivers. Young children, particularly infants and toddlers, react both to the trauma that they experience and the trauma that the adults they are attached to experience. In situations where spousal abuse is occurring, young children quickly become victims even when they are only witnessing violence and are not the physical recipient. The inability to develop trust and autonomy can be difficult for children who have witnessed domestic violence or are victims. Future relationships with other adults and peers can be impaired due to the inability to trust others.

The effects of trauma associated with domestic violence can impact a child at any age. Trauma-specific symptoms can interfere with normal growth in development. Children, particularly preschoolers who witness violence at a young age, may have a tendency toward violence and impulsivity. A child may be hypervigilent and overly sensitive to sounds or noises. Many of the effects of domestic violence can interfere with the ability to learn and develop. Preschoolers may also experience difficulty separating from caregivers, fearful avoidance reactions, and provocative behavior. Some preschoolers exposed to violence have sleep difficulties and withdraw socially (Osofsky, 2004).

It is difficult to determine what a young child will remember. What is known is that children remember traumatic events better than other events in their lives.

They have more difficulty with the sequence of events and their memories may be more fragmented, but the memories are there (Groves, 2000). The effects of the trauma also depend on the extent of the emotional involvement of the child, the level of their language development, and the security that the child has to an attachment caregiver. The length of the **violence** also plays a role in how detrimental it is to the child (Groves, 2002).

Chronic exposure to violence can lead to intense rage that can lead to aggressive behaviors. Some children become frightened by the violence and develop passive tendencies. Many children exposed to violence have difficulty in the area of academic performance. Many children seem to develop symptoms of posttraumatic stress disorder (PTSD) in response to witnessing violence. Symptoms that can develop include repetitive traumatic dreams, cognitive confusion, and re-enactment of the traumatic event through play and intrusive memories or thoughts (Groves, 2002).

There are many strategies that teachers and other adults can use to support young children who have been exposed to domestic violence. Children learn from what they see so it is important for teachers and other adults in their lives to model appropriate behaviors. Children who have witnessed or been victims of domestic violence need to learn ways to problem solve difficult situations and handle conflict and anger (Kearney, 1999). These children need consistency and structure for their behavior and logical consequences for not following rules that do not involve physical punishment. Many of these young children have difficulty developing trust in relationships, so they need consistent attention and appropriate affection.

Adults involved with children who have witnessed domestic violence should create an emotionally safe environment for the child. The child's classroom and home should be a place to which the child feels that he or she can come without anxiety. Cooperation should be encouraged rather than competition. Listening to what the child has to say is one factor that will help to promote trust (Kearney, 1999). Children should also be alerted to changes that will be taking place in the classroom or at home so they know what to expect. Allowing children to complete activities in a variety of ways and letting them know that there is no one way to do something is important to accepting the child and building self-esteem.

Osofsky (1997) argues that teachers should receive specific training on how to deal with children who have been exposed to domestic violence. Preservice teachers should receive college level training, and teachers in the schools should receive in-service training on a regular basis. Training should cover three content areas: development and the effects of domestic violence on children at various ages; resilience and coping in children; and helping teachers focus on their own reactions and experiences with domestic violence.

Teacher training should include exposure to the general development of children and how domestic violence can affect children at each stage of development. Discussions of how children's development can regress as well as how to talk with parents about sensitive issues should take place with teachers. Teachers should be trained on how to file a report of abuse or neglect and to talk with children about a violent incident. Teachers should also receive information about conflict resolution and mediation skills.

Child resilience is another important component of training for teachers and other staff who work with young children. All children will respond differently to domestic violence, and research on resilience presented during teacher training can facilitate understanding this concept. Some children are able to cope better than others and if teachers have an understanding of this, it can counteract teachers' feelings of hopelessness (Osofsky, 1997).

The third component of the training should provide teachers with self-awareness concerning their own feelings and reactions to domestic violence. The topic can be emotional and overwhelming, so it is important to allow teachers permission to discuss how they feel with others and seek support from colleagues and supervisors when dealing with domestic violence issues in the classroom (Osofsky, 1997).

Communities that work together to respond to domestic violence by linking services to help victims and families can make a difference on the impact of the violence. Multidisciplinary teams consisting of mental health providers, police, and educators and early childhood educators can contribute to responding early and working with the family as a system rather than as isolated individuals (Osofsky, 2004).

In order to help victims of domestic violence, prevention and intervention are important for reducing the short and long-term effects on young children. Early referral is an important factor and can make a difference in the intervention process in a child's life. As soon as a child has been exposed to a traumatic event, referral to intervention services can help the child to begin to process information and make sense of feelings. Ensuring that children feel safe is an important element that should be in place before effective interventions can occur (Osofsky, 2004).

Further Readings: Groves, Betsy M. (2002). *Children who see too much*. Boston: Beacon, Press; Kearney, Margaret (1999). The role of teachers in helping children of domestic violence. *Childhood Education* 75, 290–296; Kishor, Sunita, and Kiersten Johnson (2004). Profiling domestic violence: A multicountry study. Demographic and health surveys: MEASURE. Available online at http://www.measuredhs.com; Osofsky, Joy D. (1997). *Children in a violent society*. New York: Guilford Press; Osofsky, Joy D. (2004). Community outreach for children exposed to violence. *Infant Mental Health Journal* 25, 478–487; Smith Slep, Amy, and Susan G. O'Leary (2005). Parent and partner violence in families with young children: Rates, patterns, and connections. *Journal of Consulting and Clinical Psychology* 73, 435–444.

Cathy Grist Litty

Down Syndrome

Down Syndrome is a developmental disability resulting from a chromosomal abnormality. It is the most common chromosomal disorder, occurring in approximately one out of every 800 to 1000 births. In the United States, approximately 5,000 children are born with Down Syndrome each year. Furthermore, it is widely believed that with the increasing number of women postponing childbirth, the number of children born with Down Syndrome will rise dramatically over the next decade or so.

The description (and hence the name) of this syndrome is attributed to John Langdon Down, an English medical doctor, who wrote about it in his monograph entitled, *Mental Affections of Childhood and Youth* (1887). However, it was Jerome Lejeune, a French physician, who confirmed the condition as a chromosomal abnormality in 1959. The disorder was commonly referred to as mongoloidism (due primarily to the facial features of those affected by the disorder). Down Syndrome is now considered the more widely accepted and appropriate name for the disorder.

Individuals with Down Syndrome evidence a common set of physical characteristics, including low birth weight, short stature, low muscle tone, a flat-appearing face with a small nose and upwardly slanting eyes, skin folds on the corners of the eyes, an oversized tongue in relation to the size of the mouth, misshapen, low-set ears and small ear canals, broad short hands with only one crease on the palm, short fingers, hyperflexibility in the joints, and a large space between the great and second toes (sometimes referred to as a sandal gap).

The cause of Down Syndrome, also known as Trisomy 21, appears to be related to the age of the mother and is associated with a malfunction in human cell division. This can occur in one of three ways. The most common malfunction is a process known as nondisjunction, where, after cell division, there is an extra chromosome (or significant portion thereof) at the 21st chromosomal pair in every cell. This may occur before or at conception and accounts for approximately 95 percent of all cases of Down Syndrome.

A second and much less common cell division malfunction is called mosaicism. This results when the nondisjunction occurs after fertilization of the ovum and during early cell division. In this case, the extra chromosome at the 21st pair occurs in some cells but not others, yielding a pattern of cells, some with forty-six chromosomes and some with forty-seven chromosomes, much like a mosaic. Mosaicism accounts for 1–2 percent of all cases of Down Syndrome.

The third cell division malfunction resulting in Down Syndrome is also rare and usually occurs by chance. It is called translocation. In translocation, a piece of the 21st chromosome separates during cell division and attaches to another chromosome. The result is the normal set of forty-six chromosomes, but additional genetic material from chromosome 21 in each cell. Translocation accounts for 3–4 percent of all cases of Down Syndrome.

A suspicion of Down Syndrome is often made at birth based on the presence of one or more of the physical characteristics commonly associated with the syndrome. However, confirmation of the diagnosis requires karyotyping, that is, arranging the chromosomes under a microscope in order to group them by size, pattern, and shape; and to count them. Through this process, the extra number 21 chromosome can be found.

Down Syndrome is a disorder that is found in all racial and ethnic groups and across all socioeconomic levels. The incidence is greatest in older mothers, although in about 5 percent of cases, Down Syndrome originates with the father. Doctors can often estimate the risk that a pregnant woman will give birth to a baby with Down Syndrome. This estimate of risk, usually carried out between fifteen and twenty weeks of gestation, is based on a number of factors, including the amount of certain substances (alphafetoprotein, human chorionic gonadotropin, and unconjugated estriol) in the mother's blood. The age of the mother is also a risk factor in that the incidence of Down Syndrome increases with older women. However, 70–80 percent of children born with Down Syndrome are born to mothers under the age of 35. Further, a woman who has already had a child with Down Syndrome has a 1 percent chance of having another child with Down Syndrome. The screening process, along with a sonogram, is about 60 percent accurate in detecting a fetus with Down Syndrome.

Three pre-natal tests can be used to more reliably determine the presence or absence of Down Syndrome in the unborn fetus. Chorionic villi sampling (CVS) can be conducted as early as eight to twelve weeks' gestation. Amniocentesis is usually performed between twelve and twenty weeks' gestation. Percutaneous umbilical blood sampling (PUBS) is performed after twenty weeks. All three procedures extract tissue from the uterus for analysis and carry a risk of miscarriage. These tests, however, are 98–99 percent accurate in diagnosing Down Syndrome in the unborn fetus.

There are a number of medical conditions associated with Down Syndrome, including greater risk for heart disease, Alzheimer's disease, and leukemia. In the early twentieth century, a child born with Down Syndrome would likely not live beyond age 10. With the discovery of antibiotics, such a child's life expectancy doubled. Treatments for the characteristic medical conditions (i.e., heart defects, leukemia) associated with Down Syndrome have improved both life expectancy and health for those affected. Further advances in medical research continue to improve outcomes for individuals with Down Syndrome and its related medical conditions, and today many individuals with Down Syndrome live well into their fifties and beyond. However, it is still uncertain as to why individuals with Down Syndrome are at greater risk for these medical problems.

Down Syndrome is a developmental disability and individuals with Down Syndrome require a variety of therapeutic interventions (such as speech and language therapy, occupational therapy, and physical therapy) to address some of the characteristics of the disorder. Those affected with Down Syndrome also have varying degrees of mental retardation. **Early intervention** services and inclusive high-quality early childhood education have proven to be invaluable strategies to promote each child's optimal development.

The passage of critical federal legislation has had a profound influence on the quality of life for individuals with Down Syndrome. The **Individuals with Disabilities Education Act** (first enacted in 1975 as P.L. 94-142, the Education of All Handicapped Children Act and most recently reauthorized in December 2004), along with other landmark legislation (the 1975 amendment to the Rehabilitation Act known as Section 504 and the Americans with Disabilities Act of 1990) have articulated the clear expectation that children and adults with disabilities, including Down Syndrome, have the right to access meaningful opportunities in education, housing, and employment; and to participate as fully as possible in their communities alongside individuals without disabilities.

Relevant provisions of the Individuals with Disabilities Education Act (IDEA), contained in Parts B and C, specify that children from infancy through age 21 are entitled to a free and appropriate public education in the least restrictive environment. These provisions encompass early intervention, early childhood, school, and vocational preparation programs; and presume that education and support services will be made available in inclusive settings.

Today, it is not only possible but desirable that children with Down Syndrome live, grow, and learn with their families and peers in their communities. For more information contact the National Down Syndrome Society at the following address:

National Down Syndrome Society
666 Broadway
New York, NY 10012
www.ndss.org

Further Readings: Down, John Langdon (1887). *Mental affections of childhood and youth*. London: Churchill; Lejeune, J., R. Turpin, and M. Gautier (1959). Le mongolisme. Premier example d'aberration autosomique humaine. *Annales de génétique* 1, 41–49; Selikowitz, Mark (1997). *Down syndrome: The facts*. 2nd ed. London: Oxford University Press.

Stephanie F. Leeds

Drug Abuse. *See* Parental Substance Abuse